Words of the World's Religions

an anthology

Robert S. Ellwood, Jr.

University of Southern California

PRENTICE-HALL, INC., *Englewood Cliffs, New Jersey* 07632

Library of Congress Cataloging in Publication Data

Main entry under title:

Words of the world's religions.

    SUMMARY: Reading selections exploring the
religious traditions of Judaism, Christianity, and
Islam, in addition to Eastern religions and those
of ancient Egypt and the Near East.
    1. Ellwood, Robert S., 1933–
BL25.W67   291   76-49545
ISBN 0-13-965004-0

© 1977 by Prentice-Hall, Inc., Englewood Cliffs, N.J. 07632

Printed in the United States of America

10 9 8

PRENTICE-HALL INTERNATIONAL, INC., *London*
PRENTICE-HALL OF AUSTRALIA PTY. LIMITED, *Sydney*
PRENTICE-HALL OF CANADA, LTD., *Toronto*
PRENTICE-HALL OF INDIA PRIVATE LIMITED, *New Delhi*
PRENTICE-HALL OF JAPAN, INC., *Tokyo*
PRENTICE-HALL OF SOUTHEAST ASIA PTE. LTD., *Singapore*
WHITEHALL BOOKS LIMITED, *Wellington, New Zealand*

CONTENTS

SNARED BIRDS OF PARADISE:
AN INTRODUCTORY
COMMENT

He who is presenting a bird should turn its head on one side; if it be a tame bird, this need not be done.
—From ancient China; *The Book of Rites*, Bk I.

Real innocence can do nothing that is trivial.
—Lawrence Durrell, *Balthazar.*

It is he who sits above the circle of the earth, and its inhabitants are like grasshoppers.
—Isaiah, 40:22.

The fullness of a culture's religion, like all high expressions of the human spirit, cannot be caught in a cage and carried away. To be sure, much of the religion may have universal appeal, and we can transmit some words which give the gist of its intellectual expression. We can peruse descriptions of the worship and social life connected with the faith.

Indeed, we can read words which, if put down by a sensitive author within or without the tradition, communicate something of its experiential flavor and its "feel." There is certainly nothing to be disparaged in the works of those gifted writers from Herodotus to Lawrence Durrell who have made cities, cultures, and faiths exotic to the reader live before the eyes in colors as bright (or brighter) than Main Street. Of equal worth is the painstaking work of those translators and scholars who put together for transcultural shipment avian bones of past societies and ways toward the sacred—bones perhaps later to be clothed in flesh and color by the pens of artists in words.

1

Yet, however excellent, these transmissions are only tame birds transported out of their habitats. Like creatures in the zoo, they are worthy of immense interest and respect for their own sakes, and they show us what a denizen of the jungle looks like. But they only much more imperfectly put us in the jungle itself.

Like a jungle, a human culture with its religion is an almost infinitely intricate network of life. Nothing in it is really trivial, even though no one thing in it is the whole of the religion either. For all details of daily life in a culture—the diet, how acquaintances greet one another, how children are educated, where economic power lies—contribute to how religious reality and everything else is experienced as surely as do the mightiest scriptures of the official faith, and condition how they are understood.

It is easy to print a translation of the Upanishads or the New Testament, and no translation however turgid (or scholarly analysis however pedantic), can wholly destroy the universal power of their words. But it is less easy to take the next step: to try to understand the religious life of real people influenced by words like these to truly grasp what it means to be a brahmin in Benares or a Baptist in Oklahoma today. Yet this step must be taken to understand (or even to try to understand) the religious life of humanity. Studying world religion is no more, and no less, than understanding ordinary but real people.

These remarks are intended as both a warning and an invitation to the reader beginning this collection of words from and about the religions of the world. The warning is that nothing only in black and white—certainly not these short passages—can communicate all of a faith or all of what it would feel like to live and die in its ambience. The invitation is to read with a receptive mind nonetheless, for the passages *are* put down in full confidence that much which is wonderful and illuminating has been written about humanity's religious adventures, and that by reading even a little of this material one can know immensely more than before about where humankind has been, and what it means to be human.

I found searching the stacks of the University of Southern California libraries, and my own library, for these selections a thoroughly absorbing and exciting task. The only pain lay in the fact that limitations of space meant that difficult decisions had to be made between possible selections, and much splendid material had to be left out. I hope many readers are inspired by the samples here to look up further material in areas of special interest. In making the selections, my intent has been to strike a balance between old and new material, between material written from inside the tradition and by outside scholars, and between scholarly and more popular writing. I have wanted to show something of the range of kinds of writing about religion that is done, as well as illustrate as much as possible of the diversity of each tradition—its popular and intellectual expressions, its impact on both men and women, its outward appearance and inner experience.

The organization of this book parallels that of my textbook in world religions, *Many Peoples, Many Faiths*. Different chapter titles are used here, however, and some single chapters in the other book are here divided into two or three chapters, even though the sequence of material and religious traditions covered is the same. But attention has been given to making that book and the present anthology complementary but not repetitious. In this book different translations, or comparable but not identical material, are offered to parallel what is quoted or cited in the other book. But there are no internal cross-references, and either book could be used independently as well as together by teachers and students.

Each chapter in this book is constructed as a unity intended to develop the topic through prefatory commentary and reading selections basically arranged in an historical manner (apart from the first and second chapters, which are not historical in structure). The chapter introduction does not touch on everything to be presented later, except in the first two chapters. In the remainder of the book, the introduction begins a discussion which proceeds, with as much continuity as possible, through the selections and their prefatory paragraphs.

I would like to express my gratitude to the many publishers and other copyright holders who kindly gave permission to use the material herein presented; this permission is acknowledged (in the case of copyright material) by the attribution at the beginning of each passage.

R.S.E.

I

STARTING OUT

Philosophers and social scientists have long debated just how religion should be defined. This is not a question of defining the "true" religion, or the basis of an individual's personal beliefs. Rather, the question is what areas of human experience and expressions of human societies may be properly described as religious. It is generally agreed there is something in the inner lives of many individuals, and the public lives of most societies, that has to do with religion. But because what may be recognized as religious often intersects other aspects of experience, it is surprisingly difficult to arrive at an exact and exclusive definition of religion. No single statement has proved entirely satisfactory or been generally accepted; maybe simple summation is not possible. Yet the word does have at least some "ordinary usage" meanings. People think they know what "looks like" or "feels like" religion. Without attempting a grand definition, let us explore what some of these things are.

First, we think of religion as having to do with that which is ultimate: God, the source, ground, and highest goal of life. Events that are ultimate for oneself in the sense that they are most determinative for the whole pattern of a life also may be called religious—even if, like being born and falling in love, they are not ostensibly religious. Therefore, we often regard them with reverence and sanctify them with rites like baptisms and weddings. We see religion in experiences that appear ultimate because they best reveal the way reality really is for us. We see religion in those commitments which are most important or ultimate and are related to one's understanding of universal ultimate reality. Conversion and mystical experience, as well as deeply felt worship, devotion, and ethical idealism, bespeak this face of religion.

Second, we think of religion as embracing the divinely sanctioned traditions and values of communities. This side was hinted at in the mention of baptisms and weddings. This is the face of religion manifested in cathedrals and temples, in painting and sculpture, in festivals like Christmas or Passover, in the strong feelings of communities about what is moral and immoral as shaped by the accepted religion, in the politics and economics of religious institutions, and in the way they make people into communities. To be sure, these roles of religions may be said to be based on divine manifestation, probably in the distant past, but the tone of a community festival, a wayside shrine, or an ethical commonplace is very different from that of the subjective intensity of a personal divine call.

Religion, then, has many aspects. It has to do with what is spoken of as ultimate, but the ultimate comes to us in many ways. It can come as inward voice or vision, and it can speak the language of the community's norms or of ancient tradition. It can speak through idea, feeling, rite, or institution. Moreover, it is rarely a bald "either/or" among these, for the relations of inner and outer in human life are complex. Our most deeply inward experiences may often stem from words and images transmitted by a tradition: on the words of scripture or on a picture of a deity or savior. Conversely, the inner life of a significant religious figure is far from only inward: it may finally name holidays, shape traditions, and then enter the inner lives of other souls.

In this first section of the book, we shall present material from throughout world religion which illustrates various of these voices in which religion speaks, inner and outer. We shall also examine major ways of looking at religion, and its main forms of expression.

INTENSITY OF FEELING AND COMMITMENT IN RELIGION

In this passage the noted American revivalist Charles Finney (1792–1875) describes his conversion to Christ and baptism by the Holy Spirit, which occurred in 1821. Soon after this experience, Finney became one of the greatest of the nineteenth-century "hell-fire" preachers; he brought sinners to their knees through every device of fervent rhetoric and psychological suasion. He was also president of Oberlin College from 1851 to 1866, and an early advocate of the education of women and the abolition of slavery. One can understand how an experience as intense as this could give one unshakable convictions, a need to convince others of them, and strength to stand against the crowd when conscience requires.

From *Memoirs*

Charles G. Finney

I went to my dinner, and found I had no appetite to eat. I then went to the office, and found that Squire W_____ had gone to dinner. I took down my bass-viol, and, as I was accustomed to do, began to play and sing some pieces of sacred music. But as soon as I began to sing those sacred words, I began to weep. It seemed as if my heart was all liquid; and my feelings were in such a state that I could not hear my own voice in singing without causing my sensibility to overflow. I wondered at this, and tried to suppress my tears, but could not. After trying in vain to suppress my tears, I put up my instrument and stopped singing.

After dinner we were engaged in removing our books and furniture to another office. We were very busy in this, and had but little conversation all the afternoon. My mind, however, remained in that profoundly tranquil state. There was a great sweetness and tenderness in my thoughts and feelings. Everything appeared to be going right, and nothing seemed to ruffle or disturb me in the least.

Just before evening the thought took possession of my mind, that as soon as I was left alone in the new office, I would try to pray again—that I was not going to abandon the subject of religion and give it up, at any rate; and therefore, although I no longer had any concern about my soul, still I would continue to pray.

By evening we got the books and furniture adjusted; and I made up, in an open fire-place, a good fire, hoping to spend the evening alone. Just at dark Squire W_____, seeing that everything was adjusted, bade me good-night and went to his home. I had accompanied him to the door; and as I closed the door and turned around, my heart seemed to be liquid within me. All my feelings seemed to rise and flow out; and the utterance of my heart was, "I want to pour my whole soul out to God." The rising of my soul was so great that I rushed into the room back of the front office, to pray.

There was no fire, and no light, in the room; nevertheless it appeared to me as if it were perfectly light. As I went in and shut the door after me, it seemed as if I met the Lord Jesus Christ face to face. It did

Charles G. Finney, *Memoirs* (New York: Fleming H. Revell, 1876), pp. 18–21.

not occur to me then, nor did it for some time afterward, that it was wholly a mental state. On the contrary it seemed to me that I saw him as I would see any other man. He said nothing, but looked at me in such a manner as to break me right down at his feet. I have always since regarded this as a most remarkable state of mind; for it seemed to me a reality, that he stood before me, and I fell down at his feet and poured out my soul to him. I wept aloud like a child, and made such confessions as I could with my choked utterance. It seemed to me that I bathed his feet with my tears; and yet I had no distinct impression that I touched him, that I recollect.

I must have continued in this state for a good while; but my mind was too much absorbed with the interview to recollect anything that I said. But I know, as soon as my mind became calm enough to break off from the interview, I returned to the front office, and found that the fire that I had made of large wood was nearly burned out. But as I turned and was about to take a seat by the fire, I received a mighty baptism of the Holy Ghost. Without any expectation of it, without ever having the thought in my mind that there was any such thing for me, without any recollection that I had ever heard the thing mentioned by any person in the world, the Holy Spirit descended upon me in a manner that seemed to go through me, body and soul. I could feel the impression, like a wave of electricity, going through and through me. Indeed it seemed to come in waves and waves of liquid love; for I could not express it in any other way. It seemed like the very breath of God. I can recollect distinctly that it seemed to fan me, like immense wings.

No words can express the wonderful love that was shed abroad in my heart. I wept aloud with joy and love; and I do not know but I should say, I literally bellowed out the unutterable gushings of my heart. These waves came over me, and over me, and over me, one after the other, until I recollect I cried out, "I shall die if these waves continue to pass over me," I said, "Lord, I cannot bear any more;" yet I had no fear of death.

How long I continued in this state, with this baptism continuing to roll over me and go through me, I do not know. But I know it was late in the evening when a member of my choir—for I was leader of the choir —came into the office to see me. He was a member of the church. He found me in this state of loud weeping, and said to me, "Mr. Finney, what ails you?" I could make him no answer for some time. He then said, "Are you in pain?" I gathered myself up as best I could, and replied, "No, but so happy that I cannot live."

He turned and left the office, and in a few minutes returned with one of the elders of the church, whose shop was nearly across the way from our office. This elder was a very serious man; and in my presence had been very watchful, and I had scarcely ever seen him laugh. When he came in, I was very much in the state in which I was when the young man went out to call him. He asked me how I felt, and I began to tell him. Instead of saying anything, he fell into a most spasmodic laughter.

It seemed as if it was impossible for him to keep from laughing from the very bottom of his heart.

MYSTICAL EXPERIENCE IN RELIGION

Mysticism is hard to define. Often the word suggests a sense of God as a glory within oneself and all things, and experiences and philosophies to go with that awareness. Mystical experiences may have a quieter, more contemplative tone than conversion or intensity of commitment experiences, but they are no less deep and life-transforming for many who know them. Jacob Boehme (1575–1624) was a German shoemaker who experienced mystical vision and wrote weighty books of mystical philosophy. Here is an account by a biographer of his early experiences; notice how the visionary perception and the manner of life seem to go together.

From *Jacob Boehme*

Hans L. Martensen

Jacob Böhme was born in 1575 at Old Seidenberg, a village near Görlitz. His parents were poor peasants, who were only able to procure for him the usual religious school teaching, together with some instruction in reading and writing. At an early age he was compelled, with other boys, to watch the cattle in the fields. He was a quiet, introspective lad, whose face bore somewhat of the dreamy expression which is frequent in poetic natures. Indeed, when very young, he was marked by a certain visionary element, by inward visions, which for himself assumed the character of outwardness and reality. Thus, when a shepherd boy, he once climbed to the top of a mountain called the "Land's Crown;" and here he saw a vaulted entrance composed of four red stones, and leading into a cavern. When he had toiled through the bushwood that surrounded the entrance, he beheld in the depth of the cave a vessel filled with money. He was seized with inward panic, as if at something diabolical, and ran

Hans L. Martensen, *Jacob Boehme* (London: Hodder and Stoughton, 1885), pp. 4–7.

away in alarm. Subsequently he often returned to the spot, accompanied by other boys. But entrance and cavern had alike vanished!

As he was not well qualified for agricultural and rural pursuits, he was apprenticed to a shoemaker. Here also something remarkable happened to him. One day, when the master and his wife were out, and he was alone in the house, a stranger entered the shop and asked for a pair of shoes. As Jacob did not consider himself empowered to conclude a bargain, seeing that his master had given him no express authority for this, he tried to release himself from the dilemma by demanding a high price for the shoes, in the hope that the man would be disinclined to buy. But the man paid the sum required, and, when he had gone out into the street, shouted, "Jacob, come forth!" Surprised that the stranger should know his name, Jacob obeyed the call, and now the stranger looked at him with a kindly, earnest, deep, soul-piercing gaze, and said, "Jacob, thou art as yet but little, but the time will come when thou shalt be great, and become another man, and the world shall marvel at thee. Therefore, be pious, fear God, and reverence His Word; especially read diligently the Holy Scriptures, where thou hast comfort and instruction; for thou must endure much misery and poverty, and suffer persecution. But be courageous and persevere, for God loves, and is gracious unto thee." Thereupon the stranger clasped his hand and disappeared. Whether all this is to be accepted as an actual occurrence or partly as a vision, we leave an open question.

After this experience Jacob became even more pensive and serious, and devoted himself to pure morality and devout meditation; nor could he refrain from words of confession and admonition when the other journeymen on the work-bench indulged in loose conversation about sacred things. Naturally, they would not listen to his exhortations; and to make an end of the disputes that followed, his master dismissed him, saying that he would have no "house-prophet" to bring discord and trouble into the house. And thus Böhme was compelled to go forth into the wide world as a travelling journeyman. During his wanderings, he discovered that the period was full of theological conflicts, and that the Evangelical Church was split into parties that mutually vilified each other, and made on him the impression of a Babel. He was afflicted with profound solicitude, and fell into manifold doubts, against which he had to struggle by seeking for himself in Holy Scripture some firm foundation on which he might stand and have full assurance. In addition to the reading of the Scriptures, he was diligent in prayer, and clave especially to Luke ix.: "How much more shall your heavenly Father give the Holy Spirit to them that ask Him!" And thus it befell him when, during his wanderings, he was again engaged by a master that, amid the labour of his hands, he was lifted into a condition of blessed peace, a Sabbath of the soul, that lasted for seven days, and during which he was, as it were, inwardly surrounded by a Divine light. Outwardly, there was nothing noticeable about him. But "the triumph that was then in my soul I can neither tell nor describe. I can only liken it to a resurrection from the dead." It was a foretaste of the tranquility that was to be vouchsafed him in contemplation.

In the year 1594 he returned to Görlitz, became a master-shoemaker in 1599, and married a tradesman's daughter, with whom he lived in happy union for thirty years, and who bore him four children. In the year 1600 he had another remarkable experience. Sitting one day in his room, his eye fell upon a burnished pewter dish, which reflected the sunshine with such marvellous splendour that he fell into an inward ecstasy, and it seemed to him as if he could now look into the principles and deepest foundations of things. He believed that it was only a fancy, and in order to banish it from his mind he went out upon the green. But here he remarked that he gazed into the very heart of things, the very herbs and grass, and that actual nature harmonized with what he had inwardly seen. He said nothing about this to any one, but praised and thanked God in silence. He continued in the honest practice of his craft, was attentive to his domestic affairs, and was on terms of good-will with all men.

LIFE STYLE AND COMMUNITY EXPRESSED IN RELIGION

Religion is not only a matter of intense transformative experience. Equally important is its function of helping ordinary people at ordinary times find guidelines for an acceptable way of life and fulfill their need for community.

The first passage below is from a famous study of life in the white-collar suburbs that mushroomed in America after World War II. It gives a vivid picture of how churches in this setting, while scarcely emphasizing intensity of commitment or unusual mystical experience, played an important role in enabling these transplanted young couples of the 1950s to find community. One cannot help but feel it also helped them discover how to live a suburban life style implicitly sanctified by religion through the models provided by the friends they were encouraged to make in church. That life style doubtless was only reinforced by the optimistic, this-worldly, culture-affirming emphases in the church's message.

The second passage, by a distinguished historian of religion, shows us that forming communities and providing models for life styles is no new role for religion: archaic religion comparably sanctified the given tribal community and the culturally acceptable way of doing the necessary things, in these cases by citing divine examples.

From *The Organization Man*

William H. Whyte, Jr.

So far, I have been talking chiefly of Park Forest, but wherever young organization people are to be found the same urge for a more socially useful church manifests itself. The fact that the current "religious revival" has a strong social basis has been widely observed, of course, but it is significant how much more clearly this social emphasis is discerned when you narrow the focus from people in general to the strata of young organization people. They need to have emphasized what others take for granted. For those who stay put in one place, the church has always been socially useful, and the by-products of church affiliation they take as a matter of course. But the transients cannot. Stability, kinship with others —they want these demonstrated, and in the here and now.

In one Protestant church in Levittown, Pennsylvania, the young minister was surprised when his congregation began to complain about the cathedral chairs with which the church was furnished. They were excellent chairs and, for a growing church, more practical than fixed pews. They conceded all this but they still complained. "At last I figured it out," he said. "The chairs *moved*. All the young people here have come from somewhere else—from up state, Philadelphia, or New Jersey, and even though the distance isn't great, they have had to break with their old home ties. They are extremely eager for stability and for any signs of it. So I figured out a compromise. We fixed up kneeling stools so that they would hold the chairs firm. I didn't hear any complaints after that."

They seek friendship, and this yen is now becoming so evident that wherever there is a transient population, it has been an irresistible temptation for the churches to make friendship their chief appeal. Symptomatically, even within the more conservative denominations recently there has been a good bit of use of advertising appeals frankly based on the how-to-win-friends theme. Here, for example, in an ad in the New York *Herald Tribune* (May 20, 1955), "spiritual force" is advertised as a means to friendships:

> Lots of acquaintances—not many friends. Is this increasingly true for you? Look at your life. You may find that it lacks those spiritual experiences which bring people together in understanding and friendship.

William H. Whyte, Jr., *The Organization Man* (New York: Simon & Schuster, 1956), pp. 377–81. Reprinted by permission of Simon & Schuster, Inc., and Jonathon Cape, Ltd. Copyright 1956 by William H. Whyte, Jr.

Participation in the activities of the neighborhood church supplies the spiritual force to weld lasting friendships. Meet future friends in church next Sunday.

A cordial welcome awaits you

YOUR NEIGHBORHOOD EPISCOPAL CHURCH.

This is a rather exceptional ad, but the sensitivity to practicality that it illustrates is growing more general. Even though they might themselves feel that spiritual considerations are basic, a considerable number of churchmen now have been persuaded they should ask people in the door by mentioning only the social and practical benefits one will find inside. A bulletin put out by the Protestant Council of New York City, to cite another somewhat exceptional example, gives this advice to speakers on its radio and television programs:

Subject matter should project love, joy, courage, hope, faith, trust in God, good will. Generally avoid condemnation, criticism, controversy. In a very real sense we are "selling" religion, the good news of the Gospel. Therefore admonitions and training of Christians on cross-bearing, forsaking all else, sacrifices, and service usually cause the average listener to turn the dial. Consoling the bereaved and calling sinners to repentance, by direct indictment of the listeners, is out of place (with designated exceptions). . . . As apostles, can we not extend an invitation, in effect: "Come and enjoy our privileges, meet good friends, see what God can do for you!"

If transients are so disinterested in theological and doctrinal matters, many churchmen ask, why have there not been more united churches of the Park Forest variety? It is true enough that there are few; this seems due not so much to strong denominational spirit on the part of younger people, however, as to strong denominational spirit on the part of the church hierarchies. At Levittown, Pennsylvania, for example, there was for a while a fair chance of making the first church there, the Dutch Reformed, a united church deliberately patterned on the Park Forest model. The minister, the Rev. Bert Bonte, was, like Park Forest's Hugo Leinberger, eager to make the church a vehicle for bringing together people of different faiths in meaningful civic, cultural, and religious activity. For a variety of reasons the effort failed, but the church is, if not in name, in fact something of a united church. Of its 325 members, only a few were raised in the Dutch Reformed Church. The rest are Methodists, Presbyterians, Lutherans, Baptists, Congregationalists, and twelve are ex-Catholics. Like Park Forest's United Protestant Church, it has become the center of community activity. "What fires young people today is the urge to co-operate," says Bonte. "The old fire of denominationalism is gone. The young people are ready for union now, but the vested interests—the bureaucrats of the church—are against it. They would stand to lose their jobs. But the young people are ready, and I think it significant that the ones who are most eager for the ecumenical movement are the best-educated ones." (Roughly 50 per cent of Bonte's congregation is college educated.)

In near-by Fairless Hills, another united church almost came into being. The Philadelphia Council of Churches sent out a chaplain, and when he discerned the popular movement on the part of the residents for a common church, the denominational authorities were persuaded to set up such a church. It was run by the Methodists, but the understanding was that it would serve all the Protestant denominations. So it continued for several years, but in time it became more a Methodist church, and while it numbers many denominations among its members, it cannot be considered a true united church—a fact that other ministers in the neighborhood take pains to emphasize.

Whether they take the form of a united church or not, however, the desires that produced the Park Forest experiment are well illustrated everywhere. Let me go back a moment to the priorities that Park Foresters indicated in 1950. They listed, in order of importance, the minister, the Sunday school, the location, the denomination, the music. Some churchmen have been shocked at this, but subsequent experience has proved that, whatever one may think of the order, it has proven rather accurate.

That the minister is of primary importance has been well borne out by the unusually heavy demand among suburbanites for personal counseling. "So many young people around makes counseling my main worry," says a forty-two-year-old minister in one package suburb. "I simply haven't time for any more, and I am getting an assistant to help me out. But the thing is, you feel you can do so much in a place like this. My last parish was in a run-down city neighborhood. I had a lot of counseling work there, but so much of it was with people who had no hope—people you knew you couldn't do very much for. But here it's different. These young people have all their adjustments to make at once, and you feel you can do so much for them. No case seems hopeless, and you're tormented by the thought that how you help them will be important for years to come."

Because of this demand the age of the ministers has been more of a factor than expected. At first glance, the ideal minister for suburbia would seem to be a man of same age as the others, and many churches have sent young men on that assumption. The age similarity does not always work out well, however. In a community where most people are the same age, and when that age is one in which they are meeting their first marital conflicts, the couples feel drawn to a man who is somewhat more fatherly than brotherly. Some young ministers have done well, but the failures— there have been very many—have been disproportionately concentrated among the younger men. Elderly ministers have their problems, too, but one of these is the heavy strain put upon them by their popularity as counselors. One elderly minister virtually suffered a breakdown—there were so few others in his age group that he had to bear an unconscionable load, and at length he left, for the burden was too much.

The second factor, Sunday school, is at times even more important than the minister. Customarily, new suburbanites approach the church through their children, and a lively youth-education program can often offset many other factors in a church's popularity. In time, the parents may join, but on the average there is a waiting period of about a year before they will themselves become regular parishioners.

The relationship between location and churchgoing has been similarly demonstrated. At Park Forest, for example, it has been found that traffic flow is a lot more important than sectarian ties in determining churchgoing habits; people tend to go to a church located between them and the center of a community, and a mainroad location is so important that placing a church only one or two blocks away will make for considerably decreased attendance. The same seems to be true elsewhere: if you plot the location of the members of a particular congregation, you will find nearness to the church a much larger factor than some ministers would like to believe. Because of the split between the two branches of the Lutheran Church, to take another example, Park Forest has two Lutheran churches, one for each branch. Despite the doctrinal differences, however, the people divide up between the two more because of geography than theology, and to all intents and purposes the two have become regional churches.

What the transients want most urgently, in short, is a sense of community—and they are coming to care far less than their elders about matters of doctrine that might get in the way. For some people, the result may be far too secular, but before one casts a stone at such as the United Protestant Church, he must first face up to the question its people can posit: *What is the alternative?* The United Protestant Church, they maintain, is at least taking the initiative in meeting the needs of the new transients as it sees them.

Are the denominations doing so? Thanks to increased mobility, they have one of the greatest proselytizing opportunities they have ever had. But they are not seizing it. So say Protestant transients, and the more religiously inclined they are, the more harsh their judgment. Neither the mystery nor the fellowship, neither the sacred nor the secular, they complain, are being pushed forward with any real vigor. Says an executive of one of America's largest apartment-house developments, "In a community like this there isn't a well-heeled older group to get a church going, so it's up to the church authorities to step in and take the initiative. But what's happened here? The churches have missed the boat. We set aside space for the three faiths to have a center. They didn't show much interest; the Episcopalians did put up a Quonset hut, and the Jews put up a temple. But that's all so far."

The writer feels no competence to enter any judgment on the spiritual issues raised by these questions. I do think, however, that this ferment, from whatever standpoint one views it, is a clear indication that the quest among the transients for a socially useful church is a deeply felt one. They do not seek fellowship simply because they cannot avoid the need. They seek it actively, and they feel that it is ultimately a moral quest.

From *Cosmos and History*

Mircea Eliade

We must add that, for the traditional societies, all the important acts of life were revealed *ab origine* by gods or heroes. Men only repeat these exemplary and paradigmatic gestures *ad infinitum*. The Yuin tribe of Australia know that Daramulun, the "All Father," invented, for their especial benefit, all the utensils and arms that they have employed down to today. In the same way the Kurnai tribe know that Mungan-ngaua, the Supreme Being, lived among them, on earth, at the beginning of time, in order to teach them to make their implements, boats, weapons, "in fact, all the arts they know."[1] In New Guinea, many myths tell of long sea voyages, "and thus they provide exemplars for the modern voyagers," as well as for all other activities, "whether of love, or war, or rain-making, or fishing, or whatever else . . . [Myth] gives precedents for the stages of construction, the tabu on sexual intercourse, etc." When a captain goes to sea, he personifies the mythical hero Aori. "He wears the costume which Aori is supposed to have worn, with a blackened face (and in a way prematurely) the same kind of *love* in his hair which Aori plucked from Iviri's head. He dances on the platform and extends his arms like Aori's wings . . . A man told me that when he went fish shooting (with bow and arrow) he pretended to be Kivavia himself."[2] He did not implore Kivavia's favor and help; he identified himself with the mythical hero.

This same symbolism of mythical precedents is to be found in other primitive cultures. In regard to the Karuk Indians of California, J. P. Harrington writes: "Everything that the Karuk did was enacted because the Ikxareyavs were believed to have set the example in story times. The Ikxareyavs were the people who were in America before the Indians came. Modern Karuks, in a quandary how to render the word, volunteer such translations as 'the princes,' 'the chiefs,' 'the angels' . . . [These Ikxare-yavs . . .] remaining with the Karuk only long enough to state and start

Mircea Eliade, *Cosmos and History* (New York: Harper & Row, 1959), pp. 32–33. Reprinted by permission of the publisher.

[1]Howitt, pp. 543, 630.

[2]F. E. Williams, cited by Lucien Lévy-Bruhl, *La mythologie primitive* (Paris, 1935), pp. 162, 163–64.

all customs, telling them in every instance, 'Humans will do the same.' These doings and sayings are still related and quoted in the medicine formulas of the Karuk."[3]

EMBODIMENT OF TRADITION IN RELIGION

These passages, by an Englishwoman who lived in China in the early decades of this century, illustrate the vast network of little observances, symbols, and attitudes which comprise religion in an old culture like traditional China. This network maintains the tradition and helps individuals to feel part of it. Notice, in the first passage, that even a change in the pattern on its own terms—the installation of a new shrine —requires traditional validation by dreams and miracles. The second passage shows us how, on a more exalted level of the same tradition, the authority of the Emperor and his court was legitimated by speaking of it as an earthly reflection of the Heavenly Ruler and his court, identified with the Pole Star and the eternal constellations that wheel around it.

From *A Chinese Mirror*

Florence Ayscough

I always think that the Chinese cook-room is one of the most interesting corners of the house. A Chinese stove is, in itself, very picturesque. Built of plastered brick, it is gaily decorated with flowers, landscapes, or historical scenes, painted in free-hand on its white surface. Huge iron pans, sunk into the top, are used for boiling rice, the front is solid and the fire is tended from behind. Half-way up the chimney-breast, so arranged as to face South, is a little niche where sits a portrait of Ts'ao Chün, Lord of the Stove, generally referred to by Occidentals as the Kitchen God.

Five days before New Year's Ts'ao Chün's portrait is placed in a green official chair made of paper; and is despatched by means of fire, to

---

[3] J. P. Harrington, cited by Lévy-Bruhl, p. 165.

Florence Ayscough, *A Chinese Mirror* (London: Jonathon Cape, Ltd.; Boston: Houghton Mifflin Co., 1925), pp. 85–88, 291–92. Reprinted by permission of the publisher and the executors of the Florence Ayscough estate.

the court of Yü Huang the Jade Emperor. This is in order that he may make his annual report on the action of the household which he is supposed to oversee. Candles to light his way, a little food for the journey, and a sheet of red paper with an auspicious inscription such as 'May fair wind attend your road' are placed before him, and just before departure his lips are smeared with something sweet and sticky in order to assure that the report he makes will be honey-mouthed. During the five days of his absence one may have the comfortable feeling that no supervision over any action is exercised, but before dawn on New Year's morning he must be reinstalled, in readiness to shoulder his duties for the coming year.

The use of Ts'ao Chün's picture is universal. I do not suppose that it is lacking from a single kitchen in China; but in our fourth courtyard there is installed in a little temple, an Empress of Heaven, and this is most unusual.

The way it all happened is this. Once, upon my return from Europe, I found that Amah, who is very fond of pilgrimages and temple ceremonies, had been presented with a little figure of the Empress of Heaven. The priest who gave it to her said that it had been miraculously saved from shipwreck, and that its spiritual qualities were most efficacious. At all events I found that the servants' hall, made and furnished with thoughtful care, had been converted into a temple for her use. I was rather nonplussed. In the first place, it seemed a pity that the whole staff should be deprived of their sitting-room, not that they minded, as comfort in our idea of the word really does not exist in the Chinese conception; in the second, crowds of people from all the country-side, began to make our house a place of pilgrimage. I could not feel that an Empress of Heaven in our midst was entirely desirable. However, she stayed, and as time went on, I often met women with trouble in their eyes coming towards the house. They carried spirit-money and bundles of incense and came to beg intervention for a sick child, a parent or a husband. The little temple which had been very bare became more furnished. Thank-offerings beautified its walls, and I heard of numerous cures attributed to the power of the little lady who sat, clothed in green silk, behind the curtains of a Heaven Palace. The wife of a municipal detective in the near-by police station, whose little son recovered after she had acted on the advice of Heaven's Empress, gave a lovely yellow hanging, beautifully embroidered with black characters.

One evening Amah appeared rather overcome, and told me the following story. It seems that an old woman had arrived from the Chinese city which lay quite five miles from our house. No one in the house had ever seen her before, but of course the staff received her politely and listened with great interest to her tale. She said that she had had a dream; that in the dream, Heaven's Empress had come before her and said: 'To the north-west, in the house of foreign people, I have a shrine, it is very nice and I am well pleased. There is, however, one thing lacking. I am entitled by rank to wear a rose-lined yellow satin coat, and the only one I have is green.' The old woman asked the Empress what size the coat should be, and received an answer before she awoke. The next morning she promptly bought the yellow satin and the rose, and made the coat. When it was finished she set off in a north-westerly direction, to find the shrine. By dusk she reached a rice shop not far away and in answer to her inquiries was directed to our house. . . .

. . . The intimate connection between the earthly sovereign and the Creator of the Universe cannot be too strongly insisted upon. The Above Ruler is supposed to occupy a circumpolar constellation composed of fifteen stars, which is called the Purple Protected Enclosure; and his representative on earth inhabits an enclosure known as the Purple Forbidden City. Monseigneur Favier in his work on Peking states that the Forbidden City is called purple because mortar of that colour was used in the construction of its walls, and this statement has often been repeated by subsequent writers. I am, however, able to find no evidence that it is correct. It is true that purple earth is supposed to have been used in building the Great Wall, which lies North of the Capital, and some confusion may have arisen between the two. At all events the Celestial Palace near the North Star is the prototype of the Imperial Palace where the Son of Heaven passed his days in magnificent retirement from the World.

Nor does the simile stop here. In the names of seven hundred and fifty-nine asterisms of the Chinese celestial sphere, the nomenclature of officials and offices of the terrestrial court are reproduced, headed by that of Heaven's Emperor, Great Ruler which is applied to the polar star. The French astronomer, Biot, remarks: 'Without doubt the creation of these analogies sprang from superstitious ideas. In any case, can one not believe that the legislators, wishing to give to their government the most efficacious conditions of stability, strove to connect the rites with Heaven itself as the most conspicuous example of immutability.'

PHENOMENOLOGICAL DESCRIPTION
OF RELIGION

Scholars have written about religion in many ways. One method is to provide a clear, empathetic, but nonpartisan description of the forms of religion just as they appear. This is commonly called the phenomenological approach, because it seeks simply to present the phenomenon of religion as it exists. Scholars whose work is characterized by this approach include Emile Durkheim, Gerardus van der Leeuw, and Mircea Eliade.

A phenomenological description of religion requires that some cate-

gories be established; they should be openly defined and impartial. For example, a clear distinction is made between the sacred and the profane. The sacred refers to all those places, times, symbols, and experiences which are imbued with superhuman power and presence. The profane is simple, ordinary, drab, daily reality, untouched by the specialness of the sacred. In this passage a French scholar, Roger Caillois, further describes these two sides of experience so essential to religion, and emphasizes that a definition of the sacred requires and includes a definition of the profane.

From *Man and the Sacred*

Roger Caillois

Every religious conception of the universe implies a distinction between the sacred and the profane and is opposed to the world in which the believer freely attends to his business and engages in activity heedless of his salvation. The domain of the sacred is one in which he is paralyzed in turn by fear and by hope—a world in which, as at the edge of an abyss, the least misstep, the least movement can doom him irrevocably. To be sure, such a distinction is not always sufficient to define the phenomenon of religion, but at least it supplies a touchstone enabling us to recognize it with greater certainty. In effect, whatever definition is proposed for religion, it is remarkable how this opposition between the sacred and the profane is involved in it, even though not coinciding with it purely and simply. For a long time now, by logical inference or direct verification, it has been observed that religious man is, above all, one for whom two complimentary universes exist—one, in which he can act without anxiety or trepidation, but in which his actions only involve his superficial self; the other, in which a feeling of deep dependency controls, contains, and directs each of his drives, and to which he is committed unreservedly. These two worlds, the sacred and the profane, are rigorously defined only in relation to each other. They are mutually exclusive and contradictory. It is useless to try eliminating this contradiction. This opposition appears to be a genuinely intuitive concept. We can describe it, analyze it into its elements, and theorize about it. But it is no more within the power of abstract language to define its unique quality than to define a sensation. Thus the sacred seems like a category of feeling. In truth,

Roger Caillois, *Man and the Sacred*, trans. by Meyer Barash, pp. 19–25. Reprinted with permission of Macmillan Publishing Co., Inc., from *Man and the Sacred* by Roger Caillois. Copyright © 1959 by The Free Press.

that is the level on which religious attitudes exist and which gives them their special character. A feeling of special reverence imbues the believer, which fortifies his faith against critical inquiry, makes it immune to discussion, and places it outside and beyond reason.

"It is the basic idea of religion," writes H. Hubert. "Myths and dogmas characteristically comprise its content, ritual reflects its qualities, religious ethics derives from it, priesthoods embody it, sanctuaries, holy places and religious monuments enshrine it and enroot it. Religion is the administration of the sacred."

We couldn't stress more forcefully the points at which the experience of the sacred animates all the various manifestations of the religious way of life. This latter is, in effect, the sum total of man's relationships with the sacred. Creeds reveal and assure permanence to these relationships. Rites are the means of proving them in practice.

MAJOR CHARACTERISTICS OF THE SACRED

The sacred is related as a common property, solid or ephemeral, to certain objects (the instruments of the cult), to certain beings (kings, priests), to certain places (temple, church, mountain peak), to certain times (Sunday, Easter, Christmas, etc.). There is nothing that cannot become its resting place and thus clothe it in the eyes of the individual or the group with an unequaled prestige. The sacred is not something that can be taken away. It is a quality that things do not possess in themselves —a mysterious aura that has been added to things. "The bird which flies," a Dakota Indian explained to Miss Fletcher, "stops to build his nest. Man, who walks, stops where he pleases. Thus it is with divinity; the sun is one place where it has lodged, trees and animals are others. That is why we pray to them, for we reach the place where the sacred has stopped, and receive its succor and blessing."

The sacred being, the consecrated object, can in no way be modified in its appearance. Nevertheless, it is transformed in moving from person to person. From this moment on, the manner of its movement undergoes a parallel modification. It is no longer possible to partake of it freely. It stimulates feelings of terror and veneration; it becomes "taboo." Contact with it becomes dangerous. Automatic and immediate punishment would strike the imprudent one, as surely as flame burns the hand that touches it. The sacred is always more or less "what one cannot approach without dying."

As for the profane, one must, for reasons of self-interest, guard against a familiarity as deadly in its speed and its effects as the contagion of the sacred is crushing. The force that man or the holy contains is always ready to escape, to evaporate like a liquid, to discharge like electricity. It is no less necessary to protect the sacred from any taint of the profane. The profane, in effect, alters its essence, causes it to lose its unique quality—the void created by the impression of the formidable and fleeting power it contains. That is why we are careful to remove from a sacred place all that pertains to the profane world. Only the priest penetrates into the holy of holies. In Australia, the place where sacred objects or *churingas* are kept is not known by all. In the mysteries of the cult for which these objects are sacred instruments, the profane are kept ignorant of their hiding place. They only know its approximate site, and if they approach its vicinity, they have to make a great detour to avoid discovering it by chance. Among the Maori, if a woman enters the area in which a sacred boat is being built, the seaworthiness of the boat is affected and it cannot be launched. The presence of a profane being serves to remove the divine blessing. A woman who walks into a sacred place destroys its sanctity.

Without doubt, the profane, in relationship to the sacred, simply endows it with negative properties. The profane, in comparison, seems as poor and bereft of existence as nothingness is to being. But as R. Hertz expresses it so aptly, it is a *néant actif* that debases, degrades, and destroys the substance in terms of which it is defined. Thus it happens that watertight compartments separate the sacred from the profane. Any contact between them is fatal. "The two categories," writes Durkheim, "cannot be brought together without thereby losing their unique characteristics." On the other hand, they are both necessary for the evolution of life—one, as the environment within which life unfolds; the other, as the inexhaustible source that creates, sustains, and renews it.

THE SACRED, SOURCE OF SUCCESS

It is from the sacred, in effect, that the believer expects all succor and success. The reverence in which he holds the sacred is composed equally of terror and confidence. The calamities that menace and victimize him, the prosperity that he desires or gains, is attributed by him to some principle that he strives to control or constrain. It is of little importance what he imagines the supreme origin of grace or his ordeals to be—the universal and omnipotent God of the monotheistic religions; protective divinities of cities; spirits of the dead; an animistic power that gives each object its appropriate function, that makes boats rapid, weapons lethal, and food nourishing. As complex or simple as one can imagine, religion implies the recognition of this force with which man must reckon. All that seems to him to contain it appears sacred, terrible, and precious. On the other hand, he regards everything from which the sacred is absent as no doubt harmless, but powerless and unalluring. One can have only disdain for the profane, while the sacred inspires a kind of fascination. At the same time, it constitutes the supreme temptation and the greatest of dangers. Dreadful, it commands caution, and desirable, it invites rashness.

Thus, in its basic form, the sacred represents a dangerous force incomprehensible, intractable but eminently efficacious. For the one who decides to have recourse to it, the problem consists of capturing and utilizing it in his best interest, while at the same time protecting himself against the risks inherent in using a force so difficult to control. The more important the goal pursued, the more is the intervention of the sacred necessary, and the more perilous is preparation for it. The sacred cannot be subdued, diluted, or divided. It is indivisible and always a totality wherever it is found. In each bit of the consecrated wafer, the divinity of Christ is present in its entirety, for the smallest fragment of a relic possesses all the power of the total relic. The profane person must be careful in his desire to appropriate this power and must take proper precautions. The infidel who lays his hand upon the tabernacle sees it wither and crumble into dust. An unprepared individual cannot bear such a transformation of energy. The substance of the sacrilege becomes turgid, its branches diffuse and twist, its flesh decomposes, it soon dies of languor or convulsions. That is why, in some tribes, one must avoid touching the person of the chief when it is deemed sacred. The clothes the chief wears, the dish from which he eats, and his uneaten food are destroyed—burnt or buried. No one, except his own children who share his sanctity, dares to pick up a feather or turban that falls from the chief's head lest illness or death result.

DESCRIPTION OF RELIGION ORIENTED TOWARD SUBJECTIVITY

Religion can be described in terms of the inward feelings it produces as well as the outward forms it takes. The distinguished scholar Rudolf Otto (1869–1937), from whose writings the following passage is taken, contended that religion begins with a sense of the "numinous"— that is, with an awareness of a reality full of mystery and inspiring awe. This is the inward feeling which accompanies the recognition of what writers like Caillois and Eliade call the sacred, though Otto perhaps puts more emphasis on the surprising, uncanny, unpredictable character of that which engenders the numinous feeling, and its sheer awesomeness. Like most subjectivity-oriented writers on religion, he is correspondingly less interested in what might be called routine or scheduled encounters with the sacred in temple and festival.

From *The Idea of the Holy*
Rudolf Otto

Ein begriffener Gott ist kein Gott.
'A God comprehended is no God.' (TERSTEEGEN.)

We gave to the object to which the numinous consciousness is directed the name *mysterium tremendum*, and we then set ourselves first to determine the meaning of the adjective *tremendum*—which we found to be itself only justified by analogy—because it is more easily analysed than the substantive idea *mysterium*. We have now to turn to this, and try, as best we may, by hint and suggestion, to get to a clearer apprehension of what it implies.

THE 'WHOLLY OTHER'

It might be thought that the adjective itself gives an explanation of the substantive; but this is not so. It is not merely analytical; it is a synthetic attribute to it; i.e. *tremendum* adds something not necessarily inherent in *mysterium*. It is true that the reactions in consciousness that correspond to the one readily and spontaneously overflow into those that correspond to the other; in fact, anyone sensitive to the use of words would commonly feel that the idea of 'mystery' (*mysterium*) is so closely bound up with its synthetic qualifying attribute 'aweful' (*tremendum*) that one can hardly say the former without catching an echo of the latter, 'mystery' almost of itself becoming 'aweful mystery' to us. But the passage from the one idea to the other need not by any means be always so easy. The elements of meaning implied in 'awefulness' and 'mysteriousness' are in themselves definitely different. The latter may so far preponderate in the religious consciousness, may stand out so vividly, that in comparison with it the former almost sinks out of sight; a case which again could be clearly exemplified from some forms of mysticism. Occasionally, on the other hand, the reverse happens, and the *tremendum* may in turn occupy the mind without the *mysterium*.

Rudolf Otto, *The Idea of the Holy*, trans. John W. Harvey, 2d rev. ed. (New York: Oxford University Press, 1950), pp. 25–30. Reprinted by permission of the publisher.

This latter, then, needs special consideration on its own account. We need an expression for the mental reaction peculiar to it; and here, too, only one word seems appropriate, though, as it is strictly applicable only to a 'natural' state of mind, it has here meaning only by analogy: it is the word 'stupor.' *Stupor* is plainly a different thing from *tremor;* it signifies blank wonder, an astonishment that strikes us dumb, amazement absolute.[1] Taken, indeed, in its purely natural sense, *mysterium* would first mean merely a secret or a mystery in the sense of that which is alien to us, uncomprehended and unexplained; and so far *mysterium* is itself merely an ideogram, an analogical notion taken from the natural sphere, illustrating, but incapable of exhaustively rendering, our real meaning. Taken in the religious sense, that which is 'mysterious' is—to give it perhaps the most striking expression—the 'wholly other' (θάτερον, *anyad*, *alienum*), that which is quite beyond the sphere of the usual, the intelligible, and the familiar, which therefore falls quite outside the limits of the 'canny,' and is contrasted with it, filling the mind with blank wonder and astonishment.

This is already to be observed on the lowest and earliest level of the religion of primitive man, where the numinous consciousness is but an inchoate stirring of the feelings. What is really characteristic of this stage is *not*—as the theory of Animism would have us believe—that men are here concerned with curious entities, called 'souls' or 'spirits,' which happen to be invisible. Representations of spirits and similar conceptions are rather one and all early modes of 'rationalizing' a precedent experience, to which they are subsidiary. They are attempts in some way or other, it little matters how, to guess the riddle it propounds, and their effect is at the same time always to weaken and deaden the experience itself. They are the source from which springs, not religion, but the rationalization of religion, which often ends by constructing such a massive structure of theory and such a plausible fabric of interpretation, that the 'mystery' is frankly excluded.[2] Both imaginative 'myth,' when developed into a system, and intellectualist Scholasticism, when worked out to its completion, are methods by which the fundamental fact of religious experience is, as it were, simply rolled out so thin and flat as to be finally eliminated altogether.

---

[1]Compare also *obstupefacere*. Still more exact equivalents are the Greek θάμβος and θαμβεῖν. The sound θ α μ β *(thamb)* excellently depicts this state of mind of blank, staring wonder. And the difference between the moments of *stupor* and *tremor* is very finely suggested by the passage, Mark x. 32. On the other hand, what was said above of the facility and rapidity with which the two moments merge and blend is also markedly true of θάμβος, which then becomes a classical term for the (ennobled) awe of the numinous in general. So Mark xvi. 5 is rightly translated by Luther 'und sie entsetzten sich', and by the English Authorized Version 'and they were affrighted'.

[2]A spirit or soul that has been conceived and comprehended no longer prompts to 'shuddering', as is proved by Spiritualism. But it thereby ceases to be of interest for the psychology of religion.

Even on the lowest level of religious development the essential characteristic is therefore to be sought elsewhere than in the appearance of 'spirit' representations. It lies rather, we repeat, in a peculiar 'moment' of consciousness, to wit, the *stupor* before something 'wholly other,' whether such an other be named 'spirit' or 'daemon' or 'deva,' or be left without any name. Nor does it make any difference in this respect whether, to interpret and preserve their apprehension of this 'other,' men coin original imagery of their own or adapt imaginations drawn from the world of legend, the fabrications of fancy apart from and prior to any stirrings of daemonic dread.

In accordance with laws of which we shall have to speak again later, this feeling or consciousness of the 'wholly other' will attach itself to, or sometimes be indirectly aroused by means of, objects which are already puzzling upon the 'natural' plane, or are of a surprising or astounding character; such as extraordinary phenomena or astonishing occurrences or things in inanimate nature, in the animal world, or among men. But here once more we are dealing with a case of association between things specifically different—the 'numinous' and the 'natural' moments of consciousness—and not merely with the gradual enhancement of one of them —the 'natural'—till it becomes the other. As in the case of 'natural fear' and 'daemonic dread' already considered, so here the transition from natural to daemonic amazement is not a mere matter of degree. But it is only with the latter that the complementary expression *mysterium* perfectly harmonizes, as will be felt perhaps more clearly in the case of the adjectival form 'mysterious.' No one says, strictly and in earnest, of a piece of clockwork that is beyond his grasp, or of a science that he cannot understand: 'That is "mysterious" to me.'

It might be objected that the mysterious is something which is and remains absolutely and invariably beyond our understanding, whereas that which merely eludes our understanding for a time but is perfectly intelligible in principle should be called, not a 'mystery,' but merely a 'problem.' But this is by no means an adequate account of the matter. The truly 'mysterious' object is beyond our apprehension and comprehension, not only because our knowledge has certain irremovable limits, but because in it we come upon something inherently 'wholly other,' whose kind and character are incommensurable with our own, and before which we therefore recoil in a wonder that strikes us chill and numb.[3]

---

[3]In *Confessions*, ii. 9. i, Augustine very strikingly suggests this stiffening, benumbing element of the 'wholly other' and its contrast to the rational aspect of the numen; the *dissimile* and the *simile*:

'Quid est illud, quod interlucet mihi et percutit cor meum sine laesione? Et inhorresco et inardesco. *Inhorresco*, in quantum *dissimilis* ei sum. Inardesco, in quantum similis ei sum.'

('What is that which gleams through me and smites my heart without wounding it? I am both a-shudder and a-glow. A-shudder, in so far as I am unlike it, a-glow in so far as I am like it.')

This may be made still clearer by a consideration of that degraded offshoot and travesty of the genuine 'numinous' dread or awe, the fear of ghosts. Let us try to analyse this experience. We have already specified the peculiar feeling-element of 'dread' aroused by the ghost as that of 'grue,' grisly horror.[4] Now this 'grue' obviously contributes something to the attraction which ghost-stories exercise, in so far, namely, as the relaxation of tension ensuing upon our release from it relieves the mind in a pleasant and agreeable way. So far, however, it is not really the ghost itself that gives us pleasure, but the fact that we are rid of it. But obviously this is quite insufficient to explain the ensnaring attraction of the ghost-story. The ghost's real attraction rather consists in this, that of itself and in an uncommon degree it entices the imagination, awakening strong interest and curiosity; it is the weird thing itself that allures the fancy. But it does this, not because it is 'something long and white' (as someone once defined a ghost), nor yet through any of the positive and conceptual attributes which fancies about ghosts have invented, but because it is a thing that 'doesn't really exist at all,' the 'wholly other,' something which has no place in our scheme of reality but belongs to an absolutely different one, and which at the same time arouses an irrepressible interest in the mind.

But that which is perceptibly true in the fear of ghosts, which is, after all, only a caricature of the genuine thing, is in a far stronger sense true of the 'daemonic' experience itself, of which the fear of ghosts is a mere off-shoot. And while, following this main line of development, this element in the numinous consciousness, the feeling of the 'wholly other,' is heightened and clarified, its higher modes of manifestation come into being, which set the numinous object in contrast not only to everything wonted and familiar (i.e. in the end, to nature in general), thereby turning it into the 'supernatural,' but finally to the world itself, and thereby exalt it to the 'supramundane,' that which is above the whole world-order.

In mysticism we have in the 'beyond' (ἐπέκεινα) again the strongest stressing and over-stressing of those non-rational elements which are already inherent in all religion. Mysticism continues to its extreme point this contrasting of the numinous object (the numen), as the 'wholly other,' with ordinary experience. Not content with contrasting it with all that is of nature or this world, mysticism concludes by contrasting it with Being itself and all that 'is,' and finally actually calls it 'that which is nothing.' By this 'nothing' is meant not only that of which nothing can be predicated, but that which is absolutely and intrinsically other than and opposite of everything that is and can be thought. But while exaggerating to the point of paradox this *negation* and contrast—the only means open to conceptual thought to apprehend the *mysterium*—mysticism at the same time retains the *positive quality* of the 'wholly other' as a very living factor in its over-brimming religious emotion.

[4]*gruseln, gräsen.*

But what is true of the strange 'nothingness' of our mystics holds good equally of the *sūnyam* and the *sūnyatā*, the 'void' and 'emptiness' of the Buddhist mystics. This aspiration for the 'void' and for becoming void, no less than the aspiration of our western mystics for 'nothing' and for becoming nothing, must seem a kind of lunacy to anyone who has no inner sympathy for the esoteric language and ideograms of mysticism, and lacks the matrix from which these come necessarily to birth. To such an one Buddhism itself will be simply a morbid sort of pessimism. But in fact the 'void' of the eastern, like the 'nothing' of the western, mystic is a numinous ideogram of the 'wholly other'.

These terms 'supernatural' and 'transcendent'[5] give the appearance of positive attributes, and, as applied to the mysterious, they appear to divest the *mysterium* of its originally negative meaning and to turn it into an affirmation. On the side of conceptual thought this is nothing more than appearance, for it is obvious that the two terms in question are merely negative and exclusive attributes with reference to 'nature' and the world or cosmos respectively. But on the side of the feeling-content it is otherwise; that *is* in very truth positive in the highest degree, though here too, as before, it cannot be rendered explicit in conceptual terms. It is through this positive feeling-content that the concepts of the 'transcendent' and 'supernatural' become forthwith designations for a unique 'wholly other' reality and quality, something of whose special character we can *feel*, without being able to give it clear conceptual expression.

THEORETICAL EXPRESSION OF RELIGION

The concluding selections in this introductory chapter present three basic forms of religious expression as defined by the historian of religion Joachim Wach (1898–1955). Wach said that in human life the religious experience is expressed and known through three forms: the "theoretical," which means its presentation in ideas, words, stories, and philosophies; the "practical," which means what is expressed in the religion through rites, worship, pilgrimage, prayer, meditation, art, and symbol; and the "sociological," referring to the kinds of institutions, groups, and leaders which arise in response to the experience. All religious systems have these three forms of expression, intimately related to one another.

To illustrate these forms of religious expression, three selections dealing with one religion have been chosen. The religion is Zoroastrianism, the faith of ancient Persia which is still practiced by the Parsees of modern Bombay and elsewhere. Stemming from the words of the prophet Zoroaster, or Zarathustra (probably 660–583 B.C.), this faith tells us there

[5]Literally, supramundane: *überweltlich.*

is a cosmic battle between the high God, Ahura Mazda, lord of all that is holy and pure, and the forces of evil. The teachings of Zoroastrianism are especially concerned with eschatology, that is, with the themes of death, judgment, the end of the world, the resurrection of the dead, and the final victory of good. In the passage below we see some of the main doctrines of Zoroastrianism presented. This selection also suggests the kind of scholarship in ancient languages and sources which is necessary to reconstruct and understand the faiths of ages past.

From *Zoroastrian Studies*

A.V. Williams Jackson

Among the nations of antiquity there seems to have been none that had a more clearly developed system of eschatology, a firmer conviction of the immortality of the soul, and a surer belief in a resurrection and a future life, than had the ancient Iranians so far as we can judge from their sacred literature. Through all the writings of Zoroastrianism runs a strain of hope that the good will be rewarded hereafter an dthe wicked punished; that right will triumph and evil will be vanquished; that the dead shall arise and live again; and that the world will be restored to perfection so that joy and happiness may reign supreme.

In the Gāthās themselves, the pious expectation of a new order of things is the motif upon which Zoroaster rings continual changes. A mighty crisis is impending; every man ought to choose the right and seek to attain the ideal state; mankind shall then become perfect and the world renovated (*fərašɔm . . ahūm, fərašōtɔma, frašōkɔrɔti* etc.). This event will be the establishment of the power and dominion of good over evil; it will be the beginning of the complete rule of the sovereignty divine—'the Kingdom (*xšaθra*) or 'the Good Kingdom' (*vohu xšaθra*) as it is called. It is at the coming of this blessed era that the resurrection of the dead will take place. A general judgment is to follow and this will be accompanied by a flood of molten metal in which the wicked will be punished, the righteous cleansed, and evil be banished forever from the earth.

In addition to the sacred literature of Iran itself we have also the testimony of early Greek writers in regard to this subject. The authority of Theopompus (flourished B.C. 338), and also of Eudemus of Rhodes (same century) in confirmation, is quoted to this effect by Diogenes Laertius (fl. c. A.D. 210), *Prooem.* (6), 9, as well as by Aeneas of Gaza (early

A.V. Williams Jackson, *Zoroastrian Studies* (New York: Columbia University Press, 1928), pp. 143–51. Notes omitted. Reprinted by permission of the publisher.

sixth cent. A.D.), *Theophrastus*, 77; and Plutarch earlier (c. A.D. 46–120), *Isis and Osiris*, ch. 47, drew likewise upon Theopompus, whom he mentions by name. The combined statements bear witness to the recognized doctrine of a coming millennium, a general resurrection of the dead, and a complete restoration of the world. A passage in Herodotus (*Hist.* 3. 62), as far back as the fifth century B.C., has been presumed to allude to the Persian doctrine of a resurrection of the dead, but this interpretation of the sentence has been questioned. With regard to the immortality of the soul we must also consider the speech which Xenophon (*Cyrop.* 8. 7. 17–22) puts into the mouth of the dying Cyrus, although this seems to have the coloring of Greek ideas .The Zoroastrian Gāthās, the Younger Avesta and the Pahlavi Books, together with later texts, have abundant references to the future life, including also the idea of the resurrection.

The fate of the soul after death and the individual judgment, as already indicated, are favorite themes in the Zoroastrian Scriptures. There are dozens of allusions to the journey of the spirit from this world to the one beyond. Only a brief mention of these can be made here. The typical passage is found in the Hātokht Nask (Yt. 22. I–36; and compare Vishtāsp Yasht, Yt. 24. 53–64). For the first three nights after the breath has left the body the soul hovers about the lifeless frame and experiences joy or sorrow according to the deeds done in this life. On the dawn of the fourth day the soul takes flight from earth amid the waftings of a perfumed breeze or stifled by a blast of stench, according as the individual has been righteous or wicked. It is then met either by a beauteous maiden or by a hideous hag. The image is in either case a reflection of the man's former life, conscience, and religion (*daēnā*). The soul thus arrives at the fateful Judgment Bridge (*činvatō peretu,* lit. 'Bridge of the Separator'). The individual judgment now takes place in the presence of the three angels, Mithra, Sraosha, and Rashnu. These are the joint-assessors before whom the life account is rendered and the good and bad deeds respectively are weighed in the balance. According to the impartial scales the final decision is rendered. The pangs of conscience experienced at this ordeal, even by the righteous soul, and its terror at the assaults of the demons may be imagined.

Next comes the awful crossing of the Chinvat Bridge, that judgment span which stretches over Hell between the divine Mount Alburz and the Dāityā peak, near the Dāityā river. This bridge plays an important role throughout all ages of Zoroastrianism. The difficulties of the passage across it are often alluded to and dilated upon from the Gāthās onward to the latest Persian writings. According to the orthodox doctrine the bridge grows broader and easier of transit, a pathway 'nine javelins' or a 'league' in breadth, as the soul of the righteous ascends over it to heaven; but it grows narrower as the wicked passes along, until it presents an edge like 'the thinness of the blade of a razor', so that the lost soul falls into the abysm of hell within the bowels of the earth.

After the individual judgment has taken place descriptions portray the progress of the righteous man on the spirit-journey through the mansions of Good Thoughts, Good Words, Good Deeds—*humata, hūxta, hvaršta*. These abodes are depicted as lying respectively in the spheres of the stars, the moon, and the sun. At last the pious soul enters into heaven, the place of 'Eternal Light' (*anaγra raočå*), or the blissful Garōnmāna, 'the house of song', the 'fair abode' (*hušiti*) which is 'the dwelling of Good Thought' (*vaŋhəuš dəmānəm manaŋhō*), that 'Best Life' (*aŋhu vahišta*), or paradise eternal, 'where Ahura Mazdāh dwells in joy.'

In sharp antithesis to this is the fearful descent of the wicked soul through the grades of 'Evil Thoughts, Evil Words, and Evil Deeds', into a Hell of darkness so thick that it can be grasped by the hand. This is a place so foul, so gloomy, so lonely, that although the suffering souls be as many and as close together 'as the hairs in a horse's mane,' still each one in despair thinks that he is alone. This scene of frightful torment which rivals Dante's Inferno is 'the house of Falsehood' (*drujō dəmānəm*), 'the dwelling of the Worst Thought' or 'the Worst Life,'—it is Hell!

With perfect logic Zoroastrianism taught also the existence of an intermediate or third place which was suited to the special cases in which the good and evil deeds, done in life, exactly balanced. This is known in Pahlavi as the place of the Hamēstakān (perhaps read *Hamyastakān?*), 'the commingled, or equilibrium.' The name is foreshadowed in the Gāthās and the idea is old. This third state, somewhat resembling a limbo, is conceived of as located between the earth and the stellar region. Here the soul suffers no torment more severe than the changes of heat and cold due to the seasons, and here it must abide awaiting the general resurrection and the final judgment day.

We turn now to the ancient Iranian doctrines of eschatology in its stricter sense, which deal with the millennium, the advent of a Saoshyant or Savior, the resurrection of the dead, the punishment of the wicked in a flood of molten metal through which the righteous pass unscathed, the purification of hell, and the establishment of a holy sovereignty that is to be the regeneration of the world. The Avesta and the Pahlavi texts often refer to this new era and rejuvenation as *frašōkərəti* and *fraškart̲* respectively. In this way the millennium is really the preparation of all mankind for eternity and the perfection of the world, a blessed consummation in which man should have a share. At the great crisis or final change of the world there will be a decisive division and separation of the evil from the good, and a complete establishment of Ahura's sovereignty, 'the Good Kingdom' (*vohu xšaθra*).

This dogma of a new heaven and a new earth' is found both in the Gāthās and in the Younger Avesta. It is decidedly a millennial doctrine which is closely associated with the belief in the coming of a Savior (*Saošyant*) and the resurrection of the dead. These teachings were recognized as characteristically 'Magian' by Theopompus and they entered into the hieratic chronology of the Bundahishn, which bounded the history of the world by a great aeon of 12,000 years (see above, Chap. VII). The Pahlavi texts call the last 3000 years of this aeon the millennia of *Aūšēṭar, Aūšēṭar-māh,* and *Sōšyans,* or *Sōšans* (Av. *Uxšaṭ∂r∂ta, Uxšaṭ-n∂mah,* and *Saošyant).* At intervals of a thousand years the three millennial prophets are born of three maidens bathing in the 'Sea of Kasaoya,' the modern Hāmūn or lake in Seistān, where some of the semen of Zarathustra is preserved.

The entire development of the idea of a Savior in Persia and the use and meaning of Av. *Saošyant,* Phl. *Sōšyans,* or *Sōšāns,* have been discussed by the present writer and by others. The author has attempted in his article in the *Biblical World* to show how much the Messiah-idea in Judaism and the Saoshyant-idea in Mazdaism, probably taught by Zoroaster himself, resemble each other. The most important passage in the Iranian scriptures concerning the events of the last days is preserved in the thirtieth chapter of the Bundahishn, which is based, according to tradition, on the lost Avestan text Dāmdāt Nask. According to this account the events connected with the resurrection of the dead (Phl. *rīstāxēz)* and the renovation of the world by the Saoshyant and his assistants, fifteen men and fifteen damsels (Bd. 30. 17) occupy fifty-seven years. Immediately after these follows the general judgment and a flood of molten metal overwhelms the earth to cleanse it from its sin. Through this white-hot stream all men must walk, but to the righteous the metal seems no more terrible than warm milk. When this ordeal is passed, all will become pure, and there will be a happy reunion never to be broken. The final conflict between the powers of good and evil will then take place; Ahriman and his hordes are routed and put down; the serpent is burned in the molten metal; hell itself is purified, the mountains pass away, and (Bd. 30. 32) 'Ormazd brings the land of hell back for the enlargement of the world; the renovation arises in the universe by his will, and the world is immortal for ever and everlasting.'

Such, in brief outline, is the Zoroastrian doctrine of the future life and the end of the world. The similarity between it and the Christian doctrine is striking and deserves more attention on the side of Christian theology, even though much has been written on this subject.

PRACTICAL EXPRESSION OF RELIGION

These two short passages deal with a ritual of Zoroastrianism, the preparation of haoma *or* homa, *a sacred plant embodying the purity of Ahura Mazda. The preparation, drinking, and offering of a liquid made from the plant is one of the most important Parsee rites. The first passage, from the* Avesta, *the Zoroastrian scripture, shows the relationship of theoretical to practical expression, because it is a scriptural validation of a rite. The second reflects the precision and solemn atmosphere of a sacred ritual. Universally, priestly rites have a formal quality, in contrast to freer, less controlled expression of devotional fervor.*

From *Avesta: The Religious Books of the Parsis*
Arthur Henry Bleeck

Creator! When is the Haŏma pure which has been brought to a dead dog or man, O pure Ahura-Mazda?
Then answered Ahura-Mazda: It is pure, O pure Zarathustra!
The prepared Haŏma has neither dissolution nor death;
Not even when it is brought to a dead body.
Only that which is not prepared, as much as four fingers long,
This shall they lay on the ground, in the midst of the dwelling,
Until a year is gone by.
After the expiration of a year, it can be used according to [his] desire by the pure man, just as before.

From *Essays on the Sacred Language,*
Writings and Religion of the Parsis
Martin Haug

The Homa twigs must next be purified. These twigs are brought from Iran by traders, and are, therefore, considered impure until they have been purified, laid aside for a year, and again purified. The puri-

Arthur Henry Bleeck, *Avesta: The Religious Books of the Parsis* (Hertford: Stephan Austin, 1864), p. 54.

Martin Haug, *Essays on the Sacred Language, Writings, and Religion of the Parsis,* edited and enlarged by E.W. West (London: Kegan Paul, Trubner & Co., Ltd., 1878), p. 399.

fication is accomplished by water and formulas. The priest takes the Homa twig (one is sufficient) in his right hand, holding a copper goblet of water in his left, from which he pours water, at intervals, over the twig as he thrice recites *khshnaothra Ahurahê mazdâo,* &c., and *a. v.* He then takes the Jîvâm in his left hand and recites *a. v.* thrice, *fravarânê* (Yas. iii. 24, to) *frasastayaêcha, haomahê ashavazanhô* (Yas. x. 1, but only these two words), *khshnaothra,* &c. (as in p. 398, lines 8-10 above, to) *mraotû,* and *ashem a. v.* thrice, each time dipping the Jîvâm and Homa, which he holds one in each hand, into the water. Then follow *y. a. v.* twice, *yasnem-cha* (Yt. i. 23, to) *âfrînâmi,* and *haomahê ashavazanhô*; these last two words must be first spoken aloud, and then repeated in a low voice as a Bâj. The Homa twig is now laid in its place, in a metal saucer on the *takht.*

The priest takes three small pieces of the Homa and one of the Urvarâm (the *hadhânaêpatãm* or pomegranate twig), and lays them on the Hâvanîm or Homa mortar which is placed, upside down, upon the *takht.* When the Varasa is to be laid in its place, in a cup on the *takht,* after being consecrated, it must be held below between the fingers.

The Homa juice is now to be prepared. The priest takes the Varasa and Jîvâm in his hands, and recites *a. v.* thrice, *fravarânê* (to) *frasastay-aêcha,* and *Zarathushtrahê Spitâmahê* (to) *mraotû.* He then dips the Varasa into a cup full of water, utters the word *ashem* twice (once aloud and once in a low voice as a Bâj), and then lays the Varasa in its proper place.

SOCIOLOGICAL EXPRESSION OF RELIGION

These two passages illustrate how religious traditions express themselves as community, and as ethical values which inhere in a community seeing itself as sacred and set apart. The first reading is transitional from practical expression, for in describing the initiation into the Zoroastrian (Parsee) community it reveals a characteristic ritual care. But the great reality one feels shining through this account is the reality of the community with its traditions which these rites reinforce. The second passage, by a modern Parsee spokesman, also refers to the importance to Zoroastrians of bringing children into their faith and community. It shows the importance to Zoroastrians of seeing their community as the holder of ethical ideals. Notice in all these passages the common theme of purity versus impurity, and of Ahura Mazda and his rites and people as the holders of purity. This motif is expressed in doctrine (the judgment and the triumph of good), rite (haoma), and sociology (the community into which one is initiated; ethical ideals).

From *History of the Parsis*

Dosabhai Framji Karaka

The investiture of the child, whether boy or girl, with the "sudra" and "kusti" takes place, according to religious injunction, any time after it has attained the age of six years and three months, but not before that age. The wearing of the "jabhla" is then discontinued, and, as in the case of the adult, the "sudra" and "kusti" are worn instead. This ceremony is performed in an imposing manner, as will be seen from the following description. The boy or girl, whom we will term the candidate, sits before a Parsi priest, who utters certain prayers and makes him or her drink three times the sacred "nirangdin," and chew part of a leaf of the pomegranate tree. The child is then bathed, after which it is dressed in a pair of trousers and cap with a clean white linen sheet wrapped round the body. In this state the candidate is taken by the priest to the hall or room where the ceremony is to be performed, and where are already assembled the "dastur" or chief priest, the relatives of the child, and a number of male and female guests invited to witness the ceremony. On this occasion all the ladies appear in their best attire and adorn themselves with fine jewellery. The assembly, composed as it is of the "dastur" and other priests dressed in their snow-white robes and turbans, of the gentlemen who wear their best clothes, and of the ladies in their brilliant dresses of many colours, is a pleasing and gay sight to behold. Throughout the performance of the ceremony strict silence prevails, which adds considerable solemnity to the occasion. The "dastur" and the priests take their places upon a rich carpet spread upon the floor, while the members of the family and guests sit around on chairs or sofas. The candidate is seated on a flat wooden stool before the "dastur," who, together with another priest, begins to recite the "patet" or prayer of repentance, in which the candidate joins if he is able to do so. After this the "dastur" requires the child to hold the "sudra" with both hands, and, placing his own upon them, causes the following confession of faith to be repeated: "Praise be to the Mazdayasnan religion, created by the holiness, the purity, and the wisdom of Ahura Mazda. The good, righteous, right religion which the Lord has sent to His creatures is that which Zoroaster has brought. The religion is the religion of Zoroaster, the religion of Ahura Mazda given to Zoroaster."

After this the "dastur" removes the linen sheet which had at first been wrapped round the child's body and puts on in place thereof the "sudra," held up to that point in the child's hands. The "dastur" then

Dosabhai Framji Karaka, *History of the Parsis*, Vol. I (London: Macmillan and Co., 1884), pp. 165–68.

passes the "kusti" round the child's waist three times, repeating the "kusti nirang," as it is called, after which the infant is reseated on the stool, and the "dastur" delivers the "hosbam," a sort of sermon in praise of honesty, truth, and purity. This over, he pronounces blessings upon the candidate, throwing over his head the whole of a mixture composed of pieces of cocoa-nut, rice, and almonds. The full ceremony occupies about an hour, and when it is concluded the head of the family gives presents of money to the "dastur" and the other priests according to their rank. After this the assembly disperses.

The boy or girl who has been thus initiated into the Zoroastrian religion is forthwith dressed in new and fine clothes, which are put on over the "sudra." Friends and relatives then hasten to present their gifts in money or dresses to the child and its parents. All the members of the family and the guests finally partake of a sumptuous feast. In the case of the rich it is usual to give a dinner-party on the same evening, when appropriate toasts are proposed and drunk.

The "sudra," which is always worn next to the skin, is made of fine linen gauze or net, while the "kusti" is a thin woollen cord, or cincture of seventy-two threads; these threads represent the seventy-two "has" or chapters of the sacred book of the Parsis, called *Yazashne.* The "sudra" means "the garment of the good and beneficial way." The "kusti" is passed round the waist three times and tied with four knots, two in front and two behind, during the chanting of a short hymn. At the first knot the person says, "There is only one God, and no other is to be compared with Him;" at the second, "The religion given by Zoroaster is true;" at the third, "Zoroaster is the true Prophet, who derived his mission from God;" and at the fourth and last, "Perform good actions, and abstain from evil ones."

From *Zoroastrianism: The Religion of the Good Life*

Rustom Masani

The fundamental principle of the creed is embodied in the triad *Humata, Hukhta, Hvarshta,* good thought, good word, good deed. The antithesis of this triad, which is the sum and substance of all morality, is *Dushmata, Duzukhta, Duzvarshta,* evil thought, evil word, and evil deed. *"To all good thoughts, words, and deeds (belongs) Paradise, so is it mani-*

Rustom Masani, *Zoroastrianism: The Religion of the Good Life* (New York: Collier Books, 1962), pp. 77–78. Reprinted by permission of Macmillan Publishing Co., and George Allen & Unwin.

fest to the pure." This is the simple admonition given in the prayer *Vispa Humata.* In another prayer the devotee says: "Henceforth let me stand firm for good thoughts, good words and good deeds, which must be well thought, must be well spoken and must be well done."

Great importance was attached by the ancient Zoroastrians to the training of the youth in civics. They considered it essential so to educate children during their most impressionable days as to deepen their concern for the common good and to stimulate and diffuse a spirit of citizenship. In the *Cyropaedia* Xenophon gives an interesting account of the schools in Iran, in which such training was given, the first of the kind recorded in history.

"In every Persian city," says Xenophon, "is a free square, from which commerce and industry are rigorously excluded, and which contains the palace and the chief municipal buildings. On one side is the school for children from five to sixteen (up to five they live at home in the nursery), on the second, the institute for youth from sixteen to the full manhood of twenty-six, on the third, that for the man of mature years, on the fourth, that for the elders who are past the age of military service. The curriculum is remarkable; there appear to be no lessons, but only debates and 'trials' dealing with the practical events of the school life and conducted under the presidency of an appointed elder. These occupy the greater portion of the day; the rest is occupied with riding and shooting on the campus." As Xenophon puts it: "The Persians send their children to school that they may learn righteousness, as we do that they may learn letters."

Some of the notable virtues on which special emphasis was laid in the scriptures and which, one might expect, could not have failed to influence the life and character of the followers of the faith, may be noted.

II

GODS AND SPIRITS,
MEN WOMEN:
PRIMITIVE RELIGION

People who are nonliterate, whose major social unit is a relatively small tribe or clan, and who do not have extensive division of labor, are commonly called "primitive." Generally their economy is based on hunting and gathering, or on simple agriculture. The religion (as we shall see) is a collection of gods, spirits, festivals, and the like not wholly rationalized into a neat system. The word "primitive" is unfortunate insofar as it suggests a disparaging assessment of a culture as crude and backward. But "primitive" really means "first." The word can be strongly positive if it is thought of as indicating culture that is "first" not only chronologically but also in the sense of being basic. It shows where we all came from, and also reveals themes fundamental to interpreting the human experience.

This is certainly the case with religion. It is difficult to make comparisons between the religions of the few primitive peoples existing today and those of the earliest men and women. Some "primitives" of today represent cultures once more complex, and all today are, like us, the product of many millenia of development. But there is no doubt that virtually every motif of the great religions of literate societies is foreshadowed in primitive religion, and that the symbols and customs of the former are shot through with carryovers from preliterate society. This is not to say that the meaning of a high god or a spring festival is the same in both cases, for it is not. But it does suggest that primitive societies provide crucial clues to perceiving human continuities.

Primitive religion is infinitely varied. But certain themes do appear widely, and all we can do in this book is present a few of them, or rather present a few passages which illustrate the way some of them were handled in some primitive situations.

Among major motifs are the concept of a god or gods making the world at the beginning, the destiny of the soul through life and death, and the response of the community to death, the festival, the initiation of youths, the highly charged relations of men and women, shamanism or the role of ecstatic religious specialists, and the sacred meaning of hunting and agriculture. Behind all of these lies an even more fundamental theme, one which we have already encountered in the discussions of the sacred and the numinous in the last chapter. This is the conviction that while human experience very often lies on a drab and ordinary level, another dimension of reality can also come within the human orbit. Whether encountered in the most intense moments of community life or alone in the wilderness, whether met in dreams or in rite, this other dimension has ties to ultimate origins and destinies, to visions and fantasies, and to the basic structures upon which society is founded. It is this dimension which primitive mankind (like the rest of mankind) has channeled through thousands of patterns.

Sometimes the other side seems far away, sometimes near at hand; sometimes bound to the cycles of nature, sometimes sudden and capricious. Often human society itself limns the pattern to follow the divisions in which biology has divided it—male and female, parents of single births and parents of twins, members of different clans, have all taken on overtones of possessing different qualities of the sacred standing over against each other.

Finally, the often-desperate struggle of primitive peoples to survive has a dual impact on religion. It means that while they can rarely afford the indulgence of living wholly for the sacred, and the arts and culture it represents, neither can they afford to overlook any source of power for survival. Religion and economic life flow together, and are parts of a psychologically unified—if not tightly systematic—world view.

Here are some passages which give examples of primitive world views and how they worked.

THE HIGH GOD

One idea found over a wide spectrum of primitive societies is of a "high god" resident in the sky. He is typically said to have first created the world and humankind, and to have laid down the fundamental moral laws incumbent upon the latter. But this sovereign deity then withdrew, leaving the spiritual scene mainly in the hands of lesser entities: masters of animals, godlets of nature, ancestral ghosts. In this passage the distinguished historian of religion Mircea Eliade describes this process.

From *The Sacred and the Profane*

Mircea Eliade

The history of supreme beings whose structure is celestial is of the utmost importance for an understanding of the religious history of humanity as a whole. We cannot even consider writing that history here, in a few pages.[1] But we must at least refer to a fact that to us seems primary. Celestially structured supreme beings tend to disappear from the practice of religion, from cult; they depart from among men, withdraw to the sky, and become remote, inactive gods (*dei otiosi*). In short, it may be said of these gods that, after creating the cosmos, life, and man, they feel a sort of fatigue, as if the immense enterprise of the Creation had exhausted their resources. So they withdraw to the sky, leaving a son or a demiurge on earth to finish or perfect the Creation. Gradually their place is taken by other divine figures—the mythical ancestors, the mother-goddesses, the fecundating gods, and the like. The god of the storm still preserves a celestial structure, but he is no longer a creating supreme being; he is only the fecundator of the earth, sometimes he is only a helper to his companion (*paredros*), the earth-mother. The celestially structured supreme being preserves his preponderant place only among pastoral peoples, and he attains a unique situation in religions that tend to monotheism (Ahura-Mazda) or that are fully monotheistic (Yahweh, Allah).

The phenomenon of the remoteness of the supreme god is already documented on the archaic levels of culture. Among the Australian Kulin, the supreme being Bunjil himself created the universe, animals, trees, and man; but after investing his son with power over the earth and his daughter with power over the sky, Bunjil withdrew from the world. He remains among the clouds, like a lord, holding a huge sword. Puluga, the supreme being of the Andaman Islanders, withdrew after creating the world and the first man. The mystery of his remoteness has its counterpart in an almost complete absence of cult; there is no sacrifice, no appeal, no thank

Mircea Eliade, *The Sacred and the Profane*, trans. Willard R. Trask (New York: Harper & Row, 1961), pp. 121–25. Copyright 1957 by Rowohlt Taschenbuch Verlag GmbH; copyright 1959 by Harcourt Brace Jovanovich, Inc., and reprinted with their permission.

[1]For basic data, cf. Eliade, *Patterns*, pp. 38–123. Cf. especially R. Pettazoni, *Dio*, Rome, 1921; *id.*, *L'onniscienza di Dio*, Turin, 1955; Wilhelm Schmidt, *Ursprung der Gottesidee*, I–XII, Münster, 1926–1955.

offering. The memory of Puluga survives in only a few religious customs—for example, the sacred silence of hunters returning to their village after a successful hunt.

The Dweller in the Sky or He Who Is in the Sky of the Selk'nam is eternal, omniscient, all-powerful, the creator; but the Creation was finished by the mythical ancestors, who had also been made by the supreme god before he withdrew to a place above the stars. For now this god has isolated himself from men, is indifferent to the affairs of the world. He has neither images nor priests. Prayers are addressed to him only in case of sickness. "Thou who are above, take not my child; he is still too young!"[2] Offerings are rarely made to him except during storms.

It is the same among many African peoples; the great celestial god, the supreme being, all-powerful creator, plays only a minor role in the religious life of most tribes. He is too far away or too good to need an actual cult, and he is invoked only in extreme cases. Thus, for example, Olorun (Owner of the Sky) of the Yoruba, after beginning the Creation of the world, deputed finishing and ruling it to a lower god, Obatala. For his part, Olorun withdrew from human and earthly affairs, and the supreme god has neither temples nor statues nor priests. Nevertheless, *he is invoked as a last resource in times of calamity.*

Withdrawn into the sky, Ndyambi, the supreme god of the Herero, has abandoned humanity to lower divinities. "Why should we sacrifice to him?" a member of the tribe explained. "We do not need to fear him, for he does not do us any harm, as do the spirits of our dead."[3] The supreme being of the Tukumba is "too great for the common affairs of men."[4] The case is the same with Njankupon among the Tshi-speaking Negroes of West Africa; he has no cult, and homage is paid to him only under unusual circumstances, in case of mamines or epidemics or after a violent storm; men then ask him how they have offended him. Dzingbe (the Universal Father), the supreme being of the Ewe, is invoked only during droughts: "O Sky, to whom we owe thanks, great is the drought; make it rain, so that the earth will be refreshed and the fields flourish!"[5] The remoteness and passivity of the supreme being are admirably expressed in a saying of the Gyriama of East Africa, which also describes their god: "Mulugu (God) is up above, the ghosts are down below!"[6] The Bantu say: "God, after creating man, no longer cares about him." And the Negritos repeat: "God has gone far away from us." The Fang

---

[2]Martin Gusinde, "Das höchste Wesen bei den Selk'nam auf Feuerland," *Festschrift W. Schmidt,* Vienna, 1928, pp. 269–274.

[3]Cf. Frazer, *The Worship of Nature,* I, London, 1926, pp. 150 ff.

[4]*Ibid.,* p. 185.

[5]J. Spieth, *Die Religion der Eweer,* Göttingen-Leipzig, 1911, pp. 46 ff.

[6]A. Le Roy, *La religion des primitifs,* 7th ed., Paris, 1925, p. 184.

peoples of the grasslands of Equatorial Africa sum up their religious philosophy in a song:

> God (Nzame) is above, man below.
> God is God, man is man.
> Each at home, each in his house.

It is useless to multiply examples. Everywhere in these primitive religions the celestial supreme being appears to have lost *religious currency*; he has no place in the cult, and in the myths he draws farther and farther away from man until he becomes a *deus otiosus*. Yet he is remembered and entreated as the last resort, *when all ways of appealing to other gods and goddesses, the ancestors, and the demons, have failed.* As the Oraons express it: "Now we have tried everything, but we still have you to help us." And they sacrifice a white cock to him, crying, "God, thou art our creator, have mercy on us."

DEATH AND THE SOUL

One of the most prevalent ideas in religion is belief that in human nature there is a quality which may be called spirit or soul. It is a consciousness and invisible power inhabiting the flesh yet able to live and act independently of it, and linked to the Other or Sacred side of reality. Soul is a power which sends mankind much trouble, yet also makes us immortal, with an eternal destiny in other worlds or reincarnate in this one.

This selection from the distinguished anthropologist John Middleton gives a vivid impression of this belief among the Lugbara people of Uganda in Africa. It shows how the rites of death and burial, and the "death dances," serve to reinforce this belief, to facilitate acceptance of the death by the kinsmen, and to incorporate it into the ongoing life of the tribe by making it a ritual and festive occasion with set procedures and by making the deceased another tutelary ancestral spirit of the tribe.

After the main passage comes a shorter passage from another book by the same author. Here he discusses more informally the field work which led up to the previous statement on Lugbara belief and practice surrounding death. The passage gives an honest and salutary impression of the difficulties which beset obtaining an accurate portrayal of what is really going on in a culture to which the writer is an outsider. It is well for us to bear in mind that such ambiguity may lie behind the most polished scholarly statements in comparative religion, and that sensitivity of a rare order is necessary even to begin to understand.

From *The Lugbara of Uganda*
John Middleton

Before discussing the cult of the dead, something should be said about the nature of man and Spirit. Lugbara regard Spirit as an all-pervasive power that stands outside men and beyond their control. It is omnipotent and timeless, and can create and destroy men and send them various sicknesses, disasters, and punishments as well as good and prosperity. Spirit is both good and evil. Spirit as a creator is known as *Adroa 'ba o'bapiri* (Spirit the creator of men), *Adroa onyiru* (good Spirit) or *Adroa 'bua* (Spirit in the sky). Spirit is invisible and "in the wind," and is not personalized, because Spirit created persons and it can hardly therefore be a person itself. Linguistically the form *Adroa* or *Adronga* is the diminutive, since it is thought to be remote from men and not come into direct contact with them.

Besides the transcendent aspect of Spirit in the sky, there is also the immanent form on the surface of the world. This is known as *Adro*, the diminutive form of which is *Adroa*. This aspect of Spirit is thought to have the form of a tall man, white in color, cut in half down the middle, and hopping about on its one leg. It lives in streams, bushland, and on mountains, and if seen will kill and eat the person who glimpses it. It is often known as *Adro onzi* (evil Spirit), and is greatly feared.[1] This aspect of Spirit comes into direct contact with men, and can harm them in many ways. *Adro* also possesses girls and gives them the power of divination. *Adro* is said to have children, *adroanzi* ("*Adro*-children"), who are spirits of various kinds that live in streams, hills, and trees; they also guard rain groves. They have the form of small men and women, and can become visible, but a man who sees them dies. *Adroa, Adro,* and the *adroanzi* are found throughout Lugbara. In addition, each clan has its own *adro*-spirit, a manifestation of the power of Spirit that was concerned in the original genesis of each clan. Clans are linked together in this way, as well as having their separate ancestors. There are no rites associated with Spirit, except for certain prayers made to it at times of famine or disaster. Spirit comes into contact with men by sending sickness and disasters, and for men to contact it they must use diviners, prophets, or other persons

John Middleton, *The Lugbara of Uganda* (New York: Holt, Rinehart and Winston, 1963), pp. 63–66, 67–70. Reprinted by permission of the publisher.

[1]One of the older-fashioned terms for a European is *Adro*, because Europeans are white and are believed to eat the people they take to hospitals and prisons.

who can communicate with it and who can interpret its various manifestations in the form of sickness, lightning, and epidemics.

When people die, they cease to be "people of the world outside" and become "people who have died" or "people in the earth." They are still "people" or "persons" (*'ba*), that is, human beings with social and moral responsibility, as contrasted to "things" (*afa*) such as clients, babies, and young women, none of whom possesses social responsibility. The dead are said to live somewhere beneath the surface of the world, but people do not know exactly what their life is like. The belief in an afterlife is shadowy and unimportant, and there are no beliefs in heaven or hell or any rewards after death for offenses or good deeds while alive. "Our ancestors" are benevolent and wish well for their descendants, whom they protect and guide, but punish for sins. Although a dead person's character and personality are remembered for a few years, he is not regarded as malevolent after death even if so regarded while alive. Ancestors are thought to be aware of what goes on among their living kin, and discuss them among themselves. It is said that they like to say: "Now our child gives us food, and we are glad." To give food is a sign of close kinship.

A living man has certain elements. He has first a body, which becomes a corpse when dead and rots away in a few years; it is unimportant and "goes nowhere" after death. When alive a body contains breath, which at death goes no one knows where. Breath is a sign of life but has no great importance in itself. More important are certain invisible and spiritual elements: the *orindi*, the *adro*, and the *tali*. Of these the most important is the *orindi*, which I translate as "soul." The soul is said to be in the heart, and is the element that makes a man act responsibly as a social being and member of a lineage. At death it leaves the body and goes to Spirit in the sky; later it is contacted by a diviner and returns to earth where it lives at a shrine set for it. It is aware of what goes on among the living, and can in some mystical manner communicate with certain of the living and can send sickness to living sinners. When back in the shrine it becomes known as *ori*, which I translate as "ghost." Any dead person, man, woman, or child, becomes an ancestor (*a'bi*), but only certain of these become ghosts. "Ancestors" are all a man's dead kinsfolk, and although no man can relate the names of all his ancestors he nonetheless knows that they have lived and that after death they are somewhere in the earth beneath him. But only those whose souls have been given shrines are ghosts. A child rarely becomes a ghost, because his soul is small, and the same applies to most women. It is men who leave sons behind to place shrines for them who become ghosts. In effect, of course, this means that only those ancestors who are remembered in genealogies are also ghosts. An ancestor who becomes a ghost does not thereby cease being an ancestor, but is rather an ancestor who in death is known to be responsible toward his dead kin; and this is expressed by his being given a shrine at which sacrifices are made to him.

After death the soul of a man may be seen by his living kin as a specter (*atri*), which is an omen that he has died unhappily and that reparation of some kind must be made to him. Usually contact is made by a diviner, and the wishes of the dead man satisfied. He then rests content and a shrine is later made to his name. It is sometimes also said that the shadow is a form of the soul, but this belief is unimportant, except that witches can harm a victim by treading on his shadow.

The other elements are the *adro* and *tali*. I need not discuss them at length here. *Adro* is put into the body at birth, or conception (it is not known which) by Spirit. It is a sign of man's divine creation, and can be translated as "spirit." After death it leaves the body and goes off into the bushland, where it becomes one of the *adroanzi* or spirits of the water, hills, or trees. The *tali* is the element that enables a man to have influence over those around him, and it increases in power during his lifetime. After death it leaves the body and lives in a shrine where all the *tali* of past members of the lineage are. *Tali* is a word used for any manifestation of the power of Spirit, such as a place where lightning has struck, or a mystical power such as rainmaking or divination.

DEATH AND BURIAL

Death marks the beginning of an elaborate *rite de passage*, for both the dead person and for his living kin. The mortuary rites of Lugbara are the only rites or ceremonies that attract large numbers of people, and are highly important in Lugbara society. Almost every other rite is the concern of a small lineage and neighborhood only, but the mortuary rites of an important man may attract people from neighboring subtribes and last for days or even weeks: I have known cases in which they were not completed for over a year. At death a man's physical body is disposed of and forgotten, and those parts of him that do not become ancestor and ghost go to the domain of Spirit, either in the sky or in the bushland. Ancestors are important only to their living kin, in particular, members of their lineage; they have no significance to other people. A dead man has relations with both living and dead kin; Lugbara know little about the latter relations, but the former are modeled on those he had with the living while he was alive. At death the kinship status of the dead person remains, but other aspects of his social personality are extinguished.

The corpse is buried with certain objects that represent his status as a man, woman, or child, as such, and with certain objects associated with any status he may have acquired outside the lineage. With a man are buried his quiver, his favorite drinking gourd, and his elder's stool if he had been an elder. These objects symbolize the positions he had held during his lifetime: the quiver that of a young man who is a warrior and hunter, the drinking gourd that of the mature man who drinks and talks with his kin and neighbors, and the stool that of the elder. In addition, if he had become an oracle operator he is buried with his rubbing-stick and pots he used for the boiling-water oracle. With a woman are buried her beads (which represent her position as a girl), the three fire stones of her hearth ("the stones where she cooked food for her husband"), and the smaller of the two grinding stones with which she has ground flour; these last two represent her status as wife and mother in her husband's lineage. The grinding stone is that which she actually held while grinding, the one she chose herself from the rounded pieces of granite in the stream bed. The larger, lower grinding stone is not vested with her personality as is this upper stone, and passes to her daughter. Her pots, gourds, and other household utensils are broken by her brother, who also scatters the grain from her granary over the compound and pulls the thatch from her hut roof. This is done "because these are her own things, but are little": she made them but her personality is not in them as it is in the other objects. Both men and women are buried with beans, simsim, and heads of eleusine, the three traditional staple crops of the Lugbara, about which there are myths that tell of their being tilled by the heroes (other crops are later importations). The burial of these objects and foodstuffs is in no way in preparation for any kind of journey to the land of the dead. Lugbara state this quite explicitly and say they are put with the corpse "because he would have eaten them. Now who will eat them? Let us pour them over the corpse." For a woman, then, her brother (her closest kinsman) destroys her possessions. The objects buried with her symbolize her status as a wife, and after death it is her status as an ancestress that remains significant in her son's lineage, not that of a wife as such. She is buried in her husband's compound, not taken back to her natal home, if she dies where she is married.

The dead person's mother, mother's sisters, and widows do not touch the corpse. They wail loudly and cover their heads and bodies with dust and earth, and they may throw themselves on the ground and roll about in the ashes of the fire of the compound, which is put out when the death occurs. The mother and the widows do not remove the dust and ashes, nor shave their heads or wash until the end of the period of mourning. Both mourning and the ashes used are called *uri* ("fear" or "respect"). These women have special cries of mourning, which are different from those used by the lineage sisters, which are in their turn different from those used by other kin and by neighbors.

Mourning affects only the immediate kin of the dead person, and especially the widow or widower, who enters into seclusion until the end of the mourning period. During this time they live in a small hut built for the purpose, and may neither wash nor shave their heads, which must remain whitened with finely powdered ashes. Other members of the immediate family, and sisters' children, are not secluded but do not shave their heads for the same period. They wear ashes on their faces for four days if the dead person was a man, or three if a woman.

The lineage sisters who touch the corpse are regarded as ritually unclean. After the burial they wash in the nearest stream before they mix with other people, and they are not allowed to oil their bodies (a sign that the pollution has not finally been removed). The mother's brothers who prepare the grave are not so polluted. They merely wash and rejoin the dancers afterward. This washing is different from that of the lineage sisters, who go formally to the stream together, often under the direction of a diviner, but the mother's brothers regard their lustration as something rather everyday.

All other kin who attend the burial shave their heads, especially those who actually enter the compound. Lugbara say this is done to be "clean," and thus not be harmed by the corpse. They may also put ashes on their heads, but usually only on their foreheads and not over the entire face. Women, however, do not wear fresh leaves as apparel, but wear those of the day before. The compound is not swept, and is left dirty until after the end of the period of mourning.

Once the corpse is buried there starts the process of changing the dead person's status from that of a living to a dead kinsman. As a dead kinsman he is both respected and feared, in much the same way as a living man when he becomes senior in lineage and family position. On the whole the dead are regarded as beneficent, the origins of law and order and custom. Their ability to send sickness to their living descendants is part of their role as the guardians of morality, and it is accepted that they do not do so wantonly or without adequate reason. But they are also feared. This is true especially of the newly dead, since it is not known what grudges they may hold toward their living kin at the time they die. A man who knows he is about to die calls his close lineage kin to him and speaks his last words, in which he is said to designate his lineage successor and to bring into the open any grudges that he may hold. In fact, the living tend to interpret the last words of a dying man as they themselves feel best for the lineage. Immediately after death the soul goes to the place of Spirit in the sky, outside the control of living men, and it is at this time that any resentment toward them by the living may be expressed openly, and they may haunt the living as specters to show that they have died with grudges. Once the dead become full ancestors and ghosts, any resentment toward them is ideally not permitted, since by then it should have been dispersed by the diviner contacting the soul. The ambivalent attitude toward a senior kinsman is largely an aspect of the relationship to him as a known individual, which lessens after his death as the memory of him fades.

Resentment may, however, be expressed overtly at his burial. The death of an important man is followed by a period when many of the obligations of kinship are temporarily in abeyance. This period is marked by permitted license in behavior between kin, and by such things as the non-sweeping of the lineage compounds.

At the burial the dead man's successor and other men of the minimal lineage concerned speak of him and recount the "words of the ancestors."

They bring certain sacred leaves, which are associated with Spirit, dip them in water, and place them on the ground. If that evening a jackal or other night creature defecates on them they know that the dead man has died with a "bad" heart, but if there is no excrement on the leaves the next morning it is a sign that he died content and by the will of Spirit, about which he cannot complain. This is done for all men who leave children. Before the grave is closed the lineage kin stand around it, address the dead man, and express any overt resentment toward him. One such address that I heard included the words:

> Now you are dead. You fear now. . . . It is good that you fear. . . . You have begotten children and done many things. . . . Now you are dead, like a pot that is broken. If your heart is bad, then tomorrow we shall see. . . . Now you are dead and your words are little. . . .

At the burial also a bull or goat must be given to the deceased's own true mother's brother. This is the "corpse beast." If the deceased is a woman, her agnates are given a beast as well, known also as "corpse beast." The burial does not take place until this is done, for until they have accepted it, the mother's brother and, if a woman, her lineage kin, are not satisfied as to the cause of death. If they are not satisfied, they usually suspect witchcraft. The dead man would then return to haunt his lineage, or a woman to haunt her husband's lineage.

DEATH DANCES

So far I have mentioned some of the events that are connected with the change of a person's status from a living to a dead member of the lineage. But he is at the center of a network of ties between lineages and groups of kin. At his death there is a rearrangement of these ties. These realignments are of relationships between the minimal lineage and other groups and are made at death dances.

The dances start after the death, usually immediately after the burial. There are two sets of dances, the *ongo* and the *abi*. *Ongo* is the generic term for "dance," and these dances are highly elaborated. There are many variations but always two main dances: the "wailing dance" and the "leaping dance." Each consists of several distinct dances with their own songs telling of the dead man's life and way of dying. As in most Lugbara songs, there is much bitter and sarcastic allusion to the failings of other lineages, and so there is a good deal of airing of grievances and thereby disposing of them.[2]

Both men and women dance, although the main dances in the center

---

[2]Lugbara themselves say that when a grievance is openly expressed anyone who later takes it up will become ashamed and lose face.

of the arena—usually a cleared space outside the compound—are done mostly by men only, the women being on the periphery. Much beer is drunk, and because men carry spears and arrows there is often fighting. Women carry wands, and senior women, those who are the first born of sets of brothers and sisters and therefore "like men," may carry quivers. In the dances men stand by generation, not by lineage or family. The team consists of the men of a lineage. Lineages which enter the arena first thereby show their seniority over other lineages, and fighting often occurs as they jostle to take their position as a previous dance ends. There may also be brawling among the dancers themselves: those of the same generation dance side by side, leaping up and down, and to jolt one's neighbor can lead to argument and fighting. These dances are not solemn occasions. Because dances may continue for days and nights at a stretch, with the drums never stopping,[3] many people are soon in a trancelike condition and normally expected behavior may be relaxed. Lugbara recognize this, saying: "Death has destroyed the words, a big man is dead and we are like children with no one to help us." This behavior is expressed in many ways: by the fluidity of lineage relationships as seen in the jostling for seniority and the fighting; by the normally forbidden seduction of clan-sisters by young men, an accepted piece of bravado that is said "to show young men who are their clan-sisters" (the implication being that with lineage ties in temporary disarray people forget their relationships); and sometimes in the reversal of sexual roles, usually by young men wearing women's leaves as apparel, women leading men's dance teams, and so forth.

While the dancing is going on, couples run out of the throng of watchers to the outskirts of the arena. There the man cries his *cere* call[4] and shoots arrows into the bush (or mimics doing so) and the woman calls her *cere*. There is no expected relationship between the pair, except that they are never husband and wife; they may be lineage or other kin, or merely close friends. The expressed purpose of this action is that it "shows" other lineages that the pair wish to avenge the death. It is done only for adult men.

The observer soon sees that death dances are of great importance. They are the occasions for the greatest coming together of kinsfolk. There is little ceremonial or ritual at birth and marriage, and no initiation ritual. Large dance are said to have been held in the past at the first harvests in the year, but they were smaller than big death dances. Other

---

[3]There are usually three drums; the "child," the "wife," and the "grandmother," and players change over from time to time without stopping the beat.

[4]The *cere* is a long, high-pitched falsetto whooping cry. Every adult man and woman has his or her own (to which words are fitted). They are traditionally called for help and at dances, and today men call them when coming home drunkenly from beer parties, so that they may be recognized in the dark, and also to show that they are "big." It is a deep insult to cry another person's *cere* except at the one occasion when a man's heir cries the dead man's call immediately after his death.

dances, *koro* and *walangaa* ("dances of play"), are recent introductions, and the traditional *nyambi* dance of women, danced at a bride's leaving her natal home, attract only a small audience. But death dances are the cause for excitement and interest over a wide area, and the continual drumming and singing are audible for miles.

From *The Study of the Lugbara: Expectation and Paradox in Anthropological Research*
John Middleton

BURIAL OF THE DEAD

My first notes on what may loosely be called Lugbara religion were made after I had visited a funeral; and although they may now seem to be very naive—and indeed they are so—it is worth my saying something about the way I described what I saw as an example of the way that I was slowly to learn about Lugbara religious practice and belief. I had walked one morning into Nyio to find one or two compounds crowded with visitors. There were many men standing in small groups, talking, arguing, and drinking beer. Elsewhere women were grinding grain and scurrying from one hut to another with baskets of food and pots of beer. The children were chattering everywhere. At first I might have stumbled upon an impromptu party, until I realized that in one compound two or three women were wailing, throwing dust and ashes upon themselves and rolling on the ashes of the fire of the previous evening. Outside the huts in the compound one or two men were tuning drums. The men glared at me and the women looked sullen and edged away. One or two of the men whom I already knew looked embarrassed and would like to have disclaimed acquaintance with me. Oguda told me that his father's brother had died that night and was to be buried that day. We went to see his father to offer our sympathy. He was already very drunk and once he saw that I was not to be put off, welcomed me profusely. I was given beer and introduced to the circle of men, most of whom were also excited and well filled with beer. I was told that inside one of the huts the body had been washed and was now wrapped in white cloth bought for the occasion, and outside the hut some men had dug a grave about five foot deep with a

John Middleton, *The Study of the Lugbara: Expectation and Paradox in Anthropological Research* (New York: Holt, Rinehart and Winston, 1970), pp. 47–50. Reprinted by permission of the publisher.

long recess at one side. After some waiting the body was taken out and lowered into the grave while the men of the immediate family stood around the grave watching. They then began to talk, clearly addressing the corpse as it lay beneath them, pointing at it and shouting angrily. My Lugbara was not good enough at that time to understand what they said, and since Oguda was by then somewhat unsteady in his speech I was not able to grasp the gist of their remarks. After twenty minutes or so the men began to fill in the grave and other men began to beat the three drums which had been tightened at the fire and were ready for play. I noticed that as soon as the dancing began small groups of men who had been standing together ran to the dance ground and danced in line holding spears and quivers. Soon another group entered the arena and took over the small dancing space. There was a good deal of argument and competition between the various groups, many of which had a second line of women. Occasionally a man and a woman would run to the edge of the ground and shout in a falsetto voice, then shoot an arrow into the bushland before returning to the dance ground. The dancing and shouting and singing were to continue all that evening until the moon went down soon after midnight.

I went home very dispirited, having seen what was clearly an event of some importance and interest but without having understood the least thing about it except that it was a funeral. The next morning there were some more dancing and singing at the same spot. But by the afternoon things had quieted and I was able to try to make some sense out of what I had seen. I sat down and tried to write a coherent account of the events. The main questions were those of the identity and the lineage and kinship relationships of the various people who had taken part. I realized that the people associated with the disposal of the body were sisters' sons of the dead man, and thus members of other lineages. The men who had stood around the grave were the men of the dead man's minimal lineage, and had indeed been cursing him and showing their "joy" that he was dead. It was only at a later date that I understood the significance of this. I was to realize that the groups of men and women who had gone to dance together each represented the members of a lineage related to the dead man in one way or another, and I was told that the dancing was to "rejoice." It became clear that I would need to know the answers to several questions. One was the significance of the lineage relationships concerned. Others were the significance of cursing the body, of rejoicing at a man's death, and obviously of various notions of death, life, and the soul of the person.

Here I am making certain points that I think are important in fieldwork. One is that although this funeral took place when I had been in the country for only a few weeks it was to be typical of many that I witnessed. I had always assumed that the fieldworker would sit with book in hand, asking clear and intelligent questions and making clear and intelligent notes. Perhaps there have been anthropologists who have worked in this way, but I rather doubt it: and if there have been, they must have worked rather too far from the hurly-burly of everyday life to have grasped much of the flavor of it. Toward the end of my stay I was perhaps to come nearer to that ideal, but it was to be at the stage when I was filling in specific points in situations of which I already knew the main structure. Also of course I was always able to take coherent notes when talking privately with informants. The difficulty was to do this when watching a disorderly and apparently chaotic scene such as that I had briefly described, and I have deliberately set down the superficial impression that I received at the time and that I had to use as a basis for further thought and investigation. Yet if I had not actually witnessed that and been confused by it, I would have missed its most important elements altogether. The important elements of course are those that the participants themselves take for granted, so that they are not always likely to remark upon them in a conversation; and since the fieldworker would be unaware of them he would be unlikely to ask about them. After visiting the funeral I realized how important were the collective emotions that were being expressed, which seemed to me to be out of place and unexpected; in our own culture we do not expect people to rejoice at death nor to shout abuse at a corpse. It was clear, therefore, that I did not understand the motives for the display of these emotions, and would also have to check very carefully whether or not I had in fact recognized them correctly. Later, when talking with people about these matters, I realized the obvious fact that they were unable to translate what I had seen into words that were adequate for my purpose. For example, it was clear that when people said they were "rejoicing," that the English word "rejoice" was not always adequate to translate the Lugbara term *aiikosi owu*. I was later to understand, after seeing many of these and similar occasions, that the Lugbara term refers not so much to joy in our sense, as to a satisfaction at recognizing and reordering a social relationship that had been broken by the death. The death causes a period of chaos and confusion. This is brought to an end when it is restructured, by the recognition of new ties of relationship between the various people and groups concerned. Such a remark, simple though it is, has a host of implications for the ways in which we see relations of kinship, lineage, and clan. So that again it became obvious to me that I could not get very far without an understanding of the basic social relationships that I have already mentioned in earlier sections.

   In later weeks and months I was to see many funerals and death dances. I found that they always followed a similar pattern, although with variation in detail. At the same time I witnessed many other rituals and also talked with many people about the beliefs that they held about them. I asked people about the elements of man, the spirit and the soul and dissolution after death, the significance of the ancestors and ghosts and their relationship to living men and to Divine Spirit. I have described all these elsewhere and need not repeat the details here. But I should say one thing that seems to me to be important. At first I would plunge virtually at random into discussion of any kind of belief that came into my head. Bit by bit a pattern began to emerge from the details that I thus collected. I realized finally that there were one or two concepts that were key ones and that if I could adequately understand these then I could make some sense of the whole. These beliefs seemed to be arranged into a scheme that covered the entire universe and the place of man within it. In this scheme there were two main concepts: One was that of *adro* and the other that of *amve*. *Adro* means "spirit" and may refer both to the Creator God, to the immanent and evil aspect of the Divinity, and to the individual spirit within the individual body. The spirit in any aspect and any manifestation was said to be *amve* or "outside." It may be outside the world or outside the cultivated fields and homesteads, or metaphorically "outside" the responsible element of a person. If something is outside, there must be something else inside, and so I came to the pattern of complementary opposites that plays so central a part in Lugbara religious belief. Once I had realized the significance of this simple but all-pervasive dichotomy in Lugbara thought, much that I was to hear and witness fell into its proper place without difficulty. It might be argued that such a dualism is widespread throughout the world (as indeed it is) and so I should have recognized it immediately. But had I done that I would have fallen into the trap of regarding Lugbara behavior as an example of something I already expected to find. But in this research situation such deductive thinking would have been misleading and dangerous: anthropology is an inductive science and one must approach field experience in its own right. From it one may later adduce generalizations, not the other way about.

INITIATION

This passage is about a Melanesian village in New Guinea. It first examines attitudes and practices related to antagonism between the sexes, a matter very prominent in Melanesian culture, but of great moment throughout all the primitive world—and in "civilized" society as well. We then read about the initiation of young men in this community. Notice that the process is a movement into a sacred situation, indicated by the special residence and dietary regulations, and is like a ritual death and rebirth. The initiation is also a time of learning the secrets of the men of the tribe, including that the "monsters" were simulated. Finally we read about the comparable rites of transition for girls, complicated as they are by belief that feminine power is the opposite of masculine; the two are like positive and negative electric charges.

From *Pagan Religion in a New Guinea Village*
H. Ian Hogbin

THE MALE CULT

The foundation of the cult was the belief that the sexes were in substance entirely different. Men, it was claimed, were akin to the spirits and could at certain times acquire the same sanctity, a state indicated by the expression *dabung,* a close equivalent of the Polynesian *tapu.* Women, on the contrary, were outside the spirits' pale—they were essentially profane and could never attain sacredness. Contact between the two was accordingly held to be ritually dangerous, though only to the men, and likely to lead to loss of virility. The cult had as its object the overcoming of this disability and bringing about the restoration of ritual purity.

The most vital of the ceremonies was concerned with blood letting, the means adopted for removing the women's contaminating influence. The penis, the organ which actually penetrated the female body when contact was at a maximum, was the obvious choice for the cut.

Incising the penis, apart from the pain and inconvenience involved —the gash had to be of some depth—was not to be undertaken lightly. Maleness was now renewed to the full, and, as a result, the affinity with the spirits was at its height. Because of the supernatural forces present, a period of preparation was necessary beforehand and some days of seclusion afterwards. During these times even the most superficial contact with women was prohibited, and the man retired to a ceremonial house. All sorts of diet taboos were imposed, too, and various other restrictions had to be observed. Fluids were barred, for instance, thirst having to be quenched by sucking a piece of sugar cane, and many varieties of fish. Further, if the food could not be eaten raw—and this was considered to be preferable—it had to be roasted on an open fire: in no circumstances could it be prepared in the normal manner by steaming or boiling.[1]

H. Ian Hogbin, "Pagan Religion in a New Guinea Village," *Oceania* 18 (1947–48), pp. 130–37. Reprinted by permission of the editor of *Oceania,* of the University of Sydney, Australia, and of the author, H. Ian Hogbin.

[1]Women were on two occasions subject to the same diet restrictions, (i) when they were in mourning, and (ii) when set apart after their first menstruation. The loss of a near kinsman was supposed to have the effect of pulling them to the brink of the spirit world (though they did not become *dabung*); and the ceremonial associated with first menstruation was obviously based on that carried out at the initiation of youths (see below).

The operation was supposed to be performed at more or less regular intervals, but many men, probably the majority, were apt to delay until jolted into remembering their growing impurity by an attack of illness. They then retired to the ceremonial house to take the preliminary precautions. These were considered to be complete after two days, and at dawn on the third the men proceeded to a lonely spot on the beach armed with a sliver of obsidian. The blood was allowed to drip into the sea, and they afterwards bound the wound up with leaves.

Most important undertakings also involved a preparatory incision for those taking part, thereby ensuring that defilement would not bring about disaster from weakness or any other cause. Warriors purified themselves before a raid, weavers before the manufacture of a large fishing net, builders before the erection of a new ceremonial house, and gardeners before engaging in collective cultivation to furnish supplies for a feast.

Other ceremonies of the cult involved the impersonation of supernatural monsters. The women and children were told that these were like enormous crocodiles but were never allowed to approach near enough to see. Instead, on hearing the monsters' "voices," they had to run into hiding, reputedly on pain of death. The noise was in fact the sound made by bullroarers.

The myth giving the origin of bullroarers relates that their special properties were discovered accidentally in a village on Mount Yambi, near the mouth of the Waria River, to the south. One of the women when chopping firewood struck off a chip which flew into the air with a whirring noise. Picking it up, she discovered that it had a slight twist, which she rightly concluded was responsible. She thereupon bored a hole through one end, attached a piece of string, and returned home twirling it round her head. The husband, interested, borrowed it to show his friends in the ceremonial house, first warning her to make no mention as yet of what had happened. The men agreed that here was an object which could well be incorporated into their cult, from which hitherto they had had difficulty in keeping the members of the other sex. They would say that it was the voice of a spirit, they decided, which women were forbidden to look upon. The difficulty was that one woman had already seen it and would no doubt laugh at them as humbugs. It was accordingly declared that she must be killed. The husband was at first reluctant but at length gave his consent when promised a substitute. He sent a message to her to bring his supper, and as soon as she stepped on the ladder of the house the men despatched her with their spears. The body was buried in secret, the rest of the women being told that she had been eaten by a fearsome spirit monster which had come into the area. From that time onwards the men alone possessed the bullroarers.

The story may perhaps give the impression that the hoaxing of the women was uppermost in the men's minds when carrying out their ritual. From my experience in other New Guinea communities where pagan rites are still being carried out I am convinced that, although this aspect of the matter cannot be ignored, it would be a mistake to pay too much attention to it.

Every ceremonial house had two bullroarers, both named, a "male" about thirty inches in length, and a "female" somewhat shorter, often only a foot. The surfaces of both were engraved with designs of mythological significance. When not in use they were preserved in a carved bowl of the most exquisite workmanship on a special shelf, and when removed for a ceremony they were reverently painted and decorated with feathers.

One of the chief occasions for the impersonation of the monsters was when a headman wished to put a taboo on certain kinds of food as a prelude to a feast. A rite to summon them from their lairs underground was carried out some time beforehand, and from then on till the date of the feast the consumption of coconuts or bananas and the killing of pigs were forbidden. They appeared, too, if a new ceremonial house was to be erected or if a leading man of a neighbouring community was ill or had died, when it was said that they had come to mourn because his kinsmen had not taken better care of him.

The bullroarers themselves were also put to special uses. A headman wishing to communicate with another village usually entrusted one to the messenger as an indication that he was on official business. The holy object gave him complete immunity from attack, for to kill or wound him would have been sacrilege. When an alliance or a truce had been concluded between two settlements, too, several bullroarers were exchanged to cement the relationship. It was said that if treachery occurred afterwards the guilty parties were liable to be the victims of supernatural vengeance.

INITIATION

Youths were excluded from the cult until physically mature, when they were put through a series of tests first and then formally initiated. So much food had to be provided for the accompanying feasts, however, that the appropriate ceremonies—there was a whole cycle, known as *sam* —could seldom take place oftener than at intervals of ten years. The younger lads involved were therefore only about fifteen, whereas the eldest were more than twenty-four. The headman gave the word as he had to supply the major part of the food.

The first procedure was the announcement of what was contemplated to the surrounding countryside. Messengers went out to invite two men from each settlement to visit the village on a certain date, and when all had assembled the headman gave notice of his intentions and presented them with bullroarers. This marked the beginning of a taboo period, during which no minor feasts could be held. Quarrelling and fighting were also outlawed, and it is said that from this time till the ceremony was over anyone found guilty of murder, adultery, or other major offences had to be killed by his own kinsfolk. The visitors later returned to their own homes, where similar taboos now operated.

The villagers next selected two old men to undertake the arduous duties of guardians (*songoboi*) during the test. Once these had been chosen a large building (*po'labu*=cave) was erected in the bush to house the boys. This had to be fairly substantial as they remained there for five or six months. A meeting then decided which lads exactly were ready. Each had to be sponsored by a man who had himself been initiated only at the last ceremonies, so that he was not a great deal older than his ward. The pair subsequently became bond-friends and were at all times mutually considerate and helpful. This institution has now disappeared, but the two were "like the dugout and outrigger float of a canoe, always together and lost if separated." The word for bond friend was *nengga'*, which is also the kinship term used by men married to a pair of sisters.

On the day fixed for the beginning of the ordeals the various sponsors sought out their wards and told them of what was about to take place. The youths had to climb on the men's backs, and the party left the village for the house in the bush in procession. Meantime the older men had lined up along the track, taking with them firebrands, sticks tipped with obsidian fragments, and bundles of nettles. These were used to administer a sound thrashing to the boys as each passed by. The sponsors did not escape unscathed, and by the time the house was reached everyone was covered in blood.

The initiands, at this stage known as *saga*, were received by the guardians, who told them that during the next few months they would be tested to see whether they were fit to be presented to the monsters as a sacrificial meal. If they proved worthy there would be no cause for fear, as they would pass through whole and be evacuated. But anyone who failed to measure up to the requirements would remain fast in the monster's belly and never be heard of again. The tests prescribed included further beatings, being kept awake for several days on end, and partial suffocation. Huge fires were lit inside the house and piles of green boughs put on top. The doors were then kept tightly closed until everyone was practically insensible.

During the whole of this period, which lasted for upwards of three months, the boys were only allowed to eat minute portions of the coarsest types of food either raw or roasted. All liquids were forbidden, though if they were thirsty permission was occasionally granted for them to chew a piece of sugar cane provided by the sponsors. The mothers and sisters handed over plates of delicious stews daily, but these were taken by the elders. There was also a ban on leaving the house at any time except just before dawn, when each youth had to bury his fæces in a deep hole. A watch was then kept to see that he did not wash himself afterwards.

At length the day arrived for the summoning of the monsters. Word had been sent out to the villages which had proclaimed the taboo, and a vast concourse of people was by this time in attendance. They remained till the last rite ended, causing severe strain on their hosts' resources.

The pretence was that the monsters lived underground, and a hole was accordingly dug from which they could emerge. At first only a faint humming was heard, and the women murmured amongst themselves that the tree roots must be scraping their flanks. Soon afterwards a man covered with earth went along to the village to announce how deep down the monsters had been but that they had at last appeared. The humming now became louder, till in the end the whole countryside rang with the booming of dozens of bullroarers.

The boys had to listen for a few days and were then brought out and shown by their guardians, with much impressive ritual, how the noise was made. A poisonous fish was later flourished in front of their mouths, and they were warned that if a word of what had been disclosed crossed their lips they would perish as assuredly as if they had swallowed a deadly toxin.

This revelation was followed by the incision rite. This time the boys were cut by one or other of the guardians, but on all subsequent occasions each person operated on himself. A long low shed had been built to represent one of the monsters, and inside the two men waited with their obsidian knives. The lads were taken in turn, each one being carried on the back of his sponsor, who also served as a support while the gash was being made. The blood, as the first which they had shed, was especially sacred, and the sponsors gathered it in leaves for use later as face paint.

The men spoke of the wound as the mark of the monster's teeth as the boy was swallowed. Informants stated that at times some of the candidates bled to death or died as a result of the cut becoming septic and that occasionally those who had offended the guardians by their weakness or disobedience were deliberately put to death. The bodies were buried in the bush, the mothers being informed that unfortunately the monsters had failed to digest their sons.

The hosts now made ready a great feast, supposedly for the entertainment of the monsters but in fact for the guests. The youths, however, were hurried back to the shelter, where they were subject to the same taboos as before. They remained shut up until the wounds were quite healed, generally a couple of months. Different men took turns swinging the bullroarers day and night, and it is claimed that the lads had barely any sleep on account of the noise. At the same time, no further tests were held, and instead the guardians delivered long moral homilies. Respect must always be paid to the elders, they said, and it was necessary for everyone to bear in mind that he now had a binding obligation to help his various kinsfolk, those on the mother's side as well as those on the father's side. They made a great point also of the rule that sexual intercourse outside wedlock was forbidden and urged the lads to avoid entanglements by concentrating on their work and refraining from sitting for long gossips in the houses of others.

Before the boys could emerge the monsters had to be sent back underground, a rite accompanied by another feast for which sometimes
hundreds of pigs were slain. The villagers liked to boast that so much
food was provided that a large quantity became rotten before it could be
eaten.

Now called *gwale*, the youths next day went to a stream and were
given a ceremonial bath by their sponsors. Richly painted and decorated,
they were then led one by one into the village, where the women welcomed them with tears of joy. A secular feast, which all could share, had
in the meantime been prepared and a platform erected outside one of
the ceremonial houses. On this the boys sat while their relatives and
friends danced and sang songs in their honour.

This concluded the celebrations, and the guests made their fare-
wells and departed. One duty alone remained, a purely private matter for
the boys' families. Most of them liked to show their appreciation of the
sponsors by showering them with gifts.

The taboo period was also over, and fighting was no longer regarded
as sinful. The ancestors used to insist that the effect of the restrictions
continued, and that peace could confidently be expected for a year or two.
This the natives today dismiss as a pious hope. Outbreaks of violence
often began, they say, before a month had elapsed.

SOCIAL CONSEQUENCES OF INITIATION

The rites made a drama of the lads' change of status. Their childhood came to an abrupt close, and, after a period when they were under
close observation, their manhood had an even more violent beginning.
The obvious intention was to impress upon them that irresponsibility
must now give way to earnest fulfillment of obligations to kinsfolk and
the community as a whole.

Informants who are themselves of middle age, while admitting all
this, insist that the ceremonies also had the effect of ensuring that at all
times due respect would be paid to the elders. So forceful a demonstration
of knowledge and power, they urge, humbled the initiates and left them
with a meekness which they never afterwards threw off.

When giving me detailed accounts of what used to take place these
older men always dwelt longest on the belabouring of the boys during
their ride on the sponsors' backs to the place of seclusion. The ostensible
function was said to be the encouragement of growth by magical means,
but they invariably added that the beating was of extra importance as a
demonstration that authority rested in the hands of the senior generations. Whether or not the blows were administered with sadistic abandon
it is now impossible to say, but everyone insisted that this was so.

The alleged laziness and moral laxity of the youths to-day, in my
opinion somewhat exaggerated, are attributed to the abandonment of the

custom, and many elders expressed a desire for its revival in some form by the mission. "I'd make the youngsters heed me," one man exclaimed. "I'd hit them till the blood flowed like rain. Then we'd see whether they'd sit talking all day instead of helping us in the gardens. They'd bring some of their money home from work, too, and not gamble it away as fast as they earn it."

It is unnecessary to point out that any changes in the young people's behaviour cannot be accounted for so simply and that many other factors must be at work.

WOMEN'S CEREMONIES

Just as men reached the highest levels of sanctity when renewing their masculinity by incising the penis, so women gravitated towards the lowest depths of the profane when their femininity was at a maximum during childbirth and menstruation. Yet though at such times the two sexes travelled in different directions and ended up poles apart, they had one thing in common: both were wrenched out of the ordinary world of every day. The women no less than the men therefore were subject to restrictions—they had to avoid all contact with males and were forbidden to eat certain foods. A ceremonial house into which they could retire was lacking, but the difficulty was overcome by preventing the menfolk from visiting the family dwelling.

As the time for the wife's delivery approached the husband pulled the floorboards aside and dug a hole underneath to receive the placenta and the blood. These preparations concluded, he withdrew to wait on the beach or at some other convenient spot. The woman was attended by certain of her female relatives, who brought firewood, water, and clean mats. Progress was announced from time to time, and as soon as the child was born a message was sent to the father telling him of its sex. He was not permitted to see it, however, or even to go near the house for several days.

The mother remained indoors for about a week devoting all her attention to the care of the infant. The only food permitted, in contrast with the raw or roasted vegetables eaten by men under a taboo, was hot soup, preferably made from the shoots of young sago palms, which her husband and brothers were expected to provide, one every alternate day. At length, if she was considered to have regained her strength fully, her kinswomen went out with their nets to catch a dish of freshwater fish. After these had been eaten her seclusion ended. She was allowed to come out of the house into the village, and the husband could now examine his offspring and perhaps nurse it for a few minutes.

The girl's entry into womanhood at her first menstruation was something of an event, the accompanying ceremonies being not unlike those carried out at initiation. At the same time, they were not nearly so elaborate, and, as only one girl passed through at a time, there was no general disturbance of village life.

On the first appearance of the blood the girl was ordered to go to bed. She was considered to be ritually cold and had thus to be heated, a process achieved with the aid of massage with warmed oil in which ginger roots had been steeped. The rubbings continued for several days, during which she did not sit up.

This was the beginning of a period of seclusion lasting for six or seven months. Permission to go outside was only granted when it became necessary to answer the calls of nature, and at such times a shroud of mats was worn as a cover not only for the head but for the whole body. If the father or brothers wished to remain in the dwelling a small compartment was made for the girl in one corner, but the men usually preferred to stay outside and eat their meals in the ceremonial house.

Unlike the youths, the girl was not called upon to undergo any ordeals, but washing and drinking were forbidden, and her diet was also confined to raw or roasted foods. Three or four girls of approximately her own age attended to her wants, companions to whom the word *nengga'* was applied, the term used by the boys and their sponsors.

When at last the father considered that he had sufficient food for a small feast he announced to his relatives that the time for emergence had come. The next morning the companions took the girl to the stream for a ritual bath. An old woman always went with the party, and on the completion of the toilet it was her duty to give a certain amount of elementary instruction in sex. Using a gourd or a green banana, she told of the male organs of generation and showed the girl how the penis would be inserted in her vagina, rupturing the hymen as she did so.

A member of the train carried the girl back to the village. Many persons, men as well as women, stood in readiness, and as the two appeared they were beaten with stalks of the ginger plant. They were afterwards expected to become bond friends, *sangung* being used for the girl herself and *ise'* for the companion. (These are not kinship terms: women married to two brothers call one another *dawatang*).

The feast took place on the following day, the girl, now known as an *aku'wi*, being painted and decorated with all the family ornaments for the occasion. The food was displayed in front of the house with a mat on the ground in front. To this she was led by her brothers, who protected her from observation with a screen of mats until she was seated and arranged to the best advantage.

When menstruating later, women were not confined quite so strictly to the house, though they rarely came outside. The beach was absolutely barred, however, on the ground that the fish might afterwards smell the contamination on the canoes drawn up above high-water mark and keep their distance. Gardening and the preparation of the family meals were also forbidden, and, to tide the husband and children over, the neighbors sent along provisions. The women cooked for themselves but had to limit their meals to hot broth.

SHAMANISM

Undoubtedly the most dramatic figure in primitive religion is the shaman. He is, roughly speaking, identical with the "witch doctor" or "medicine man" of older literature, but today the shaman's role is much more profoundly understood and appreciated. Far from being only a prescientific healer if not a charlatan (though he may be these), the shaman is also psychiatrist, visionary, initiate, artist, communicator with the gods and the dead, master of techniques of ecstasy, and custodian of the tribal language and lore. His is a special vocation which, typically, involves a degree of apparent instability. As a young man or woman the future shaman may seem given to fits, possession, dissociation, and melancholy. He may have symptoms we would interpret as schizophrenic, and at the least he goes through times of pain and difficulty. But in shamanistic societies, these are signs of election by the spirits: it is they who are haunting and seizing him. His task is to pass through a powerful initiation, alone or under the guidance of a senior shaman, by which he gains mastery over the spirits rather than being torn apart by them. Then he will be able to enter the Other World which has been made accessible to him on his own volition, to heal or recover lost souls or communicate with the gods.

The first passage below gives an account of shamanism from the Arctic region. The second account tells us of the life and background of Ramón, a modern mara'akate or shaman of the Huichol Indians in Mexico. The most sacred rite of the Huichol is pilgrimage to Wirikuta, a special land where peyote is found. The pilgrimage is led by a mara'akate, and culminates in a very sacred, sacramental partaking of peyote to receive divine visions.

From *Shamanism: The Beginnings of Art*

Andreas Lommel

The shaman's psychological experiences in a trance are always expressed in images from the real world. Such events then live on in human memory as miracles.

Andreas Lommel, *Sharmanism: The Beginnings of Art,* trans. Michael Bullock (New York: McGraw-Hill, 1967), pp. 84, 97. Reprinted by permission of the publisher.

The journeys of the shaman into the beyond, his diving down into psychic depths, an experience which we are scarcely capable of repeating, the real result of which, the pacification of the group psyche, the increase in certainty and confidence, remains incomprehensible to us, are generally experienced and reported as a journey to the dead in the underworld, the beyond.

To reach the Land of the Dead the Greenland shaman has to go down to the bottom of the sea, whose realm (mythologically conceived) is separated from the Land of the Dead by a river—the frontier between the Land of the Dead and the world of the living. 'Finally they reached the frontier between the sea and the country beneath the sea, which is formed by a foaming brook; in order to cross it they had to jump over large, sharp-pointed stones that were completely covered by wet seaweed and had such a slippery gleam that no one dared cross . . . With the aid of the spirits, the shaman jumped over these obstacles. The spirits encouraged him and called out to him: "If you do not dare to make this jump, and turn back, you will never reach the Land of the Dead; your journey will always end at these stones." Then the shaman dared to make the jump and to his great astonishment the seaweed proved not to be so slippery at all.' The same author gives an account of steps which the Greenland shaman has to climb in order to enter the World of the Dead. 'The shaman . . . came upon a stairway with three high steps. They were so high that he was only just able to swing himself up from one to the other, and they were slippery with human blood that trickled over them. The shaman climbed the slippery steps with great difficulty and at the continual risk of his life and came to a wide, wide plain, the plain of heaven . . . The way back was without obstacles and he had no bloody steps to overcome.'

Among the Salish Indians of the northwest coast of America the shaman goes through an imaginary voyage by water, in order to recover the lost and stolen soul of a sick man. The voyage across the great sea (River of the Dead), which divides the living from the dead, is made with a crew of ten shamans; the steersman is the spirit of the officiating shaman. The remainder stand during the ceremony in two rows of four, each with a paddle in his hand with which he makes paddling movements. Thus the voyage by boat is made clearly visible to the spectators. After a long voyage they come to the Land of the Dead, the narrows of a river on which the spirits dwell. They fish and hunt, having the same way of life as humans; unlike humans, they walk with crossed legs. By this they may be recognized as spirits. Among primitive peoples the next world is almost always very like this world; the same conditions of life are projected on to the next world.

The first obstacle which the shaman has to overcome in the Land of the Dead is a raging torrent. As the dead are accustomed to do, he lays a tree trunk across the river and crosses it as though by a bridge. While he is overcoming this (imaginary) obstacle, he lays his paddle on the ground and walks carefully along it, balancing carefully so as not to fall. The next difficulty is a viscous river that is crossed in a canoe. There follows a struggle with a man who refuses to tell him the way.

As he enters the Land of the Dead he comes into conflict with the spirits, who defend themselves with torches of burning cedarwood. This imaginary battle is portrayed by boys of the tribe, who rush up with torches and throw them at the invaders of the spirit kingdom. According to Indian informants, the participants sometimes suffer serious injury.

Finally the threshold of the Kingdom of the Dead is ceremoniously closed, so that the spirits who have been robbed of the sick man's soul cannot take revenge. When the sick man's spirit has been found the song of this spirit is sung on the return journey. When the sick man hears this music he jumps up and is cured.

We have an account from Siberia on the same subject:

When the evil spirits in the north carry away a person's soul the shaman performs the seance and sets out for their country with various gifts. Formerly old, hump-backed women with putrid bones in their joints set out on the road to the north. They travelled down the Lena in boats and settled on Mount Jokuo.

In addition, the shamans mentioned in particular two old women whom they also drive out of sick people: Tanyakhtaakh Laabyralaan, 'Laabyralaan with a stick,' and Toruoskalaakh Soluonnyay-Khotun, 'the Lady Soluonnyay who has a stick.' [The informant is wrong in counting Soluonnyay among the northern spirits. She is usually reckoned one of the nine heavenly virgins, who assist horses and bring madness. G.V.K.]

As offerings to these spirit women nine coarse cakes are cooked and vodka is poured into wooden goblets. A pig and a turkey are made of wood. In addition the skin of a polecat is used, a rope plaited of white and black hair, and finally a two-pronged wooden fork. When these women travelled north they took all these things with them.

Among the spirits there lives a girl with a crooked face who serves as a watchman. When the shaman approaches voices ring out:

'There he goes, the shaman with his heavy load, with valuable presents. Before him he is driving cattle, behind him he is pulling sacrificial animals on a rope . . . '

'Ay, here comes our eldest son (the shaman is their son because his soul was brought up among them). Quick, catch him! . . . '

Then shouts ring out: 'Suu, saa!' (These are cries uttered when herding cattle). Then the cattle he has brought are driven into a pen.

The shaman begins to speak before them, saying that such and such a human prince has fallen sick and has sent these gifts . . . 'Give me his soul!'

The spirits, satisfied with the gifts he has brought, order the soul to be set free, saying: 'Ay, go and open the door of the prison in which the sick man's soul lies!'

Sometimes the spirits refuse to release the soul. Then the shaman expresses anger and despair . . . He rolls about round the fireplace, turns into a wasp and flies into the cow byre. There lies a bright blue bull. The wasp stings the bull on the nose. The bull snorts and the soul, which lay prisoner in the bull's nostril, falls out. The shaman seizes it at once and flies hurriedly away with it.

From *Peyote Hunt*

Barbara G. Myerhoff

Ramón was from San Sebastián, a community in the Sierra, where his family remained. He had a deeply religious heritage; his paternal grandfather in his day had been one of the most important shaman-priests or *mara'akate* (plural, *mara'akate;* singular, *mara'akame*). When we met, Ramón was an aspiring mara-akame himself, having made three out of the necessary five annual peyote pilgrimages to Wirikuta, the Huichol sacred land. He had preserved his grandfather's frayed headband and wore it on his hat or tied around his box of sacred implements. Ramón's mother was also a learned and religious woman and had made many trips to Wirikuta. And Ramón's younger sister, Concha, was the only practicing woman mara'akame in the Sierra at that time. One of Ramón's texts tells of his family and early life. It begins:

> More or less my age is forty, as I am speaking to you here. Perhaps, I am close to forty. When my mother brought me into this world, I came, I don't know from where. But once I started growing up—I must have been five or six years old—my father left us alone. Alone he left us, to make do for ourselves. My mother brought us up according to how one must do such things, as Tayaupá, as Tatewarí gave her the ability, the will, the love.[1]

Because of the father's departure, the family suffered great hardship, and even among other Huichols they were exceptionally poor. While still very young, Ramón became aware that his life would not be an ordinary one:

> I began to have those dreams. Sometimes it would happen when I was asleep, sometimes awake, when it was day. It happened one night that

Barbara G. Myerhoff, *Peyote Hunt* (Ithaca: Cornell University Press, 1974), pp. 31–36. Reprinted by permission of the publisher.

[1]Tayaupá, also known as Our Father Sun, and Tatewarí, known as Our Grandfather Fire, are two of the major deities in the Huichol pantheon. The latter is especially important in the shamanic complex.

Tayaupá spoke to me. He said, "Look, son, do not worry. You must grow a little more so you can go out and become wise, so that you can support yourself." He said, "Do not worry son. It will be good with you one day." I heard everything. I saw my life. And then I was very happy. I was still a small boy, five, six, seven years old. I would wake up happy because Tayaupá would say to me, "You are going to do this and that and the other. You will make fine things, things of color. You will understand this and that. It is for this that you were born." At first, I was frightened. I did not know. I began to reflect. I began to listen to them, to those old men when they told our stories, that which is our history.

When Ramón was around eight years old, he was bitten on the foot by a poisonous snake and nearly died. His grandfather the mara'akame was summoned and revealed that the snakebite was sent as punishment because Ramón's father had failed to fulfill a promise he had made to the deities to journey to Wirikuta. The grandfather sucked out the poison, cleansed Ramón with his sacred feathers, and chanted all that night and the following day. Then he revealed to the boy that Tatewarí had chosen him to become a mara'akame. If he lived, his grandfather said, it would be a sign that this was Ramón's destiny.

The boy was in terrible pain and completely paralyzed for over six months. But he didn't die and little by little began to be able to drag himself about and finally to walk. During this period of his life he spent much time alone and began to reflect on what his grandfather had revealed. He grew more serious and began to accept the idea of becoming a mara'akame. His mother was very supportive, and when his courage failed she sustained and consoled him. This was clearly a turning point in his life.

From this time on, Ramón was set apart.

I started to think, to understand: "Oh, this is what they told me, that I was to become a mara'akame." And then some people said, "Ah, what is that boy going to be good for? He will never be able to help us in anything. Always he goes alone, always he is reflecting." I would be embarrassed, but what is one to do? And I would think to myself, "Whatever those great ones say, whatever Tatewarí and Tayaupá say, that is the correct thing. If one does it that way one will do it well." That is how I did it, learning this way and that, how one cures, how one goes to Wirikuta, how one learns all those stories of ours which are our history. How one makes the sacred things, the offerings. All that. It takes many years, much thought, to do such things. Much work, much sacrifice. Now I see that I grew up well.

And indeed, the work of a mara'akame is extraordinarily demanding, intellectually, physically, and spiritually. It requires great religious knowledge, social skill, dramatic and aesthetic gifts, for the mara'akame must undertake the sacred, ecstatic journey to other worlds, to command the spirits, communicate with the deities, defend his patients, and interpret the supernatural to his people. It is a role that very few can hope to fill, as will be seen.

Ramón continually struggled to earn a living in the Sierra but was forced to leave his family and work on mestizo haciendas far from his home to support them. While still in his teens, lonely and far from home, he met Lupe, who had contracted to work in the same plantation as Ramón in Nayarít, and after a time they married.

The young couple tried to support themselves by working the scant arable land near the homes of their families in the Sierra but again and again they found it necessary to leave and find work in distant places. Unencumbered by children, they finally decided to attempt earning a living by selling handiwork in Guadalajara, which they had done on previous occasions. Settling on a bit of vacant land on the outskirts of the city in 1966, they erected a tiny hut, a thatched ramada for shade, and cultivated a half acre of maize and beans. The little household was on the Zacatecas road, the road which many Huichols use when walking into the city from the mountains, and inevitably Ramón's home became a meeting and resting place for visitors from the Sierra. Here, Ramón began regular work as a folk artist for a government institute promoting indigenous arts and crafts.

Lupe's position as mara'akame's wife was a precise and demanding one which she took with the greatest seriousness; she "completed" the mara'akame, as she put it. She was required to be exemplary in Huichol morals and well trained in custom and lore, but in addition she assisted Ramón in his frequent supernatural activities. At times of vulnerability, when the mara'akame's special animal helpers were off guard, for example, she would "stand at his back and protect him from sorcerers." When I first met Lupe she had never been to Wirikuta and Ramón was actively preparing her for this experience. He considered her a student of Huichol religion and took special pains with her training in anticipation of the momentous and dangerous experience of her first peyote hunt.

FESTIVITY AND RITUAL CLOWNS

An important part of the spiritual culture in most primitive societies are ceremonial dances which mark the turning of the seasons, impersonate gods and spirits, and provide occasions for celebrating the community— together with its ancestors and tutelary gods—as a unity. The following is a famous passage from a classic work on primitive religion which interprets one aspect of ceremonial dance in some American Indian cultures— the "ritual clowns." These personages do not hesitate to mimic for laughs even the shamans. In so doing, they illustrate the primitive ability to include such aspects of human life as humor and dance within the ambience of the sacred, and ritually to create cosmic unity by presenting the normal and its opposite side by side. Out of such acts as this is the impressive spiritual cohesion of primitive societies made.

From *Primitive Religion*
Robert H. Lowie

Whether the Maidu of the Sacramento Valley in central California are holding a spiritistic meeting or celebrating one of their ceremonial dances, the clown has a part officially not less recognized than the shaman's. He apes the shaman's actions and speeches, tries to make his audience laugh, and gives an exhibition of gluttony only checked with great difficulty by the shaman's reproaches. This character is strongly reminiscent of certain functionaries in the ritual of the Pueblo tribes of Arizona and New Mexico. I have myself seen clowns of the Tewa village on the First Hopi Mesa entertaining spectators by their voracity, practical joking, and every other kind of farcical action while a serious masquerade dance was going on, and even mimicking the priests in aspersing the mummers with corn meal. But perhaps the most instructive data are supplied by the Zuñi of New Mexico, and a brief description of the relevant data seems desirable.

All Zuñi males enter a rain-making and mask-wearing society, which is ceremonially distinct from a series of medical and magical associations admitting both sexes and without compulsory membership. Buffoonery is intimately connected with both types of religious activity. During the public performances of the Masked Dancers appear a group of annually chosen clowns, the Koyemshi, who mimic the celebrants, deride one another's appearance, indulge in obscene raillery, play games, pretend being frightened at some child in the crowd, fall to loggerheads with one of the fraternities, and otherwise seek to amuse the spectators. Notwithstanding their distinctness from the Koyemshi in point of organization, the doctoring fraternity known as Newekwe (Galaxy) is often connected with the Koyemshi in public pleasantries. This association is plausible enough considering the comic pantomime correlated with both groups. The Newekwe, however, have as a distinctive feature obligatory eating of filth, members vying with one another as to the amount consumed. This is only one of a series of equally repulsive actions, from our point of view, such as the drinking of urine and the biting off of the heads of living mice. Nevertheless, this same organization practices the typical rituals of other

Robert H. Lowie, *Primitive Religion* (New York: Liveright Publishing Co., 1948), pp. 315–19. Notes Omitted. Copyright © 1924 by Boni & Liveright, Inc. Copyright renewed 1952 by Robert H. Lowie. Reprinted by permission of the publisher.

sacred fraternities, erects an altar, indulges in ceremonial smoking, and constructs prayer plumes.

Among the Plains Indians the contrast is of a rather different kind. Thus, in the Crazy Dance of the Arapaho the performers "act in as extravagant and foolish a manner as possible, and are allowed full license to do whatever they please": they annoy every one in camp, some impersonate animals which their comrades shoot at, aiming backward over their shoulders; indeed, all do directly the opposite of what would be expected from a rational being. Thus, if a dancer is carrying a heavy load he pretends that it is negligible, while a light one is treated as though it were a terrible burden; and all members "talk backward," that is, say exactly the opposite of what they mean. Further, the Crazy Dancers rush into a fire specially built for the purpose and trample it out. They have a root possessing the virtue of paralyzing man and beast: using it against a rattlesnake, for example, they can make him unable to coil. These features recur in varying combinations among many tribes of the same region, as a few examples will amply demonstrate. The Crow had "Crazy Dogs" who said the reverse of what they meant and were pledged to foolhardiness in battle. In the Dog society of the Hidatsa the officers distinguished from the rank and file as "Real Dogs" also used backward speech, were expected to be particularly brave, and acted contrary to normal ways, for instance, by walking about practically naked in the winter time. They also took out meat from a kettle of boiling water without injury to their arms or hands. This last-mentioned trick was in the highest degree characteristic of the Heyoka organization of the Dakota, whose general motto was to defy natural conduct and normal custom. They would pretend to be cold in summer and hot in winter, would assist women in cooking, might face west instead of east in a Sun Dance, and altogether played the part of buffoons. Nevertheless, the society had a definitely religious setting. The members theoretically modeled themselves on a being or group of beings from whom the organization derived its name, and participation depended on a particular type of vision,—indeed, was compulsory for those having such visions lest they be killed by thunder.

I am of opinion that the phenomena cited proceed from diverse psychological motives and that successful grappling with the question at issue will only begin when we cease to lump together all so-called clownish behavior under a single head. For one thing, the fire-dance of the Arapaho and the kettle-trick of the Dakota and Hidatsa are probably not to be confounded with buffoonery at all. True, they imply an apparently irrational defiance of the laws of nature. In reality, however, the point of these performances lies in the immunity of the actors from the effects that would normally be expected; in other words, they are demonstrating their supernatural powers, a thing very different from clownishness. Secondly, the reckless bravery of certain men in the military societies, such as the Hidatsa Real Dogs, is also in the nature of a demonstration, though of a different sort: the actor proves that he possesses in an exalted degree a trait incumbent on all tribesmen in milder form. Yet in this case we can see how comic elements might easily develop incidentally. Suppose that the name "Crazy Dog" is once applied to a Crow who has undertaken the vow of foolhardiness; then the very name will suggest certain modes of conduct and correlated modes of treatment. "As these dogs act when they see a cow, so he acted in sight of the buffalo. . . . When they went on a hunt, the people regarded him as a dog." The mad ignoring of danger obligatory in sight of the foe might be extended to like conduct in camp: as a Crazy Dog walked straight towards the enemy irrespective of consequences, so he would ride directly into the midst of a group of tribesmen unless shooed away as a dog. The suggestions of the word "crazy" would also account for backward speech and all manner of eccentricity. In this way, some of the farcical proceedings can be interpreted not as the effect of religious degeneration but as casual ramifications of *military* ideas; and they appear in the religious context merely because these military ideas are linked with religious ones.

As for the buffoonery of the Koyemshi, we may fall back upon a principle previously used to account for ceremonial amplification. If some slapstick sort of comedy exists in a tribe independently of sacred connections and is more or less regularly evoked by a specific condition, then the occurrence of the proper cue in the course of some holy ritual may set in motion the machinery of clownishness without any one's resenting the intrusion as anomalous.

All this must be taken as purely tentative and at best covers only a part of the field. It is, however, useful to point out the existence of problems and also that they are at least in principle not altogether insoluble.

HUNTING AND RELIGION

For most primitive societies, hunting as the source of much of the livelihood is a crucial and sacred matter. It requires the delicate adjustment of several spiritual forces. For a good hunt, there must be right alignment of the spiritual powers within the community, right propitiation of the animals sought, and a proper regard for the powers controlling the forest. The following passage gives an unforgettable impression of this process in Africa in recent times. Something of the spiritual ferment of modern Africa can be gathered from the fact that a new "anti-sorcery" cult called Kabengabenga, and Christian converts, were among the forces which had to be reconciled to make hunting successful. The Lele are a Bantu-speaking people in the Congo area of Africa, living in the south-central part of what is now Zaire along the Kasai River, a major tributary of the Congo. The pangolin, the main symbol in this passage, is an armored nocturnal mammal growing up to three feet long. The duiker is a small antelope.

From *Animals in Lele Religious Thought*

Mary Douglas

HUMANS, ANIMALS, AND SPIRITS

Lele religion is based on certain assumptions about the interrelation of humans, animals, and spirits. Each has a defined sphere, but there is interaction between them. The whole is regarded as a single system. A major disorder in the human sphere is presumed to disturb the relations which ought to exist between all the parts. Major disorders in the other spheres are not expected to occur.

Animals live their lives, each behaving according to its kind. Their sphere does not impinge on the human sphere. No animal will molest a human, enter a human habitation, or steal chickens and goats, unless made to do so by sorcery. Nor will an animal become a victim to a hunter unless the spirits are willing. For their part, humans cannot expect to intervene in animal affairs, even to sight or pursue, still less to kill an animal, unless their relations with the spirits are harmonious. The approval of the spirits is assured if human relations with each other are peaceful and if ritual is correctly performed. The goodwill of the spirits notwithstanding, the hunter's success may be spoilt by sorcery.

The hunt is the point at which the three spheres touch. Its significance far surpasses its primary object—the supply of meat. The whole range of human aspirations—for food, fertility, health, and longevity—is controlled by the spirits and may be thwarted by sorcery. If the hunt fails, the Lele fear that their other enterprises also are in danger. Not only do they feel angry at a wasted day and meatless fare, but they feel anxious for the recovery of the sick, for the efficacy of their medicines, for their whole future prosperity.

In the delicate balance between humans, animals, and spirits, certain humans and certain animals occupy key positions of influence. Among humans, the Begetters' group honours those who have been blessed with a child. At their initiation rites ribald songs mock the sterile. The Pangolin cult honours those who have been blessed with children of both sexes; the Twin cult honours those who have been blessed with multiple births. The qualification for membership of any these cults is not something which a man can achieve by his own efforts. He must have been

Mary Douglas, "Animals in Lele Religious Thought," *Africa* 27 (1957): 51–56. Reprinted by permission of the International African Institute, and of the author.

chosen by the spirits for his role as mediator between the human and the supernatural. In theory, the candidates for the Diviners' Group are also believed to have been made aware of their vocation in a dream or by spirit-possession, though in practice men are known to fake this qualification. Once initiated these men have access to magical powers which can be used on behalf of their fellows.

In the animal world certain creatures mediate between animals and humans. Among these the pangolin is pre-eminent. It has the character of a denatured fish: a fish-like creature which lives on dry land, which bears its young after the manner of humans, and which does not run away from humans. In order to see the full significance of its fish-like scales, one should know more of the symbolic role of fish for the Lele.

Fishes belong so completely to the watery element that they cannot survive out of it. Bringing fish out of the water and the forest into the village is an act surrounded with precautionary ritual. Women abstain from sexual intercourse before going fishing. Fish and fishing gear, and certain water-plants, cannot be brought into the village on the day they are taken from the water unless ritual is performed. The woman who is carrying the fish sends a child ahead to fetch a live firebrand with which she touches the fish. The other things are left for one night in the grassland before being taken into the village.

I might interpret this behaviour by saying that they wish to avoid any confusion of the dry and the watery elements, but this would not be a translation of any Lele explanation. If asked why they do it, they reply: 'To prevent an outbreak of coughing and illness,' or, 'Otherwise the furry animals (*hutapok*) will get in and steal our chickens, and coughing will break out among our children.' But these are merely elliptical references to the communion between spirit, animal, and human spheres. The furry animals which steal chickens and cause illness are not ordinary carnivorous animals, but sorcerers' familiars, whose access to the sphere of living humans is made more difficult if the proper distinctions between human and animal, day and night, water and land,[1] are correctly observed.

In accordance with the symbolism relating fishes with fertility and with spirits, pregnant women and novices for initiation must totally avoid eating fish. Certain fishes are more specially associated with spirits than others, and diviners are supposed to avoid eating them. Fishes do nothing to bridge the gap between human society and the creatures of the forest. Unprepared contact with them is potentially dangerous and is hedged with ritual. People in a marginal ritual condition avoid them altogether. But pangolins, part fish, part animal, friendly to humans, are apt for a mediatory role. This, I suggest, is the context of the underlying assumptions by means of which the Lele cult of pangolins is intelligible to themselves. This is why killing and eating pangolins, with proper ritual ob-

---

[1] I have given an outline of the most important of these distinctions as they appear in ritual, in 'The Lele of the Kasai', in *African Worlds*, ed. Daryll Forde, 1954.

servances, are believed to bring animals in droves to the hunter's arrows and babies to women.

PANGOLIN RITUAL

In a village of forty men and fifty women, all the adult male pagans save one were Begetters, sixteen were initiated Diviners, three men and their wives were Twin Parents, four men were Pangolin initiates. I was present and able to record the results of a number of hunts in the dry season of 1953.

All the villages to the north, and many to the south of my village had adopted a new anti-sorcery cult, Kabengabenga, which was sweeping across the whole Kasai district. It promised hunting success, health, and long life to its initiates by threatening automatic death to anyone who attempted sorcery after initiation. Men and women in Kabengabenga villages brought pressure to bear on their kinsmen in other villages to follow their example and rid themselves of sorcery, and those who hesitated were accused by the initiates of culpable neglect if any of their kinsmen fell ill or died. Deaths in Kabengabenga villages were attributed to the boomerang action of the cult magic, so that anyone who died was held to be convicted of attempted sorcery. The mission and the Administration had taken strong action to stop the spread of the Kabengabenga cult, and in our own village the young Christians threatened to run away if the village were initiated.

Tension was running high in the village. Hunting failures, personal or communal, were attributed to sorcery; so also was sickness. Scarcely a night passed without someone shouting warnings to unnamed sorcerers to desist, to leave the sick to recover, to leave the hunter in peace to kill his quarry. They were begged to consider the reputation of the village in the eyes of other villages. One old man declared: 'The villages to the north and the villages to the south have taken Kabengabenga. They are all watching us. They used to say: "The men of Lubello kill quantities of game, without taking Kabengabenga." Now we go out hunting, and we come back empty-handed. That is a disgrace. They watch us and say we have sorcerers in our midst.'

Alternative explanations for misfortunes were offered. The senior Pangolin man said after a strange woman had entered the village recently, it was discovered that she had borne twins; no twin-rites had been performed to prevent her entry from spoiling the village; the twin-parents should now perform rites and send the village on a hunt that would make good the breach of the twin-ritual.

On 6 August the twin-parents duly consulted together. A twin-parent is supposed to be an 'owner' of the village (*muna bola*) in the sense that his or her anger would render hunting fruitless unless a rite of blessing were performed. One of them, therefore, drew attention to her ulcerated leg, and protested that, in spite of the callous disregard of others in the village, she held no grudge against them for their neglect. If she had been heard to complain, it was in pain, not in anger. She performed the ritual of blessing. Instructions were given for a hunt for the next day.

7 August. The hunt was moderately successful; although four duikers escaped, two small 'blue duikers,' one water chevrotain, and one young bay duiker were killed. The success was attributed to the performance of the twin-ritual.

There was no more communal hunting until 12 August. Individual hunters complained of their lack of success, and considered the village to be 'bad.' The senior official diviner of the village, the *ilumbi*, was informally approached and asked to take up his magic for the next hunt. It required some courage and tact to ask him to do this, as he was widely thought to be the sorcerer responsible for the bad condition of the village. On the eve of the hunt, he ordered those who had quarrelled to pay fines, and announced that he would do magic. Before the hunt one of the Pangolin men spoke a blessing, in case his grief at the obstinate and rude behaviour of the young Christians should spoil the hunt. They drew three covers, saw little game, killed only one adult and one young 'blue duiker'—a quite negligible bag. The *ilumbi* felt discredited. He announced that the animals which he had seen by divination had been escaping behind the hunters; next time he would do different magic.

13 August. In the dawn an old man got up and harangued the sorcers, asking what they ate if they didn't like animal meat? Dogs? People? What? He warned them that he did not consent to the illness of children in the village.

During the day it transpired that the twin-ritual was still outstanding. The village had been tricked into believing that the successful hunt on 7 August had been the result of twin-rituals whereas, in fact, the junior *ilumbi*, himself a twin-parent, had persuaded the others to let him try a 'spirit magic' which had been highly successful a month earlier. Everyone was angry at the deception. The senior Pangolin man, who had originally diagnosed that a breach of twin-ritual had 'spoilt the village,' declared that if only the twin-parents had been frank, the diviners themselves would have stepped in to perform the necessary twin-rites. Twins *(mayehe)* and spirits *(mingehe)* are all the same, he said, and initiated diviners do not need to beget twins in order to do twin-rites. Angriest of all was the senior *ilumbi*, hurt in his pride of magic, who now saw the reason for the failure of the hunt he had arranged on 12 August. More serious than being made to look a fool, he had looked like a sorcerer chasing away the game. In the next village the *ilumbi* had been hounded out for failure to produce game, and in the old days he would have been made to take the poison ordeal. He was obliged to dissemble his anger, as the village could be 'spoilt' by the ill will of any of its ritual officers.

In the next week men refused to go on a communal hunt as the village seemed obviously 'bad,' i.e. infected with sorcery. Individual hunters had some success: a duiker was caught in a trap, a man chanced on a wild sow just after she had farrowed and easily shot her and killed her young; and a large harnessed bush-buck was shot. In spite of these successes, there was an atmosphere of frustration and acrimony in the village.

On 24 and 27 August the women went on two long fishing expeditions. While they were away there was little food, and work in the village just ticked over till their return. On 28th two pangolins were killed. When the women came back the atmosphere in the village had changed overnight to one of general rejoicing. The village evidently was felt to be vindicated in the eyes of its Kabengabenga critics. A neighbouring village asked to be allowed to send a candidate for initiation into the Pangolin cult. Among the ritual specialists annoyance about the overdue twin-rite still rankled, but the Pangolin rites had to take precedence now.

The junior Pangolin man announced on behalf of the initiates that the village was 'tied' (*kanda*), that is, that sexual intercourse was banned until after the eating of the pangolin and the shedding of animal blood in the hunt that should follow the feast. Etiquette appropriate to the presence of a chief in the village was to be observed. He used the words: *Kum ma wa*: The master is dead. Let no one fight.' *Kum* can be translated as master or chief. Unfortunately a quarrel between children dancing broke out, adults took sides, and blows were struck. A fine had to be paid to the Pangolin group for this breach of ritual peace.

29 August. A meeting was called. The village was in a ferment because a man had been caught seducing the wife of the senior Pangolin man. The latter refused to carry on with Pangolin initiation and feast.

30 August. There was a spate of early-morning speeches. The senior Pangolin man was reproached for turning household affairs into village affairs, and for making the village suffer for his private wrong. Someone pointed out that if the pangolins were left to rot, the people of the next village, who wanted their candidate vested with Pangolin power, would think we had refused to eat the pangolin to spite them. All those who had quarrelled were roundly taken to task in public speeches. All were convinced that to go hunting while the senior Pangolin man was feeling angry would be useless.

31 August. Village opinion, originally sympathetic to the senior Pangolin man, now turned against him. He was insisting that full adultery damages should be paid before he proceeded with the Pangolin rites. There was anxiety lest the pangolins should go bad; they had already been dead five days. If they were to go bad without being eaten with proper ritual, the whole village would go 'hard' and suffer for a long time, until Pangolin magic had been done again. Repeated injunctions were made to keep the peace until the pangolin hunt. Two more cases of fighting occurred.

2 September. Fines for fighting were all paid up, and the major part of the adultery damages had been given. Ritual was performed to make the way clear for hunting the next day. The two *ilumbi*, the four Pangolin men, and the twin-parents met and agreed to do two rites: twin-ritual and Pangolin ritual, for the hunt.

3 September. Before the hunt, two twin-parents aired their grievances; one on account of her ulcerated leg, which she felt no one took trouble to diagnose and cure; the other complained that her husband had abandoned her for a new young wife. Her husband's colleagues replied for him that it was nonsense to suppose that a man would leave a woman through whom he had attained three of God's callings or vocations (*mapok manjambi*). He was, through her, an initiate of the Begetters, of Twins and of the Pangolin. She was reminded of the danger to the village if a woman who was in these three senses one of its 'owners' were allowed to nurse her anger.

The hunt that followed this concerted ritual effort was a failure. Seven animals in all were seen, but only two small duikers were killed. There was great anger and agreement that the village was bad. However, blood had been shed and the Pangolin feast could proceed. After the Pangolin rites had been performed, people assured each other, we should all see great quantities of game being brought back. The pangolin would draw animals to the village. The next day was fixed for the feast.

That very afternoon a third pangolin was killed. There was great satisfaction. 'Just as we were saying "Tomorrow we shall eat pangolin, and invest new members" . . . behold, another pangolin comes into the village!' They spoke as if the pangolin had died voluntarily, as if it had elected to be the object of Pangolin ritual and to offer itself for the feast of initiates; as if it had honoured this village by choosing it.

At night the junior Pangolin man announced that no one was to fight, above all no one was to fight secretly. 'If you must fight, do it openly and pay up. He who fights tonight, let him be rich. The fine will be twenty raffia cloths.'

5 September. The Pangolin feast and initiation rite were eventually held. I was unfortunately unable to see the rites. I was told that emphasis was laid on the chiefship of the pangolin. We call him *kum*, they said, because he makes women conceive. They expressed shame and embarrassment at having eaten a *kum*. No one is allowed to see the pangolins being roasted over the fire. The tongues, necks, ribs, and stomachs were not eaten, but buried under a palm-tree whose wine thenceforth becomes the sole prerogative of the Begetters. Apparently the new initiate was made to eat some of the flesh of the first two pangolins which were in process of decay; the more rotten parts, together with the scales and bones, were given to the dogs. The senior initiates ate the flesh of the more recently killed animal. All were confident that the hunt on the following day would be successful.

6 September. The hunt went off in good heart, twenty men and eight dogs. It was an abject failure. Powerful sorcery was evidently at work, since all ritual had been duly performed. People discussed the possible significance of a leopard that had been heard to bark in the precincts of the village that night, and of leopard tracks that had been seen on the way to the hunt. The leopard is one of the forms which the *ilumbi* is supposed to be able to take, and the *ilumbi* was suspected of having gone ahead of the hunters in leopard's guise, and scared off the game. The *ilumbi* himself, realizing that suspicions of sorcery were again directed at him, suggested that he would gladly go with the rest of the village to take Kabengabenga magic, if only the Christians did not hold such strong objections. He evidently saw it as a means of clearing his own name. In his youth he had twice taken the poison ordeal and confounded his accusers. He also suggested to me privately that he might leave the village and live elsewhere, as his enemies had never forgiven him for the disputes over women in which he had been embroiled.

In the meanwhile, the village was still 'tied:' the ban on sexual intercourse had not been lifted since 28 August, and could not be until blood had been shed in a hunt following the feast of Pangolin initiates.

9 September. A hunt took place in which one small duiker was killed. The ritual requirement was fulfilled, and the ban on sexual intercourse was lifted, but from every other point of view it was felt to have been a failure.

AGRICULTURE AND RELIGION

The development of agriculture was among the latest and most important events in the saga of preliterate humanity. To the archaic farmer, all steps in the annual process of planting, cultivating, and harvesting are fraught with sacred meaning and likely to be attended with special rituals to help the plants, the all-important givers of life by means of their own "deaths" at harvest, through a crucial transition. This passage describes traditional agricultural rituals after rice planting and transplanting among the Bontoc Igorots of the Philippine Islands. (Transplanting is a crucial step in rice cultivation.) An ato is a small residential and social unit of some twenty families, the fawi is the men's ceremonial building. Runo is a tall stalked plant which has sacred significance—as we see here, it marks the path to the sacred fawi, and as pud-i-pud two stalks of runo are planted on the path leading to the terraced fields (sementeras) to warn all Igorot they must not pass these fields at harvesttime unless they are engaged in that sacred and crucial work. Palay is unhusked rice. Inana is the first season of the year. Basi and tapui are fermented beverages. Anito are spirits of the departed; notice their role in agricultural rites. An olla is a jar. Lumawig is the supreme God, who dwells in the sky and is prayed to for fruitage and increase among humans, animals, and plants. He is worshipped particularly at a monthly ceremony by a hereditary class of priests called Patay.

From *The Bontoc Igorot*

Albert Ernest Jenks

CEREMONIES CONNECTED WITH AGRICULTURE

Pochang

This ceremony is performed at the close of the period Pa-chog', the period when rice seed is put in the germinating beds.

It is claimed there is no special oral ceremony for Po-chang'. The proceeding is as follows: On the first day after the completion of the period Pa-chog' the regular monthly Pa'-tay ceremony is held. On the second day the men of ato Sigichan, in which ato Lumawig resided when he lived in Bontoc, prepare a bunch of runo as large around as a man's thigh. They call this the "cha-nûg'," and store it away in the ato fawi, and outside the fawi set up in the earth twenty or more runo, called "pa-chi'-pad—the pûd-i-pûd' of the harvest field.

The bunch of runo is for a constant reminder to Lumawig to make the young rice stalks grow large. The pa-chi'-pad are to prevent Igorot from other pueblos entering the fawi and thus seeing the efficacious bundle of runo.

During the ceremony of Lĭs-lĭs, at the close of the annual harvest of palay, both the cha-nûg' and the pa-chi'-pad are destroyed by burning.

Chaka

On February 10, 1903, the rice having been practically all transplanted in Bontoc, was begun the first of a five-day general ceremony for abundant and good fruitage of the season's palay. It was at the close of the period I-na-na'.

The ceremony of the first day is called "Su-yâk'." Each group of kin —all descendants of one man or woman who has no living ascendants— kills a large hog and makes a feast. This day is said to be passed without oral ceremony.

The ceremony of the second day was a double one. The first was called "Wa-lĭt'" and the second "Mang'-mang." From about 9.30 until 11 in the forenoon a person from each family—usually a woman—passed

Albert Ernest Jenks, *The Bontoc Igorot* (Manila: Bureau of Public Printing, 1905), pp. 207–11.

slowly up the steep mountain side immediately west of Bontoc. These people went singly and in groups of two to four, following trails to points on the mountain's crest. Each woman carried a small earthen pot in which was a piece of pork covered with basi. Each also carried a chicken in an open-work basket, while tucked into the basket was a round stick about 14 inches long and half an inch in diameter. This stick, "lo'-lo," is kept in the family from generation to generation.

When the crest of the mountain was reached, each person in turn voiced an invitation to her departed ancestors to come to the Mang'-mang feast. She placed her olla of basi and pork over a tiny fire, kindled by the first pilgrim to the mountain in the morning and fed by each arrival. Then she took the chicken from her basket and faced the west, pointing before her with the chicken in one hand and the lo'-lo in the other. There she stood, a solitary figure, performing her sacred mission alone. Those preceding her were slowly descending the hot mountain side in groups as they came; those to follow her were awaiting their turn at a distance beneath a shady tree. The fire beside her sent up its thin line of smoke, bearing through the quiet air the fragrance of the basi.

The woman invited the ancestral anito to the feast, saying:

"A-ni'-to ad Lo'-ko, su-ma-a-kay'-yo ta-in-mang-mang'-ta-ko ta-ka-ka'-něn si mu'-těg." Then she faced the north and addressed the spirit of her ancestors there: "A-ni'-to ad La'-god, su-ma-a-kay'-yo ta-in-mang-mang'-ta-ko ta-ka-ka'-něn si mu'-těg." She faced the east, gazing over the forested mountain ranges, and called to the spirits of the past generation there: "A-ni'-to ad Bar'-lǐg su-ma-a-kay'-yo ta-in-mang-mang'-ta-ko ta-ka-ka-něn si mu-těg."

As she brought her sacred objects back down the mountain another woman stood alone by the little fire on the crest.

The returning pilgrim now puts her fowl and her basi olla inside her dwelling, and likely sits in the open air awaiting her husband as he prepares the feast. Outside, directly in front of his door, he builds a fire and sets a cooking olla over it. Then he takes the chicken from its basket, and at his hands it meets a slow and cruel death. It is held by the feet and the hackle feathers, and the wings unfold and droop spreading. While sitting in his doorway holding the fowl in this position the man beats the thin-fleshed bones of the wings with a short, heavy stick as large around as a spear handle. The fowl cries with each of the first dozen blows laid on, but the blows continue until each wing has received fully half a hundred. The injured bird is then laid on its back on a stone, while its head and neck stretch out on the hard surface. Again the stick falls, cruelly, regularly, this time on the neck. Up and down its length it is pummeled, and as many as a hundred blows fall—fall after the cries cease, after the eyes close and open and close again a dozen times, and after the bird is dead. The head receives a few sharp blows, a jet of blood spurts out, and the ceremonial killing is past. The man, still sitting on his haunches, still clasping the feet of the pendent bird, moves over beside his fire, faces his dwelling, and voices the only words of this strangely cruel scene. His eyes are open, his head unbending, and he gazes before him as he earnestly asks a blessing on the people, their pigs, chickens, and crops.

The old men say it is bad to cut off a chicken's head—it is like taking a human head, and, besides, they say that the pummeling makes the flesh on the bony wings and neck larger and more abundant—so all fowls killed are beaten to death.

After the oral part of the ceremony the fowl is held in the flames till all its feathers are burned off. It is cut up and cooked in the olla before the door of the dwelling, and the entire family eats of it.

Each family has the Mang'-mang ceremony, and so also has each broken household if it possesses a sementera—though a lone woman calls in a man, who alone may perform the rite connected with the ceremonial killing, and who must cook the fowl. A lone man needs no woman assistant.

Though the ancestral anito are religiously bidden to the feast, the people eat it all, no part being sacrificed for these invisible guests. Even the small olla of basi is drunk by the man at the beginning of the meal.

The rite of the third day is called "Mang-a-pu'-i." The sementeras of growing palay are visited, and an abundant fruitage asked for. Early in the morning some member of each household goes to the mountains to get small sprigs of a plant named "pa-lo'-ki." Even as early as 7.30 the pa-lo'-ki had been brought to many of the houses, and the people were scattering along the different trails leading to the most distant sementeras. If the family owned many scattered fields, the day was well spent before all were visited.

Men, women, and boys went to the bright-green fields of young palay, each carrying the basket belonging to his sex. In the basket were the sprigs of pa-lo'-ki, a small olla of water, a small wooden dish or a basket of cooked rice, and a bamboo tube of basi or tapui. Many persons had also several small pieces of pork and a chicken. As they passed out of the pueblo each carried a tightly bound club-like torch of burning palay straw; this would smolder slowly for hours.

On the stone dike of each sementera the owner paused to place three small stones to hold the olla. The bundle of smoldering straw was picked open till the breeze fanned a blaze; dry sticks or reeds quickly made a small, smoking fire under the olla, in which was put the pork or the chicken, if food was to be eaten there. Frequently, too, if the smoke was low, a piece of the pork was put on a stick punched into the soil of the sementera beside the fire and the smoke enwrapped the meat and passed on over the growing field.

As soon as all was arranged at the fire a small amount of basi was poured over a sprig of pa-lo'-ki which was stuck in the soil of the sementera, or one or two sprigs were inserted, drooping, in a split in a tall, green runo, and this was pushed into the soil. While the person stood beside the efficacious pa-lo'-ki an invocation was voiced to Lumawig to bless the crop.

The olla and piece of pork were at once put in the basket, and the journey conscientiously continued to the next sementera. Only when food was eaten at the sementera was the halt prolonged.

A-sĭg-ka-cho' is the name of the function of the fourth day. On that day each household owning sementeras has a fish feast.

At that season of the year (February), while the water is low in the river, only the very small, sluggish fish, called "kacho," is commonly caught at Bontoc. Between 200 and 300 pounds of those fish, only one in a hundred of which exceeded 2½ inches in length, were taken from the river during the three hours in the afternoon when the ceremonial fishing was in progress.

Two large scoops were used to catch the fish. They were a quarter of a mile apart in the river, and were operated independently.

At the house the fish were cooked and eaten.

When this fish meal was past the last observance of the fourth day of the Cha'-ka ceremonial was ended.

The rite of the last day is called "Pa'-tay." It is observed by two old Pa'-tay priests. Exactly at high noon Kad-lo'-san left his ato carrying a chicken and a smoldering palay-straw roll in his hand, and the unique basket, tak-fa', on his shoulder. He went unaccompanied and apparently unnoticed to the small grove of trees, called "Pa-pa-tay' ad So-kok'." Under the trees is a space some 8 or 10 feet across, paved with flat rocks, and here the man squatted and put down his basket. From it he took a two-quart olla containing water, a small wooden bowl of cooked rice, a bottle of native cane sugar, and a head-ax. He next kindled a blaze under the olla in a fireplace of three stones already set up. Then followed the ceremonial killing of the chicken, as described in the Mang'-mang rite of the second day. With the scarcely dead fowl held before him the man earnestly addressed a short supplication to Lumawig.

The fowl was then turned over and around in the flame until all its feathers were burned off. Its crop was torn out with the fingers. The ax was struck blade up solid in the ground, and the legs of the chicken cut off from the body by drawing them over the sharp ax blade, and they were put at once into the pot. An incision was cut on each side of the neck, and the body torn quickly and neatly open, with the wings still attached to the breast part. A glad exclamation broke from the man when he saw that the gall of the fowl was dark green. The intestines were then removed, ripped into a long string, and laid in the basket. The back part of the fowl, with liver, heart, and gizzard attached, went into the now boiling pot, and the breast section followed it promptly. Three or four minutes after, the bowl of rice was placed immediately in front of the man, and the breast part of the chicken laid in the bowl on the rice. Then followed these words: "Now the gall is good, we shall live in the pueblo invulnerable to disease."

The breast was again put in the pot, and as the basket was packed up in preparation for departure the anito of ancestors were invited to a feast of chicken and rice in order that the ceremony might be blessed.

At the completion of this supplication the Pa'-tay shouldered his basket and hastened homeward by a different route from which he came.

If a chicken is used in this rite it is cooked in the dwelling of the priest and is eaten by the family. If a pig is used the old men of the priest's ato consume it with him.

The performance of the rite of this last day is a critical half hour for the town. If the gall of the fowl is white or whitish the palay fruitage will be more or less of a failure. The crop last year was such—a whitish gall gave the warning. If a crow flies cawing over the path of the Pa'-tay as he returns to his dwelling, or if the dogs bark at him, many people will die in Bontoc. Three years ago a man was killed by a falling bowlder shortly after noon on this last day's ceremonial—a flying crow had foretold the disaster. If an eagle flies over the path, many houses will burn. Two years ago an eagle warned the people, and in the middle of the day fifty or more houses burned in Bontoc in the three ato of Pokisan, Luwakan, and Ungkan.

If none of these calamities are foretold, the anito enemies of Bontoc are not revengeful, and the pueblo rests in contentment.

HEADHUNTING

Headhunting is generally found only in archaic agricultural societies, and is known in only a minority of them. Nonetheless it provides insight into human nature in general. Headhunting cultures attach value to a man's taking the head of someone from another community and ritually preparing it, in distinction from war or raids of the usual sort. This passage describes headhunting among the Iatmul of New Guinea, a Melanesian people. The overtones of sexual antagonism in headhunting's demonstration of male potency, and the quasi-religious transmission of fertility and blessing by the act, are apparent. Notice how headhunting shades into concern with the eagle symbol of the unified community, the naven or ceremonial feast performed by kinsmen to celebrate the accomplishments of a child (and which included transvestite elements), the "beautiful dances," the blessing of ancestors, and the fundamental values of pride and shame upon which the society is grounded. Headhunting is, of course, among the most unpleasant aspects of primitive society—although one would not have to look long to see scarcely veiled "civilized" parallels to the values and attitudes which produced the custom.

From *Naven*

Gregory Bateson

In the business of head-hunting, the masculine ethos no doubt reached its most complete expression; and though at the present time the ethos of head-hunting cannot be satisfactorily observed, there is enough left of the old system to give the investigator some impression of what that system implied. Lacking observations of actual behaviour my description must, however, be based on native accounts.

The emphasis here was not on courage; no better *coup* was scored for a kill which had entailed special hardship or bravery. It was as good to kill a woman as a man, and as good to kill by stealth as in open fight. An example will serve to illustrate this set of attitudes: In a raid on one of the neighbouring bush villages a woman was killed and her daughter was taken by the killer (Malikindjin) and brought back to Kankanamun. He took her to his house, where for a while he hid her, thinking of adopting her into his household. But she did not remain there. He took her to the ceremonial house and a discussion arose as to her fate. She pleaded that she should be pitied: "You are not my enemies; you should pity me; later I will marry in this village."

One of the young men, Avuran-mali, son of her captor, cut into this discussion, and in a friendly way invited her to come down to the gardens to get some sugar-cane. Accordingly he and the girl went down to the gardens together with one or two of the younger boys, among them my informant, Tshava, who was then a small boy. On arriving there, Avuran-mali speared her. (The duty of cleaning the skull fell to Tshava. An enemy skull must never be touched, and Tshava had some difficulty in detaching a ligament. He therefore discarded the tongs, seized the end of the ligament in his teeth and pulled at it. His father saw him and was very shocked; but Tshava said to me: "The silly old man! How was I to know?"—an attitude towards taboos which is not uncommon among the Iatmul).

But in spite of the lack of "sportsmanship," the activity of head-hunting was to a considerable extent a "sport." There was no clear rule that you must have a grudge against a man before you killed him, nor against a village before raiding it; though a majority of the killings were certainly regarded as vengeance. In general the fighting and killing was confined to the killing of foreigners, i.e. members of other villages, especially of villages against whom a feud existed. But even this rule was not too strictly interpreted; a woman, married into the village, might for purposes of head-hunting be considered a foreigner. I even came across one case in which a man wore a tassel for killing his own wife in revenge for a kill accomplished by members of the village from which she had come.

Two main motives informed this system, the personal pride of the individual and his pride and satisfaction in the prosperity and strength of his community. These two motives were closely tangled together. On the purely personal side, the successful homicide was entitled to special ornaments and paints and to the wearing of a flying fox skin as a pubic apron; while the apron of stripped *Dracaena* leaves was the reproach of the man who had never killed. The homicide was the hero of the most elaborate *naven* and the proud giver of feasts to his *lanoa nampa* (husband people). Lastly, he was admired by the women; and even to-day the women occasionally make scornful remarks about the calico loin-cloths worn by the young mēn who should strictly still be wearing *Dracaena* aprons like those which were given them when they were little boys being initiated.

The association of personal pride with success in head-hunting and of shame with failure is brought out too in the behaviour of those whose relatives had been killed. Their first duty was the taking of *nggambwa* (vengeance). The rings of cane worn in mourning for the killed individual may not be put aside until vengeance has been achieved; and a pointed reference to an unavenged relative is one of the most dangerous insults that one Iatmul can use in ranting against another—an insult which is felt to be specially aggravating now that head-hunting is forbidden.

Indeed so serious is the condition of those who are unable to secure revenge, that it produces *ngglambi* in the group and may lead to the sickness and death of its members.

This spreading of clan dysphoria resulting from the unavenged insult to the pride of the clan may be contrasted with the "sociological" phrasings of the benefits which successful head-hunting confers upon the community. Here, as is usual in sociological phrasings, the matter is expressed in tangled symbolism, but may be made clear by an artificial separation of the various components of the system:

1. The enemy body was, if possible, brought back to the village and was there ritually killed by a man wearing a mask which represents an eagle. Thus the kill symbolically became the achievement not only of the individual homicide but of the whole village.

2. The natives articulately say that the eagle is the *kau* of the village. *Kau* is a word which means "a raiding party", "a fighting force", "an expression of anger", etc. The eagle is also represented on the finial of the ceremonial house (cf. *Oceania*, 1932, Plate VIII), and at the ceremony with which this

eagle is put in place, the bird speaks. He looks out over the enemy country and sees them there as "birds preening themselves" or as "fish jumping in the water"—ready to be killed.

3. The natives say that prosperity—plenty of children, health, dances and fine ceremonial houses—follows upon successful head-hunting.

4. Prosperity is also dependent upon the *mbwan*, those ancestral[1] spirits which are represented by standing stones.

5. The heads of the killed were placed upon the *mbwan* and in some cases their bodies were buried under the *mbwan*.

6. The standing stones are phallic symbols, e.g. in the shaman's jargon the phrase for copulation is *mbwan tou-*, "setting up a standing stone".

7. The male sexual act is definitely associated with violence and pride.

Running through this plexus of cultural details we can clearly see the general position of head-hunting as the main source of the pride of the village, while associated with the pride is prosperity, fertility and the male sexual act; while on the opposite side of the picture but still a part of the same ethos, we can see the association of shame, mourning and *ngglambi*.

Closely linked with these emphases upon pride and shame is the development of the spectacular side of head-hunting. Every victory was celebrated by great dances and ceremonial which involved the whole village. The killer was the hero of these and he was at the same time the host at the feasts which accompany them. Even the vanquished assented to the beauty of the dances, as appears from a text collected in Mindimbit describing the typical series of events on a raid:

(After the fighting) they leave off. Then he (the killer, standing in his canoe and holding up the head which he has taken from the enemy) asks "I am going to my beautiful[2] dances, to my beautiful ceremonies. Call his name." (The vanquished reply) "It is so-and-so that you have speared." (Or the victor will say) "This one is a woman" and they (the vanquished) will call her name (and they will cry to the victors) "Go. Go to your beautiful dances, to your beautiful ceremonies."

[1]The *mbwan* are regarded as ancestors and are classified roughly with the *angk-au* or potsherd spirits. But in some cases at least, the *mbwan* are really the spirits not of deceased ancestors but of killed enemies. Perhaps they are thought of as ancestors because of their activity in promoting the proliferation of the community.

[2]In this text the phrase which I have translated as "beautiful dances, beautiful ceremonies" is of considerable interest. The native word for "beautiful" is *yigen*, a common Iatmul word which is used to describe an admired face or spectacle. The same word also occurs in the adverb *yigen-mbwa*, "gently", the opposite of *nemwan-pa*, "violently" (literally, "greatly"). The whole phrase is *yigen vi, yigen mbwanggo*, a poetical form built up out of the common everyday phrase *vi mbwanggo*, "a (triumphant) war dance". In this phrase, *vi* is the word for a particular sort of spear with many points, used in warfare, and *mbwanggo* is the ordinary word for any dance or ceremony. In the traditional diction this phrase is divided into two parallel phrases, a common trick of Iatmul poetic genius. (Cf. also *yigen kundi*, "quiet singing".)

III

FIRE, FATE, AND LOVE:
THE SPIRITUAL ADVENTURE
OF HINDUISM

Like a broad river, the Hindu religious tradition has flowed down the centuries of India's history. The clear springs of its origin are in a remote, mythic past. Over the years Hinduism has cut certain deep channels, but has also spread out into numberless eddies and pools. The diversity of Hinduism cannot but impress the observer of its galaxy of colorful divine forms, processions and festivals, holy men and priests, all emerging out of a way of life at once sensuous and circumscribed. It is all inseparable from the traditional culture and social order of India; the whole idea of the religion of India being an "ism" called "Hinduism" ("Hindu" is based on the same root as "India") is a construction of Westernized scholarship.

Yet despite the diversity and the artificiality of trying to make India's religion into one thing, certain themes do run through the spirituality of India past and present.

One is the theme of sacrificial fire. Fire, or its equivalent in emotional and psychological heat, is recognized as transformative, changing tainted and ordinary clay into gods and food for gods. In ancient India (and to this day in rites done by the brahmin priests), fire sacrifices accompanied by hymns from the Rig Veda carried food to the gods. This outer fire was then "interiorized" into the yogic inner fire of asceticism and concentration which burned away impurities of flesh and soul to isolate the divine within. Finally, the warmth of rapturous devotion could bring a lover of God in any form into freedom, even transform him into a form of God himself.

For what fire reveals is oneness, the One in the many. As Agni, the fire of the sacrifice, he is the messenger bearing the sacrifices up to the gods, and so uniting heaven, atmosphere, and earth. In the yogi, spiritual fire is transformed into the One within. As the fire of devotion, it makes the two one in love. The quest for a transformation which reveals oneness beneath the separate things underlies much of India's religion and philosophy alike.

A second main theme is that the social order is, in its own way, an expression of oneness. The many separate persons, and classes, which make up society are like the cells and organs of one body. The sanctity of the social order is as important to traditional Hinduism as the quest for ultimate realization of the One beyond it. Indeed, the One can be found in selfless devotion to the social good. At different stages of life, devotion to one's role in society or to the ultimate quest are most prominent, according to traditional patterns.

A third theme is diversity of spiritual paths. In living religiously within the social order, and even more in questing the One, different paths are followed by different people within Hinduism. The matter is not as schematic as some writers have made it seem, but there are those for whom the wisdom of the ancient philosophical books like the Upanishads and meditations to go with it are most useful, and those for whom devotion to the gods has the highest appeal. For some people the special postures and breathing exercises accompanied by concentration which are called yoga are very helpful, but others use only chants or the effusive rituals of offerings and festivals. But all serious techniques for spiritual growth have in common that they are disciplines, and should be undertaken after initiation and guidance by a guru, or teacher who himself is competent in them.

Religion in India today, as everywhere, is changing. Mohandas K. Gandhi, the spiritual heart of the Indian independence movement, showed that its ancient wisdom can be combined with modern concepts of political freedom and human dignity. Other modern Hindu saints have showed the relevance of important aspects of this tradition to the spiritual malaise of Western man, and have established noteworthy India-based movements in Europe and America. Fully to understand Hinduism, though, it is necessary to understand it in the many forms it takes on the soil of India itself.

THE RIG VEDA

The oldest of the Vedas or scriptures of Hindu India is the Rig Veda. It goes back at least to the time some three thousand years ago when Indo-European or Aryan cattle-herders, cousins of the Persians and the ancestors of most of the modern Europeans, pushed into India from central Asia. The priests of these folk were the brahmins, and the Rig Veda comprises hymns offered by the brahmins (called hotar in the ritual setting) as they performed the intricate sacrificial rites by which it was believed they sustained the cosmos and acquired power to give boons to mankind. The focus of the sacrifice was fire, Agni (compare our word "ignite"). Fire represented the world's transforming cycles of creation and destruction, and conveyed oblations to the gods. One of the most popular gods was Indra, heroic patron of the Indo-European people, who consumed vast quantities of the sacred drink Soma, slew the monster Vritra when he withheld water from Earth, and wielding his thunderbolt accompanied his people into battle against the forts of the indigenous people in India. Here we see, from the Rig Veda, a hymn to Agni and one to Indra, together with a hymn to Night which further reveals the poetic power of this literature. We see also the celebrated hymn of creation which suggests that metaphysical profundity which would be developed more as time went on.

From *Hindu Scriptures*

Nicol MacNicol

TO AGNI

1. I laud Agni, the chosen priest, god, minister of sacrifice,
   The hotar, lavishest of wealth.

2. Worthy is Agni to be praised by living as by ancient seers:
   He shall bring hitherward the gods.

3. Through Agni man obtaineth wealth, yea, plenty, waxing day by day,
   Most rich in heroes, glorious.

4. Agni, the perfect sacrifice which thou encompassest about
   Verily goeth to the gods.

5. May Agni, sapient-minded priest, truthful, most gloriously great,
   The god, come hither with the gods.

6. Whatever blessing, Agni, thou wilt grant unto thy worshipper,
   That, Angiras, is indeed thy truth.

Nicol MacNicol, *Hindu Scriptures* (London: J.M. Dent & Sons, 1938), pp. 1, 6, 36–37. First published by E.J. Lazarus & Co., Benares. Notes omitted.

7. To thee, dispeller of the night, O Agni, day by day with
      prayer
   Bringing thee reverence, we come;

8. Ruler of sacrifices, guard of law eternal, radiant one,
   Increasing in thine own abode.

9. Be to us easy of approach, even as a father to his son;
   Agni, be with us for our weal.

TO INDRA

1. I will declare the manly deeds of Indra, the first that he
      achieved, the thunder-wielder.
   He slew the dragon, then disclosed the waters, and cleft the
   channels of the mountain torrents.

2. He slew the dragon lying on the mountain: his heavenly
      bolt of thunder Tvashtar fashioned.
   Like lowing kine in rapid flow descending, the waters glided
   downward to the ocean.

3. Impetuous as a bull, he chose the soma, and in three sacred
      beakers drank the juices.
   Maghavan grasped the thunder for his weapon, and smote
   to death this firstborn of the dragons.

4. When, Indra, thou hadst slain the dragon's firstborn, and
      overcome the charms of the enchanters,
   Then, giving life to Sun and Dawn and Heaven, thou foundest
   not one foe to stand against thee.

5. Indra, with his own great and deadly thunder, smote into
      pieces Vritra, worst of Vritras.
   As trunks of trees, what time the axe hath felled them low
   on the earth, so lies the prostrate dragon.

6. He, like a mad, weak warrior, challenged Indra, the great,
      impetuous, many-slaying hero.
   He, brooking not the clashing of the weapons, crushed—
   Indra's foe—the shattered forts in falling.

7. Footless and handless still, he challenged Indra, who smote
      him with his bolt between the shoulders.

Emasculate yet claiming manly vigour, thus Vritra lay with scattered limbs dissevered.

TO NIGHT

1. With all her eyes the goddess Night looks forth approaching many a spot:
   She hath put all her glories on.

2. Immortal, she hath filled the waste, the goddess hath filled height and depth:
   She conquers darkness with her light.

3. The goddess as she comes hath set the Dawn her sister in her place:
   And then the darkness vanishes.

4. So favour us this night, O thou whose pathways we have visited
   As birds their nest upon the tree.

5. The villagers have sought their homes, and all that walks and all that flies,
   Even the falcons fain for prey.

6. Keep off the she-wolf and the wolf; O Ūrmyā, keep the thief away:
   Easy be thou for us to pass.

7. Clearly hath she come nigh to me who decks the dark with richest hues:
   O morning, cancel it like debts.

8. These have I brought to thee like kine. I Night, thou child of heaven, accept
   This laud as for a conqueror.

THE SONG OF CREATION

1. Then was not non-existent nor existent: there was no realm of air, no sky beyond it.
   What covered in, and where? and what gave shelter?
   Was water there, unfathomed depth of water?

2. Death was not then, nor was there aught immortal: no sign
was there, the day's and night's divider.
That one thing, breathless, breathed by its own nature:
apart from it was nothing whatsoever.

3. Darkness there was: at first concealed in darkness, this All
was indiscriminated chaos.
All that existed then was void and formless: by the great
power of warmth was born that unit.

4. Thereafter rose desire in the beginning, Desire, the primal
seed and germ of spirit.
Sages who searched with their heart's thought discovered the
existent's kinship in the non-existent.

5. Transversely was their severing line extended: what was
above it then, and what below it?
There were begetters, there were mighty forces, free action
here and energy up yonder.

6. Who verily knows and who can here declare it, whence it
was born and whence comes this creation?
The gods are later than this world's production. Who
knows, then, whence it first came into being?

7. He, the first origin of this creation, whether he formed it all
or did not form it,
Whose eye controls this world in highest heaven, he verily
knows it, or perhaps he knows not.

THE UPANISHADS

*The Upanishads are the latest and most philosophical of the Vedic
scriptures. The most important date from perhaps 500 to 100 B.C. They
are commentaries revealing what seemed to brahmin thinkers to be the
deeper meaning of the religion implied by the sacrifices; the main thrust
is that beneath the world of changing appearances is the one Existent or
Life, called Brahman. Brahman is the source of all things; by knowing
him with the help of a wise teacher, one can turn to a life close to the
wellsprings of true joy. In this passage, from the Chandogya Upanishad
(one of the oldest, from around 500 B.C.), a brahmin father is instructing
his son Svetaketu. The father emphasizes, in the famous words "You are
that," the great Upanishadic truth that on the level of atman, his ultimate self at the roots of being and consciousness, the son like all beings
is Infinite Reality.*

From *A Source Book of Advaita Vedanta*

Eliot Deutsch and J.A.B. van Buitenen

9. "Just as the bees prepare honey by collecting the juices of all manner of trees and bring the juice to one unity, and just as the juices no longer distinctly know that the one hails from this tree, the other from that one, likewise, my son, when all these creatures have merged with the Existent they do not know, realizing only that they have merged with the Existent.

"Whatever they are here on earth, tiger, lion, wolf, boar, worm, fly, gnat, or mosquito, they become that.

"It is this very fineness which ensouls all this world, it is the true one, it is the soul. *You are that*, Svetaketu."

"Instruct me further, sir."

"So I will, my son," he said.

10. "The rivers of the east, my son, flow eastward, the rivers of the west flow westward. From ocean they merge into ocean, it becomes the same ocean. Just as they then no longer know that they are this river or that one, just so all these creatures, my son, know no more, realizing only when having come to the Existent that they have come to the Existent. Whatever they are here on earth, tiger, lion, wolf, boar, worm, fly, gnat or mosquito, they become that.

"It is this very fineness which ensouls all this world, it is the true one, it is the soul. *You are that*, Svetaketu."

"Instruct me further, sir."

"So I will, my son," he said.

11. "If a man would strike this big tree at the root, my son, it would bleed but stay alive. If he struck it at the middle, it would bleed but stay alive. If he struck it at the top, it would bleed but stay alive. Being entirely permeated by the living soul, it stands there happily drinking its food.

"If this life leaves one branch, it withers. If it leaves another branch, it withers. If it leaves a third branch, it withers. If it leaves the whole tree, the whole tree withers. Know that it is in this same way, my son," he said, "that this very body dies when deserted by this life, but this life itself does not die.

Eliot Deutsch and J.A.B. van Buitenen, *A Source Book of Advaita Vedanta* (Honolulu: The University Press of Hawaii, 1971), pp. 14–16. Reprinted by permission of the publisher. This passage is translated by J.A.B. van Buitenen.

"This is the very fineness which ensouls all this world, it is the true one, it is the soul. *You are that,* Svetaketu."

"Instruct me further, sir."

"So I will, my son," he said.

12. "Bring me a banyan fruit."

"Here it is, sir."

"Split it."

"It is split, sir."

"What do you see inside it?"

"A number of rather fine seeds, sir."

"Well, split one of them."

"It is split, sir."

"What do you see inside it?"

"Nothing, sir."

He said to him, "This very fineness that you no longer can make out, it is by virtue of this fineness that this banyan tree stands so big.

"Believe me, my son. It is this very fineness which ensouls all this world, it is the true one, it is the soul. *You are that,* Svetaketu."

"Instruct me further, sir."

"So I will, my son," he said.

13. "Throw this salt in the water, and sit with me on the morrow." So he did. He said to him, "Well, bring me the salt that you threw in the water last night." He looked for it, but could not find it as it was dissolved.

"Well, taste the water on this side.—How does it taste?"

"Salty."

"Taste it in the middle.—How does it taste?"

"Salty."

"Taste it at the other end.—How does it taste?"

"Salty."

"Take a mouthful and sit with me." So he did.

"It is always the same."

He said to him, "You cannot make out what exists in it, yet it is there.

"It is this very fineness which ensouls all this world, it is the true one, it is the soul. *You are that,* Svetaketu."

"Instruct me further, sir."

"So I will, my son," he said.

14. "Suppose they brought a man from the Gandhāra country, blind-folded, and let him loose in an uninhabited place beyond. The man, brought out and let loose with his blindfold on, would be turned around, to the east, north, west, and south.

"Then someone would take off his blindfold and tell him, 'Gandhāra is that way, go that way.' Being a wise man and clever, he would ask his way from village to village and thus reach Gandhāra. Thus in this world a man who has a teacher knows from him, 'So long will it take until I am free, then I shall reach it.'

"It is this very fineness which ensouls all this world, it is the true one, it is the soul. *You are that*, Svetaketu.'

"Instruct me further, sir."

"So I will, my son," he said.

15. "When a man is dying, his relatives crowd around him: 'Do you recognize me? Do you recognize me?' As long as his speech has not merged in his mind, his mind in his breath, his breath in Fire, and Fire in the supreme deity, he does recognize.

"But when his speech has merged in the mind, the mind in the breath, the breath in Fire, and Fire in the supreme deity, he no longer recognizes.

"It is this very fineness which ensouls all this world, it is the true one, it is the soul. *You are that*, Svetaketu."

"Instruct me further, sir."

"So I will, my son," he said.

16. "They bring in a man with his hands tied, my son: 'He has stolen, he has committed a robbery. Heat the ax for him!' If he is the criminal, he will make himself untrue. His protests being untrue, and covering himself with untruth, he seizes the heated ax. He is burnt, and then killed.

"If he is not the criminal, he makes himself true by this very fact. His protests being true, and covering himself with truth, he seizes the heated ax. He is not burnt, and then set free.

"Just as he is not burnt—that ensouls all this world, it is the true one, it is the soul. *You are that*, Svetaketu."

This he knew from him, from him.

YOGA

One method for attaining awareness of the true self taught in ancient India was that combination of an austere and disciplined way of life, postures and breathing exercises, and concentrated meditation known as yoga. As we have noted, it can be thought of as an internal sacrifice. This passage is from the most important of all yoga texts, the Yoga Sutras of Patanjali, from about 100 B.C. The first part summarizes the basic idea of yoga, the control of the fluctuations of mind caused by ignorance, together with the attachments which keep us from the calm joy of knowing who we really are. The second part outlines the earlier of the eight "limbs" or steps of yoga as a means to that end, the isolation of the true

self. (The translation used below, in order to emphasize the translators'
view of the continuity of upanishadic with yogic thought, renders the
true self "atman" rather than "purusha," the term used in the original.)

From *How to Know God: The Yoga*
Aphorisms of Patanjali

Swami Prabhavananda and Christopher Isherwood

1. Austerity, study, and the dedication of the fruits of one's work
to God: these are the preliminary steps toward yoga.

2. Thus we may cultivate the power of concentration and remove
the obstacles to enlightenment which cause all our sufferings.

3. These obstacles—the causes of man's sufferings—are ignorance,
egoism, attachment, aversion, and the desire to cling to life.

4. Ignorance creates all the other obstacles. They may exist either
in a potential or a vestigial form, or they may have been temporarily
overcome or fully developed.

5. To regard the noneternal as eternal, the impure as pure, the
painful as pleasant and the non-Atman as the Atman—this is ignorance.

6. To identify consciousness with that which merely reflects consciousness—this is egoism.

7. Attachment is that which dwells upon pleasure.

.   .   .

28. As soon as all impurities have been removed by the practice of
spiritual disciplines—the "limbs" of yoga—a man's spiritual vision opens
to the light-giving knowledge of the Atman.

29. The eight limbs of yoga are: the various forms of abstention
from evil-doing (yama), the various observances (niyamas), posture
(asana), control of the prana (pranayama), withdrawal of the mind from

Swami Prabhavananda and Christopher Isherwood trans., *How to Know God:
The Yoga Aphorisms of Patanjali* (Hollywood: The Vedanta Press, 1969), aphorisms
1–7, 28–55. Commentary omitted. Reprinted by permission of The Vedanta Society of
Southern California.

sense objects (pratahara), concentration (dharana), meditation (dhyana) and absorption in the Atman (samadhi).

30. Yama is abstention from harming others, from falsehood, from theft, from incontinence, and from greed.

31. These forms of abstention are basic rules of conduct. They must be practiced without any reservations as to time, place, purpose, or caste rules.

32. The niyamas (observances) are purity, contentment, mortification, study and devotion to God.

33. To be free from thoughts that distract one from yoga, thoughts of an opposite kind must be cultivated.

34. The obstacles to yoga—such as acts of violence and untruth—may be directly created or indirectly caused or approved, they may be motivated by greed, anger or self-interest, they may be small or moderate or great, but they never cease to result in pain and ignorance. One should overcome distracting thoughts by remembering this.

35. When a man becomes steadfast in his abstention from harming others, then all living creatures will cease to feel enmity in his presence.

36. When a man becomes steadfast in his abstention from falsehood he gets the power of obtaining for himself and others the fruits of good deeds, without having to perform the deeds themselves.

37. When a man becomes steadfast in his abstention from theft, all wealth comes to him.

38. When a man becomes steadfast in his abstention from incontinence, he acquires spiritual energy.

39. When a man becomes steadfast in his abstention from greed, he gains knowledge of his past, present and future existences.

40. As the result of purity, there arises indifference toward the body and disgust for physical intercourse with others.

41. Moreover, one achieves purification of the heart, cheerfulness of mind, the power of concentration, control of the passions and fitness for vision of the Atman.

42. As the result of contentment, one gains supreme happiness.

43. As the result of mortification, impurities are removed. Then special powers come to the body and the sense-organs.

44. As the result of study, one obtains the vision of that aspect of God which one has chosen to worship.

45. As the result of devotion to God, one achieves samadhi.

46. Posture (asana) is to be seated in a position which is firm but relaxed.

47. Posture becomes firm and relaxed through control of the natural

tendencies of the body, and through meditation on the Infinite.

48. Thereafter, one is no longer troubled by the dualities of sense-experience.

49. After mastering posture, one must practice control of the prana (pranayama) by stopping the motions of inhalation and exhalation.

50. The breath may be stopped externally, or internally, or checked in mid-motion, and regulated according to place, time and a fixed number of moments, so that the stoppage is either protracted or brief.

51. The fourth kind of pranayama is the stoppage of the breath which is caused by concentration upon external or internal objects.

52. As the result of this, the covering of the Inner Light is removed.

53. The mind gains the power of concentration (dharana).

54. When the mind is withdrawn from sense-objects, the sense-organs also withdraw themselves from their respective objects and thus are said to imitate the mind. This is known as pratyahara.

55. Thence arises complete mastery over the senses.

THE LAWS OF MANU

Hindu thought has never been content only to present means of inner spiritual realization, but has continually wrestled also with the problem of the relation of the social order and the workaday world to the Absolute it knows underlies what appears on the surface. The social order must also be an expression of the One, and ways must exist to know the One through it. Regarding as sacred the caste system—the division of society into different groups, largely hereditary—was the most significant way of doing this. Each caste had its traditional vocations, rituals, prohibitions, and above all rigorous restrictions concerning marriage and sharing food with persons of other castes. This made society like a giant body, with each individual like a cell and each caste like an organ of the body. Society reflected the oneness of the universe, rather than just being a collection of stray parts. This passage, from the influential text called the Laws of Manu, expressed about 100 B.C. this vision of a hierarchical yet linked society as a cosmic body. It deals only with the four varnas or major categories: brahmins or priests and scholars; kshatriyas or knights and rulers, vaishyas or traders and craftsmen; and shudras or peasants. The actual caste system is tremendously more complex. These broad categories are subdivided into innumerable jati (gâti) or subcastes, which are the functional units. This passage emphasizes most the impressive dignity and responsibility of brahmins (brahmanas). Elsewhere the Laws of Manu endeavor to reconcile responsibility to the social order with the quest for liberation by teachings about the stages of life; when one has finished a life as a student and householder, he is to give up material attachments and place in the world to follow the ultimate quest under his guru or spiritual master.

From *The Laws of Manu*
G. Buhler

But in order to protect this universe He, the most resplendent one, assigned separate (duties and) occupations to those who sprang from his mouth, arms, thighs, and feet.

To Brhâma*n*as he assigned teaching and studying (the Veda), sacrificing for their own benefit and for others, giving and accepting (of alms).

The Kshatriya he commanded to protect the people, to bestow gifts, to offer sacrifices, to study (the Veda), and to abstain from attaching himself to sensual pleasures;

The Vai*s*ya to tend cattle, to bestow gifts, to offer sacrifices, to study (the Veda), to trade, to lend money, and to cultivate land.

One occupation only the lord prescribed to the Sûdra, to serve meekly even these (other) three castes.

Man is stated to be purer above the navel (than below); hence the Self-existent (Svayambhû) has declared the purest (part) of him (to be) his mouth.

As the Brâhma*n*a sprang from (Brahman's) mouth, as he was the first-born, and as he possesses the Veda, he is by right the lord of this whole creation.

For the Self-existent (Svayambhû), having performed austerities, produced him first from his own mouth, in order that the offerings might be conveyed to the gods and manes and that this universe might be preserved.

What created being can surpass him, through whose mouth the gods continually consume the sacrificial viands and the manes the offerings to the dead?

Of created beings the most excellent are said to be those which are animated; of the animated, those which subsist by intelligence; of the intelligent, mankind; and of men, the Brâhma*n*as;

Of Brâhma*n*as, those learned (in the Veda); of the learned, those

G. Buhler, trans., *The Laws of Manu* (Oxford: The Clarendon Press, 1886), pp. 24–28. Notes omitted.

who recognise (the necessity and the manner of performing the prescribed duties); of those who possess this knowledge, those who perform them; of the performers, those who know the Brahman.

The very birth of a Brâhmana is an eternal incarnation of the sacred law; for he is born to (fulfil) the sacred law, and becomes one with Brahman.

A Brâhmana, coming into existence, is born as the highest on earth, the lord of all created beings, for the protection of the treasury of the law.

Whatever exists in the world is the property of the Brâhmana; on account of the excellence of his origin the Brâhmana is, indeed, entitled to it all.

The Brâhmana eats but his own food, wears but his own apparel, bestows but his own in alms; other mortals subsist through the benevolence of the Brâhmana.

In order to clearly settle his duties and those of the other (castes) according to their order, wise Manu sprung from the Self-existent, composed these Institutes (of the sacred law).

A learned Brâhmana must carefully study them, and he must duly instruct his pupils in them, but nobody else (shall do it).

A Brâhmana who studies these Institutes (and) faithfully fulfils the duties (prescribed therein), is never tainted by sins, arising from thoughts, words, or deeds.

He sanctifies any company (which he may enter), seven ancestors and seven descendants, and he alone deserves (to possess) this whole earth.

(To study) this (work) is the best means of securing welfare, it increases understanding, it procures fame and long life, it (leads to) supreme bliss.

In this (work) the sacred law has been fully stated as well as the good and bad qualities of (human) actions and the immemorial rule of conduct, (to be followed) by all the four castes (varna).

The rule of conduct is transcendent law, whether it be taught in the revealed texts or in the sacred tradition; hence a twice-born man who possesses regard for himself, should be always careful to (follow) it.

A Brâhmana who departs from the rule of conduct, does not reap the fruit of the Veda, but he who duly follows it, will obtain the full reward.

The sages who saw that the sacred law is thus grounded on the rule of conduct, have taken good conduct to be the most excellent root of all austerity.

The creation of the universe, the rule of the sacraments, the ordinances of studentship, and the respectful behaviour (towards Gurus), the most excellent rule of bathing (on return from the teacher's house),

(The law of) marriage and the description of the (various) marriage-rites, the regulations for the great sacrifices and the eternal rule of the funeral sacrifices,

The description of the modes of (gaining) subsistence and the duties

of a Snâtaka, (the rules regarding) lawful and forbidden food, the purification of men and of things,

The laws concerning women, (the law) of hermits, (the manner of
gaining) final emancipation and (of) renouncing the world, the whole
duty of a king and the manner of deciding lawsuits,

The rules for the examination of witnesses, the laws concerning husband and wife, the law of (inheritance and) division, (the law concerning)
gambling and the removal of (men nocuous like) thorns,

(The law concerning) the behaviour of Vai*s*yas and Sûdras, the
origin of the mixed castes, the law for all castes in times of distress and
the law of penances,

The threefold course of transmigrations, the result of (good or bad)
actions, (the manner of attaining) supreme bliss and the examination of
the good and bad qualities of actions,

The primeval laws of countries, of castes (*gâti*), of families, and the
rules concerning heretics and companies (of traders and the like)—(all
that) Manu has declared in these Institutes.

As Manu, in reply to my questions, formerly promulgated these
Institutes, even so learn ye also the (whole work) from me.

THE BHAGAVAD GITA

*In modern times the most consequential statement of the relation
between the social order and the Absolute has been the text known as
the Bhagavad Gita, the "Divine Song." It is also from around 100 B.C.,
and is actually a part of the great epic, the* Mahabharata. *The Bhagavad
Gita is a dialogue on a field of battle between the king, Arjuna, and
Krishna, God in human form who is his charioteer. Arjuna is troubled
because he must, as a* kshatriya *and king, go forth to kill his kinsmen.
Krishna responds that one kills only the outer form, for the true self is
deathless. He replies also with the teaching known as karma-yoga, so
important to the pacifist Gandhi, that if one works for the good without
attachment to the results of one's actions but just for the good's own sake,
this is the same as yogic renunciation. Finally Krishna shows himself in
his divine splendor, as the eternal Lord before whom all else is passing
away.*

*The following passage is from a beautiful version of the Bhagavad
Gita which was very influential in popularizing Eastern thought in England and America in the nineteenth century. It gives some instruction in
practicing meditative yoga, but presses also the supreme value of karma-
yoga. Then it hints at the even greater worth of bhakti, loving devotion,
a new spiritual path then emerging in India.*

From *The Song Celestial*

Sir Edwin Arnold

Krishna

Therefore, who doeth work rightful to do,
Not seeking gain from work, that man, O
    Prince!
Is Sânyasi and Yôgi—both in one!
And he is neither who lights not the flame
Of sacrifice, nor setteth hand to task.

Regard as true Renouncer him that makes
Worship by work, for who renounceth not
Works not as Yôgin. So is that well said
"By works the votary doth rise to saint,
And saintship is the ceasing from all works;"
Because the perfect Yôgin acts—but acts
Unmoved by passions and unbound by deeds,
Setting result aside.

                    Let each man raise
The Self by Soul, not trample down his Self,
Since Soul that is Self's friend may grow Self's
    foe.
Soul is Self's friend when Self doth rule o're Self,
But Self turns enemy if Soul's own self
Hates Self as not itself.[1]
                    The sovereign soul
Of him who lives self-governed and at peace
Is centred in itself, taking alike
Pleasure and pain; heat, cold; glory and shame.
He is the Yôgi, he is *Yûkta*, glad
With joy of light and truth; dwelling apart
Upon a peak, with senses subjugate
Whereto the clod, the rock, the glistering gold
Show all as one. By this sign is he known
Being of equal grace to comrades, friends,
Chance-comers, strangers, lovers, enemies,

Sir Edwin Arnold, *The Song Celestial* (Boston: Roberts Brothers, 1891), pp. 62–71.
[1]The Sanskrit has this play on the double meaning of *Âtman*.

Aliens and kinsmen; loving all alike,
Evil or good.

                    Sequestered should he sit,
Steadfastly meditating, solitary,
His thoughts controlled, his passions laid away,
Quit of belongings. In a fair, still spot
Having his fixed abode,—not too much raised,
Nor yet too low,—let him abide, his goods
A cloth, a deerskin, and the Kuśa-grass.
There, setting hard his mind upon The One,
Restraining heart and senses, silent, calm,
Let him accomplish Yôga, and achieve
Pureness of soul, holding immovable
Body and neck and head, his gaze absorbed
Upon his nose-end[2] rapt from all around,
Tranquil in spirit, free of fear, intent
Upon his Brahmacharya vow, devout,
Musing on Me, lost in the thought of Me.
That Yôjin, so devoted, so controlled,
Comes to the peace beyond,—My peace, the peace
Of high Nirvana!

                    But for earthly needs
Religion is not his who too much fasts
Or too much feasts, nor his who sleeps away
An idle mind; nor his who wears to waste
His strength in vigils. Nay, Arjuna! call
That the true piety which most removes
Earth-aches and ills, where one is moderate
In eating and in resting, and in sport;
Measured in wish and act; sleeping betimes,
Waking betimes for duty.

                    When the man,
So living, centres on his soul the thought
Straitly restrained—untouched internally
By stress of sense—then is he *Yûkta.* See!
Steadfast a lamp burns sheltered from the wind;
Such is the likeness of the Yôgi's mind
Shut from sense-storms and burning bright to
    Heaven.
When mind broods placid, soothed with holy wont;
When Self contemplates self, and in itself
Hath comfort; when it knows the nameless joy
Beyond all scope of sense, revealed to soul—

2So in original.

Only to soul! and, knowing, waves not,
True to the farther Truth; when, holding this,
It deems no other treasure comparable,
But, harbored there, cannot be stirred or shook
By any gravest grief, call that state "peace,"
That happy severance Yôga; call that man
The perfect Yôgin!

      Steadfastly the will
Must toil thereto, till efforts end in ease,
And thought has passed from thinking. Shaking off
All longings bred by dreams of fame and gain,
Shutting the doorways of the senses close
With watchful ward; so, step by step, it comes
To gift of peace assured and heart assuaged,
When the mind dwells self-wrapped, and the soul
 broods
Cumberless. But, as often as the heart
Breaks—wild and wavering—from control, so oft
Let him re-curb it, let him rein it back
To the soul's governance; for perfect bliss
Grows only in the bosom tranquillized,
The spirit passionless, purged from offence,
Vowed to the Infinite. He who thus vows
His soul to the Supreme Soul, quitting sin,
Passes unhindered to the endless bliss
Of unity with Brahma. He so vowed,
So blended, sees the Life-Soul resident
In all things living, and all living things
In that Life-Soul contained. And whoso thus
Discerneth Me in all, and all in Me,
I never let him go; nor looseneth he
Hold upon Me; but, dwell he where he may,
Whate'er his life, in Me he dwells and lives,
Because he knows and worships Me, Who dwell
In all which lives, and cleaves to Me in all.
Arjuna! if a man sees everywhere—
Taught by his own similitude—one Life,
One Essence in the Evil and the Good,
Hold him a Yôgi, yea! well-perfected!

Arjuna:

Slayer of Madhu! yet again, this Yôg,
This Peace, derived from equanimity,
Made known by thee—I see no fixity
Therein, no rest, because the heart of men

Is unfixed, Krishna! rash, tumultuous,
Wilful and strong. It were all one, I think,
To hold the wayward wind, as tame man's
   heart.

Krishna:

Hero long-armed! beyond denial, hard
Man's heart is to restrain, and wavering;
Yet may grow restrained by habit, Prince!
By wont of self-command. This Yôg, I say,
Cometh not lightly to th' ungoverned ones;
But he who will be master of himself
Shall win it, if he stoutly strive thereto.

Arjuna:

And what road goeth he who, having faith,
Fails, Krishna! in the striving; falling back
From holiness, missing the perfect rule?
Is he not lost, straying from Brahma's light,
Like the vain cloud, which floats 'twixt earth and
   Heaven
When lightning splits it, and it vanisheth?
Fain would I hear thee answer me herein,
Since, Krishna! none save thou can clear the doubt.

Krishna:

He is not lost, thou Son of Prithâ! No!
Nor earth, nor heaven is forfeit, even for him,
Because no heart that holds one right desire
Treadeth the road of loss! He who should fail,
Desiring righteousness, cometh at death
Unto the Region of the Just; dwells there
Measureless years, and being born anew,
Beginneth life again in some fair home
Amid the mild and happy. It may chance
He doth descend into a Yôgin house
On Virtue's breast; but that is rare! Such birth
Is hard to be obtained on this earth, Chief!
So hath he back again what heights of heart
He did achieve, and so he strives anew
To perfectness, with better hope, dear Prince!
For by the old desire he is drawn on
Unwittingly; and only to desire
The purity of Yôga is to pass

Beyond the *Sabdabrahm*, the spoken Ved.
But, being Yôgi, striving strong and long,
Purged from transgressions, perfected by births
Following on births, he plants his feet at last
Upon the farther path. Such an one ranks
Above ascetics, higher than the wise,
Beyond achievers of vast deeds! Be thou
Yôgi, Arjuna! And of such believe,
Truest and best is he who worships Me
With inmost soul, stayed on My Mystery!

SHANKARA'S ADVAITA VEDANTA

An extremely important philosophical tradition in India has been the interpretation of the upanishadic teaching about the One Existent or Brahman called Advaita Vedanta. "Advaita" means "nondualist" and "Vedanta" means the end or summation of the Vedas. Advaita Vedanta presses home in an uncompromising way its perception that all seeming opposites, and indeed all separate things, can be reduced to a deeper unity, so finally only One exists. The One is then our own true being, and beside it all separate persons and objects and even gods are but Maya or misperceptions. The greatest spokesman for Advaita Vedanta was Shankara (c. 700–750 A.D.). Here is a passage from one of his more popular and devotional works.

From *Shankara's Crest-Jewel of Discrimination*
Swami Prabhavananda and Christopher Isherwood

I, the Atman, am Brahma.[1] I am Vishnu. I am Shiva.[2] I am this universe. Nothing is, but I am.

Swami Prabhavananda and Christopher Isherwood, trans., *Shankara's Crest-Jewel of Discrimination (Viveka Chudamani)* (New York: New American Library, 1970), pp. 90–93. Reprinted by permission of The Vedanta Society of Southern California. Copyright 1947 by the Vedanta Press, Hollywood, Ca.

[1]Brahma, one of the Hindu trinity, the creator, as distinct from Brahman, God in his impersonal, absolute aspect.

[2]The Hindu trinity: Brahma, the creator; Vishnu, the preserver; Shiva, the destroyer.

I dwell within; I am without. I am before and behind. I am in the south and I am in the north. I am above and I am below.

The wave, the foam, the eddy and the bubble are all essentially water. Similarly, the body and the ego are really nothing but pure consciousness. Everything is essentially consciousness, purity and joy.

This entire universe of which we speak and think is nothing but Brahman. Brahman dwells beyond the range of Maya. There is nothing else. Are jars, pots and vessels distinct from the clay of which they are made? Man drinks the wine of Maya, becomes deluded and begins to see things as separate from each other, so that he talks of "you" and "I."

The scripture says: "The Infinite is where one sees nothing else, hears nothing else, knows nothing else." In the Infinite, the scripture tells us, there is no duality—thereby correcting our false idea that existence is manifold.

I am Brahman, the supreme, all-pervading like the ether, stainless, indivisible, unbounded, unmoved, unchanging. I have neither inside nor outside. I alone am. I am one without a second. What else is there to be known?

What more remains to be said? I am none other than Brahman. Brahman is this universe and all things that exist within it. The scriptures declare that there is nothing else but Brahman. Those who are illumined by the knowledge "I am Brahman" renounce their attachment to this apparent universe. It is certain indeed that these illumined ones live in constant union with Brahman, the pure blissful consciousness.

Renounce all earthly hopes and physical pleasures by ceasing to identify yourself with the gross body. Next, you must cease also to identify yourself with the subtle body. Realize that you are Brahman, whose form is bliss eternal, whose glories the scriptures declare. Thus you may live in union with Brahman.

As long as man loves this mortal body, he remains impure, he is troubled by his enemies in all manner of ways, he is still subject to rebirth, disease and death. But if he will meditate upon the Atman as pure, unchangeable, the essence of goodness, he will be delivered from all evil. The scriptures also confirm this truth.

Cease to identify yourself mistakenly with all those coverings, such as the ego, etc., which overlie the Atman. Brahman alone remains—supreme, infinite, changeless, the one without a second.

When the mind is completely absorbed in the supreme Being—the Atman, the Brahman, the Absolute—then the world of appearances vanishes. Its existence is no more than an empty word.

The world of appearances is a mere phantom; there is but one Reality. It is changeless, formless and absolute. How can it be divided?

There is neither seer nor seeing nor seen. There is but one Reality —changeless, formless and absolute. How can it be divided?

There is but one Reality—like a brimming ocean in which all

appearances are dissolved. It is changeless, formless and absolute. How can it be divided?

Into it, the causes of our delusion melt away, as darkness melts into light. It is supreme, absolute, one without a second. How can it be divided?

There is but one supreme Reality. It is the very self of unity. It cannot possibly be divided into many. If multiplicity is real, and not merely apparent, why does no one ever experience it while enjoying dreamless sleep?

The universe no longer exists after we have awakened into the highest consciousness in the eternal Atman, which is Brahman, devoid of any distinction or division. At no time—either past, present or future—is there really a snake within the rope or a drop of water in the mirage.

The scriptures declare that this relative universe is only an appearance. The Absolute is non-dual. In dreamless sleep, also, the universe disappears.

It is our delusion which superimposes the universe upon Brahman. But the wise know that this universe has no separate reality. It is identical with Brahman, its ground. The rope may appear to be a snake, but the apparent difference between rope and snake only lasts as long as delusion persists.

This delusion of difference has its origin in the gross mind. When the mind is transcended, it ceases. Therefore let your mind be absorbed in contemplation of the Atman, the reality, your inmost essence.

BHAKTI

The following passage follows the thought of Narada, whom tradition makes the sage author of some influential early medieval texts on bhakti or devotional religion. The passage suggests something of the tone and power of this path of liberation into the One through loving devotion to one of the personal deities. The great majority of Hindus follow mainly the bhakti way and are in effect monotheists of one of the great Hindu deities such as Vishnu, Krishna, Shiva, or Shakti. While of course the average devotee does not approach his faith in such an analytic manner as this—indeed, an impulsive disregard of all calculation is part of its spirit—we can see here that bhakti is by no means unsophisticated, but has produced deep thought full of philosophical and psychological subtlety.

From *Bhagavata Religion: The Cult of Bhakti*
Jadunath Sinha

Nārada describes eleven forms of devotion. Though devotion is one in kind, still it appears in eleven forms. It assumes the forms of love for the attributes and greatness of God, for His beauty, for His worship, and for His recollection; love for Him of a servant, a friend, a parent, and a beloved wife; love of self-consecration to Him; love of absorption in Him; and love of the pang of separation from Him. This aphorism beautifully describes the different grades of religious consciousness. At first we are overwhelmed with the consciousness of our own finitude, and of the infinitude and majesty of God; and we adore Him as a superhuman Power. Then we come into more intimate touch with Him as the supreme Person (Purusottama), and cultivate personal relationship with Him. We love the sweetness of His transcendent beauty; we adore Him with all our heart; and we love His sweet memories. Then our love of God matures into personal love. First of all, the devotee serves the Lord as a servant serves his master. Then he approaches Him nearer, and loves Him as a friend. Then he rises higher, and manifests parental affection for the loved One, as a father for his son. And, at last, even the vestige of remoteness between them vanishes altogether. The two become one in spirit, and the devotee develops all the marks of a devoted wife's love for her beloved husband. Then the devotee consecrates his whole being to the beloved Lord, loses himself in Him, and feels His living presence everywhere. And, finally, he feels the pang of separation from his Beloved, which is the highest consummation of love. Union is tinged with selfishness. Separation is selfless. Even in separation higher union is felt. The devotee is eternally united with Him in his separation from Him.

Nārada lays stress on constant servitude and unswerving wifely love to God. We should cultivate love and love alone for God, rising above the three forms of secondary devotion. The *Nārada Pañcarātra* mentions the servitude to the Lord as the chief means of liberation. It does not mention friendship, parental affection, and wifely love. In later devotional literature, five kinds of personal relationship with the Lord are clearly mentioned: quietness (*śānta*), servitude (*dāsya*), friendship (*sakhya*), parental affection (*vātsalya*), and sweet wifely love (*mādhurya*).

Jadunath Sinha, "Bhagavata Religion: The Cult of Bhakti," in Haridas Bhattacharyya, ed., *The Cultural Heritage of India*, Vol. 4 (Calcutta: The Ramakrishna Mission Institute of Culture, 1956), pp. 152–56. Notes omitted. Reprinted by permission of the publisher.

The inherent qualities of the preceding sentiment are included in the succeeding one.

Nārada enjoins the following practices for the attainment of devotion:

Evil company should be shunned by all means, because it excites lust, anger, infatuation, lapse of memory, and loss of intelligence, and finally leads to utter ruin. These passions are natural to man. But when they are fanned by evil company, they assume huge proportions. Conversation with those who are not devotees, touching their bodies, sleeping and eating with them, all pollute our souls with sins, and we should fly away from them as we do from poisonous snakes.

Wealth and sex are the two rocks on which many souls are shipwrecked. Atheists disturb our faith in God. So we should not listen to talks about women, wealth, and the character of atheists.

We should give up egoism, pride, and other passions. We should not set up our finite will against the divine will. God hates the egotists, and is fond of meekness.

We should not indulge in vain discussion about God. It is absolutely useless, as it can never lead us to certainty.

Devotion to God arises from the renunciation of all objects of enjoyment and of every attachment for them. He who uproots all earthly attachments gives up acquiring and preserving objects of enjoyment.

These are the negative methods which prepare the mind for the attainment of devotion. Besides these, Nārada prescribes the following positive methods for the culture of devotion:

We should study the treatises on devotion, and constantly think of their teachings. We should perform those duties which are enjoined by them. We should observe non-injury to living beings, truthfulness, purity of body and mind, kindness, and cultivate faith in God and other excellences of character. We should also develop the nine marks of devotion mentioned above.

We should incessantly pray to God. The attraction for the objects of enjoyment can be overcome not by directing our attention to them, but by constant prayer to God. We have very little time left at our disposal for prayer after what is spent in the pursuit of pleasure, pain, desire, gain, and the like. But how is the desire for prayer awakened?

Devotion is obtained, principally, by the grace of the great souls who are devoted to God, or from the least touch of divine compassion. The company of the great is difficult of attainment. But once we have an access to their company, it is bound to awaken devotion in us. The companionship of devotees is attained by the grace of God alone. The grace of God is followed by the response of the devotees, since there is no distinction between God and His men. The *Gītā says*, 'I dwell in them, and they dwell in me' (IX. 29).

We should strive after love of God alone. Being invoked, He will quickly reveal Himself to us and fill us with His influence. He will give us a taste of His infinite sweetness.

Nārada describes the results of the culture of devotion in glowing language:

By attaining devotional love a person becomes fulfilled, immortal, and contented. He becomes free from the wheel of births and deaths, as they are due to desire. He does not crave for anything, since all his desires are fulfilled in God; he does not lament for the loss of anything, for in God he gains everything; he does not hate anybody, since his consuming love of God burns up the very roots of hatred; he does not delight in any earthly object of enjoyment, because his heart is soaked in divine love; he does not become zealous for worldly achievements, since by attaining love of God he has attained everything. He becomes intoxicated with joy, absolutely quiet, and completely self-satisfied. The devotee becomes God-intoxicated. The clamour of his passions and cravings being drowned, he becomes absolutely quiet. Communing with the Lord of his heart, he delights in himself (ātmārāma), sees Him alone, hears Him alone, and thinks of Him alone. His sense-organs, mind, and intellect are all directed towards God. He realizes Him through his whole being. He is filled with the presence of God. He feels His presence everywhere. He offers his whole being to God. He belongs to Him, and not even to himself.

Srī Krṣna says, 'I am like one who is not free (asvatantra iva). I am entirely dependent on my devotees (bhakta-parādhīna). My heart is given over to my saintly devotees. I am their beloved. I have no liking either for myself or for my immortal consort, Lakṣmī, without the association of my saintly devotees whose sole refuge I am. How can I leave them who have renounced their wives, home, children, relations, wealth, and this world and the next, and completely surrendered themselves to me? They do not know anything other than me, nor do I know anything else but them' (Bhā., IX 4. 63–68).

KRISHNA

One of the most popular of all bhaktic deities is Krishna. In the Bhagavad Gita and the Mahabharata he has the role of a warrior and sublime teacher. Medieval sources present him as God moving in a somewhat different way. He is charming and seemingly diffident, yet also all-powerful and all-understanding, a combination making of him a fascinating mystery. As a youth he was surrounded by the gopis or milk-maids, who represent ideal devotees in their utter self-abandonment to the Lord. This devotion transcends caste. One can see below the lushly romantic quality of Krishna devotion, yet at the same time perceive how earthly desires are transformed by Krishna to heavenly, and earthly delights foreshadow the heavenly delights which await the true devotee in Krishna's paradise. This passage is from a translation and "summary study" of the tenth canto of the account of Krishna called the Srimad Bhagavatam (from around the sixth century A.D.) by the spiritual head of the International Society for Krishna Consciousness (the "Hare Krishna" movement), which has brought Krishna devotion to America. The movement affirms Krishna as the Supreme Personality of Godhead.

From *Krsna, The Supreme Personality of Godhead*

A.C. Bhaktivedanta Swami Prabhupada

The scorching heat of the autumn sunshine was sometimes intolerable, and therefore the clouds in the sky appeared in sympathy above Krsna and Balarāma and Their boy friends while They engaged in blowing Their flutes. The clouds served as a soothing umbrella over Their heads just to make friendship with Krsna. The wanton aborigine girls also became fully satisfied when they smeared their faces and breasts with the dust of Vrndāvana, which was reddish from the touch of Krsna's lotus feet. The aborigine girls had very full breasts, and they were also very lusty, but when their lovers felt their breasts, they were not very satisfied. When they came out into the midst of the forest, they saw that while Krsna was walking, some of the leaves and creepers of Vrndāvana turned reddish from the *kuṅkuma* powder which fell from His lotus feet. His lotus feet were held by the *gopīs* on their breasts, which were also smeared with *kuṅkuma* powder, but when Krsna travelled in the Vrndāvana forest with Balarāma and His boy friends, the reddish powder fell on the ground of the Vrndāvana forest. So the lusty aborigine girls, while looking toward Krsna playing His flute, saw the reddish *kuṅkuma* on the ground and immediately took it and smeared it over their faces and breasts. In this way they became fully satisfied, although they were not satisfied when their lovers touched their breasts. All material, lusty desires can be immediately satisfied if one comes in contact with Krsna consciousness.

Another *gopī* began to praise the unique position of Govardhana Hill in this way: "How fortunate is this Govardhana Hill, for it is enjoying the association of Lord Krsna and Balarāma who are accus-

A.C. Bhaktivedanta Swami Prabhupada, *Krsna, The Supreme Personality of Godhead*, Vol. I (Los Angeles: Bhaktivedanta Book Trust, 1970), pp. 150–51. Reprinted by permission of the publisher.

tomed to walk on it. Thus Govardhana is always in touch with the lotus feet of the Lord. And because Govardhana Hill is so obliged to Lord Kṛṣṇa and Balarāma, it is supplying different kinds of fruits, roots and herbs, as well as very pleasing crystal water from its lakes, in presentation to the Lord." The best presentation offered by Govardhana Hill, however, was newly grown grass for the cows and calves. Govardhana Hill knew how to please the Lord by pleasing His most beloved associates, the cows and the cowherd boys.

Another *gopī* said that everything appeared wonderful when Kṛṣṇa and Balarāma travelled in the forest of Vṛndāvana playing Their flutes and making intimate friendship with all kinds of moving and nonmoving living creatures. When Kṛṣṇa and Balarāma played on Their transcendental flutes, the moving creatures became stunned and stopped their activities, and the nonmoving living creatures, like trees and plants, began to shiver with ecstasy.

Kṛṣṇa and Balarāma carried binding ropes on Their shoulders and in Their hands, just like ordinary cowherd boys. While milking the cows, the boys bound the hind legs with a small rope. This rope almost always hung from the shoulders of the boys, and it was not absent on the shoulders of Kṛṣṇa and Balarāma. In spite of Their being the Supreme Personality of Godhead, They played exactly like cowherd boys, and therefore everything became wonderful and attractive. While Kṛṣṇa was engaged in tending the cows in the forest of Vṛndāvana or on Govardhana Hill, the *gopīs* in the village were always absorbed in thinking of Him and discussing His different pastimes. This is the perfect example of Kṛṣṇa consciousness: to somehow or other remain always engrossed in thoughts of Krsna. The vivid example is always present in the behavior of the *gopīs;* therefore Lord Caitanya declared that no one can worship the Supreme Lord by any method which is better than the method of the *gopīs*. The *gopīs* were not born in very high *brāhmaṇa* or *kṣatriya* families; they were born in the families of *vaiśyas,* and not in big mercantile communities but in the families of cowherd men. They were not very well educated, although they heard all sorts of knowledge from the *brāhmaṇas,* the authorities of Vedic knowledge. The *gopīs'* only purpose was to remain always absorbed in thoughts of Kṛṣṇa.

SHIVA

Hindu devotional deities can be divided into two great families, that of Vishnu and that of Shiva. Vishnu in many respects is like the western monotheistic (especially Christian) God. He rules from heaven, works on behalf of good, and is relatively decorous. From time to time he takes human form, as in Rama and Krishna, to set ill to rights from within the world.

*Shiva is stranger and more comprehensive. He embraces both crea-
tion and destruction and can appear as a mad dancer or a wild-haired
yogin. His consort is equally vivid and unpredictable. But he—and she—
are ultimately on the side of good, for they represent the world with all
its extremes of good and horror as manifested God, and the depths of
God as the Absolute beyond the world.*

From *Cradle Tales of Hinduism*

Sister Nivedita

THE STORY OF SHIVA, THE GREAT GOD

In wild and lonely places, at any time, one may chance on the Great
God, for such are His most favoured haunts. Once seen, there is no
mistaking Him. Yet He has no look of being rich or powerful. His skin
is covered with white wood-ashes. His clothing is but the religious
wanderer's yellow cloth. The coils of matted hair are piled high on the
top of His head. In one hand He carries the begging-bowl, and in the
other His tall staff, crowned with the trident. And sometimes He goes
from door to door at midday, asking alms.

High amongst the Himalayas tower the great snow-mountains, and
here, on the still, cold heights, is Shiva throned. Silent—nay, rapt in
silence—does He sit there, absorbed and lost in one eternal meditation.
When the new moon shines over the mountain-tops, standing above the
brow of the Great God, it appears to worshipping souls as if the light
shone through, instead of all about Him. For He is full of radiance, and
can cast no shadow.

Wrapped thus into hushed intensity lies Kailas, above Lake Manas-
arovara, the mountain home of Mahadeva, and there, with mind hidden
deep under fold upon fold of thought, rests He. With each breath of
His, outward and in, worlds, it is said, are created and destroyed. Yet
He, the Great God, has nothing of His own; for in all these that He has
created there is nothing—not kingship, nor fatherhood, nor wealth, nor
power—that could for one moment tempt Him to claim it. One desire,
and one alone, has He, to destroy the ignorance of souls, and let light
come. Once, it is said, His meditation grew so deep, that when He awoke

Sister Nivedita, *Cradle Tales of Hinduism* (Calcutta: Advaita Ashrama, 1968), pp.
27–30. Reprinted by permission of the publisher.

He was standing alone, poised on the heart's centre of all things, and the universe had vanished. Then, knowing that all darkness was dispelled, that nowhere more, in all the worlds, was there blindness or sin, He danced forward with uplifted hands, into the nothingness of that uttermost withdrawnness, singing, in His joy, "Bom! Bom!" And this dance of the Great God is the Indian Dance of Death, and for its sake is He worshipped with the words "Bom! Bom! Hara! Hara!"

It is, however, by the face of the Great God that we may know Him once for all, beyond the possibility of doubt. One look is enough, out of that radiance of knowledge, one glance from the pity and tenderness in His benign eyes, and never more are we able to forget that this whom we saw was Shiva Himself. It is impossible to think of the Great God as being angry. He "whose form is like unto a silver mountain" sees only two things, insight and want of insight, amongst men. Whatever be our sin and error, He longs only to reveal to us its cause, that we may not be left to wander in the dark. His is the infinite compassion, without one shadow or stain upon it.

In matters of the world, He is but simple, asking almost nothing in worship, and strangely easy to mislead. His offerings are only bael-leaves and water, and far less than a handful of rice. And He will accept these in any form. The tears of the sorrowful, for instance, have often seemed to Him like the pure water of His offering. Once He was guarding a royal camp at night, when the enemy fell upon Him, and tried to kill Him. But these wicked men were armed with sticks of bael-wood, and as they beat Him again and again with these, He, smiling and taking the blows for worship, put out His hand, and blessed them on their heads!

He keeps for Himself only those who would otherwise wander unclaimed and masterless. He has but one servant, the devoted Nandi. He rides, not on horse or elephant, but on a shabby old bull. Because the serpents were rejected by all others, did He allow them to twine about His neck. And amongst human beings, all the crooked and hunchbacked, and lame and squint-eyed, He regards as His very own. For loneliness and deformity and poverty are passwords sufficient to the heart of the Great God, and He, who asks nothing from any one, who bestows all, and takes nothing in return, He, the Lord of the Animals, who refuses none that come to Him sincerely, He will give His very Self, with all its sweetness and illumination, merely on the plea of our longing or our need!

Yet is this not the only form in which Shiva may come to the soul of man. Sometimes the thing that stands between us and knowledge is unspeakably dear. Yet is the Great God ever the Destroyer of Ignorance, and for this, when our hour comes, He will arise, as it were, sword in hand, and slay before our eyes our best beloved. In the middle of His brow shines forth the great Third Eye of spiritual vision, with which He pierces to the heart of all hypocrisy and shams. And with the light that flashes from this eye, He can burn to ashes at a glance that which is untrue. For foolish as He may be in matters of the world, in spiritual things He can never be deceived. In this aspect, therefore, He is known as Rudra the Terrible; and to Him day after day men pray, saying, "O Thou the Sweetest of the Sweet, the Most Terrible of the Terrible!"

So runs the tale. And yet in truth this thought of the Great God is but half of that conception which is known to the intuition of man as the divine. Two things there are which we see as God. One is knowledge, insight—Jnana, as it is called in India—and this, carried to its utmost height, is Shiva or Mahadeva. But some see God rather in power, energy, beauty, the universe about us. Indeed, without both of these, either becomes unthinkable. Hence Shiva has ever a consort in Maha Shakti, the Primal Force. Amongst the pictures made, and the tales told, of Her, are those of Sati, and Uma, and the Great Death. She is Gauri, the Golden One, the fair, the light of the sunrise shining on the mountain snows. And she dwells ever in Kailas, as the wife and devoted worshipper of that Mahadeva, or Spiritual Insight, who goes amongst men by the name of Shiva, the Great God.

TANTRA

Tantrism is a form of worship and spiritual realization which emerged in both Hinduism and Buddhism in the early middle ages. It is a complex combination of yoga, ritual, and devotion designed to arouse powerful, initiatory energy by which one can realize God in oneself and all things. Tantric sadhanas or practices are often performed in small, quasi-secret groups and employ powerful psycho-physical techniques. Tantrists realize that, when there is careful preparation and controlled conditions, the doing of things ordinarily forbidden by society and the arousal of sexual energy can have potent transformative effects on the psyche. Thus their rituals employed, more often symbolically than actually, these things. They recognized that sexuality is the most powerful and unitive natural force in ordinary human experience, and so used it to symbolize or actualize the union of the individual, and of the phenomenal world, with the Absolute. An actual sexual rite like that described below is not typical or frequent, but it does express much of the psychology and atmosphere of the tradition. Aided by citations from tantric literature, we see that the male (sadhaka) and female (shakti) in this sacramental sexual union are identified with Shiva and his shakti or consort, and so with the Absolute (Shiva) and the world (shakti). These two are then made one, and the energy aroused used for spiritual transformation.

From *Tantra Yoga*

Nik Douglas

Sadhana can either be practiced alone, with a partner or in a circle (*Chakra*). When performed in a circle (generally of four, five, seven, nine, twelve, sixteen or thirty-two couples) the Guru (or most senior *Sadhaka*) and his Shakti remain in the middle and are "worshipped" as the individual Gurus of each of the members of the circle. Those that are not already married will be married according to the tradition:

> "Saiva marriage celebrated in the Chakra is of two kinds. One kind is terminated with the Chakra and the other is lifelong." . . .
>
> *Mahanirvana Tantra*

. . . The Sadhana begins with both partners bathing, all the time thinking of the cosmic purpose of the Sadhana. The Shakti is anointed with perfume (generally of musk, patchouli or sandal) and is garlanded with flowers. Incense and lamps (candles) are lit and the Guru is "worshipped" with offerings of flowers, lamps, incense etc. The couple will repeat the Mantra of initiation and generally the Mantra of the "Deity" (*Devata*) to be invoked. If the Shakti has not been previously initiated she will be initiated with the Mantra *Hrim*, whispered into the ear. This will be followed by meditation on the four Tantric "seats" (*Pitths*), both as the directions, and as the four main Chakras of the Subtle body. This is the *Sandhya*.

The next stage is *Tarpana*, or "purification of the Elements". This will take place generally in front of a fire, accompanied by *Pranayama* (Breath-movement), *Mudra* (ritual gestures) and the *Bija-Mantras* (internally repeated) of the elements to be purified. The seat will then be purified and the couple will sit in *Asana*, side by side. The *Asana* used at this stage is generally *Padmasana* ("Vajrasana"), *Virasana* ("half-lotus") or a similar comfortable position.

The ritual-proper commences with the installation of the *Patras* (the bowls used to hold the ingredients). These are of specific form and material (copper, silver, gold), according to the tradition of the Sadhana, and are placed upon "bases" of *Yantras* which are "drawn" (*Rekha*) accompanied by *Mantras, Mudra* and *Pranayama*. The ritual here varies

Nik Douglas, *Tantra Yoga* (New Delhi: Munshiram Manoharlal, 1971), pp. 83–88. Reprinted by permission of the publisher.

greatly from Sadhana to Sadhana, according to the type and purpose of the practice . . .

> "The worshipper should then, in the space between himself and the Yantra, draw a triangle with the Bija *Hrim* in its centre, and outside the triangle in the order here stated, a circle, a hexagon and a square. The excellent disciple should then worship in the four corners of the square the four *Pitths*, with the Mantras formed of their respective names . . . "
>
> "Then the six parts of the body should be worshipped in the six corners of the hexagon. Then worship the *Devata* of the triangle with the Mantra *Hrim* and *Namah*. Wash the receptacle with the Mantra *Namah*, and place it on the *Mandala*, and worship it in the ten *Kalas* . . . "
>
> "Then, taking the vessel (*Patra*) of offering and purifying it with the Mantra *Phat*, place it on the tripod . . . "
>
> *Mahanirvana tantra*

Hemp (*Vijaya*) is generally taken just prior to the installation of the vessels. It is taken either as a drink, a sweet or sometimes smoked. The body organs are purified by Mantra, and the *Kundalini-Shakti* is visualised "ready to rise" from the lower regions. The ingredients (*Shuddhi*) . . . Meat, Fish, Grain, Wine . . . or their substitutes (Ginger, Lemon, Rice, Bhang), are placed in the bowls, accompanied by Meditation of their true meaning, Mantras of purification, and gestures of propitiation (*Mudra*) . . .

> "Meat, fish, parched food, fruits, roots, or anything else offered to the *Devata* along with wine, are called *Shuddhi*."
>
> *Mahanirvana tantra*

> "Bring into this great cup, which is full of wine, the essence of ambrosia produced from the essence of all that is in this world with its differing kinds of taste. I offer as oblation into the Fire of the Supreme Self the excellent nectar of Thisness with which the cup of I-ness is filled."
>
> *Mahanirvana tantra*

> "We eat meat and drink wine. The true followers come all together, but the frauds are kept far away by fear. We take that fourfold preparation and musk and camphor. Herbs and special meat we eat with relish."
>
> *Hevajra tantra*

Mediating on the wine as ambrosia (*Amrit*) and the food (usually a very small quantity in one bowl) as representing offerings to the Deity (*Devata*) . . . offerings of the animal (Meat), aquatic (Fish), and vegetable (Grain) worlds [and representing the *Tattva*-essence of evolved Spirit (*Jiva*)] . . . the *Sadhaka* and *Shakti* will take the bowl of wine in one hand, and some *Shuddhi* (food-offering) in the other, and will together first offer it to the "invoked" Deity (*Kundalini*) by bringing the two bowls together up from the base (*Mandala*, Platform, Seat) to the head (*Sahasrara-Chakra*), accompanied by visualisation of the *Kundalini-Devi* (*Kundalini-Shakti* as Goddess) rising up through the Centres (each one visualised with the *Bija-Mantras* mentally repeated) to union in the Etheric of the head . . .

"Then let them take up each his own cup and meditate on the *Kula-Kundalini*, who is Divine Consciousness, and who is spread from the *Muladhara*-lotus to the tip of the tongue, and, uttering the *Mula-Mantra*, let each, after taking the others' permission, offer it as oblation to the mouth of the *Kundali*."

Mahanirvana tantra

"From the *Muladhara* go up to the *Brahmarandhra* again and again; Bliss issues out of this meeting of the *Kundalini-Shakti* and the Moon of full Consciousness. What flows from this lotus in the supreme Ether is the wine, the real wine to be tasted by man; what is drunk otherwise, is only liquor."

Kularnava tantra

"The yogin who delights in the drink of Yoga, becomes drunk with no other drink."

Hevajra tantra

The wine and other ingredients are then taken by the *Sadhaka* and the *Shakti*, until . . .

" . . . the sight or the mind is not affected."

Mahanirvana tantra

The hands are then washed, and the final Tattva (*Maithuna:* Union) is proceeded with.

The Shakti is wrapped in a red robe (of silk or wool) and anointed. Water is sprinkled over her (sometimes wine) and incense may be lit. Then the Sadhaka touches (*Nyasa*) her forehead, eyes, nostrils, mouth, lobes of the ear, hollow of the throat, breasts, arms, hands, navel, thighs, yoni, knees and feet with the right hand whilst pronouncing the *Matrikas* (letters of the Sanskrit alphabet) and also the *Bija-Mantra* of the Deity (*Devata*). She must be seen "as the Goddess incarnate".

Then, in seated posture, the *Shakti* will be taken by the *Sadhaka* . . . *Linga* and *Yoni*, *Vajra* and *Padma*, *Shiva* and *Shakti* will become one. The Unity (*Samarasa*) is the essence of the Sadhana. It is the True Yoga . . . Union.

"Twofold is the Innate, for Wisdom is the Woman, and Means is the Man . . . "

"Neither passion nor absence of passion is found there, nor yet a middle state. Because of its freedom from all three the Innate is called Perfect Enlightenment."

"At the union of *Vajra* and lotus (*Linga* and *Yoni*), earth arises there from that contact with the quality of hardness. From the flow of semen (*Shukra*) water arises, and fire from the friction. Wind comes from the motion, and space corresponds to the Bliss."

"The *Yogin* is Means and Compassion, and the *Yogini* Wisdom and Voidness, for she is deprived of causation. The thought of Enlightenment is the undivided Unity of Compassion and Voidness."

Hevajra tantra

Once in Union (*Maithuna*) with the Yogini, the Yogi aims to retain the sperm. Though there is movement it is not excessive. The Buddhist Tantras lay great emphasis on the retention of the sperm, except in a special case where insemination (fertilisation) is the special reason for the Sadhana, which is then performed in order to incarnate a "high" compassionate being in the womb of the Yogini. There is an enormous "esoteric" commentary on the stabilisation of "Breath, Thought and Semen". Many of the Tibetan Yoga doctrines (Dream-Yoga, Light-Yoga, Heat-Yoga, Transformation-Yoga) deal extensively with this basis. Stabilisation of Breath (through Pranayama), Thought (through Meditation) and Semen (through Maithuna-Sadhana) brings about Realisation of the four Joys (*Ananda, Paramananda, Viramananda* & *Sahajananda*) and the four kinds of Wisdom, which are inseparable from Voidness. Realisation of Voidness is the essence of Mahayana Buddhism, and therefore the essence of Vajrayana Tantric practice. The "Thought of Enlightenment" (*Bodhicitta*) is the subtle manifestation of the stabilisation of Breath, Thought and Semen. This "nectar" (*Amrit*) so produced, pervades the bodies of the Yogi and Yogini whilst in Union together, bringing indescribable joy to their Being. This is the state of true *Samadhi* . . . freed from the bonds of *Samsara*. Absolutely separate from the world of duality, yet existing *because of* that very duality . . .

"There is Moon and Sun and between them is the Seed. This last is that Being whose nature is Joy Supreme."

"Great knowledge abides in the body, free of all falsification, but although it pervades all things and exists in the body, it is not in the body that it arises."

Hevajra tantra

TEMPLE WORSHIP

Not all Hindu worship, of course, is in the context of pursuing a personal spiritual path. Like all religions, Hinduism has its public sanctuaries, its community festivals, its pilgrimages, its rituals for birth, mar-

riage and death. Rituals in the home, properly performed by the head of the household every morning before the home shrine, are very important and are observed by many devout Hindus who seldom worship in the temples. It is the colorful temple worship, however, which presents the most public face of Hinduism and is the topic of this passage. By temple protocol the imaged deity, who would be regarded by the more philosophic as an object of bhaktic adoration and so a means to liberation, is treated like a king in his court, and the attentions given him are modelled on those offered an Indian maharajah of old.

From *Religious Practices of the Hindus*

Sivaprasad Bhattacharyya

In addition to the worship in the home, the religious disposition of man has spread itself to the world around him, to the temple and the pilgrimage. It is impossible to think of an Indian village without a shrine—it is an amenity which has been given priority of consideration in the selection of one's home from time immemorial. Because of the role of water in religious practices, shrines have been erected on river banks whenever possible. Where there is no river, big tanks serve the same purpose of purifying the worshiper through a dip in the water. Associated with shrines and temples there are pavilions where are held discourses on religion, readings from the scriptures, especially the Purāṇas, and musical entertainment of a religious nature. The wayside shrines help people no less than wayside inns and taverns, and house village deities which receive worship from the local people as well as from the pilgrim.

The institution of temples which are of more than local importance can be explained in many ways. From the earliest times the status and worth of deities were conceived on the model of kings among men, and as the kings built great palaces for themselves a demand arose for similar great temples. Sometimes a temple was built to house the relics of a saintly person belonging to one of the sects; at other times the temple grew up in connection with one of the monastic orders. Many great temples have grown up at places made sacred by legend.

Through the centuries, the technical skill and artistic creativity of the Hindus have been revealed in a genius for architecture which has created temples of singular felicity. Broadly speaking, a temple compound is made up of a pyramidal gateway, a terrace, a courtyard with a metallic

Sivaprasad Bhattacharyya, "Religious Practices of the Hindus," in Kenneth W. Morgan, ed., *The Religion of the Hindus* (New York: Ronald Press Company, 1953), pp. 185–88. Reprinted by permission of the publisher.

bell hung high above it, the temple building proper with an inner shrine, and within that the most sacred inner room where the chief image is kept. The larger temples usually have a high wall surrounding the court-yard, a big tank near the temple, a kitchen, and a tapering spire. The sacred inner room where the image is kept is usually small and not well lighted; it is the cave in which the deity is lying, symbolic of the heart of the devotee. The tapering spire is meant to represent the upward ascent of the spirit of the devotee to the vicinity of the Lord who is poised above everything.

DAILY CEREMONIES IN THE TEMPLE

There is a regular daily schedule in temple worship which is followed as strictly as the schedule is followed in the worship of the family deity in the home. It begins with the auspicious lamp ceremony at the last eighth of the night when the deity is awakened with sweet, solemn music and the recitation of scriptural prayers. The awakening ceremony is followed by the bathing ceremony an hour or so after sunrise; in Śiva shrines it is the linga which is bathed; for the other deities, a substitute which is often hidden from public view is bathed, or the ceremony is performed with the sālagrāma or the yantra. After the bath comes the anointing ceremony when sandal paste is offered pro-fusely, and then the deity is worshiped with japa of appropriate mantras for some time. At midday the image is screened from public view and offered cooked food, followed by a fire offering if the Vedic code of worship is insisted on. After that the deity enjoys the midday rest and should not be disturbed, though this is not always possible at big temples where pilgrims come at all times and occasionally interrupt the rest for an anointing and decorating ceremony.

In the afternoon, before sunset, refreshment is offered to the deity in big temples—at Pūri, the deity is offered refreshment or food fifty-two times during the day! At dusk, the lamp ceremony is performed elabo-rately, followed by the offering of food for the night. The day ends with the lying down ceremony; after another elaborate lamp ceremony, the god is dressed in right royal fashion with beautiful clothes, flowers, and vilva leaves, and put to rest for the night.

In the daily worship in the temple the ceremonial stages of conse-cration, invocation, and sending away are dispensed with because the image is permanently installed. In Śiva worship, no cooked food is offered; in other temples care is taken to see that the food offered to the deity is in no way inferior to that which a well-to-do person in the locality takes for himself. Regularly, hymns and prayers are read during the day, especially during the early hours of the morning and during the midday and evening worship. Only priests who are versed in Vedic studies may perform the bathing and fire ceremonies; ordinary worship with japa is done by officiating priests who are next in rank to the chief priests; prayers in Sanskrit are recited by one group of priests, while decorating and anointing are done by other priests who in some temples may even be non-Brāhmans.

CARE OF THE TEMPLE IMAGE

Much of the attention in the service in temples is concentrated on the image, for the care of the image is considered to be a religious obligation. From the time of the awakening of the deity with auspicious music and the lamp ceremony until the lying down ceremony at night, these teams of devout technicians and experts perform the daily duties to which they have been assigned. The anointing with sandal paste, especially in Śiva temples, is an admirable operation performed with exemplary patience. On special days there are fire offerings and sprinkling ceremonies on a grand scale. The placing of the golden sacred thread, particularly on important occasions, the putting on of the silken apparel in the case of Vishṇu and Śakti images, the lamp ceremony when done at nightfall before retiring—all these are spectacular demonstrations. Thousands of pilgrims flock to have a look at the form of the Lord on such occasions when it is royally attired, for it is really an achievement in the art of decoration with flowers, clothes, and jewels: a lovely figure, kingly and saintly.

The pilgrims who come to the temple offer flowers, scents, special cooked foods, garlands, ornaments, and sometimes they sacrifice animals, as at Kālighāt in Calcutta. They provide lighted lamps at the threshold to the inner sacred room, and attain special merit by arranging for the repetition of mantras and the reading of the scriptures. Going around the temple, always with the right side toward the deity, or prostrating one's self all around the temple or the courtyard is frequently done to appease the deity or to fulfill a vow. Providing for the singing of kīrtanas and bhajanas or the production of religious dramas is a popular means of adoring the deity.

A MODERN HINDU SPIRITUAL MASTER

India is still a land which produces figures believed to have very special divine power, and able to attract large numbers of followers and sometimes international fame. These masters are said to have transcended all hindrances to the divine within, so that they radiate its strength and wisdom. Sometimes this spiritual state seems to appear spontaneously; more often it is the result of initiation by another great teacher together with years of disciplined training. Here is a careful account by a modern American scholar of one such teacher living in India today, Swami Muktananda, best known for his ability to impart a powerful spiritual energy called shakti-pat.

From *Swami Muktananda and the Enlightenment Through Shakti-Pat*
Charles S.J. White

I subsequently returned to India and was able to gather materials for a preliminary description of Muktānanda's history and present activities. I have also taken this occasion to speculate on the noumenal area of his experience and influence. What follows is presented somewhat schematically to give a sense of the structure that one might expect to be able to extrapolate, for example, in a comparative study together with other similar data.

1. Muktānanda was born into a wealthy family in the vicinity of Mangalore in Mysore State. His mother was a pious woman who had made a pilgrimage to Dharmasthala to invoke the aid of a form of Siva, known as Manjunāth Mahādev, to have a son. She was told afterward by a Sadhu to repeat the mantra, Om Nāmaḥ Śivāya, and her prayer would be granted. (The same mantra is used by the devotees of Muktānanda in the ashram at Ganespuri today to assist in the work of arousing the Kuṇḍalinī.)

2. The mother was taken in labor while she was at the washbasin under a tree in the compound of her house. The baby emerged so swiftly that she did not have time to catch it before it fell into the washbasin. The time was dawn on May 16, 1908, the full moon day of the month of Vaiśākh: very auspicious. They named him Kṛṣṇa.[1]

Charles S. J. White, "Swami Muktananda and the Enlightenment Through Shak-tiPat," *History of Religions* 13 (May 1974), pp. 312–19. Reprinted by permission of the author and the University of Chicago Press. Copyright 1974 by the University of Chicago.

[1]Amma, *Swami Muktananda Parmahansa* (hereafter *SMP*) (Bombay: Vora & Co., for Shree Gurudev Ashram, 1969), pp. 1–2. Other works published by the ashram include: Swami Muktananda Parmahansa, *Gurukripa* (Bombay: V.P. Bhagwat, 1970), *Soham-Japa* (New Delhi: Siddha Yoga Dham, 1969); Dwarka Khosla, *A Visit to Shree Gurudev Ashram* (Bombay: Radha Raman Printing Press, 1963); *Svādhyāya Sudhā* (Bombay:

3. The story goes that as a boy and youth he was stronger, more handsome, and more aggressive than his peers and bored with formal education but highly intelligent. "Nor did any theories or dogmas interest him; for he was one who could be convinced only by actual observation and direct experience."[2] At fifteen, by chance at a festival, he met Swāmi Nityānanda who was afterward to direct the final stages of his spiritual development. Nityānanda embraced Kṛṣṇa and gently stroked his cheeks. He then strode away and they did not meet again for many years.[3] A pious home life had already aroused interest in a religious vocation, so six months after the encounter with Nityānanda Kṛṣṇa left to become a sadhu.

4. Unlike certain other saints in India his full realization did not occur until middle age, while the process leading up to it included instruction under several different gurus.

a) Among the saints, siddhas, and sadhus with whom he took training of some sort as a young man—including Sanskrit language, study of the scriptures, yoga practice, and other subjects—his first teacher was Siddharuddha Swāmi, from whom he received initiation as sannyasī and his religious name, Muktānanda. Thus his formal entrance into the ascetic life was under the direction of a monk trained in the disciplines of sakti.[4] In 1929 he began to wander through India, staying here and there with various teachers. In all, during this period he mentions having met sixty great saints. Besides his first guru, among others there were "Popat Maharaj at Satana, Upasani Baba at Sakori, Swami Prakashananda at Gondal, Sitaram Bairagi at Dwarkabet, Bhagari Baba at Lasalgaon, Narayan Maharaj at Kedgaon, Mauni Baba at Chikhali, Chaitanya Swami at Paithan, Munsoji Baba at Varad, Prembhikshu at Jamnagar, Ramana Maharshi at Tiruvannamalai, Jagannath Baba at Ahmedabad and a saint at Howrah (Calcutta) who was known to subsist on stones."[5] In the reports about his experiences, in the latter part of his first phase he received special attention from two saints who noted his impending realization. The one, Zipruanna, a naked ascetic who passed his days seated on a refuse heap, healed Muktānanda's incessant headaches by licking the latter's head and, through water that had been poured on

---

Nirnayasāgar Press, 1968); *Hamāre Pyāre Bābā* [Picture study of Muktānanda]; *Guru-vani* or *Shree Gurudev-Vani* (hereafter *GV*), parts in English, Hindi, and Marathi, vol. 2 (July 1965); vol. 3 (July 1966); vol. 4 (July 1967); vol. 5 (July 1968); vol. 6 (July 1969); vol. 7 (July 1970); vol. 8 (July 1971); *Swami Muktananda Parmahansa Sixtieth Birthday Commemoration Volume* (hereafter *Sixtieth*) (Ganeshpuri: Shree Gurudev Ashram, 1968); *Shree Gurudev-Vani*, Special Number, May 1971.

2*SMP*, p. 3. See *Bhagavata Purāṇa*, bk. 10 on *Śri Kṛṣṇa* or *The Gospel of Śri Rama-krishna* for a more modern comparison.

3*SMP*, p. 4. A different version of this initial meeting with Nityānanda appears in V. D. Khatri, "The Boy Named Krishna," *GV* 7 (July 1970): 67 ff.

4*SMP*, p. 6.

5Ibid., p. 26. See Swāmi Muktananda, *Guru* (New York: Harper & Row, 1971), p. 37.

Zipruanna's foot, helped Muktānanda to cure a woman in an advanced stage of tuberculosis. Of Muktānanda, Zipruanna said, "Your fame will touch the highest heaven."[6] Another saint, Harigiri Bābā, said of Muktānanda shortly before the last and crucial stage of the sadhana began, "You have now to live in a palatial building. Cast away your ochre clothes and wear silken garments instead. You are no longer a *sannyasin*, but a *maharaja*. You shall not ask but only give."[7]

b) Muktānanda has discussed in detail the special relationship that developed between himself and the saint known as Bhagavān Nityānanda. Nityānanda became for Muktānanda his guru, both in the sense that he received final initiation from him and in a very special manner when it became clear that Muktānanda was the "chosen disciple." The date of his initiation was August 14, 1957. On that occasion Nityānanda gave his own sandals to him—the closest physical objects to the lotus feet of the guru. The presentation of the initiatory symbol marked a turning point in the quality of Muktānanda's noumenal experience which now began to conform with that of the Siddha Paramparā, the adepts in Kuṇḍalinī. He writes of what happened: "[Nityānanda] looked into my eyes. Watching carefully, I saw a ray of light entering me from his pupils. It felt hot, like burning fever. Its light was dazzling, like that of a high-powered bulb. As that ray emanating from Lord Nityānanda's pupils penetrated mine, I was thrilled with amazement, joy and fear. I was beholding its color, and also chanting 'Guru Om.' It was a full unbroken beam of divine radiance. Its color kept changing from molten gold to saffron, to a shade deeper than the blue of a shining star. I stood utterly transfixed."[8]

From shortly after the time that this experience occurred, Muktānanda lived away from Ganeshpuri in very intense *sādhana* until his realization was complete. After he returned to Ganeshpuri, when the devotees of Nityānanda were preparing a small temple to enshrine an image of their guru to worship after his passing, which they expected would be soon, on November 16, 1956 they were directed instead to install Muktānanda in the temple with ceremonies appropriate to a divinity. Thereafter, the two saints lived side by side in the ashram until Nityānanda's death on August 8, 1961. Since then Muktānanda has directed the ashram and greatly expanded both its size in respect to property holdings and its activities with increasing numbers of devotees.

5. In regard to the organization of the ashram and related subjects I have firsthand knowledge—having visited Ganeshpuri and Shri Gurudev Ashram in July of 1971 and having met Swāmi Muktānanda. Moreover, it was possible to engage in extended discussions with several of the

---

[6]*SMP*, p. 19. For photographs of Zipruanna and Harigiri Bābā see *GV* 4 (July 1967): 33.

[7]*SMP*, p. 20.

[8]*Guru*, p. 50.

devotees who had been initiated. The ashram has attracted people from all over India and among them large numbers of the elite of Bombay who come, particularly on weekends, to have *darśan* of Muktānanda and to join temporarily in the ashram's religious life. There is also a considerable group of Western devotees, including several who have been living in the ashram for a year or more since it was established. The emotional atmosphere of this sanctuary for those who are experiencing Kuṇḍalinī awakening is no doubt very exalted. At the edge of the road with rice fields making a half-moon around it and everything, including the little jungle at a distance behind, washed and hearteningly green in the monsoon rain, to the observer the ashram gave a sense of cleanliness, order, and peace. Muktānanda rules as Guru Mahārāj and demands conformity to the horarium, which is somewhat similar to that of a monastic house in the West. Seeing him, listening to his remarks, hoping for some favorable sign bestowed on oneself constitute the framework of the relationship that the individual devotee develops with the guru.

6. We have already mentioned the "royal" style of Muktānanda. He has been described by some as "virile," and by that is meant that he has a commanding, masculine personality. He speaks directly and even coarsely at times to express his ideas, but on the other hand his erudition and skill in expression in written form are often commented on as well. In this he contrasts with Nityānanda who was illiterate; likewise, in his personal habits, Muktānanda favors silken *lūngīs* and has taken pains to make the ashram attractive with plants, an enclosed garden, a spacious meditation hall and dining room, and so on. In personal manner Muktānanda is often said to be "restless," and one observes this in his sudden appearances and disappearances around the grounds, his quick walk, the changing expressions on his face, and his penchant for unexpected excursions to holy places in the region or for calling the people to vary the routine of services during the day with some novel celebration. He usually wears dark glasses, and it is reported that he does so because he perceives the spiritual quality of the world and of the persons who come to see him in varying degrees of a kind of light which hurts the physical eyes. He does not have the reputation of being able to produce phenomena, or at least he does not particularly cater to demands that he do such, although the psychic experiences which his followers say stem from his powers are remarkable enough.

7. There are several persons at the ashram who undoubtedly have a much closer bond with the guru than do others. Chief among these is a very bright woman, a former professor of Sanskrit, who serves as the leader of the woman devotees and is in charge of some of the other internal operations of the ashram. She is called Amma, or Mother, and has written about the tantric *sādhana* taught by Muktānanda. She has been at Ganeshpuri since before the time that the two saints lived together there in the fifties. Since she is a person of great personal refinement and charm, her allegiance to this saint is an instance of the testi-

mony of the distinguished disciple to the worthiness of the master. A young, former English professor, Mr. Jain, who serves as Muktānanda's interpreter and has been in the ashram for several years, is also high in the ranking of the disciples. Among others of them one might mention an American girl, now called Uma, who met Muktānanda in New York City during his American tour and was able, through a combination of seemingly miraculous circumstances, to come to Ganeshpuri to live permanently. Indeed, I was able to talk with several young Western men and women, including married couples who felt called to be followers of Muktānanda and reside with him. Reports of the experiences of some of the disciples appear in *Shree Gurudev-Vani.*[9]

8. As Muktānanda's reputation grows and he becomes known in wider and wider circles, no doubt he will be increasingly called upon to serve in the role of guru to society. If one might compare him with the somewhat more famous Sathya Sāi Bābā, one would say that his social role is likewise less well developed. It is difficult to completely clarify these aspects of the demands upon the Hindu saint, but they may be compared with the tasks that some of the clergy in Western countries, particularly famous prelates or evangelists, are called upon to perform.[10]

Beyond such activities, Muktānanda is a man who can capture the attention of the reading public. In his own right he has published in Hindi a spiritual memoir, entitled *Citsakti Vilās,* which was translated and abridged in the American version, *Guru.* Members of the ashram, but particularly Amma and Mr. Jain, are likewise skilled writers.[11] In this regard, as compared with the majority of the saints one would find in India, Muktānanda may be thought of as more clearly employing his intellectual gifts to reach a literate public. This is true also in the ques-

---

[9]*Guruvani* (see n. 8).

[10]The following quotation from an issue of the *Shree Gurudev Ashram Newsletter* illustrates these impositions (March 4, 1972):

"Once again Gurudev made a 'lightning tour'—this time to Aurangabad. At the request of Ramnath Dhoot on the occasion of the opening of his new factory, Dhoot Chemo Plast Pvt. Ltd., Baba and a small group of devotees went there to perform the opening ceremony. . . . The Dhoot family had been devoted to Baba for many, many years and are often Baba's hosts in Bombay and other parts of India. . . . After taking *prasad* and resting at Ahmednagar, the party went to the factory for the ceremonies. There Baba was welcomed by Baba Saheb Pavar, Chairman of the Gangapur Co-op. Sugar Factory. Many people had gathered for Baba's *darshan,* including Shri Zakaria, Maharashtra Minister for Health.

"First they worshipped Baba. Then Baba cut the ribbon and pressed the button. The machines started amidst cheers of 'Sadgurunath Maharaj Ki Jaya!' Afterwards, Baba spoke a few words. He told the devotees gathered there, 'With whatever love and pride you decorate your worldly life, apply that same love and pride to the inner Self.' "

[11]*GV,* Special Number, pp. 123 ff.; *Sixtieth,* pp. 1, 29 ff.; *GV,* vol. 8, pp. 15, 61 ff.; vol. 7, pp. 12, 27 ff.; vol. 6, pp. 23, 32 ff.; vol. 5, pp. 1, 22 ff.

tion-and-answer series, published from transcriptions of conversations with the disciples.[12]

9. As far as the further development of the cult is concerned, it is clear already that Muktānanda has been adopted as guru and avatar by a proliferating body of followers and that he will experience the fame of a national celebrity. Besides the testimonials of both Eastern and Western disciples appearing in ashram publications, independent writings of disciples attest to the master's influence. There is a temple, Shree Gurudev Dhyan Mandir, in Johannesburg, South Africa, where devotions are held regularly in honor of Muktānanda; and his cult is observed in various places in India and the United States at the present time.[13] It should be emphasized that this is happening while the saint is still alive.

NOUMENAL ASPECTS

Muktānanda in a unique manner has described his inner states both in his Hindi and English writings on the subject. As the devotees point out, what is unusual about Muktānanda's "way" is that, for the first time, the secret initiations and experiences of the Sakti Pāt, the yoga of the goddess, of the primordial energy of Śiva, is presented openly in a manner suitable to universal acceptance. We often speak of this kind of yoga as Kuṇḍalinī Yoga.[14]

[12]Published in *Shree Gurudev Ashram Newsletter* [hereafter *SGAN*], no. 2; and vol. 1, no. 4.

[13]See *GV*, vol. 6, p. 66; vol. 5, p. 65; and Dharam Yash Dev, "My Pilgrimage to Ganeshpuri," also published in *Bhavan's Journal*, vol. 18, no. 12 (January 9, 1972).

[14]Some important remarks on this subject and its relation to the experiences of the devotees of Muktānanda are contained in a small pamphlet prepared by Amma under the title, "Dhyan-Yoga and Kundalini-Yoga," pp. 1–3: "What is Kundalini? Kundalini is Shakti, the Divine Power. It is Chiti, the Consciousness. It is Jnana, Knowledge. All creation is its manifestation. It creates the world of its own free will. It permeates the world and is the life and essence of all existing things. . . . The Chiti Shakti projects itself in different forms, sentient and insentient, for the harmonious working of this world. This entire Universe is its Lila (play) for which there is neither reason nor purpose. Of this finite world of changing experiences it is the Primal cause, changeless, finite and all-pervading . . . In the Tantras, Kundalini is described as lying in the human body at the base of the spinal column, in the Muladhar, being coiled in three and half circles in serpentine form blocking the entrance to the Sushumna nadi with its mouth. When this sleeping Kundalini is awakened it raises its hood. The door of the Sushumna is opened and the Kundalini ascends upwards along the Sushumna piercing through the six chakras (centres) situated in it. When it reaches the highest centre, called Sahasrara, in the crown of the head, it unites with the Lord Shiva. This union brings ineffable joy of Blissful Beatitude. The process by which this state is achieved by awakening of the Kundalini, is known as the Kundalini Yoga. . . . With the awakening of the Kundalini, the process of Nadi-shuddhi (purification of the nerves) starts by itself and it gives various mysterious experiences to the sadhaka, who himself is struck with wonder by them. When aroused, the Kundalini becomes activated

When we look through the reports of Muktānanda's and his disciples' experiences, we find that there is conformity to the technical theory. For instance, one might recall the passage quoted previously from the letter of my friend who experienced the initiation very emotionally. As regards its further physical effects, he goes on in the same letter to say the following:

> Now when I visit a temple, a samādhi or dargāh [Hindu or Muslim saint's tomb, respectively], I become acutely aware of the shakti present there, to the extent that my body shakes very violently. Near Ganeshpuri is a very old Devi temple—Vajreshvari—and when I visited it, I found myself doing the mūla-bandha. Since then I have been doing the uddi-yāha-bandha and the jālandhara-bandha at various times. I have found that the samādhi of Dyāneshvar at Ālandī is particularly powerful in this respect. As I approach the temple my body starts to shake and by the time I reach the sanctum sanctorum it is uncontrollable. Dyāneshvar is there for me. The pūjari throws some water on me and my body twists and writhes even more —such is the power of the shakti.

A devotee writing about his and a friend's experiences after being initiated at the ashram mentions equally striking results.

> We sat for meditation after the recitation of the Vishnu Sahasra Nama. Within half an hour I could notice some movements in my body: I was swinging from left to right, and back and forth. My entire body was trembling as if I had received an electric shock or there was an earthquake. I felt a heaviness in my head and it touched the ground. I was in that condition for about an hour. I felt a kind of wheel moving or whirling in the stomach at high speed. I had some visions of Lord Ganapati and Lord Dattatreya. My eyes had become red and tears rolled down the cheeks.

> Even when I got up my body was trembling and I could not keep my balance. Shri Zarapakar could sit for about half an hour only and in that period he said he saw some colours, a flame, and visions of Lord Dattatreya, Swami Vivekananda and others. He also felt heaviness in his head especially between the two eye-brows. His eyeballs were sometimes rotating and then fixed between the two eyebrows.[15]

---

and with the prana (life force) it rises upwards. As each centre opens the Shakti manifests itself according to the characteristics of the centres, which during the meditation appear as lotuses, each with a different number of petals. The Sadhaka also gets uncommon experience of the gross and subtle levels of his being. . . . The experiences in the gross body are such as tremors, heat, electric shocks, perspiration, tears, thrill of joy, palpitation, involuntary suspension of breath or deep breathing, revolving of eyeballs. . . . The experiences in the subtle body are such as visions of deities and divine beings, receiving instructions from them; hearing sounds like those of conch, bell, flute, drum, thunder. . . . Under the guidance of the Guru, the sadhaka should proceed with the spirit of surrender allowing the Shakti to manifest itself unobstructed while himself remaining as a witness to its working. He should not try to avert an experience through fear. The Shakti is intelligent. It is aware of its own activity. Hence nothing ever goes wrong. Besides, the Guru is always there to control its flow. It should be borne in mind that the divine working of the Kundalini and the centres is not the subject of anatomy or physiology."
15GV, vol. 6, p. 68.

MOHANDAS K. GANDHI

No other nation has come to independence in quite the same way as did India in 1947. More than of any other man, that victory was the work of Mohandas Gandhi, who long had campaigned for political goals through "soul force." He and his followers had fasted, offered nonviolent resistance, and lectuerd, inspired by the yogic asceticism and the karma-yoga ideal of India's spiritual tradition, as well as by western thinkers like Ruskin, Thoreau, and Tolstoy. Both by renewing it and shifting its emphases, Gandhi illustrated the continuing life of the Hindu tradition. In this passage, Gandhi summarizes his commitments on several points of importance to him: the need for a new attitude of confident fearlessness in a servile nation, doing away with the degrading "untouchable" status of that miserable fifth of the nation lowest on the caste scale, the importance of education in the Indian languages, the dignity and importance of manual labor, and of course the interaction of religion and politics.

From *Mahatma Gandhi's Ideas, Including Selections from his Writings*

C.F. Andrews

THE VOW OF FEARLESSNESS

I found, through my wanderings in India, that my country is seized with a paralysing fear. We may not open our lips in public: we may only talk about our opinions secretly. We may do anything we like within the four walls of our house; but those things are not for public consumption.

If we had taken a vow of silence I would have nothing to say. I suggest to you that there is only One whom we have to fear, that is God. When we fear God, then we shall fear no man, however high-placed he may be; and if you want to follow the vow of Truth, then fearlessness is

C.F. Andrews, *Mahatma Gandhi's Ideas, Including Selections from his Writings* (London: George Allen & Unwin; New York: The Macmillan Co., 1930), pp. 108–11.

absolutely necessary. Before we can aspire to guide the destinies of India we shall have to adopt this habit of fearlessness.

And then we have also

THE VOW REGARDING THE 'UNTOUCHABLES'

There is an ineffaceable blot that Hinduism to-day carries with it. I have declined to believe that it has been handed down to us from immemorial times. I think that this miserable, wretched, enslaving spirit of 'untouchableness' must have come to us when we were at our lowest ebb. This evil has stuck to us and still remains with us. It is, to my mind, a curse that has come to us; and as long as that curse remains with us, so long I think we are bound to consider that every affliction in this sacred land is a proper punishment for the indelible crime that we are committing. That any person should be considered untouchable because of his calling passes my comprehension; and you, the student world, who receive all this modern education, if you become a party to this crime, it were better that you received no education whatsoever.

EDUCATION THROUGH THE VERNACULARS

In Europe every cultured man learns, not only his own language, but also other languages.

In order to solve the problem of language in India we in this Ashram must make it a point to learn as many Indian vernaculars as possible. The trouble of learning these languages is nothing compared to that of mastering English. How dare we rub off from our memory all the years of our infancy? But that is precisely what we do when we commence our higher life through the medium of a foreign tongue. This creates a breach for which we shall have to pay dearly. And you will see now the connection between this education and untouchability—this persistence of the latter in spite of the spread of knowledge and education. Education has enabled us to see the horrible crime, but we are seized with fear, and therefore we cannot take this doctrine to our homes.

THE VOW OF KHADDAR[1]

You may ask, 'Why should we use our hands?' You may say, 'Manual work has got to be done by those who are illiterate. I can only occupy

---

[1] Khaddar is home-spun and home-woven cloth. The vow of Khaddar would be to spin with one's own hands and to wear nothing but home-spun garments.

myself with reading literature and political essays.' We have to realize the dignity of labour. If a barber or shoemaker attends a college he ought not to abandon his profession. I consider that such professions are just as good as the profession of medicine.

Last of all, when you have conformed to these rules you may come to

THE RELIGIOUS USE OF POLITICS

Politics, divorced from religion, has absolutely no meaning. If the student world crowd the political platforms of this country, that is not necessarily a healthy sign of national growth; but this does not mean that you, in your student life, ought not to study politics. Politics are a part of our being; we ought to understand our national institutions. We may do this from our infancy. So in our Ashram every child is taught to understand the political institutions of our country and to know how the country is vibrating with new emotions, with new aspirations, with new life. But we want also the steady light, the infallible light of religious faith; not a faith which merely appeals to the intelligence, but a faith which is indelibly inscribed on the heart. First we want to realize our religious consciousness, and immediately we have done that the whole department of life is open to us; and it should then be a sacred privilege of all, so that when young men grow to manhood they may do so properly equipped to battle with life. To-day what happens is this: much of the political life is confined to the students, but immediately they cease to be students they sink into oblivion, seeking miserable employments, knowing nothing about God, nothing of fresh air or bright light, or of real vigorous independence, such as comes out of obedience to those laws that I have placed before you on this occasion.

IV

IN THE WAKE
OF THE AWAKENED ONE:
THE VOYAGE OF BUDDHISM

The Buddhist way began within the great tradition of Indian spirituality, and in some respects has never ceased to be a part of its legacy. Yet it is a part which has touched the lives of more people outside of India than within it; one might call Buddhism an "export version" of India, carrying in portable form its concentrated essence.

According to traditional Buddhist belief, the faith began in this way. (The following account contains much that is clearly legendary, but is nonetheless important, for it reflects the way hundreds of millions of Buddhists down the centuries have understood their supreme teacher).

Some twenty-five hundred years ago, a son was born to a king of kshatriya rank in the foothills of the Himalayas. His personal name was Siddhartha, his family name was Gautama, his clan was the Sakya, but he is best known by the title he later attained: the Buddha, meaning "the Enlightened One" or "the One Who has Awakened." (Compared to his state of consciousness, the latter title means, most of the rest of us are asleep and lost in dreams even when we think we are awake.)

He was, we are told, no ordinary child: wonderful signs accompanied his birth, and an old brahmin told the king that his son would become either a world-emperor or a Buddha. Hoping to swerve him toward the former vocation, the father caused vast pleasure-palaces to be built with high walls around them, lest the young prince see the anguish of the world and be so moved by compassion as to want to teach mankind rather than rule. But to no avail: in his late twenties the future Buddha left the walls to see four sights: an old man, a dying man, a corpse, a wandering holy man. From then on he would not rest till he had learned how one can find meaning in life in the face of its inevitable careening toward senility, suffering, and extinction. Emulating the mendicant, he set out on a quest for this all-important answer.

He tried extreme asceticism and the dicta of various teachers, but found them all unsatisfactory. Finally, we are told, the young quester seated himself under a spreading fig-tree, and vowed not to arise until he had attained full enlightenment. He passed through the deepest reaches of trance, and found the wisdom he sought.

It can be summarized in this way. The cause of suffering is attachment to particular things, including attachment to particular ideas and concepts and even to oneself conceived of as a separate individual self. Indeed, attachment to one's own ego-structure is, for Buddhism, the root of suffering and evil. All these desires or attachments are futile, for all things, including our separate particular selves, are transitory aggregates. By blowing out the flames of attachment, then, the suffering will cease.

The way to do this is to attain a state of equilibrium between all pairs of opposites, between all particularized things, veering toward no partial thing or concept on the winds of desire. This is the Middle Way. The best way to find it is through meditation, which creates in the mind calm freedom. This the Buddha lived and taught.

Buddhism developed two main streams: Theravada, found in southeast Asia; and Mahayana, prevalent in China, Tibet, Japan, Korea, and adjacent areas. Theravada is in a sense more conservative, emphasizing formal methods of meditation and study for the monks, and for the laity religious and charitable activities which make merit that will gain one a better state in this and future lives.

Mahayana is more diverse. It could be called a multi-media Buddhism, for within it are many paths toward equilibrium and freedom: meditation, chanting, devotion, magical evocation, faith. It teaches that the "Buddha-nature"—reality as the Buddha saw it—is in all things, so any act which causes one to wake up to his own true nature also fills him with the wisdom which enables him to set sail toward the farther shore of existence, unconditioned reality.

THE BUDDHA'S DAILY LIFE

This passage, from the commentary on the ancient scriptures by the great scholar Buddhaghosa (early fifth century A.D.), gives the conventional interpretation of the Buddha's life after his enlightenment. Notice the overtones suggesting he is a supernatural being, though not a god. In the middle watch of the night he taught gods even as he had taught human beings by day, and in the last watch his gaze moved like a searchlight over the face of the earth to find deserving beings.

From *Buddhism in Translations*

Henry Clarke Warren

Habits are of two kinds, the profitable, and the unprofitable. Of these, the unprofitable habits of The Blessed One had been extirpated by his attainment of saintship at the time he sat cross-legged under the Bo-tree. Profitable habits, however, remained to The Blessed One.

These were fivefold: his before-breakfast habits; his after-breakfast habits; his habits of the first watch of the night; his habits of the middle watch of the night; his habits of the last watch of the night.

His before-breakfast habits were as follows:—

The Blessed One would rise early in the morning, and when, out of kindness to his body-servant and for the sake of bodily comfort, he had rinsed his mouth and otherwise cared for his person, he would sit retired until it was time to go begging. And when it came time, he would put on his tunic, girdle, and robes, and taking his bowl, he would enter the village or the town for alms. Sometimes he went alone, sometimes surrounded by a congregation of priests; sometimes without anything especial happening, sometimes with the accompaniment of many prodigies.

While, namely, the Lord of the World is entering for alms, gentle winds clear the ground before him; the clouds let fall drops of water to lay the dust in his pathway, and then become a canopy over him; other winds bring flowers and scatter them in his path; elevations of ground depress themselves, and depressions elevate themselves; wherever he places his foot, the ground is even and pleasant to walk upon, or lotus-flowers receive his tread. No sooner has he set his right foot within the city-gate than the rays of six different colors which issue from his body race hither and thither over palaces and pagodas, and deck them, as it were, with the yellow sheen of gold, or with the colors of a painting. The elephants, the horses, the birds, and other animals give forth melodious sounds; likewise the tom-toms, lutes, and other musical instruments, and the ornaments worn by the people.

By these tokens the people would know, "The Blessed One has now entered for alms;" and in their best tunics and best robes, with perfumes, flowers, and other offerings, they issue forth from their houses into the street. Then, having zealously paid homage to The Blessed One with

Henry Clark Warren, *Buddhism in Translations* (Cambridge, Massachusetts: Harvard University Press, 1896), pp. 91–95. Notes omitted. Reprinted by permission of the publisher.

the perfumes, flowers, and other offerings, and done him obeisance, some would implore him, "Reverend Sir, give us ten priests to feed;" some, "Give us twenty;" and some, "Give us a hundred priests." And they would take the bowl of The Blessed One, and prepare a seat for him, and zealously show their reverence for him by placing food in the bowl.

When he had finished his meal. The Blessed One, with due consideration for the different dispositions of their minds, would so teach them the Doctrine that some would become established in the refuges, some in the five precepts, some would become converted, some would attain to the fruit of either once returning, or of never returning, while some would become established in the highest fruit, that of saint-ship, and would retire from the world. Having shown this kindness to the multitude, he would rise from his seat, and return to the monastery.

On his arrival there, he would take his seat in a pavilion, on the excellent Buddha-mat which had been spread for him, where he would wait for the priests to finish their meal. When the priests had finished their meal, the body-servant would announce the fact to The Blessed One. Then The Blessed One would enter the perfumed chamber.

These, then, were his before-breakfast habits.

Then The Blessed One, having thus finished his before-breakfast duties, would first sit in the perfumed chamber, on a seat that had been spread for him by his body-servant, and would wash his feet. Then, taking up his stand on the landing of the jeweled staircase which led to the perfumed chamber, he would exhort the congregation of the priests, saying,—

"O priests, diligently work out your salvation; for not often occur the appearance of a Buddha in the world and existence among men and the propitious moment and retirement from the world and the opportunity to hear the true Doctrine."

At this point some would ask The Blessed One for exercises in meditation, and The Blessed One would assign them exercises suited to their several characters. Then all would do obeisance to The Blessed One, and go to the places where they were in the habit of spending the night or the day—some to the forest, some to the foot of trees, some to the hills, and so on, some to the heaven of the Four Great Kings, . . . and some to Vasavatti's heaven.

Then The Blessed One, entering the perfumed chamber, would, if he wished, lie down for a while, mindful and conscious, and on his right side after the manner of a lion. And secondly, his body being now refreshed, he would rise, and gaze over the world. And thirdly, the people of the village or town near which he might be dwelling, who had given him breakfast, would assemble after breakfast at the monastery, again in their best tunics and their best robes, and with perfumes, flowers, and other offerings.

Thereupon The Blessed One, when his audience had assembled, would approach in such miraculous manner as was fitting; and taking his seat in the lecture-hall, on the excellent Buddha-mat which had been spread for him, he would teach the Doctrine, as suited the time and occasion. And when he perceived it was time, he would dismiss the audience, and the people would do obeisance to The Blessed One, and depart.

These were his after-breakfast habits.

When he had thus finished his after-breakfast duties, he would rise from the excellent Buddha-seat, and if he desired to bathe, he would enter the bath-house, and cool his limbs with water made ready by his body-servant. Then the body-servant would fetch the Buddha-seat, and spread it in the perfumed chamber. And The Blessed One, putting on a tunic of double red cloth, and binding on his girdle, and throwing his upper robe over his right shoulder, would go thither and sit down, and for a while remain solitary, and plunged in meditation. After that would come the priests from here and from there to wait on The Blessed One. And some would propound questions, some would ask for exercises in meditation, and some for a sermon; and in granting their desires The Blessed One would complete the first watch of the night.

These were his habits of the first watch of the night.

And now, when The Blessed One had finished his duties of the first watch of the night, and when the priests had done him obeisance and were departing, the deities throughout the entire system of ten thousand worlds would seize the opportunity to draw near to The Blessed One and ask him any questions that might occur to them, even such as were but four syllables long. And The Blessed One in answering their questions would complete the middle watch of the night.

These were his habits of the middle watch of the night.

The last watch of the night he would divide into three parts, and as his body would be tired from so much sitting since the morning, he would spend one part in pacing up and down to free himself from the discomfort. In the second part he would enter the perfumed chamber, and would lie down mindful and conscious, and on his right side after the manner of a lion. In the third part he would rise, and taking his seat, he would gaze over the world with the eye of a Buddha, in order to discover any individual who, under some former Buddha, with alms-giving, or keeping the precepts, or other meritorious deeds, might have made the earnest wish.

These were his habits of the last watch of the night.

THE BUDDHA'S ENTRY INTO NIRVANA

In this passage from the Mahaparinibbana Sutta, or Scripture of the Entry into Nirvana, we read of the great teacher's death. The Buddha's

final words say in effect that a human being is a compound, and all com-
pounds must come apart sooner or later. He then passed through higher
and higher stages of meditation, even as he had on the night of his en-
lightenment, but this time not to return again to normal consciousness.
After his decease, he was no more in any conditioned form, but his disci-
ples remained to celebrate the direction whither he went.

From *Buddhist Suttas*

T.W. Rhys Davids

Then the Blessed One addressed the brethren, and said: 'Behold
now, brethren, I exhort you, saying, "Decay is inherent in all component
things! Work out your salvation with diligence!" '

This was the last word of the Tathâgata!

Then the Blessed One entered into the first stage of deep meditation. And rising out of the first stage he passed into the second. And rising out of the second he passed into the third. And rising out of the third
stage he passed into the fourth. And rising out of the fourth stage of
deep meditation he entered into the state of mind to which the infinity
of space is alone present. And passing out of the mere consciousness of
the infinity of space he entered into the state of mind to which the infinity of thought is alone present. And passing out of the mere consciousness of the infinity of thought he entered into a state of mind to which
nothing at all was specially present. And passing out of the consciousness
of no special object he fell into a state between consciousness and unconsciousness. And passing out of the state between consciousness and unconsciousness he fell into a state in which the consciousness both of sensations and of ideas had wholly passed away.

Then the venerable Ânanda said to the venerable Anuruddha: 'O
my Lord, O Anuruddha, the Blessed One is dead!'

'Nay! brother Ânanda, the Blessed One is not dead. He has entered
into that state in which both sensations and ideas have ceased to be!'

Then the Blessed One, passing out of the state in which both sensations and ideas have ceased to be, entered into the state between consciousness and unconsciousness. And passing out of the state between
consciousness and unconsciousnes he entered into the state of mind to
which nothing at all is specially present. And passing out of the consciousness of no special object he entered into the state of mind to which

T.W. Rhys Davids, trans., *Buddhist Suttas* (Oxford: The Clarendon Press, 1881),
pp. 114–19. Notes omitted.

the infinity of thought is alone present. And passing out of the mere consciousness of the infinity of thought he entered into the state of mind to which the infinity of space is alone present. And passing out of the mere consciousness of the infinity of space he entered into the fourth stage of deep meditation. And passing out of the fourth stage he entered into the third. And passing out of the third stage he entered into the second. And passing out of the second he entered into the first. And passing out of the first stage of deep meditation he entered into the second. And passing out of the second stage he entered into the third. And passing out of the third stage he entered into the fourth stage of deep meditation. And passing out of the last stage of deep meditation he immediately expired.

When the Blessed One died there arose, at the moment of his passing out of existence, a mighty earthquake, terrible and awe-inspiring: and the thunders of heaven burst forth.

When the Blessed One died, Brahmâ Sahampati, at the moment of his passing away from existence, uttered this stanza:

> 'They all, all beings that have life, shall lay
> Aside their complex form—that aggregation
> Of mental and material qualities,
> That gives them, or in heaven or on earth,
> Their fleeting individuality!
> E'en as the teacher—being such a one,
> Unequalled among all the men that are,
> Successor of the prophets of old time,
> Mighty by wisdom, and in insight clear—
>   Hath died!'

When the Blessed One died, Sakka, the king of the gods, at the moment of his passing away from existence, uttered this stanza:

> 'They're transient all, each being's parts and
>   powers,
> Growth is their nature, and decay.
> They are produced, they are dissolved again:
> And then is best, when they have sunk to rest!'

When the Blessed One died, the venerable Anuruddha, at the moment of his passing away from existence, uttered these stanzas:

> 'When he who from all craving want was free,
> Who to Nirvâna's tranquil state had reached,
> When the great sage finished his span of life,
> No gasping struggle vexed that steadfast heart!
> All resolute, and with unshaken mind,

He calmly triumphed o'er the pain of death.
E'en as a bright flame dies away, so was
His last deliverance from the bonds of life!'

When the Blessed One died, the venerable Ānanda, at the moment of his passing away from existence, uttered this stanza:

'Then was there terror!
Then stood the hair on end!
When he endowed with every grace—
The supreme Buddha—died!'

When the Blessed One died, of those of the brethren who were not yet free from the passions, some stretched out their arms and wept, and some fell headlong on the ground, rolling to and fro in anguish at the thought: 'Too soon has the Blessed One died! Too soon has the Happy One passed away from existence! Too soon has the Light gone out in the world!'

But those of the brethren who were free from the passions (the Arahats) bore their grief collected and composed at the thought: 'Impermanent are all component things! How is it possible that [they should not be dissolved]?'

BUDDHIST TEACHING

Here we see the teaching on key points attributed by the scriptures to the Buddha himself. First, we read that a human being is a compound of five "attachment groups," that is, bundles of elements or skandhas: form, sensation, perception, predispositions, consciousness. Then we see that these have come together and perpetrate their suffering-laden existence because of desire for pleasure and existence; when desire is stilled this burden is laid down. To put it another way, beings prone to pain come into being when consciousness seeks a resting-place in form and feeling, but when consciousness has no such resting-place, it becomes free, quiet, and blissful. This bliss is found in the Middle Way, which on its profoundest level means being free of attachment either to being or non-being. The whole process is summarized in the twelve steps of coming into being and their reversal. We then see that Nirvana (Nibbana) is unconditioned reality, unbounded by any definition or ignorance or wave of feeling—yet although little can be said of it in language, it is utterly greater than anything in this world of wavering, falling change.

From *Buddhism in Translations*

Henry Clarke Warren

—Translated from the Samyutta-Nikāya

Thus have I heard.

On a certain occasion The Blessed One was dwelling at Sāvatthí in Jetavana monastery in Anāthapiṇḍika's Park. And there The Blessed One addressed the priests.

"Priests," said he.

"Lord," said the priests to The Blessed One in reply.

And The Blessed One spoke as follows:—

"I will teach you, O priests, the burden, the bearer of the burden, the taking up of the burden, and the laying down of the burden.

"And what, O priests, is the taking up of the burden?

"Reply should be made that it is the five attachment-groups. And what are the five? They are: the form-attachment-group, the sensation-attachment-group, the perception-attachment-group, the predisposition-attachment-group, the consciousness-attachment-group. These, O priests, are called the burden.

"And who, O priests, is the bearer of the burden?

"Reply should be made that it is the individual; the venerable So-and-so of such-and-such a family. He, O priests, is called the bearer of the burden.

"And what, O priests, is the taking up of the burden?

"It is desire leading to rebirth, joining itself to pleasure and passion, and finding delight in every existence,—desire, namely, for sensual pleasure, desire for permanent existence, desire for transitory existence. This, O priests, is called the taking up of the burden.

"And what, O priests, is the laying down of the burden?

"It is the complete absence of passion, the cessation, giving up, relinquishment, forsaking, and non-adoption of desire. This, O priests, is called the laying down of the burden."

Thus spake The Blessed One; and when The Happy One had so spoken, The Teacher afterwards spoke as follows:—

Henry Clarke Warren, *Buddhism in Translations* (Cambridge, Massachusetts: Harvard University Press, 1896), pp. 159–60, 162–63, 165–66. Notes omitted. Reprinted by permission of the publisher.

"The five groups form the heavy load,
And man this heavy load doth bear;
This load 't is misery to take up,
The laying down thereof is bliss.

"He who this heavy load lays down,
Nor any other taketh up,
By extirpating all desire
Shall hunger lose, Nirvana gain."

Thus have I heard.

On a certain occasion The Blessed One was dwelling at Sāvatthí in Jetavana monastery in Anāthapiṇḍika's Park. And there The Blessed One addressed the priests.

"Priests," said he.

"Lord," said the priests to The Blessed One in reply.

And The Blessed One spoke as follows:—

"Not to seek for anything, O priests, is to be free; to seek for anything is not to be free.

"If consciousness abide, O priests, it is because of a seeking for form that it abides, and supported by form, and resting in form, and taking delight therein, it attains to growth, increase, and development. When consciousness abides, O priests, it is because of a seeking for sensation, . . . perception, . . . the predispositions, that it abides, and supported by the predispositions, and resting in the predispositions, and taking delight therein, it attains to growth, increase, and development.

"It is impossible, O priests, for any one to say that he can declare either the coming, or the going, or the passing out of an existence, or the springing up into an existence, or the growth, or the increase, or the development of consciousness apart from form, apart from sensation, apart from perception, apart from the predispositions.

"If passion for form, O priests, is abandoned, then through the abandonment of passion the support is cut off, and there is no resting-place for consciousness. If passion for sensation, . . . for perception, . . . for the predispositions is abandoned, then through the abandonment of passion the support is cut off, and there is no resting-place for consciousness.

"When that consciousness has no resting-place, does not increase, and no longer accumulates karma, it becomes free; and when it is free, it becomes quiet; and when it is quiet, it is blissful; and when it is blissful, it is not agitated; and when it is not agitated, it attains Nirvana in its own person; and it knows that rebirth is exhausted, that it has lived the holy life, that it has done what it behooved it to do, and that it is no more for this world." . . .

. . . The world, for the most part, O Kaccāna, holds either to a belief in being or to a belief in non-being. But for one who in the light of the highest knowledge, O Kaccāna, considers how the world arises, belief in the non-being of the world passes away. And for one who in the light of the highest knowledge, O Kaccāna, considers how the world ceases, belief in the being of the world passes away. The world, O Kaccāna, is for the most part bound up in a seeking, attachment, and proclivity [for the groups], but a priest does not sympathize with this seeking and attachment, nor with the mental affirmation, proclivity, and prejudice which affirms an Ego. He does not doubt or question that it is only evil that springs into existence, and only evil that ceases from existence, and his conviction of this fact is dependent on no one besides himself. This, O Kaccāna, is what constitutes Right Belief. . . .

. . . That things have being, O Kaccāna, constitutes one extreme of doctrine; that things have no being is the other extreme. These extremes, O Kaccāna, have been avoided by The Tathāgata, and it is a middle doctrine he teaches:—

On ignorance depends karma;
On karma depends consciousness;
On consciousness depend name and form;
On name and form depend the six organs of sense;
On the six organs of sense depends contact;
On contact depends sensation;
On sensation depends desire;
On desire depends attachment;
On attachment depends existence;
On existence depends birth;
On birth depend old age and death, sorrow, lamentation, misery, grief, and despair. Thus does this entire aggregation of misery arise.

But on the complete fading out and cessation of ignorance ceases karma;
On the cessation of karma ceases consciousness;
On the cessation of consciousness cease name and form;
On the cessation of name and form cease the six organs of sense;
On the cessation of the six organs of sense ceases contact;
On the cessation of contact ceases sensation;
On the cessation of sensation ceases desire;
On the cessation of desire ceases attachment;
On the cessation of attachment ceases existence;
On the cessation of existence ceases birth;
On the cessation of birth cease old age and death, sorrow, lamentation, misery, grief, and despair. Thus does this entire aggregation of misery cease.

From *Some Sayings of the Buddha*

F.L. Woodward

Then on that occasion the Exalted One, seeing the application of it, uttered these solemn words:

'There is, brethren, a condition wherein there is neither earth, nor water, nor fire, nor air, nor the sphere of infinite space, nor the sphere of infinite consciousness, nor the sphere of the void, nor the sphere of neither perception nor non-perception: where there is no "this world" and no "world beyond": where there is no moon and no sun. That condition, brethren, do I call neither a coming nor a going nor a standing still nor a falling away nor a rising up: but it is without fixity, without mobility, without basis. THAT IS THE END OF WOE:

Hard to behold THE SELFLESS, so 'tis called.
Not easy is it to perceive the Truth.
But craving is pierced through by one who knows:
He who sees all clings not to anything.'

And again, on that occasion, the Exalted One uttered these solemn words:

'There is, brethren, an unborn, a not-become, a not-made, a not-compounded. If there were not, brethren, this that is unborn, not-become, not-made, not-compounded, there could not be made any escape from what is born, become, made, and compounded.

But since, brethren, there is this unborn . . . therefore is there made known an escape from what is born, become, made, and compounded.'

And again, on that occasion, the Exalted One uttered these solemn words:

'In him who depends (on others), there is wavering. In him who is independent, there is no wavering. Where there is no wavering, there is tranquillity. Where there is tranquillity, there is no passionate delight. Where there is no passionate delight, there is no coming and going (in rebirth). Where there is no coming and going (in rebirth), there is no falling from one state to another. Where there is no falling from one state to another

F.L. Woodward, *Some Sayings of the Buddha* (New York: Oxford University Press, 1973), p. 220. Reprinted by permission of the publisher.

there is no "here," no "beyond," no "here-and-yonder." THAT IS THE END OF WOE.'

THE CEASING OF BECOMING IS NIBBANA.

BUDDHIST MEDITATION

The supreme means to this nirvanic tranquillity is meditation, for it cuts into the flames of desire and releases that calmness of mind which permits right understanding. Here, a modern Buddhist writer clearly describes how meditation is practiced by Theravada monks.

From *Buddhism in Theravada Countries*
The Ven. Balangoda Ananda Maitreya

MEDITATION

Two things, O brethren, are conducive to knowledge. What are the two? Tranquillity and insight. When tranquillity is developed, what happens? Mind is developed. When mind is developed, what happens? Whatever passion there is is abandoned. When insight is developed, what happens? Right understanding is developed. When right understanding is developed, what happens? Whatever ignorance there is is abandoned. The mind soiled with passion is not freed. When there is soiling through ignorance, right understanding is not developed. Thus through unstaining of passion there is freedom of mind, and through unstaining of ignorance there is freedom of right understanding. (Anguttara Nikaya.)

These words of the Buddha make it clear that the only way to culture and the perfection of the mind is meditation, and that meditation is of two kinds—the kind which leads to tranquillity (*Samatha*) and the kind which leads to insight (*Vipassana*).

The meditation which leads to tranquillity is based on practices which were to a large extent known and used by ascetics before the

The Ven. Balangoda Ananda Maitreya, "Buddhism in Theravada Countries," in Kenneth W. Morgan, ed., *The Path of the Buddha*. New York: Ronald Press Company, 1956), pp. 144–52. Reprinted by permission of the publisher.

appearance of the Buddha. Because such practices bring a calmness and serenity to the mind and help to turn the mind away from depravities, and because the habit of fixing the mind on an object is useful for the development of mental processes, the Buddha recommended to his followers the way of meditation which leads to tranquillity. By itself, this method is not sufficient, but it serves as a useful preparation for the second kind of meditation, the meditation which leads to insight.

According to *The Path of Purity (Visuddhi Magga)*, by Buddhaghosha, there are forty subjects of meditation suggested to followers of the Dhamma for the development of tranquillity. The disciple should choose for his meditation the subjects which suit his temperament and character, making the selection under the guidance of a competent teacher if possible, but in the end relying upon his experience as a guide. People are divided into six classes according to their temperament—the lustful, the hot-tempered, the easily deluded, the self-confident, the quick-witted, and those of discursive mind.

The forty subjects of meditation are divided into the ten devices, the ten impurities, the ten recollections, the four sublime states, the four immaterial states, the one notion, and the one analysis.

The ten devices:

1. Earth device—a circle made of dawn-colored clay, generally a span and four inches in diameter
2. Water device—a bowl of clean water
3. Fire device—a bright flame appearing through a hole
4. Air device—the perception of air shaking and swaying the top of a tree
5. Blue device—a circle of blue cloth or the like
6. Yellow device—a circle of yellow cloth or the like
7. Red device—a circle of red cloth or the like
8. White device—a circle of white cloth or the like
9. Light device—a light falling through a circular hole
10. Space device—a limited space of a prescribed dimension, seen through an opening

The ten impurities:

1. A swollen corpse
2. A discolored, blue-green corpse
3. A corpse full of pus
4. A fissured corpse
5. A corpse mangled by dogs or other animals
6. A corpse with dismembered limbs
7. A corpse with its limbs partly destroyed and scattered
8. A corpse covered here and there with blood

9. A worm-infested corpse
10. A skeleton

The ten recollections are the recollection of:

1. The virtues of the Buddha
2. The merits of the Dhamma
3. The Order of the Holy Disciples of the Buddha
4. The merits of the observation of the precepts
5. The merits of liberality
6. The equality between one's self and the deities in regard to the virtues
7. Death—that is, mindfulness of the fact that everyone is subject to inevitable death
8. The body—that is, mindfulness regarding the body
9. Respiration—that is, mindfulness of respiration
10. Peace of mind—that is, cognition of the attributes of peace of mind

The four sublime states are the development of:

1. Universal love, amity (*metta*)
2. Compassion (*karuna*)
3. The happiness of others
4. Equanimity

The four immaterial stages are the attainment of:

1. Infinite space
2. Infinite consciousness
3. Nothingness
4. Neither perception nor nonperception

The one notion is meditation on the loathsomeness of food.
The one analysis is the analysis of the four primary elements.
Of these forty exercises in meditation which lead to tranquillity,
the ten impurities and the mindfulness regarding the body are suitable
for a person of lustful temperament. The four sublime states and the
four color devices are suitable for the hot-tempered. The mindfulness as
to respiration is suitable for men of discursive mind and for those who
are easily deluded. The first six recollections are suitable for the person
to whom confidence comes easily. For those who are quick-witted, the
suitable exercises are mindfulness as to death, the cognition of the
attributes of peace of mind, meditation on the loathsomeness of food,
and the one analysis. The remaining exercises are suitable for all. In
choosing a device as an object of meditation, those who are easily deluded

should choose a wide one, and a person of discursive nature should choose a little one of a span and four inches in diameter.

There are three stages of the meditation which leads to tranquillity. The first stage is called the preliminary stage and can be attained by any one of the forty meditations. The second stage is called the accessory stage and can be attained through the first eight recollections, the one notion, and the one analysis. The third stage is called the stage of absorption and can be attained through using the rest of the forty meditations. There are nine levels of the stage of absorption (jhana), five (or four, according to another classification) belonging to the realm of form, and four belonging to the formless realm. The levels of absorption pertaining to the realm of form can be attained through the ten devices and the respiration exercise. Meditation on the ten impurities and mindfulness concerning the body will attain only the first level of the realm of form; meditation on the first three sublime practices—love, compassion, and the happiness of others—will attain only the first four levels of absorption in the realm of form; meditation on the fourth sublime practice—equanimity—will bring attainment of the fifth level of absorption in the realm of form. Meditation which relies on the four immaterial states will attain the four levels of absorption belonging to the formless realm.

As an example, let us now consider a brief account of the way in which meditation on the earth device is used in the meditation which leads to tranquillity.

First, the beginner must establish himself perfectly in pure conduct so there will be no distractions caused by his actions, and he will be sure that his self-restraint is not endangered from any side. At the same time, he should so guard the gates of his senses that he may not be attracted or fascinated by anything which is perceived by his senses. Then he should be constantly mindful of himself and be self-possessed in all his movements. By such preliminary practices he reaches the state of being content with whatever happens to be his lot, and his mind becomes inclined toward simplicity and fewness of wants. It is only after that preparation that he can select a proper object for meditation, as recommended by his spiritual teacher, and begin to practice meditation.

If he selects the earth device for his object, he must make the device with clay the color of the dawn which he smears on a piece of cloth or some convenient surface in a circle a span and four inches in diameter. Then he places the circle at a distance of about a yard and a half from his seat. He gazes at it and repeats its name all the time, trying to grasp it by the mind. When it is thoroughly grasped by the mind an image of it appears before the mind, and as he continues to look at it and grasp it the after-image arises. The after-image then appears to be bursting the grasped mental image and is a thousand times more brilliant than it was at first; this is called the transformed after-image. By a repetition of the process of grasping the image of the earth device and then the after-image, the process of mental hindrances subsides.

When he sees in himself the absence of mental hindrances, joy arises and, because of the joy, interest arises. When the mind is interested, the body becomes calm. When he experiences the calmness, he experiences comfort, and his mind becomes concentrated. Then, free from low and sensuous mental states, he enters upon the first absorption (jhana) which is endowed with initial and sustained application, interest, and comfort born of quietude. After mastering this absorption, he goes on further in his practice and brings about the quiescence of initial and sustained application and attains to the second level of absorption which is endowed with inward placidity, unification of the mind, interest, and comfort born of concentration. This, too, he masters and continues his practices and attains to the third level of absorption at which interest fades and he becomes equable and mindful and feels bodily comfort. Again, as a result of further practice, he rejects ease and pain and enters upon the fourth level of absorption which is endowed with equanimity and individualization.

When he has elevated his mind by passing through those four levels of absorption, he can, if he likes, develop his super-normal powers such as clairvoyance, thought reading, remembrance of past lives, levitation, and such. Whether or not he decides to develop these powers, he can go on with his meditation, for those powers are not of any help in attaining the next levels of absorption. A person who sees the evils of the physical body, whether gross or subtle, and prefers to exist purely in a mental state—to be a spirit—follows the path that leads to such a state. Such a person sees the disadvantages even of the level of absorption he has thus far attained and attempts to go farther.

To attain the next levels of absorption, he spreads the object of the previous absorption—that is, the transformed after-image—as far and wide as possible throughout the space he can imagine; then he removes it so that he may see the empty space. Then he fixes his mind on the very same mental space and repeatedly turns to it and impinges on it until his mind becomes firmly fixed in the mental space, and thus he attains to the first level of the formless absorption. He masters that level by entering it and rising from it over and over again, and then if he wishes to rise higher, he takes for his object the consciousness which was fixed on the infinite space and attempts to fix the mind on this new object. After some effort, he succeeds in fixing his mind on the consciousness with which he viewed the mental space and attains the second level of absorption in the realm of the formless. After the mastery of this level, he tries to elevate the mind to a more subtle level. He stops attending to the object of infinite consciousness and attempts to fix his mind on its absence—on "nothingness." When he is successful, he attains the third level of absorption in the formless, known as the realm of nothingness.

When he has mastered the third level, he attempts to attain the fourth stage of formless absorption which is the culmination of the meditation which leads to tranquillity. He enters the third level of formless absorption and rises from it and observes the condition of his immediately previous absorption-consciousness. As he repeatedly reflects upon that condition, his mind becomes most subtle and he attains to the state of mind which is called "neither consciousness nor unconsciousness." It is called that because the grossness of consciousness is absent, and it exists in the most subtle form ever possible.

The persons who have attained to any of the four levels of the formless absorption are destined to be reborn in comparable pure mental states or realms. When the force of their meditation which elevated them to that state has been exhausted, they will come down again and be born among men. Thus it is seen that the attainments of the method of meditation which leads to tranquillity are still worldly, and that is why they were not highly praised by the Buddha.

Thus far we have described the first of the two kinds of meditation, the meditation which leads to tranquillity. Let us turn now to the second kind of meditation, the meditation which leads to insight. This is Buddhist meditation, the meditation which leads the follower further and further away from worldliness and awakens the mind to awareness of the real nature of the living being. Some persons develop insight and attain Arahatship by starting with the meditation which leads to tranquillity and gaining insight from one of the levels of absorption—they are known as those who have made tranquillity of the mind their vehicle. But none of the levels of absorption discussed above is absolutely necessary to Arahatship because even without it some are able to attain Arahatship—they are called the dry-visioned, the ones who attained Arahatship by the meditation which leads to insight.

In the meditation which leads to tranquillity there are forty exercises, but in the meditation which leads to insight, there are only three—meditation on the impermanence, suffering, and nonsubstantiality (anicca, dukkha, and anatta) of life in the world.

The meditator who seeks to practice the meditation which leads to insight, if he has already developed any of the levels of absorption, enters any stage of absorption and from it analyzes the factors and qualities of that stage and tries to understand their impermanence, suffering, and nonsubstantiality. If he has not attained any level of absorption, he will analyze his own life. Either way, he will see by analyzing his own self that the so-called being or self is nothing but a process or flux of mental and material states which are interdependent. By analysis he sees that they are but a stream of causes and effects. Then he examines and scrutinizes the nature of the causes and effects very minutely, and at last he realizes the voidness or emptiness of the life of all living beings, either human or divine. The whole universe appears to him as a mere flux, as mere vibrations which are void of any entity. With the attainment of this realization, craving for such an existence wanes, vanishes, and ceases to be. The opposite side of this illusory existence dawns before his mind, and the path which he has been following reaches its culmination. This, in Buddhist terminology, is the Realization of the Four Truths.

The Realization of the Four Truths occurs four times. On the first occasion, the meditator discerns the ill, the suffering, of life; then the false view concerning the ego-entity and any scepticism concerning the Buddha and all his teachings vanish away from him forever, Nibbana gleams before his mind, and all the eight factors of the Path appear together in his mind. This experience is called the Entering of the Stream, for anyone who reaches this state will never fall back into worldliness and is destined to become an Arahat. That fourfold experience —the understanding of suffering, loss of false views, glimpse of Nibbana, and grasping of the Eightfold Path—occurs within one flash of thought and is immediately followed by two or three thought-moments in which he experiences the bliss of Nibbana. Those moments are called the fruit-consciousness of the Stream-winner's Path. After those thought-moments he engages in retrospection, reviewing the Holy stage of the Path which has been attained, the fruits enjoyed, Nibbana intuited, the mental depravities already got rid of in the first stage, and the depravities to be got rid of in the future.

When in that retrospection he sees the depravities to be removed, he goes on with his practice of contemplation, and on the second occasion he discerns once more the ills of existence and consequently slackens his sensual attachment, his anger, and delusion; he sees Nibbana and develops the Path. When one has attained this second stage, he is called a Once-returner because, since he has lessened his attachments that much, he will be reborn only once in the sensual world. This brief thought-moment is followed by its fruit-consciousness two or three times, and then he engages in the process of retrospection as before. As he sees in his retrospection that his realization is still not perfect, he continues his contemplation, and at the moment of reaching the next stage he sees the ills of existence clearer than before, eradicates desire for sensual pleasure, and ends all ill will; he sees Nibbana face to face, and the factors of the Path appear unitedly in his mind at one moment. Because he will never be reborn to the sensual plane after this insight, he is called a Never-returner. This thought-moment at the third stage of progress is followed by its fruit-moments and by the process of retrospection.

Through the process of retrospection after attaining the third stage of insight he sees that there are still some mental depravities to be removed, so he returns to his usual practice of meditation. Now at last he reaches the culmination of his meditative practice; he realizes perfectly the ills of existence, eradicates all the remaining weaknesses of the mind, sees Nibbana as it is, and all the factors of the Path appear in his mind simultaneously. This stage is called the Path of Arahatship. It also is followed by its fruit-consciousness two or three times, and then follows the process of retrospection upon the Path, its fruition, Nibbana, and the eradication of all passions.

A person who has attained to this final stage has become an Arahat and has nothing more to do for he has now reached the end of the Path. He is free of passion and lives a selfless life doing his pure service to frail mortals. This stage of insight is the goal of the Path expounded by the Buddha.

THE HEART SUTRA

This short but intensely packed bit of Buddhist scripture is one of the basic texts of Mahayana, and presents some of its most important insights. Mahayana began its separate destiny around 100 A.D., and this writing derives from not long after. It extols two of the oldest Mahayana themes.

The first is the motif of the "Perfection of Wisdom" (Prajna-paramita) or Wisdom Which Has Gone Beyond, gone to the Other Shore, Nirvana—that is, wisdom which is sheer, direct insight without resting-place in any distorting attachment or preconception, and so is able to see things as they are. It sees even the skandhas as empty—without separate existence but interrelated with the universe—and all pairs of opposites as false polarizations between which one must thread the Middle Way. The "five heaps" are the five skandhas.

The second theme is the idea of the bodhisattva, "Enlightenment Being," like Avalokita. He is a coming Buddha and is one who fully grasps these things, and so is fearless. He is full of the Perfection of Wisdom and is free of attachment even to his own attainment. He has no "thought-coverings" or distorting preconceptions, and so recognizes that all is interdependent. Since he is attached to nothing, nothing could be taken away from him, so he is afraid of nothing, and victoriously goes toward the Other Shore.

From *Buddhist Scriptures*

Edward Conze

THE HEART SUTRA

I. The invocation

Homage to the Perfection of Wisdom, the lovely, the holy!

Edward Conze, *Buddhist Scriptures* (Harmondsworth, Middlesex, England: Penguin Books, 1959), pp. 162–64. Reprinted by permission of the publisher. Copyright 1959 by Edward Conze.

II. The prologue

Avalokita, the holy Lord and Bodhisattva, was moving in the deep course of the wisdom which has gone beyond. He looked down from on high, he beheld but five heaps, and he saw that in their own-being they were empty.

III. The dialectics of emptiness. First stage

Here, O Sariputra, form is emptiness, and the very emptiness is form; emptiness does not differ from form, form does not differ from emptiness; whatever is form, that is emptiness, whatever is emptiness, that is form. The same is true of feelings, perceptions, impulses, and consciousness.

IV. The dialectics of emptiness. Second stage

Here, O Sariputra, all dharmas are marked with emptiness; they are not produced or stopped, not defiled or immaculate, not deficient or complete.

V. The dialectics of emptiness. Third stage

Therefore, O Sariputra, in emptiness there is no form, nor feeling, nor perception, nor impulse, nor consciousness; no eye, ear, nose, tongue, body, mind; no forms, sounds, smells, tastes, touchables or objects of mind; no sight-organ-element, and so forth, until we come to: no mind-consciousness-element; there is no ignorance, no extinction of ignorance, and so forth, until we come to: there is no decay and death, no extinction of decay and death; there is no suffering, no origination, no stopping, no path; there is no cognition, no attainment, and no non-attainment.

VI. The concrete embodiment and practical basis of emptiness

Therefore, O Sariputra, it is because of his indifference to any kind of personal attainment that a Bodhisattva, through having relied on the perfection of wisdom, dwells without thought-coverings. In the absence of thought-coverings he has not been made to tremble, he has overcome what can upset, and in the end he attains to Nirvana.

VII. Full emptiness is the basis also of Buddhahood

All those who appear as Buddhas in the three periods of time fully awake to the utmost, right and perfect enlightenment because they have relied on the perfection of wisdom.

VIII. The teaching brought within reach of the comparatively unenlightened

Therefore one should know the Prajñaparamita as the great spell, the spell of great knowledge, the utmost spell, the unequalled spell, allayer of all suffering, in truth—for what could go wrong? By the Prajña-paramita has this spell been delivered. It runs like this: Gone, Gone, Gone beyond, Gone altogether beyond, O what an awakening, All Hail! This completes the Heart of Perfect Wisdom.

THE LOTUS SUTRA

This great and immensely influential Mahayana text from perhaps 300 A.D. represents the Buddha, called the Tathagata or "He who has gone thus," as the Jina (Gina) or Hero and as actually an infinite, universal quality. This quality is unchanging of itself, but as accommodations it takes the form of Buddhas appearing in historical periods, like Gautama the Buddha, and teaches doctrines in different words for different sorts of people. But he who is truly wise and near to Nirvana sees that all these words or "laws" by which we try to catch the moon in a net, and indeed all that appears, are like dreams and echoes, so equally false and equally true.

From *The Saddharma-Pundarika or The Lotus of the True Law*
H. Kern

As the rays of the sun and moon descend alike on all men, good and bad, without deficiency (in one case) or surplus (in the other);

So the wisdom of the Tathâgata shines like the sun and moon, leading all beings without partiality.

As the potter, making clay vessels, produces from the same clay pots for sugar, milk, ghee, or water;

Some for impurities, others for curdled milk, the clay used by the artificer for the vessels being of but one sort;

As a vessel is made to receive all its distinguishing qualities according to the quality of the substance laid into it, so the Tathâgatas, on account of the diversity of taste,

Mention a diversity of vehicles, though the Buddha-vehicle be the only indisputable one. He who ignores the rotation of mundane existence, has no perception of blessed rest;

H. Kern, *The Saddharma-Pundarika or The Lotus of the True Law* (Oxford: The Clarendon Press, 1884), pp. 136–41. Notes omitted.

But he who understands that all laws are void and without reality (and without individual character) penetrates the enlightenment of the perfectly enlightened Lords in its very essence.

One who occupies a middle position of wisdom is called a Pratyekagina (i.e. Pratyekabuddha); one lacking the insight of voidness is termed a disciple.

But after understanding all laws one is called a perfectly-enlightened one; such a one is assiduous in preaching the law to living things by means of hundreds of devices.

It is as if some blind-born man, because he sees no sun, moon, planets, and stars, in his blind ignorance (should say): There are no visible things at all.

But a great physician taking compassion on the blind man, goes to the Himâlaya, where (seeking) across, up and down,

He fetches from the mountain four plants; the herb Of-all-colours-flavours- and-cases, and others. These he intends to apply.

He applies them in this manner: one he gives to the blind man after chewing it, another after pounding, again another by introducing it with the point of a needle into the man's body.

The man having got his eyesight, sees the sun, moon, planets, and stars, and arrives at the conclusion that it was from sheer ignorance that he spoke thus as he had formerly done.

In the same way do people of great ignorance, blind from their birth, move in the turmoil of the world, because they do not know the wheel of causes and effects, the path of toils.

In the world so blinded by ignorance appears the highest of those who know all, the Tathâgata, the great physician, of compassionate nature.

As an able teacher he shows the true law; he reveals supreme Buddha-enlightenment to him who is most advanced.

To those of middling wisdom the Leader preaches a middling enlightenment; again another enlightenment he recommends to him who is afraid of the mundane whirl.

The disciple who by his discrimination has escaped from the triple world thinks he has reached pure, blest Nirvâna, but it is only by knowing all laws (and the universal laws) that the immortal Nirvâna is reached.

In that case it is as if the great Seers, moved by compassion, said to him: Thou art mistaken; do not be proud of thy knowledge.

When thou art in the interior of thy room, thou canst not perceive what is going on without, fool as thou art.

Thou who, when staying within, dost not perceive even now what people outside are doing or not doing, how wouldst thou be wise, fool as thou art?

Thou are not able to hear a sound at a distance of but five yoganas, far less at a greater distance.

Thou canst not discern who are malevolent or benevolent towards thee. Whence then comes that pride to thee?

If thou hast to walk so far as a kos, thou canst not go without a beaten track; and what happened to thee when in thy mother's womb thou hast immediately forgotten.

In this world he is called all-knowing who possesses the five transcendent faculties, but when thou who knowest nothing pretendest to be all-knowing, it is an effect of infatuation.

If thou are desirous of omniscience, direct thy attention to transcendent wisdom; then betake thyself to the wilderness and meditate on the pure law; by it thou shalt acquire the transcendent faculties.

The man catches the meaning, goes to the wilderness, meditates with the greatest attention, and, as he is endowed with good qualities, ere long acquires the five transcendent faculties.

Similarly all disciples fancy having reached Nirvâna, but the Gina instructs them (by saying): This is a (temporary) repose, no final rest.

It is an artifice of the Buddhas to enunciate this dogma. There is no (real) Nirvâna without all-knowingness; try to reach this.

The boundless knowledge of the three paths (of time), the six utmost perfections (Pâramitâs), voidness, the absence of purpose (or object), the absence of finiteness;

The idea of enlightenment and the other laws leading to Nirvâna, both such as are mixed with imperfection and such as are exempt from it, such as are tranquil and comparable to ethereal space;

The four Brahmavihâras and the four Sangrahas as well as the laws sanctioned by eminent sages for the education of creatures;

(He who knows these things) and that all phenomena have the nature of illusion and dreams, that they are pithless as the stem of the plantain, and similar to an echo;

And who knows that the triple world throughout is of that nature, not fast and not loose, he knows rest.

He who considers all laws to be alike, void, devoid of particularity and individuality, not derived from an intelligent cause; nay, who discerns that nothingness is law;

Such a one has great wisdom and sees the whole of the law entirely. There are no three vehicles by any means; there is but one vehicle in this world.

All laws (or the laws of all) are alike, equal, for all, and ever alike. Knowing this, one understands immortal, blest Nirvâna.

THE BODHISATTVA PATH

No image is more characteristic of Mahayana Buddhism than the bodhisattva, that "being destined for enlightenment" who has gone beyond by the mastery of the perfection of wisdom. Their transcendent compassion has made bodhisattvas objects of story and worship in Mahayana countries, for to those far behind them they seem like gods. Yet they were once humans like us; their serene state and vast power to work good was attained arduously. Here a modern scholar relates the nature of the bodhisattva's progress, beginning with the dawning of a desire for bodhi (awakening or enlightenment) and the nurturing of bodhicitta (the thought of enlightenment).

From *Buddhist Religion: A Historical Introduction*
Richard H. Robinson

The way begins with the teaching of a Buddha, a bodhisattva, or some other spiritual friend. Seeds of virtue are planted in the mind of the hearer, and from much hearing he comes to perform good deeds, through which he acquires more and more roots of goodness. After many lives, thanks to the infused grace of the various teacher-saviors and the merit earned by responding to them, a person becomes able to put forth the thought of enlightenment. The two motives for this aspiration are one's own desire for bodhi, and compassion for all living beings who suffer in saṃsāra. Initially the motivation is both egotistic and altruistic, but along the path one realizes the sameness of self and others, and transcends the duality of purpose. Arousing the thought of bodhi is an extremely meritorious deed. It cancels past bad karma, increases merit, wards off bad rebirths, and assures good ones. In these respects, it corresponds to "winning the stream" in Early Buddhism, since the stream-winner, too, will never be reborn in the woeful destinies and is confirmed in the course to enlightenment. "Arousing the thought" is a decisive conversion experience with profound psychological effects. It is compared to a pearl, to the ocean, to sweet music, to a shade-giving tree, to a convenient bridge, to soothing moonbeams, to the sun's rays, to a universal panacea, and to an infallible elixir.

The new bodhisattva proceeds to consolidate his bodhicitta and advance on the path by cultivating good qualities and working for the welfare of living beings. He makes a set of vows or earnest resolutions. Some vows are quite general, for instance: "When we have crossed the stream, may we ferry others across. When we are liberated, may we lib-

Richard H. Robinson, *Buddhist Religion: A Historical Introduction* (Encino: Dickinson Publishing Company, 1970), pp. 55–58. Reprinted by permission of the publisher.

erate others." Some bodhisattvas' vows are very specific and pragmatic, for example those of Dharmākara, who later became the Buddha Amitābha. He made three or four dozen vows, in the form "May I not attain supreme, perfect enlightenment until such-and-such a benefit is assured beings who are born in my Buddha-country." Taking the precepts is an Early Buddhist forerunner of Mahāyāna vow-making in that it is a formal act of commitment and involves a greater forfeiture of merit if one transgresses than if one had not made a vow. Bodhisattva vows are usually binding until the end of the bodhisattva career, a matter of eons. Even when the great bodhisattva has passed beyond dualistic cognitions and intentions, he is motivated, as if on automatic pilot, by the force of his original vows.

The bodhisattva is supposed to declare his vows in the presence of a Buddha, which means that he must wait until a Buddha appears in the world. The Tathāgata then gives the bodhisattva a prediction that after x number of ages he will become a Buddha of such-and-such a name, reigning in such-and-such a Buddha-country, which will have such-and-such excellences. Ordinary bodhisattvas who have not yet had the good fortune to be born in the same generation as a Buddha make their vows in the presence of other human bodhisattvas, or even with the Buddhas and bodhisattvas of the ten directions as their witnesses.

The six perfections are the main course of the bodhisattva career. As we have noted these virtues are all advocated in the Early Buddhist Canon, and extreme instances of them are extolled in the Jātakas. Mahāyāna differs from Hīnayāna in making the extremes the model for ordinary devotees.

A virtue is practiced to perfection when the most difficult acts are executed with a mind free from discriminatory ideas, without self-consciousness, ulterior motives, or self-congratulation. The perfect giver, for example, doesn't think "I give," and has no fictive concepts about the gift, the recipient, or the reward that ensues from the act. Thus the perfection of wisdom (prajñā-pāramitā) is necessary in order to attain the other five perfections.

The perfection of donation (dāna) consists of giving material things, Dharma-instructions and one's own body and life to all beings, then in turn transferring or reassigning the ensuing merit to supreme enlightenment and the welfare of other beings, rather than allowing it to earn one future bliss in the world. The bodhisattva practices dāna, and instigates others to do likewise.

The perfection of morality (śīla) consists of following the ten good paths of action, transferring the merit, and instigating others to do likewise. The ten are: not killing, stealing, or fornicating; not lying, slandering, speaking harshly, or chattering frivolously; and not having covetous thoughts, hostile thoughts, or false views.

The perfection of patience (kṣānti) is founded in nonanger and nonagitation. It means patient endurance of hardship and pain, forbearance and forgiveness toward those who injure and abuse the bodhisattva, and patient assent to difficult and uncongenial doctrines.

The perfection of vigor (*vīrya*) means unremitting energy and zeal in overcoming one's faults and cultivating virtues, in studying Dharma and the arts and sciences, and in doing good works for the welfare of others. Vīrya is derived from *vīra* ("a martial man, a hero"). It corresponds to right effort, the sixth member of the Holy Eightfold Path of Early Buddhism, but more explicitly signifies heroic endeavor to benefit other living beings.

The perfection of meditation (*dhyāna*) consists of entering all the meditative trances, concentrations, and attainments, yet not accepting rebirth in the paradises to which such states normally destine one in the next life.

The perfection of wisdom (*prajñā-pāramitā*) is personified as a goddess, because *prajñā* is grammatically feminine. She is the mother of all the Buddhas, since through her they become enlightened ones. A famous hymn endows her with feminine traits and maternal loving-kindness.

The *Prajñā-pāramitā Sūtras* say over and over again that the doctrine that things neither arise nor cease is supremely difficult, that it causes fear and aversion in the tender-minded, and that the bodhisattva who can accept it is a great hero (*mahāsattva*). Three degrees of assent (*kṣānti*) are distinguished. The first is acceptance of the words of the teaching. The second is conforming assent, attained in the sixth bodhisattva-bhūmi, and consisting of an intense but not definitive conviction. The third is patient acceptance that the dharmas are nonarising. It is said by later texts to be attained in the eighth bhūmi, and it is concomitant with reaching the nonrelapsing state. We have seen that the nonreturner is the second highest level of holy person in Early Buddhism, and that the stream-winner is assured of not falling back into the states of woe. The Mahāyāna concept of nonrelapsing is a reworking of the old ideas.

The early bhūmi theory seems to have recognized just seven bodhisattva stages, with acceptance that the dharmas are nonarising and that the nonrelapsing states occur in the seventh bhūmi. The number of bhūmis was increased from seven to ten about 200 A.D. Variant lists of stations and stages circulated for a while, but eventually the following became standard:

(a) The stage of the "lineage," where the beginner strives to acquire a stock of merit and knowledge. It extends from the first thought of enlightenment until the "experience of heat," the first signpost of success in meditation.

(b) The stage of "practicing with conviction." Here the bodhisattva cultivates four "factors of penetration," namely "meditative heat," "climax," "patience," and "highest mundane dharma." These meditative experiences overcome and expel the antithesis between subject and object, and lead to nondiscriminative knowledge.

(c) The ten bodhisattva stages, namely: (1) the joyful, (2) the stainless, (3) the illumining, (4) the flaming, (5) the very-hard-to-conquer, (6) the face-to-face, (7) the far-going, (8) the immovable, (9) good-insight, and (10) Dharma-cloud. In each successive stage, one of the pāramitās is supposed to be practiced concertedly. Four pāramitās were added to the early list of six for the sake of symmetry: (7) skill in means, (8) vows, (9) power, and (10) knowledge. The first bodhisattva-bhūmi corresponds to the path of vision, which follows immediately after "highest mundane dharma," and is characterized by nondual awareness.

(d) The Buddha-stage follows the diamond-like samādhi which is the last event on the "path of cultivation." This concentration plays an important role in Abhidharma, too, where it is realized by the bodhisattva as he sits on the Diamond Throne, and in it he fulfills the perfections of dhyāna and prajñā in the moment just before he attains bodhi. It is this samādhi which destroys all the residues of defilement. Mahāyāna doctrine maintains that the terminal path consists in awareness that the causes of suffering have been destroyed and will never arise again. In other words, the bodhisattva's final realization is identical with the arhant's.

There were some differences of opinion about the duration of the bodhisattva career, but the prevalent view was that it takes three immeasurable kalpas: one to or through the first bodhisattva-bhūmi, one from there through the seventh bhūmi, and one for bhūmis eight to ten.

VAJRAYANA

Mahayana Buddhism has developed many strains. Some, like Zen and Pure Land, we will examine later in connection with China and Japan. Now we will look at another form, Vajrayana (meaning the Diamond or Thunderbolt Vessel). Vajrayana is also spoken of as tantric or esoteric Buddhism. It reached its greatest flowering in the mountain-rimmed fastness of Tibet.

Vajrayana was deeply influenced by the Yogacara Buddhist philosophy, which teaches that the phenomenal world as we see it is projected out of mind. In reality, it says, there is only pure consciousness, the diamond-like Clear Light. Vajrayana teaches how to get beneath the phenomenal world to the pure consciousness by initiation into psychophysical techniques of altering ordinary perception. The relation of spiritual master or guru (lama in Tibet) and disciple is very important. So is the evocation of deities (Buddhas, bodhisattvas, initiatory females, and so forth). The point of the evocation is to learn experimentally that all forms come out of mind and are not as real as pure consciousness, and to use the evoked entities (Yidam in Tibet) as guides representing one's highest self to the fullest realization of one's true nature. The following passage, by a European lady who spent many years in Tibet, describes the process. A tsams *is a hermitage, a* kyilkhor *a magic circle or mandala, a* gomti *a yogic posture.*

From *Magic and Mystery in Tibet*

Alexandra David-Neel

The master orders his disciple to shut himself in *tsams* and to meditate—taking his *Yidam* (tutelary deity) as object of his contemplation.

The novice dwelling in strict seclusion, concentrates his thoughts on the *Yidam,* imagining him in the shape and form ascribed to him in books and images. Repeating certain mystic formulas and constructing a *kyilkhor* are parts of the exercise of which the aim is to cause the *Yidam* to appear to his worshipper. At least, such is the aim that the master points out to the beginner.

The pupil breaks his contemplation during the time strictly necessary to eat[1] and the very short time allowed for sleep. Often the recluse does not lie down and only dozes in one of those *gomti* which have been described in a previous chapter.

Months and even years may elapse in that way. Occasionally the master inquires about the progress of his pupil. At last a day comes when the novice informs him that he has reaped the fruit of his exertion: the *Yidam* has appeared. As a rule, the vision has been nebulous and lasted only a little while. The master declares that it is an encouraging success, but not as yet a definitive result. It is desirable that the recluse should longer enjoy the hallowed company of his protector.

The apprentice *naljorpa* cannot but agree, and continues his effort. A long time again elapses. Then, the *Yidam* is "fixed"—if I may use that term. He dwells in the *tsams khang* and the recluse sees him as always present in the middle of the *kyilkhor.*

"This is most excellent," answers the master when he is informed of the fact; "but you must seek a still greater favour. You must pursue

Alexandra David-Neel, *Magic and Mystery in Tibet* (Secaucus, N.J.: University Books, 1965), pp. 283–87. Reprinted by permission of the publisher.

[1]Generally the recluse has only one meal a day, but drinks buttered tea several times. However, during such periods of retreat some ascetics subsist on water and roast barley flour only.

your meditation until you are able to touch with your head the feet of the *Yidam,* until he blesses you and speaks to you."

Though the previous stages have taken long to be effected they may be considered the easiest part of the process. The following are much more arduous to attain, and only a small minority of novices meet with success.

These successful disciples see the *Yidam* taking on life. They distinctly feel the touch of his feet when, prostrated, they lay their head on them. They feel the weight of his hands when he blesses them. They see his eyes moving, his lips parting, he speaks. . . . And lo! he steps out of the *kyilkhor* and walks in the *tsams khang*.

It is a perilous moment. When wrathful demi-gods or demons have been called up in that way, they must never be allowed to escape from the *kyilkhor,* whose magic walls hold them prisoners. Set free out of due time, they would revenge themselves on the person who has compelled them to enter this prison-like consecrated circle. However, the *Yidam,* though his appearance may be dreadful and his power is to be feared, is not dangerous because the recluse has won his favour. Consequently, he may move about as he pleases in the hermitage. Even better, he may cross its threshold and stand in the open. Following his teacher's advice, the novice must find out if the deity is willing to accompany him when he walks out.

This task is harder than all previous ones. Visible and tangible in the obscure hermitage fragrant with incense, where the psychic influences born from a prolonged concentration of thought are working; will the *Yidam's* form be able to subsist in quite different surroundings under the bright sunlight, exposed to influences which, instead of supporting it, will act as dissolving agents?

A new elimination takes place amongst the disciples. Most *Yidam* refuse to follow their devotee into the open. They remain obstinately in some dark corner and sometimes grow angry and avenge themselves for the disrespectful experiments to which they have been submitted. Strange accidents occur to some anchorites, but others succeed in their undertaking and wherever they go enjoy the presence of their worshipful protector.

"You have reached the desired goal," says the *guru* to his exultant disciple. "I have nothing more to teach you. You have won the favours of a protector mightier than I."

Certain disciples thank the lama and, proud of their achievement, return to their monastery or establish themselves in a hermitage and spend the remainder of their life playing with their phantom.

On the contrary, others trembling in mental agony prostrate themselves at their *guru's* feet and confess some awful sin. . . . Doubts have arisen in their mind which, in spite of strenuous efforts, they have not been able to overcome. Before the *Yidam* himself, even when he spoke to them or when they touched him, the thought has arisen in them that they contemplated a mere phantasmagoria which they had themselves created.

The master appears afflicted by this confession. The unbeliever must return to his *tsams khang* and begin training all over again in order to conquer his incredulity, so ungrateful to the *Yidam* who has favoured him.

Once undermined, faith seldom regains a firm footing. If the great respect which Orientals feel for their religious teacher did not restrain them, these incredulous disciples would probably yield to the temptation of giving up the religious life, their long training having ended in materialism. But nearly all of them hold on to it, for if they doubt the reality of their *Yidam,* they never doubt their master's wisdom.

After a time the disciple repeats the same confession. It is even more positive than the first time. There is no longer any question of *doubt;* he is thoroughly *convinced* that the *Yidam* is produced by his mind and has no other existence than that which he has lent him.

"That is exactly what it is necessary for you to realize," the master tells him. "Gods, demons, the whole universe, are but a mirage which exists in the mind, 'springs from it, and sinks into it.' "2

THE TIBETAN BOOK OF THE DEAD

The best-known classic of Tibetan Buddhism and of Vajrayana is the Bardo Thodol, known in the West as the Tibetan Book of the Dead. It is a text of instructions to be given a deceased person as he passes through the after-death state preparatory to his attaining either release or reincarnation. The basic premise is that beside ordinary consciousness there is an alternative state called the Bardo. The Bardo state is met in the womb, in dreams, in meditation, and after death. In it the realities of one's true nature are faced; it is a state accessible to infinite bliss and surrealistic terror.

A second premise is that the after-death Bardo reality takes three successive forms: the Chikhai Bardo, the Clear Light beyond all forms; the Chonyid Bardo, the level of transcendent forms like those of the yidam; and the Sidpa Bardo, which one passes through in reentry through the portals of birth into this or another world. After death one first confronts the Clear Light; if he cannot recognize it as his true nature and so become one with it, he faces next the Chonyid Bardo. Here he meets one by one, and then all together, on successive days the great cosmic Buddhas of Vajrayana. First he meets them in tranquil form, then if he cannot accept them as arising from his own thoughts and so find

2A declaration continually repeated by Tibetan mystics.

liberation through them, he confronts them again in terrifying form. If he cannot accept that either as coming from his own nature, he is led back to rebirth. The following passage describes the Clear Light, the bardo states, and one buddhic deity, Vairocana, in both tranquil and terrifying aspect. Notice the tantric influence in Vairocana's being embraced by a consort representing wisdom; together they are a totality or Father-Mother deity.

From *The Tibetan Book of the Dead*

Frank J. MacHovec

FIRST STATE OF THE CHIKHAI BARDO

(NAME OF DECEASED), The time has come for you to enter the Chikhai Bardo. Your breathing will soon cease. You will be able to see The Primary Clear Light. You will perceive a great void, like a boundless ocean, without waves, beneath a cloudless sky. Your mind will float freely, alone, unaided. At this instant, know thyself, as I know you.

Repeat three or seven times to impress this teaching on the dying one. As death comes, continue:

Do not let your mind wander. Listen carefully, for this is the hour of your death. Use death as an advantage, the opportunity to achieve Buddhahood. Do this by keeping your mind clear of all thought except thoughts of love and goodness. Seek the light of Truth, the goodness of enlightenment. Concentrate, for it is the time of The Primary Clear Light. Meditate thus: 'Even if I do not fully realize or understand it, I accept the Chikhai Bardo. I will earnestly try to be one with it, not only for my own benefit, but for the benefit of all humanity.' If death has not yet come and there is still time to think, keep these teachings in mind, and also remember inspiring religious experiences from your previous life.

Repeat this again to prevent the dying one's mind from wandering. When death unmistakably comes, continue:

You are facing The Primary Clear Light. Be alert and attentive to

Frank J. MacHovec, trans., *The Tibetan Book of the Dead* (Mount Vernon, N.Y.: The Peter Pauper Press, 1972), pp. 20–25, 35–36. Reprinted by permission of the publisher.

all that happens. You can now see and hear ultimate reality, the all-good, the dharmakaya, the first state of Buddhahood. Your mind is no longer restricted to your body. It can join with the great stream of universal consciousness. It can be one with the unborn, with perfect enlightenment, with Buddhahood. You can be beyond birth, beyond death, free, immortal. You can be one with The Primary Clear Light. Know that life is unreal and death is also unreal. Only what you experience is real. It alone is the Truth, the Light. Because you no longer experience yourself as real, as mortal, you can be one with the Buddha, one with the dharmakaya. Recognize this, accept this, be one with this teaching and you will instantly achieve Buddhahood.

SECOND STATE OF THE CHIKHAI BARDO

Repeat the previous teaching three or seven times. Since you cannot know if the deceased has achieved Buddhahood, call the deceased by name three times and continue:

If you have not seen The Primary Clear Light, know that you can still achieve Buddhahood through the clear light of the Chonyid Bardo which will soon follow. Meditate now on your favorite deity or on the Compassionate Buddha. Think of Him as if He were with you now. Avoid the influence of bad karma. Concentrate and do not be distracted.

THE CHONYID BARDO

In this Bardo there will be frightening karmic illusions. It is important to prepare the deceased for them. He or she can see and hear but no one can see or hear the spirit of the deceased. Call the deceased by name and continue:

Listen carefully, with undivided attention. Do not be distracted. There are six Bardo states: three are involved with life; three are involved with death. The first is in the womb awaiting birth; second, the dream-state; third, mystic balance (samadhi) and holy meditation (dyhana); fourth, at the moment of death; fifth, karmic illusions after death; and sixth, seeking rebirth. You will experience the three Bardos of death: Chikhai Bardo, at the moment of your death; Chonyid Bardo, intermediate state of karmic reality; and Sidpa Bardo, seeking rebirth. Of these, you have already passed through the Chikhai Bardo. The Primary Clear Light shone upon you but you were unable to recognize it and be one with it, and so you are now in the Chonyid Bardo.

Listen carefully, be attentive and alert. Death has come to you. It is time for you to depart this world. While you must face this reality alone, know that you are not the only one, for death comes to all. Do not cling to life because of sentiment or fear to go on. You do not have the power to stay. There is no value whatever to aimlessly wandering as a lonely spirit. Think on these teachings and the Compassionate Buddha from whence they come. They are meant to help you. Listen carefully so you can be saved from fear and terror in the Chonyid Bardo. Do not forget these teachings. Meditate thus:

> When karmic illusions dawn upon me
> And fear and terror grow within me,
> May I realize they are but reflections from within
>   myself;
> May I realize they are a natural part of the Bardo
>   of death;
> May I realize this moment as one of great
>   opportunity;
> May I accept good and evil karmic illusions as
>   my own.

Think on these words, as you go into the Chonyid Bardo. Then, when illusions come, you will be able to understand them. Do not forget this secret insight. When your mind and body separated, you were able to see The Primary Clear Light. It is said that it is like a mirage, subtle but bright, dazzling in its radiance. Do not be afraid, for it is the same kind of light which you also radiate. So be comfortable with it. Within this light there is also the sound of ultimate reality, like a thousand simultaneous thunder claps. Do not be afraid of it, for this, too, is the same kind of sound which you also generate. Accept it as such. The being you are now is a spirit and not a body. It is mind and thought rather than flesh and blood. Know that no sights or sounds can hurt you. Remember that, for now, you cannot die again. Remember, too, that these illusions arise from your own thoughts. Realize this is part of the Chonyid Bardo. If you cannot recognize your own thoughts from your previous life, and from within your present mind, the good and the evil, if you forget these teachings which are meant to help you, the sights and sounds of karmic illusion will surely terrify you. If you disregard the secret insight of these words you will wander aimlessly frightened and terrified, through the Chonyid Bardo and perhaps through other worlds.

The death Bardos take 49 days, calculated from the first day the deceased realizes he or she is dead. This realization takes three and one half days which are not counted in the 49. Call the deceased by name at the beginning of each day's teachings.

1ST DAY. For three and a half days you have been unaware of what was happening to you. Concentrate, be alert, so you will now recognize what happens. Realize that your existence and your perception have changed. You will see sights and hear sounds unlike those of earthly existence. They will arise first from the mandala of the heart center, the realm of enlightened realization. From mandala center you will see Vairocana, the White Buddha of the central realm. His body is dazzling white and he radiates pure blue light. He sits on a lion throne, holding the 8-spoked wheel, embraced by Akasadhatis, Divine Mother of space and the heavens. The blue light shines so brightly you can hardly look at it. Bad karma within you may cause you to fear this pure light. Accept it, believe in it, pray to it, for it can save you from a painful Bardo. The pure blue light will be mixed with the dull white light of the devas, the gods. Avoid the dull white light for it can mislead you and interrupt your journey. Meditate thus:

> When wandering in ignorance,
> Seeking the enlightenment of universal
>   consciousness,
> May the pure blue light of Vairocana inspire and
>   strengthen me;
> May the Divine Mother Akasadhatis comfort and
>   sustain me;
> May I be spared a long and painful Bardo;
> May I achieve Buddhahood.

Pray with sincerity, humility, and deep faith, and you will be one with Vairocana in the central realm of universal consciousness. . . . .

8TH DAY. Be attentive and listen carefully. It is the day of Buddha-Heruka, the Buddha of Masculinity, of the mind-mandala center. He comes because you could not be one with the deities which came before. He is dark brown and radiantly aflame. He has three heads, each with three widely opened eyes, six arms, and four feet. His left face is red, his right is white, the middle, dark brown. His heads are adorned with skulls and symbols of sun and moon. He wears a garland of black snakes strung with human heads. His first right hand holds a wheel, the second holds a sword, the third, a battle-axe. His first left hand holds a bell, the second holds a skull, the third, a plow. He has a frightening stare, his eyes blink rapidly, his teeth protrude and overlap. He speaks in loud piercing tones. His hair bristles and is radiant red-brown. He is embraced by the Divine Mother Krotishvarima, Mother of Femininity, her right arm around his neck, her left hand holding a blood-filled red shell to his mouth. The shell makes a crackling thunderous sound. Both bodies radiate brightly, each with a flaming sceptre. One leg of each is bent, the other straight. They are borne on a platform carried by horned half-eagles half-humans. Fear not, do not be confused. It is really Father-Mother Vairocana. Know that they arise from your own thoughts. Recognize them, accept them, be one with them, and you will achieve Buddhahood.

V

HEAVEN, EARTH, AND THE WAY: RELIGIOUS TRADITIONS OF CHINA

It is often said that traditional China had three religions: Confucianism, Taoism, and Buddhism. Certainly these are three areas that must be studied to understand Chinese thought and life. But it also must always be borne in mind that these are not like three great "denominations" into which all Chinese were divided. Instead, many ordinary Chinese had some relationship to all three, worshipped at temples associated with all three, and were affected by the values of all three. Even more important, the religious practices closest of all to the ordinary people, such as veneration of ancestors and worship of the gods of village and soil, are not directly identifiable with any of the three "religions" but are more of an all-pervasive background.

Also in the background of all three as they appear in China are certain common basic assumptions. One is that humankind and the universe make up a great, incomprehensibly vast unity called the Tao or the Way. By getting in harmony with the Tao, one can find a fulfilled existence. But the question was where is the Tao best found.

Confucianism is the way of life deriving from the rituals and lore of ancient China as interpreted by the Master Kung (Confucius, 551–479 B.C.) and his disciples. It emphasized that the Tao and the supreme human good is found in a good society, based on right relationships between people. A human being alone, Confucianists thought, is scarcely human; it is in relationships that humanity is realized and so the human Tao is best expressed. The most basic relationship is that of father and son, "filial piety." On it are built the family system, the veneration of ancestors, and the role of the emperor as "father" of his people and mediator between them and Heaven, for all these are extensions of the filial relationship. Confucianism was given practical and sociological expression in the ancestral cultus, the temples of Confucius whose formal and archaic rites were attended mainly by officials and schoolboys, and in the rites of the emperor.

Taoism probably derives from shamanism and popular magic reaching back into prehistory. But the philosophical side of this tradition was historically articulated first in the book called the *Tao te ching* (The book of the Way and its power), attributed to an older contemporary of Confucius called Lao-tzu. This book sees society and its relationships and conventions as corrupting, and advocates living in profound harmony with nature; in nature and in the depths of the self was the Tao found. Because of its rejection of Confucian rationalism and moderation, romantic and occult elements clustered around the Taoist tradition. What served personal needs, from the poet's vision to the peasant's desire to exorcise evil spirits, fitted better with Taoism than sober Confucian social virtue. Taoism acquired a colorful pantheon of deities; a priesthood who performed lavish rites; and a collection of esoteric alchemical, yogic, and magical practices intended to produce immortality and control spirits. Behind it all lay a vision of the Tao so great that it exceeded not only what reason and society could comprehend, but even the widest limits of imagination. The Taoist spirit believed it was better to risk believing and experiencing too much than too little.

Buddhism has become deeply embedded in Chinese culture, although it has always had about it a whiff of the Indic and exotic, which has both created trouble and added to its appeal. It also borrowed a great deal from China, particularly Taoism. But Chinese Buddhism was always kept distinct by its scriptures of Indic origin, and its monasticism. Even though Buddhist monasticism was imitated by Taoism, there was always a certain tension between it and Confucian society.

Chinese Buddhism ended up coalescing around two major strands, Pure Land and Ch'an. Both are Mahayana, and both in different ways emphasize "sudden enlightenment"—assertion that nirvanic consciousness is pure and indivisible, so attaining it cannot really be a gradual process but is experienced as a sudden grace or flash of insight.

Pure Land Buddhism is a tradition which stresses dependence upon the help of the cosmic Buddha called Amitabha. Ages ago, it was said, Amitabha had vowed to bring all who called upon his name into his Western Paradise, a world wonderful in itself and from which access to Nirvana was easy. Amitabha (Omito in China) is a cosmic-consciousness Buddha who really personifies the Clear Light like Vairocana and others in the Tibetan Book of the Dead. Pure Land Buddhism has been very popular among the laity in China.

Ch'an, called Zen in Japan, is more monastic in orientation. It stresses meditation as the best technique for realization. Beyond that, the Ch'an tradition emphasizes "direct pointing." Rather than depending on scriptures and images, it wants to see the "Buddha nature" in all things directly, including seeing it as one's own true nature. To produce this realization beyond words, Ch'an masters combined meditation, work, and the brainsplitting "shock therapy" of blows, bizarre behavior, and the illogical puzzles known (in Japanese) as koans.

Over against these three strands of Chinese religion is the basic unity of Chinese spiritual culture.

TAOISM AND BUDDHISM IN TAIWAN

This passage is by an American student of religion in Taiwan, the most important place since the Communist revolution where traditional Chinese religion is preserved. It illustrates the complexity and unity of popular religion. Among the Buddhist objects of worship, Guan-in (also Kwanyin) is a bodhisattva, actually the same as Avalokita in the Heart Sutra, but feminized in China and Japan and considered a "goddess of mercy"; Amida is the Amitabha of Pure Land; Sakyamuni Buddha is the historical Gautama Buddha.

From *Gods, Ghosts, and Ancestors*
David K. Jordan

One question that is often asked about religion in Taiwan is whether the people are Taoists or Buddhists, and perhaps it will prove easiest to begin consideration of Taiwanese religion by answering this reasonable question. There is something called Taoism, with certain tradition and religious specialists and books associated with it; and it is Chinese. There is also something called Buddhism, with certain traditions, religious specialists and books. It is different from Taoism, but in most ways it is equally Chinese. There is in addition to these two traditions, with their specialists and their books, a corpus of beliefs and practices, the folk religion, which has variously been described as Confucian (which it is not), as animistic and as popular. All three of these strains, Taoism, Buddhism, and folk religion, have contributed heavily to Chinese religious life, and their interpenetration is so extensive as to prevent a thoroughgoing sorting of the elements one might associate with each in its "pri-

David K. Jordan, *Gods, Ghosts, and Ancestors* (Berkeley: University of California Press, 1972), pp. 27–30. Reprinted by permission of the publisher. Copyright 1972 by The Regents of the University of California.

mal" state. It is important that we note how closely these three strains are mixed. At the same time, however, there are certain traits that still carry a specifically Taoist and Buddhist tinge, and, most important, there are separate Taoist and Buddhist clergies whom village people call upon to perform certain rituals. Both the pantheons and the personnel of the Taoist and Buddhist faiths must be clearly distinguished from each other and from folk religion if we are to understand the dynamics of religion in Taiwan today.[1]

Buddhism has a hierarchy of supernatural beings which is, as I understand it, clearly and explicitly worked out, if not by a universal Buddhist church, at least by individual schools. Taoism also has a hierarchy of supernatural beings which is, as I understand it, worked out in some detail. These supernatural beings include some gods worshipped only by the Taoist priests, for they are founders of various schools of Taoist philosophy, alchemy, and magic. Both clergies engage in worship of the beings in their respective hierarchies, but only certain members of either hierarchy are worshipped by the people at large.

In the Buddhist religion, popular worship is confined almost entirely to three figures: Guan-in, the Amida Buddha, and the Śākyamuni Buddha, in that order of popularity. The arhats are represented in many temples by tiny statues on the wall of a room devoted to Guan-in, where they are more items of pious and conventional decoration than objects of worship.

In the case of the Taoist figures, the intergrading with popular religion is more complete. The primary difference is that the masses ignore (and are ignorant of) the deified magicians, and the priests pay little attention to most of the popular gods, although either side would acknowledge the importance of all these beings as gods. The pantheons are intellectually continuous.

---

[1]Contemporary Chinese writers unanimously distinguish Buddhism and Taoism from other beliefs, which are variously treated. For Jiang Jia-jiin (1957, 1959) the classification of religions in Taiwan is Taoism, Buddhism, Christianity, and "popular beliefs," the last category including nature worship, divination, and a variety of other things. For Lii Tian-chuen (1956) the categories are Taoism, Buddhism, Christianity, and "common beliefs," but unlike Jiang Jia-jiin's "popular beliefs" this last category includes cults of three popular gods, two of whom Jiang Jia-jiin (1959) specifically classes as Taoist. For Her Lian-kwei and Wey Huey-lin (1966) the category of popular beliefs is itself composed of Taoism, Buddhism, Lay Buddhism, and individual cults of various historical figures (e.g., Guangong, Jenq Cherng-gong) plus the cults of patron gods, plus many other subdivisions each given equal rank with the rest. A separate category of wizardry includes all practitioners other than orthodox Buddhist and Taoist clerics, and this is considered separate from the category of popular beliefs. Approximately the same format is followed in Her Lian-kwei's contribution to the Taiwan provincial gazeteer (Her Lian-kwei, 1955).

What is more significant than the particular classifications of these authors is their agreement that whatever Buddhism and Taoism may be, they are not the whole story, and that some additional categories are necessary to include the parts of Taiwanese folk belief that they are unwilling to subsume under one or the other of these major traditions.

The Taiwanese Buddhist clergy dwell in monasteries, and the Buddhist monastery-temples are therefore clearly understood to be Buddhist, despite various practices not historicaly a part of Buddhism (such as the use of divination blocks and *chhiam*-papers).[2] Taoist priests, on the other hand, practice in public temples, which they neither own nor control, or in the houses of their clients. Taoist priesthood is entirely a private practice, like that of an American lawyer or physician.[3] There is no such thing as a Taoist temple, over and against a folk temple, in the way that there are distinctive Buddhist temples, for the "Taoist" temples (that is, the places where Taoist rites are performed) *are* the folk temples.[4] These temples, because they are public, folk temples, often contain Buddhist images as well as non-Buddhist ones,[5] but Buddhist temples do not ordinarily contain non-Buddhist images.

The Buddhist faith is considered foreign in some way, and Chinese delight in explaining that it is ultimately Indian. Buddhist clerics dress in grey or white or brown robes of distinctive cut, and are celebate and vegetarian, whereas Taoist priests are indistinguishable from the remainder of the population, have families, and eat what they please except during particular rites.

All of this sounds rather complicated. In practice it is very simple. There is a set of village beliefs and practices related to the supernatural. There are, in addition, two traditions represented by clergy. Both clergies are outside the village, and are related to village religion only in being outside specialists called in to perform needed rituals, particularly funerals and temple festivals, but also exorcism and other rites. These occasions are not frequent, and the liturgies and rites the priests perform are

[2] The one religion introduced during the Japanese period and still surviving in Taiwan is *Tenrikyō*. The first postwar Japanese *Tenrikyō* missionary arrived in Taiwan during my stay there and was dismayed, as I was, to discover that since the war the Taiwanese *Tenrikyō* adherents had introduced divination blocks into the temple. In one *Tenrikyō* home I even found a carved joss representing "the *Tenrikyō* god" rather than the mirror used as a semi-mystical symbol of *Tenri-ō-no-mikoto* in Japan.

[3] This situation does not seem to be typical for China as a whole. In many parts of the country there have been Taoist institutions very similar to the Buddhist monasteries, as well as a variety of types of Buddhist religious organizations. In Taiwan, however, the Taoist clerics are a dwindling handful of men who are not associated in formal organizations.

[4] The term *Taoist* is often used in Taiwan to cover everything that is not Buddhist. Christian, or Moslem, and I have often slipped into this usage myself. The usage is convenient and harmless, as long as we remember what it means.

[5] It is widely held that during the Japanese years, the government resolved to destroy all Chinese temples. Buddhist figures were placed in them, and it was pointed out that they were now Buddhist temples, and hence Japanese. The Japanese were apparently convinced, it is said, for they did not burn the temples. Even the most recent temples, however, are still built with niches or even halls for Guan-in, often surrounded by the arhats, so it is difficult to accept this historical incident as the explanation for the presence of Buddhist figures today. Basically, certain Buddhist figures are objects of popular and not merely Buddhist worship, and as such they are (naturally enough) placed in popular temples.

not understood by anyone who is not a priest. In the Taoist case the liturgy is typically secret; in the Buddhist case it is heavily sanskritized and requires an extensive special education before it is intelligible.

THE BOOK OF RITES

The Li Chi (or Li Ki), called in English the Book of Rites, is a part of one of the five books traditionally believed to be authored or edited by Confucius, and its oldest sources certainly date back even before his time. On the other hand, substantial portions of it are later than Confucius. But its importance to understanding Confucian thought and ancient and traditional Chinese ways is immense. This passage inculcates proper behavior by children toward parents, and so is illustrative of "filial piety."

From *The Sacred Books of China*

James Legge

The sovereign and king orders the chief minister to send down his (lessons of) virtue to the millions of the people.

Sons, in serving their parents, on the first crowing of the cock, should all wash their hands and rinse their mouths, comb their hair, draw over it the covering of silk, fix this with the hair-pin, bind the hair at the roots with the fillet, brush the dust from that which is left free, and then put on their caps, leaving the ends of the strings hanging down. They should then put on their squarely made black jackets, knee-covers, and girdles, fixing in the last their tablets. From the left and right of the girdle they should hang their articles for use:—on the left side, the duster and handkerchief, the knife and whetstone, the small spike, and the metal speculum for getting fire from the sun; on the right, the archer's thimble for the thumb and the armlet, the tube for writing instruments, the knife-case, the larger spike, and the borer for getting fire from wood. They should put on their leggings, and adjust their shoe-strings.

(Sons') wives should serve their parents-in-law as they served their

James Legge, *The Sacred Books of China, Part II: The Li Ki, I-X* (Oxford: The Clarendon Press, 1885), pp. 449–51. Notes omitted.

own. At the first crowing of the cock, they should wash their hands, and rinse their mouths; comb their hair, draw over it the covering of silk, fix this with the hair-pin, and tie the hair at the roots with the fillet. They should then put on the jacket, and over it the sash. On the left side they should hang the duster and handkerchief, the knife and whetstone, the small spike, and the metal speculum to get fire with; and on the right, the needle-case, thread, and floss, all bestowed in the satchel, the great spike, and the borer to get fire with from wood. They will also fasten on their necklaces, and adjust their shoe-strings.

Thus dressed, they should go to their parents and parents-in-law. On getting to where they are, with bated breath and gentle voice, they should ask if their clothes are (too) warm or (too) cold, whether they are ill or pained, or uncomfortable in any part; and if they be so, they should proceed reverently to stroke and scratch the place. They should in the same way, going before or following after, help and support their parents in quitting or entering (the apartment). In bringing in the basin for them to wash, the younger will carry the stand and the elder the water; they will beg to be allowed to pour out the water, and when the washing is concluded, they will hand the towel. They will ask whether they want anything, and then respectfully bring it. All this they will do with an appearance of pleasure to make their parents feel at ease. (They should bring) gruel, thick or thin, spirits or must, soup with vegetables, beans, wheat, spinach, rice, millet, maize, and glutinous millet,—whatever they wish, in fact; with dates, chestnuts, sugar and honey, to sweeten their dishes; with the ordinary or the large-leaved violets, leaves of elm-trees, fresh or dry, and the most soothing rice-water to lubricate them; and with fat and oil to enrich them. The parents will be sure to taste them, and when they have done so, the young people should withdraw.

THE BOOK OF CHANGE

Another of the five books, and perhaps in places the oldest of all extant Chinese texts of any length, is the I Ching *or* Book of Change. *This text, which has recently become popular in the West, is a book used for divination. But it is more than just a manual of fortune-telling. Underlying the* I Ching's *enigmatic sayings is a subtle philosophy picturing the world as interlocking, continually changing, and a place where the wise man is both virtuous and flexible. The heart of the* I Ching *is a set of sixty-four "hexagrams"—patterns made of six lines, some solid and some broken. The solid lines represent* yang, *the expansive masculine force which is one side of the Tao; the broken lines are* yin, *the recessive, yielding feminine power which is the other side of reality. All events can be characterized by one or two of these sixty-four combinations. To use the* I Ching, *one determines, by a rather complicated method of draw-ing sticks or throwing coins, which are operative in the situation one is inquiring about, and then endeavors to relate the text for those hexa-grams to the matter at hand. The following passage gives an account of consultation of the* I Ching *by a modern English author from his intro-duction to his translation of the book; next are presented the texts for the two hexagrams he discusses.*

From *I Ching*

John Blofeld

My interest in the *I Ching* was fully awakened towards the end of 1962 at about the time when hostilities between India and mainland China commenced in the Tibetan border region. Before long, the news-papers in Bangkok (where I live) were prophesying that the Chinese armies would continue their rapid advance, swoop down onto the plains of India and perhaps occupy some major cities there before India's friends could come to her defence. The contrary view was never expressed in the newspapers that came to my notice. As I had been very happy both in China and India and felt a keen affection for both peoples, I was deeply disturbed; finally, in a spirit of sincere enquiry, I consulted the *Book of Change*. The answer was so contrary to other people's predictions that I decided to write it down word for word. I do not have the record by me now; but, as far as I remember, my interpretation, which was closely based upon the actual wording of the book, ran something like this, though it was considerably longer and more detailed. An army in the hills (the Chinese) was looking down upon the marshy plain below (India). If its leaders were wise, they would halt their attack at the very momen when everything was going well for them, refrain from advanc-ing further and perhaps withdraw in some places. A week or two later this is precisely what happened. Moreover, the *I Ching* had given reasons for this advice, namely that the lines of communication were already too long for safety; that the opponent (India) was likely to receive powerful support from its friends; that the moral value of calling a halt before any necessity for it became generally apparent would be greater in the long run than fresh military gains; and several other reasons which I cannot now recall. I remember that every one of them was later adduced in news-

From *I Ching*, translated and edited by John Blofeld, Copyright © 1965 by George Allen & Unwin Ltd. Reprinted by permission of the publishers, E. P. Dutton & Co., Inc., and of George Allen & Unwin, Ltd., London, pp. 27–29, 179–81, 108–9.

paper articles to explain the unexpected behaviour of the Chinese and I vividly recall the astonishment of my friends when I showed them what I had written down in advance of the newspapers. It could of course be claimed that a good deal of the accuracy of my answer was due to my particular interpretation of the actual words below the two hexagrams and the two moving lines involved; but, as I had not at all expected the Chinese to call a halt or reasoned out the possible reasons for their doing so, it is hard to see how I could have made myself the dupe of autosuggestion.

The following is a reconstruction from memory of the way in which I obtained these results. The response consisted of Hexagram 48 plus moving lines in the first and second places of that hexagram plus Hexagram 63 (which results when those lines 'move' and thus become their own opposites).

Hexagram 48 signifies a well. My knowledge of the Indo-Tibetan borderlands, where the mighty Himalayas slope sharply down to the dead flat plain of north India, led me promptly to equate India with the well and to think of the Chinese as looking down into it from above. Of the two component trigrams, one has 'bland' or 'mild' among its meanings, while the other means 'water.' Taking water, the contents of the well, to be the people of India, I found it easy to think of bland or mild as representing their declared policy of non-violence and neutrality. Thus, the significance of these two trigrams convinced me that I had been right to suppose that the well represented India (or the whole of that country except for the Himalayan border region). The Text attached to that hexagram contained three ideas which seemed to me appropriate to the situation. That the well suffers no increase or decrease suggested that India would lose no territory lying south of the mountainous frontier region; the rope's being too short suggested that the Chinese could not safely extend their lines of communication further than they had already done; otherwise, their 'pitcher' would be broken, i.e. they would suffer a serious reverse or defeat.

Next, I examined the texts and commentaries attached to the two moving lines (lines 1 and 2) of that hexagram. The commentary on the first of them suggested that a further Chinese advance would not succeed and that the time had come for a wise commander to 'give up,' i.e. to halt and perhaps to withdraw somewhat. The commentary on the second moving line suggested that, in addition to the tactical reason for halting already given, there was also a strategic or political reason, namely China's inability to win a favourable response from other countries, hostile, friendly or neutral as the case might be.

The main Text and Commentary of Hexagram 63 reinforced the conclusions I had reached. 'Success in small matters' suggested that the Chinese would not forfeit their local gains in the Himalayan region. The reward promised for persistence in a *righteous* course appeared enigmatic, until I remembered that the Chinese had never accorded recognition to the McMahon Line; thus they could argue (and certainly believed) that they had a legal claim to certain border areas, to which past Chinese governments had also laid claim; whereas there could be no shadow of legality to back up an advance into the Indian plains (i.e. down into the well). The last sentence of the main Commentary attached to this hexagram states: 'It is clear that good fortune will accompany the start; but, ultimately, affairs will be halted amidst disorder because the way peters out.' The last four words of this passage are often taken to mean: 'thenceforth, heaven's blessing is (or will be) withdrawn.' In other words, for the Chinese to advance into the plains with no moral claim whatsoever to support them would be to court disaster. Thus, in a nutshell, the whole response conveyed to me the idea that the Chinese would gain local successes, but that there were tactical, strategic and moral reasons for supposing that no further advance could be made with impunity.

My second example concerns a time just a few days after this prediction had been fulfilled. Flushed with this and some other successes, I soon put a question that was suggested by an incident described in C. G. Jung's preface to Wilhelm's version. I asked the *I Ching* whether I could now consider myself as a qualified interpreter of its oracles and freely make use of its power to influence the lives of those of my friends who had faith in it. In other words, the question resulted from an impure motive—self-esteem! The answer was as salutary as it was deflating. In effect I was informed that one who sought to interpret the *Book of Change* for people who would rely upon his reading of the answers must possess a considerable number of intellectual and moral virtues, several of which were named directly or by implication. The really shattering sentence came at the end. According to my interpretation the *Book of Change* added: 'Do you really suppose that you have these qualities in any marked degree?' My cheeks could not have been redder if I had been unexpectedly reproved by a living person whose high opinion I particularly desired.

HEXAGRAM 48
CHING   A WELL

Component trigrams:
Below: SUN, *wind, wood, bland, mild.*
Above: K'AN, *water, a pit.*

TEXT   A Well. A city may be moved, but not a well.[1] A well suffers from no decrease and no increase; but often, when the people come to draw water there, the rope is too short or the pitcher gets broken before reaching the water[2]—misfortune!

COMMENTARY ON THE TEXT Where (the pitchers are put) into the water to draw it up—such is a well. That a well gives nourishment without suffering depletion and that a city may be moved, but not a well, are both implied by the firm line in the centre (of the upper trigram). The rope's being too short indicates failure to achieve results; the breaking of the pitcher presages a positive misfortune.

SYMBOL This hexagram symbolizes water over wood.[3] The Superior Man encourages the people with advice and assistance.

THE LINES

6 FOR THE BOTTOM PLACE The muddy water at the well bottom is undrinkable; an old well attracts no animals. COMMENTARY The first clause signifies that our affairs take a downward trend; the second, that it is time to give up.

9 FOR THE SECOND PLACE Perch dart from the water in the well hole; the pitcher is worn out and leaks.[4] COMMENTARY This is indicated by the failure of this line to win response (from the other lines).

9 FOR THE THIRD PLACE The well has been cleaned out; to my heart's sorrow, no one drinks from it, though it could well be used to supply drinking water. The King is wise and it is possible for the people to share his good fortune.[5] COMMENTARY The first sentence implies activities which call forth pity; the second, that we should accept our good fortune.

6 FOR THE FOURTH PLACE The well is being tiled—no error! COMMENTARY For it is under repair.[6]

9 FOR THE FIFTH PLACE The well is cool; its water tastes like water from an icy spring.[7] COMMENTARY This is indicated by the suitable position of this line, which is central (to the upper trigram).

6 FOR THE TOP PLACE The well-rope lies unconcealed—confidence and supreme good fortune! COMMENTARY The supreme good fortune presaged here is in the nature of a great achievement.

NOTES (1) The building of a city depends upon ourselves; but wells cannot be moved to places where nature supplies no water. The implication is that our activities are limited by natural conditions. (2) What we desire is there for the taking, but we may not succeed in getting it. (3) A reference to the component trigrams. Wood may signify the bottom of a bucket or the wooden lining of an ancient well. (4) We are doubly unfortunate in that natural conditions (signified by fish in the water) and our own ineptitude or misfortune combine to ensure our failure. (5) If we fail now, it is not for lack of opportunity but because we do not make use of opportunity. (6) We are likely to suffer a necessary delay, but the situation is hopeful. (7) All goes well with us.

HEXAGRAM 63
CHI CHI   AFTER COMPLETION

The component trigrams:
Below: LI, *fire, brilliance, beauty.*
Above: K'AN, *water, a pit.*

TEXT   After Completion—success in small matters! Persistence in a right-eous course brings reward. Good fortune at the start; disorder in the end![1]

COMMENTARY ON THE TEXT   This hexagram presages success in small matters. That right persistence will be rewarded is indicated by the correctness and suitable arrangement of the firm and yielding lines. Since the yielding (line 2) is central (to the lower trigram), it is clear that good fortune will accompany the start; but, ultimately, affairs will be halted amid disorder because the way peters out.[2]

SYMBOL   This hexagram symbolizes water above fire.[3] The Superior Man deals with trouble by careful thought and by taking advance precautions.

THE LINES

9 FOR THE BOTTOM PLACE   He brakes the wheel of his chariot and gets the rear part wet—no error! COMMENTARY   This passage means that (since we manage to stop at the right moment) we are not to blame (for what happens).

6 FOR THE SECOND PLACE   The lady loses the blind from her chariot window. She should not go in search of it, for she will recover it in seven days. COMMENTARY   Her getting it back after seven days suggests that restraint or (moderation) will be rewarded.

9 FOR THE THIRD PLACE   The Illustrious Ancestor (namely, the Emperor Wu Ting, 1324 BC) carried out a punitive expedition in Kuei Fang (literally, the Land of Devils) and conquered it after three years—men of mean attainments would have been useless![4] COMMENTARY   His taking three years to conquer it indicates great fatigue.[5]

6 FOR THE FOURTH PLACE   Amidst the fine silk are ragged garments[6]—be

NOTES   (1) Perhaps persistence may help to lessen the disorder that threatens to come upon us after some initial success.   (2) Hence, we should not try to advance very far. 'The way peters out' can also be taken to mean that our stock of merit becomes exhausted.   (3) A reference to the component trigrams.   (4) The Land of Devils was probably a territory inhabited by non-Chinese tribes. The implication is that only a man of outstanding capability should attempt any difficult task now.   (5) Even if we do feel capable of undertaking an extremely difficult task, we must expect it to occupy us for so long as to make us feel exhausted.   (6) This corrupt passage is variously interpreted in the additional commentaries. In any case it signifies a need for caution.

cautious throughout the livelong day! COMMENTARY   This indicates that doubt and suspicion are now prevalent.

9 FOR THE FIFTH PLACE   In terms of benefits, the neighbour to the east gained less from sacrificing an ox than the neighbour to the west obtained from carrying out the spring sacrifice. COMMENTARY   Because the former's sacrifice (though bigger) was less timely.[7] The benefits obtained by the neighbour to the west betoken that good fortune is on its way to us.

6 FOR THE TOP PLACE   His head gets wet—trouble! COMMENTARY   But this sort of trouble can scarcely last long.[8]

THE CONFUCIAN BOOK OF
THE BALANCED LIFE

The Chung Yung, *whose name means something like "living a balanced life" and has been called by translators "The Mean" and "Genuine Living," is attributed by tradition to Confucius' grandson. It presents a normative and very influential summary of Confucian thought. In this version of part of it, "Nature" is the translation of Tao. Notice that maturation means developing the Tao wtihin one in harmony with the universal Tao. This cannot be done apart from mankind, for one's own Tao is expressed through right relationships with others, especially the "five relationships." Virtue leads one to be able to take responsibility in society.*

From *The Heart of Confucius: Interpretations of Genuine Living and Great Wisdom*
Archie Bahm

PERSONAL SOURCE OF SOCIAL HARMONY

What Nature provides is called "one's own nature." Developing in accordance with one's own nature is called "the way of self-realization." Proper pursuit of the way of self-realization is called "maturation."

Archie Bahm, *The Heart of Confucius: Interpretations of Genuine Living and Great Wisdom* (New York: Harper & Row, 1971), pp. 69–71, 78–79, 92–95. Notes omitted. Reprinted by permission of John Westherhill, Inc.

(7)   This is one of the favourite themes of the *Book of Change*, namely, the importance of timeliness. A small effort at the right time will win for us more benefit than a gigantic effort at the wrong time.
(8)   We must expect some trouble, but perhaps not very serious and not likely to endure.

One's own nature cannot be disowned. If it could be disowned, it would not be one's own nature. Hence, a wise man pays attention to it and is concerned about it, even when it is not apparent and when it does not call attention to itself.

One's external appearance is nothing more than an expression of his invisible interior, and one's outward manifestation reveals only what is inside. Therefore the wise man is concerned about his own self.

Being unconcerned about [attitudes toward others and by others involving] feeling pleased, angered, grieved, or joyful is called "one's genuine personal nature." Being concerned [about such attitudes], each in its appropriate way, is called "one's genuine social nature."

This "genuine personal nature" is the primary source from which all that is social develops. This "genuine social nature" is the means whereby everyone obtains happiness.

When our "genuine personal nature" and "genuine social nature" mutually supplement each other perpetually, then conditions everywhere remain wholesome, and everything thrives and prospers. . . .

NATURE'S WAY IS SELF-CORRECTING

Nature's way is not something apart from men. When a man pursues a way which separates him from men, it is not Nature's way.

In the *Book of Verses* it is written: "When one molds an axe handle, his pattern is not far away." The model for the handle is in the hand which grasps it, [even though] when we compare them, they appear different. So likewise, the wise man influences men by appealing to their natures. When they revert [to nature's way], he stops.

When one develops his nature most fully, he finds that the principles of fidelity and mutuality are not something apart from his nature. Whatever you do not want done to you, do not do to others.

SOCIAL RELATIONSHIPS

The nature of social [i.e., mutual] relationships may be illustrated by five [social relationships], and the traits needed to fulfill them [may be summarized as] three.

The relationships are those 1) between sovereign and subject, 2) between father and son, 3) between husband and wife, 4) between elder brother and younger brother, and 5) between friend and friend associating as equals. These five exemplify the nature of all social relationships.

The three traits—concern *(chih)*, good will *(jen)*, and conscientiousness *(yung)*—are required in all social relationships. In effect, the way in which these [three] traits function is unitary.

Some persons seem born with social aptitudes. Some acquire them by learning from teachers. And some develop them through trial-and-error experiences. But no matter how obtained, they operate in the same way.

Some persons express their concern for others spontaneously, some by calculating the rewards in prospect, and some by reluctantly forcing themselves. But when concern [and good will and conscientiousness] for others is expressed, then [regardless of whether they are expressed spontaneously, calculatingly, or reluctantly] the results are the same.

To be fond of learning is close to having wisdom (chih). To try hard is close to having good will (jen). To have feelings of guilt contributes to conscientiousness (yung).

When a person understands these traits, then he knows how to develop his character. When he knows how to develop his character, then he knows how to guide others. When he knows how to guide others, then he knows how to govern the whole country, including its states and communities.

THE BOOK OF THE WAY
AND HOW TO LIVE IT

In this translation of the Tao te ching, Tao *is translated as the Way. But we see that the constant or universal Tao cannot be given a meaningful name, for it is before all beginnings. We see too that all comparisons, preferring one thing to another, are ridiculous before it, for it is better characterized by emptiness and nongrasping. The person close to the Tao lives in that same manner. So does the ruler who keeps his people from making comparisons which would give rise to dissatisfaction, and otherwise seeks not to interfere with the course of nature in his state. The Way is spoken of in paradoxical language to indicate its subtle, indirect, yet irresistible power: it is "empty," "a valley," "darkly visible." Notice also it is called the "mysterious female"; its way of producing the myriad things is like giving birth.*

From *Lao Tzu: Tao Te Ching*
D.C. Lau

I

    1   The way that can be spoken of
      Is not the constant way;

D.C. Lau, trans., *Lao Tzu: Tao Te Ching.* (Harmondsworth, Middlesex, England: Penguin Books, 1963), pp. 57–66. Reprinted by permission of the publisher. Copyright 1963 by D.C. Lau. Notes omitted.

The name that can be named
Is not the constant name.
2 The nameless was the beginning of heaven and
    earth;
The named was the mother of the myriad creatures.
3 Hence always rid yourself of desires in order to
    observe its secrets;
But always allow yourself to have desires in order
    to observe its manifestations.
3a These two are the same
But diverge in name as they issue forth.
Being the same they are called mysteries,
Mystery upon mystery—
The gateway of the manifold secrets.

II

4 The whole world recognizes the beautiful as the
beautiful, yet this is only the ugly; the whole world
recognizes the good as the good, yet this is only the
bad.
5 Thus Something and Nothing produce each other;
The difficult and the easy complement each other;
The long and the short off-set each other;
The high and the low incline towards each other;
Note and sound harmonize with each other;
Before and after follow each other.
6 Therefore the sage keeps to the deed that consists
in taking no action and practises the teaching that
uses no words.
7 The myriad creatures rise from it yet it claims no
    authority;
It gives them life yet claims no possession;
It benefits them yet exacts no gratitude;
It accomplishes its tasks yet lays claim to no merit.
7a It is because it lays claim to no merit
That its merit never deserts it.

III

8 Not to honour men of worth will keep the people
from contention; not to value goods which are hard
to come by will keep them from theft; not to display

what is desirable will keep them from being unsettled of mind.

9 Therefore in governing the people, the sage empties their minds but fills their bellies, weakens their wills but strengthens their bones. He always keeps them innocent of knowledge and free from desire, and ensures that the clever never dare to act.

10 Do that which consists in taking no action, and order will prevail.

IV

11 The way is empty, yet use will not drain it.
   Deep, it is like the ancestor of the myriad creatures.

12 Blunt the sharpness;
   Untangle the knots;
   Soften the glare;
   Let your wheels move only along old ruts.

13 Darkly visible, it only seems as if it were there.
   I know not whose son it is.
   It images the forefather of God.

V

14 Heaven and earth are ruthless, and treat the myriad creatures as straw dogs; the sage is ruthless, and treats the people as straw dogs.

15 Is not the space between heaven and earth like a bellows?
   It is empty without being exhausted:
   The more it works the more comes out.

16 Much speech leads inevitably to silence.
   Better to hold fast to the void.

VI

17 The spirit of the valley never dies.
   This is called the mysterious female.
   The gateway of the mysterious female
   Is called the root of heaven and earth.

Dimly visible, it seems as if it were there,
Yet use will never drain it.

VII

18 Heaven and earth are enduring. The reason why
heaven and earth can be enduring is that they do not
give themselves life. Hence they are able to be long-
lived.
19 Therefore the sage puts his person last and it comes
first,
Treats it as extraneous to himself and it is preserved.
19a Is it not because he is without thought of self that he
is able to accomplish his private ends?

VIII

20 Highest good is like water. Because water excels in
benefiting the myriad creatures without contending
with them and settles where none would like to be,
it comes close to the way.
21 In a home it is the site that matters;
In quality of mind it is depth that matters;
In an ally it is benevolence that matters;
In speech it is good faith that matters;
In government it is order that matters;
In affairs it is ability that matters;
In action it is timeliness that matters.
22 It is because it does not contend that it is never at fault.

IX

23 Rather than fill it to the brim by keeping it upright
Better to have stopped in time;
Hammer it to a point
And the sharpness cannot be preserved for ever;
There may be gold and jade to fill a hall
But there is none who can keep them.
To be overbearing when one has wealth and
position

Is to bring calamity upon oneself.
To retire when the task is accomplished
Is the way of heaven.

X

24　When carrying on your head your perplexed bodily
　　　soul can you embrace in your arms the One
　　And not let go?
　　In concentrating your breath can you become as
　　　supple
　　As a babe?
　　Can you polish your mysterious mirror
　　And leave no blemish?
　　Can you love the people and govern the state
　　Without resorting to action?
　　When the gates of heaven open and shut
　　Are you capable of keeping to the role of the female?
　　When your discernment penetrates the four quarters
　　Are you capable of not knowing anything?
25　It gives them life and rears them.
26　It gives them life yet claims no possession;
　　It benefits them yet claims no gratitude;
　　It is the steward yet exercises no authority.
　　Such is called the mysterious virtue.

THE EIGHT IMMORTALS

The Taoist tradition, exalting romantic feeling and transcendence of reason, went far beyond the mystical naturalism of the Tao te ching. *It ended up with lore about yogic and mystical techniques for becoming one with the Tao and so immortal. A numerous troupe of colorful gods—all of whom had once been human but had attained immortality, and with it fairy-tale powers—frolicked and reverberated in its popular consciousness. Sovereign over the gods and immortals was the Jade Emperor, King of the heavenly court and identified with the Pole Star. But few Taoist figures were more popular than the "Eight Immortals," the subjects of much Chinese art and countless tales. The following traditional account of them gives something of the flavor of this side of popular Taoism.*

From *Encyclopedia of Chinese Symbolism and Art Motives*

C.A.S. Williams

The Eight Immortals of Taoism are described as follows:

1. Chung-li Ch'üan, the Chief of the Eight Immortals, is said to have lived under the Chou dynasty, 1122–249 B.C., and to have obtained the secrets of the elixir of life, and the powder of transmutation. He is generally depicted as a fat man with a bare belly, sometimes holding a peach in his hand, and always grasping his emblem, a fan, with which he is believed to revive the souls of the dead. "Fairylike stories say he married a young and beautiful wife, and retired to his native place to lead the life of a philosopher. One day walking in meditation in the country, he noticed a young woman in deep mourning, sitting near a grave and fanning the freshly upturned soil. When asked the reason, she said that her late husband implored her not to remarry until the soil on his grave dried. Having found an admirer, she wanted the grave to be dry as soon as possible, and was assisting in carrying off the moisture by fanning it. Chung-li Ch'üan offered her his help. Taking her fan, he invoked spirits to his aid, struck the tomb with the fan, and it became absolutely dry. The widow thanked him gaily, and walked away, leaving her fan, which Chung-li Ch'üan kept. When his young wife saw the fan, she wanted to know whence it came. On hearing the story she became very indignant, protesting that she would never behave so, and that the widow must be a monster of insensibility. These words gave the magician an idea to test her feelings. With the aid of powerful spells he pretended to be dead, at the same time assuming the shape of a handsome young man, and making love to the supposed widow, who in a few days agreed to marry him. The young man said to his betrothed that he needed the brain of her late husband to make a powerful potion, and the widow opened the coffin to comply with her lover's request. To her horror her former husband suddenly came to life, while her admirer disappeared into thin air. Unable to survive her shame, she hung herself, while Chung-li Ch'üan set the house on fire, taking out of it only the fan and the sacred book called Tao-teh King" [Tao te ching].

2. Chang Kuo-lao, 7th and 8th century A.D., a recluse who had supernatural powers of magic, such as rendering himself invisible, etc. He

C.A.S. Williams, *Encylopedia of Chinese Symbolism and Art Motives* (New York: The Julian Press, 1960), pp. 150–54. Reprinted by permission of the publisher.

used to be accompanied by a white mule, which carried him immense distances, and, when not required, was folded up and put away in his wallet; when he wished to resume his travels he squirted some water upon the wallet and the beast at once appeared; he generally rode the animal backwards. His emblem is the *Yü Ku*, a kind of musical instrument in the shape of a bamboo tube or drum with two rods to beat it. The Emperor Ming Huang wished to attach him to his court, but Chang Kuo could not give up his wandering life. On the second summons from court he disappeared and entered on immortality without suffering bodily dissolution.

3. Lü Tung-pin, *circa* A.D. 750, a scholar and recluse who learnt the secrets of Taoism from Chung-li Ch'üan, the Chief of the Eight Immortals, and attained to immortality at the age of 50. He is the patron saint of the barbers, and is also worshipped by the sick. In his right hand he holds a Taoist fly-brush, and his emblem, a sword, is generally slung across his back. He was exposed to a series of temptations, ten in number, and having overcome them, was invested with a sword of supernatural power, with which he traversed the earth, slaying dragons, and ridding the world of various forms of evil for upwards of 400 years.

4. Ts'ao Kuo-chiu, said to be the son of Ts'ao Pin, A.D. 930–999, a military commander, and brother of the Empress Ts'ao Hou of the Sung dynasty. He wears a court head-dress and official robes, and his emblem is a pair of castanets, which he holds in one hand. He is a patron saint of the theatrical profession. The castanets are said to be derived from the court tablet, authorising free access to the palace, to which he was entitled owing to his birth.

5. Li T'ieh-kuai is represented as a beggar leaning on an iron staff, for the following reason. He attained so much proficiency in magic during his life on earth that he was frequently summoned to the presence of Laocius in the celestial regions. In such cases he went there in spirit, leaving his body, apparently dead, in charge of his disciple. Once, when he was absent longer than usual, his disciple, who was called away to his mother's bed of sickness, decided that his master was really dead this time; so he burned the body and went home. When Li T'ieh-kuai returned from the Hills of Longevity, he discovered that he had no body into which to enter. Hastily he cast around for somebody recently dead, but all he could find was the body of a lame beggar in a nearby wood. He entered into it, and is always represented as a beggar with an iron crutch and a pilgrim's gourd from which a scroll is escaping, emblematic of his power to set his spirit free from the body. His emblem is the pilgrim's gourd, and he is sometimes represented standing on a crab or accompanied by a deer.

6. Han Hsiang-tzŭ, nephew of Han Yü, a famous scholar who lived about A.D. 820. He is credited with the power of making flowers grow and blossom instantaneously. He was a favourite pupil of Lü Tung-pin, who carried him to the supernatural peach-tree, from which he fell and be-

came immortal. His emblem is the flute, and he is the patron of musicians. He wandered in the country, playing his flute and attracting birds and even beasts of prey by the sweet sounds. He did not know the value of money, and, if given any, used to scatter it about on the ground.

7. Lan Ts'ai-ho. "Generally regarded as a woman and represented as dressed in a blue gown, with one foot shod and the other bare, waving a wand as she wanders begging through the streets." She continually chanted a doggerel verse denouncing this fleeting life and its delusive pleasures. Her emblem is the flower-basket which she carries, and she is the patron saint of the florists.

8. Ho Hsien-ku, 7th century A.D. Daughter of a shopkeeper of Ling-ling, Hunan. Having eaten of the supernatural peach, she became a fairy. She used to wander alone in the hills, and lived on powdered mother-of-pearl and moonbeams, which diet produced immortality. Once she got lost in the woods and was in great danger from a malignant demon; but Lü Tung-pin appeared at the critical moment and saved her, using his magic sword. She disappeared when summoned to the court of the Empress Wu, A.D. 625–705. Her emblem is the lotus, which she carries in her hand. Sometimes she is represented poised on a floating petal of the lotus, with a fly-whisk in her hand. She assists in house management.

THE JADE EMPEROR'S BIRTHDAY

Religious Taoism has its temples, monasteries, priests, and festivals replete with the vivid and fantastic quality one would expect from such a tradition. The following passage, by a writer of Russian exile background who lived in China in the 1920s and 1930s and who visited many Taoist centers, describes the celebration in a monastery of an important Taoist holiday, the birthday of the Jade Emperor, sovereign of heaven. Notice that both the atmosphere and clientele suggest a counterbalance to Confucian propriety.

From *The Monastery of Jade Mountain*
Peter Goullart

It was already dark when Abbot Lichun called for us and led us to the top of the monastery to enable us to see the climax of the festival.

Peter Goullart, *The Monastery of Jade Mountain* (London: John Murray, 1961), pp. 79–82. Reprinted by permission of the publisher.

From the little upper terrace it looked as if the whole immense structure was on fire. Long tongues of flame shot from the great incense burners in front of the Jade Emperor's Hall as more and more incense sticks and joss paper were thrown in by hundreds of worshippers. Masses of paper money and paper representations of earthly objects, offerings for the gods and the departed, were burning in huge heaps, sending sparks into the night sky, and smoke rose in dense columns. There was the sound of drums and bells and the deafening hubbub of milling crowds. Thousands of red candles burned in the halls and galleries before the different deities, and the waves of heat and the smell of incense were carried upwards on the breeze. Priests in red vestments began a slow dance on the terrace of the main hall, each holding a red paper lantern in the shape of a lotus flower. There was a clashing of cymbals, a wail of trumpets and flutes and the tinkling of innumerable little bells.

We went down to join the religious procession which was slowly forming around the dancing monks. Down the galleries it started and through lesser courtyards; rich and poor, peasants and city dwellers all followed in one happy, excited crowd, some men playing flutes, others clashing cymbals or strumming on *pipas*. As there was no lighting, most people carried candles and lanterns. The monks stopped now and then before bevies of gods and chanted a short litany followed by a ritual dance. Country-folk gaped good-naturedly at elegantly dressed and be-jewelled Shanghai ladies and whispered to each other on seeing smartly clad men and well-groomed monks accompanying them. There was no malice in the looks of the simple people; only a naïve admiration for the beautiful women and handsome men who made the occasion of the gay festival also one for a few amours on the side. These provided an endless and delicious topic for gossip when the simple folk returned to their villages and drab lives. Everybody could enjoy himself according to his lights, provided he kept within the well-defined standard of behaviour and etiquette.

The procession now turned down into the subterranean passages under the monastery. It was dark and suffocatingly hot here from so many burning candles, but the people happily jostled along together. Unescorted ladies got a few winks from some braves in smart hats but they did not seem to mind, and some merry widows purposely walked close to Koueifo and myself, pressing themselves close against us in the recesses of the cave. Now and then, I noticed, some couples quietly drifted into narrow and unlighted branch passages. Soon we emerged on to an open platform outside the monastery, where the priests sang and danced a short compline and then dispersed.

We were asked to join in the dinner which was provided for the pilgrims and guests staying at the Upper Tower of Literature. It was a sumptuous feast as befitted the dignity of a reception at the Jade Emperor's Court. Of course, the ingredients were all donations from the villagers, pooled together, and the wine, decanted from a battery of jars standing by the wall, flowed freely.

Due to a lack of tables and space, we were seated together with local farmers and rubbed elbows with people sitting at surrounding tables. There was little room, but everybody was in good humour and nobody complained. There were dishes of live and cooked shrimps, turtles and eels roasted with garlic and ham, chickens and ducks and traditional roast pork. In this Chengyi Taoistic establishment there was no ban on meat and wine and its superb chefs utilized everything which was good to eat or to drink.

Koueifo and I loved to eat together with simple farmers, as did most of the well-born Chinese, and to eat here, together with the peasants of the Soochow countryside, was an honour and a privilege for they were the true aristocracy of the country. Here was the seat of real Chinese civilization and culture and it was these same people who had produced the men who had ascended high in the Imperial Government, during so many centuries, and returned to the soil to surrender their rank and power in exchange for the peace and beauty of village life. Not a mile away was an estate where a retired Prime Minister of China was living in rural simplicity.

There was great hilarity at the dinner-table and we were toasted and urged to drink not only by our immediate neighbours but also by men and women at other tables. Some succulent pieces of a duck or chicken were placed in our bowls and there was much laughter and talk in the sonorous dialect of the place. It sounded to me like music to hear these people speak so softly and melodiously. The decorum and propriety of their behaviour was so correct and yet so free and natural that nothing better could be observed in any of Shanghai's drawing-rooms.

There was a noise of similar festivities coming from other sections of the monastery. The crops had been bountiful and the weather good. All these people were gathered not to pray to the gods for any favour but in gratitude for the continued flow of the good things of life, for the virility of their lovers and the apparent constancy of their husbands, the fruitfulness of their wives and the goodly number of their offspring. The concubines thanked the gods for the possibility of a child from their old and seemingly sterile masters, a blessing which might be realized after their visit to the monastery. The sing-song girls were grateful for the secrets of a new bliss which they would carry to their jaded patrons.

In this upsurge of joy and content, amidst these simple pleasures of eating and drinking, I felt that all sense of time and reality had disappeared. I looked at Abbot Lichun, he appeared carefree and gay and his face was pink. Lifting his cup he toasted all of us.

'Drink, drink!' he exclaimed. 'A happy moment of life, like tonight, which may never be recaptured again, is pure meditation according to our Taoistic concept,' and he emptied the cup. We all followed suit.

After the tables had been cleared, some people produced mahjongg chips and Koueifo joined a group. I retired, but outside the gambling, music and laughter continued until the small hours.

ANCESTRISM

This passage describes some customs regarding death and ancestors observed by an anthropologist studying a Chinese village that goes under the name of West Town. Note the intimate involvement of ancestrism with daily and family life.

From *Under the Ancestor's Shadow*
Francis L.K. Hsu

ANCESTOR FESTIVALS

Each household has a family shrine. The shrine is situated in the central portion of the second floor of the west wing of the home. It is installed on the ground floor only when the house is a one-story structure. Occasionally the shrine is for ancestors only, but more often it houses a number of popular gods.

Ancestors are represented in such a shrine either on a large scroll or on separate tablets. The scroll is a large sheet of mounted paper containing names, sex, and titles of the ancestors who are (theoretically) within *wu fu,* or five degrees of mourning. As mentioned in Chapter II, this rule is not always observed. On the scroll of a poor and illiterate Ch family only a small number of the ancestors were represented, because "the old scroll was destroyed by fire and these are the only ones we can remember." On the scroll of a Y family many ancestors beyond the five degrees were represented, because they "have not had another scroll made yet." The tablets are made of wood, but if there is no time to have one made, a paper one will be substituted.

The popular gods in all family shrines are three: *Kuan Kung* (the warrior from Three Kingdoms), Confucius, and one or more Buddhas. A fourth popular figure is the Goddess of Mercy or Fertility. As a rule these gods are represented by images. In addition, there are often other spiritual figures in family shrines which the family members cannot identify. In at least one shrine there was a large tablet for Confucius as

Francis L.K. Hsu, *Under the Ancestors' Shadow* (Stanford: Stanford University Press, 1967), pp. 182–84, 186–88. Reprinted by permission of the publisher.

well as his supposed image. Before the shrine is an offering table, on which there are two incense burners, one for ancestors and one for the gods, two candlesticks, and a flower vase or two. At the foot of the table are two round straw cushions for the kneeling worshiper.

Incense is offered in each burner daily, usually by a woman of the house. This act is performed every morning just before breakfast. There is no offering of food except on occasions of marriage, birth, division of the family, and during the ancestor festival.

The festival occurs around the 15th of the Seventh Moon, but in effect it begins on the 1st of the month and ends on the 16th. On the 1st of the month the portion of the house containing the shrine is cleared of non-essential articles and cleaned. Offerings of the following items are made: fruit, preserves, candies, two or more bowls containing growing rice sprouts, one or more dishes containing fragrant wood, some lotus or other flowers in the vase, and a number of dishes or bowls of cooked food. Red candles are inserted in the candlesticks. A new cloth, as well as a front cover, is placed on the offering table. If the tablets are encased, their covers are removed. The offerings and arrangements may be made by both men and women. The offerings may be replaced with fresh ones from time to time throughout the fifteen days.

If the family can afford it, as many West Town families can, one or more priests are invited to read scriptures and perform certain rituals before the shrine during this period. Such priests may be hired for one day or for several days, depending on how much the family is willing to spend. The greater the number of priests and the longer they are utilized, the more beneficial it will be for the dead and for the living. If only one priest is hired, he sits on a stool at the right of the offering table. His equipment consists of a wooden "fish," a pair of cymbals, many volumes of scriptures, the family's complete genealogical record, as well as the names and birthdays of all its living members. These data are written on a long folder of yellow paper. The priest recites the scriptures and performs all the pertinent rites continuously for the entire period of his employment, stopping only for meals and opium, but uninterrupted by the family's work on the shrine.

The function of the priest in connection with the dead ancestors was clear to all informants: to report the names of the dead to superior deities and to uplift them by scripture reading so that they will be able to proceed to the Western Heaven of Happiness as soon as possible. The reason for a complete list of the names of the family's living members is not clear to all. Some insist that it is to bless the living; others say that it will make the dead happier by showing them what worthy descendants they have. . . .

. . . When the offerings and homage at the family altar terminates, the same dishes are taken by a male member of the household (or branch of the household) to the clan temple. There the food is briefly offered at the main altar, and the male who delivers it kowtows a number of times. After this, the offering food is taken back to the house, and all members of the household come together to feast on it. If it is not enough for everyone, more food will be added until all are satisfied. Male and female members of the household eat at the same table.

During the day incense sticks are inserted at numerous places in the family home: on the lintels of all portals, special parts of the walls, and in many sections of the courtyard. During the ceremony at the family altar practically equal amounts of homage are given to ancestors and to the gods beside them. In some families the offering dishes are placed between the two groups. In others, identical offerings are placed before each group. In some families, all kowtows are intended to be shared by both; in others, all members prostrate themselves twice, once before each group.

After the meal the *shu pao* (burning the bags) ceremony begins. Each bag contains a quantity of silver ingots and bears the names of a male ancestor and his wife, of the descendants who are providing the bag for them, and the date on which this is burned, together with a brief plea entreating the ancestors to accept it. . . .

Shortly after the household ceremony and sometimes while it is still going on, the worship in the clan temples begins. Families who have no clan temples omit this ceremony; those who have them, never fail to perform it. Although this is more formal than the worship at the family altar, the degree of formality varies from clan to clan.

CH'AN

The "meditation" school of Buddhism known as Ch'an in China and Zen in Japan is famous for its pithy anecdotes of famous masters. Often they are examples of "direct pointing"—a passing of Zen awakening to a disciple by means of illogicality, shock, or illustration of the Buddha-nature's reality everywhere beyond all concepts. Here are some examples. The fact that Ch'an is a Buddhism deeply influenced by Taoism is suggested by the use of the word Tao. The stories are from the "Golden Age" of Ch'an in China, the T'ang dynasty (618–907 A.D.). The hossu *is a whisk carried by priests as a symbol of authority.*

From *Manual of Zen Buddhism*
D.T. Suzuki

A monk asked: "What is the meaning of the First Patriarch's coming from the West?"

D.T. Suzuki, *Manual of Zen Buddhism* (New York: Grove Press, 1960), pp. 106–7, 110–12. Reprinted by permission of Grove Press, Inc. All rights reserved.

Master: "Ask the post over there."

Monk: "I do not understand you."

Master: "I do not either, any more than you."

Ta-tien asked: "According to an ancient sage it is a dualism to take the Tao either as existing or as not-existing. Please tell me how to remove this obstruction."

"Not a thing here, and what do you wish to remove?"

Shih-t'ou turned about and demanded: "Do away with your throat and lips, and let me see what you can say."

Said Ta-tien, "No such things have I."

"If so, you may enter the gate."

Tao-wu asked: "What is the ultimate teaching of Buddhism?"

"You won't understand it until you have it."

"Is there anything over and above it whereby one may have a new turn?"

"Boundlessly expands the sky and nothing obstructs the white clouds from freely flying about."

"What is Zen?" asked a monk.

"Brick and stone."

"What is the Tao?"

"A block of wood." . . .

. . . P'ang the lay-disciple asked one day when Ma-tsu appeared in the pulpit: "Here is the Original Body altogether unbedimmed! Raise your eyes to it!" Ma-tsu looked straight downward. Said P'ang, "How beautifully the master plays on the first-class stringless lute!" The master looked straight up. P'ang made a bow, and the master returned to his own room. P'ang followed him and said, "A while ago you made a fool of yourself, did you not?"

Someone asked: "What is the Buddha?"

"Mind is the Buddha, and there's no other."

A monk asked: "Without resorting to the four statements and an endless series of negations, can you tell me straightway what is the idea of our Patriarch's coming from the West?"

The master said: "I don't feel like answering it today. You go to the Western Hall and ask Shih-tsang about it."

The monk went to the Western Hall and saw the priest, who pointing at his head with a finger said, "My head aches today and I am unable to explain it to you today. I advise you to go to Brother Hai."

The monk now called on Hai, and Hai said: "As to that I do not understand."

The monk finally returned to the master and told him about his adventure. Said the master: "Tsang's head is black while Hai's is white."

A monk asked: "Why do you teach that Mind is no other than Buddha?"

"In order to make a child stop its crying."

"When the crying is stopped, what would you say?"

"Neither Mind nor Buddha."

"What teaching would you give to him who is not in these two groups?"

"I will say, 'It is not a something.' "

"If you unexpectedly interview a person who is in it what would you do?" finally, asked the monk.

"I will let him realize the great Tao."

The master asked Pai-chang, one of his chief disciples: "How would you teach others?"

Pai-chang raised his *hossu*.

The master remarked, "Is that all? No other way?"

Pai-chang threw the *hossu* down.

A monk asked: "How does a man set himself in harmony with the Tao?"

"I am already out of harmony."

Tan-yuan, one of Ma-tsu's personal disciples, came back from his pilgrimage. When he saw the master, he drew a circle on the floor and after making bows stood on it facing the master. Said Ma-tsu: "So you wish to become a Buddha?"

The monk said: "I do not know the art of putting my own eyes out of focus."

"I am not your equal."

The monk had no answer.

One day in the first month of the fourth year of Chen-yuan (788). while walking in the woods at Shih-men Shan, Ma-tsu noticed a cave with a flat floor. He said to his attendant monk, "My body subject to decomposition will return to earth here in the month to come." On the fourth of the second month, he was indisposed as he predicted, and after a bath he sat cross-legged and passed away.

THE SACRIFICE TO HEAVEN

The Chinese emperor's supreme religious rite was the sacrifice to heaven he performed at the great Altar of Heaven in Peking in the middle of the night at the winter solstice. In theory, only the emperor could worship heaven and earth, the ultimate ancestors, directly. All others could worship only their own ancestors and the gods and Buddhas who had once been human. This passage describes the worship of heaven toward the end of the Manchu or Ch'ing dynasty (1644–1911) at its period of greatest development; the sacrifice has not been performed since the end of that dynasty marked the end of imperial China.

From *Folkways in China*

Lewis Hodous

Outside of the Tartar city of Peking in the Chinese city is situated a large park in which stands the altar of Heaven. The enclosure has an area of over a square mile and consists of an outer court and an inner court shaded by old cypress trees. The whole is surrounded by a wall which is curved at the north end in the same manner as the walls around graves.

The round mound or the altar of Heaven is built of white marble and consists of three concentric terraces approached by stairs of nine steps to each terrace from the four points of the compass. The top terrace is 90 feet in diameter, the second terrace is 150 feet, and the lower terrace is 210 feet. The top terrace has a circular stone in the centre. In the first circle are nine stones, then eighteen. There are nine such circles. The outermost circle contains eighty-one stones. The terraces and stairs are flanked by carved balustrades. In the sides of the terraces there are 360 panels. These measurements are multiples of the odd numbers from one to nine, which symbolize Heaven.

The circular court about the altar, 335 feet in diameter, is surrounded by a low wall covered with blue tiles. At each cardinal point of the compass there is an opening with three doors. The circular court is surrounded by a square court 549 feet on each side. In the south-west corner of this court stood three masts with lanterns. The south-east corner is occupied by a large furnace of green tiles in which the bullock was burned. Nearby are eight iron braziers for burning the offerings of silk.

North of the altar a small round building with a conical roof of blue tiles contains the tablets and tabernacles of Shangti and the ancestors. On one side among the trees stands a group of buildings employed

Lewis Hodous, *Folkways in China* (London: Arthus Probsthain, 1929), pp. 220–25, 235. Reprinted by permission of the publisher.

to store the sacrificial implements. On the other side is the hall of abstinence in which the emperor kept vigil before the great sacrifice. Outside of the south gate of the square court on the east side was the place of the dressing tent of the emperor. It was provided with a fireplace for the purpose of warming the tent.

On the north side of the altar is a covered circular building on a foundation of three circular terraces. This is often wrongly called the temple of Heaven. It was the temple in which the emperor prayed for a good year.

All the rites and ceremonies of State of the last dynasty were in charge of the Board of Rites. It had two presidents, one Manchu and one Chinese, and four vice-presidents, two Manchus and two Chinese, and numerous petty officials. The sacrifice to Heaven was in charge of the Court of Supreme Imperial Sacrifices. This court had two presidents, one Manchu and one Chinese, and two vice-presidents, one Manchu and one Chinese, and a large number of under-officials and secretaries. It looked after all the sacrifices offered by the emperor, or his proxies.

In sacrifices of the first class the one who officiated and his assistants purified themselves for three days. For a sacrifice of the second class they purified themselves for two days. Accordingly three days before the sacrifice early in the morning the Court of Sacrificial Worship, being a department of the Court of Supreme Imperial Sacrifices, brought the abstinence tablet to the emperor. This tablet was two inches long and one inch wide covered with yellow paper. It had inscribed upon it in Chinese and Manchu the day of abstinence. It was worn on the breast. The Emperor issued a proclamation to all his officials regarding the practice of abstinence as follows: "In a certain year, month, day, at the winter solstice, I shall sacrifice to Shangti of August Heaven at the round mound. Now all officials purify your heart, cleanse your desires. Let all exalt their duty. Should anyone be disrespectful the dynasty has a fixed punishment. Be respectful. Do not be remiss." This proclamation was posted in the main hall of the yamens. All officials of the seventh rank and above practised abstinence in their official residences.

Those who practised abstinence did not occupy themselves with public affairs, nor with criminal cases. They did not attend banquets and abstained from music, sexual intercourse, wine, and vegetables with a strong odour such as onions. They did not visit the sick, nor did they go to the tombs of their ancestors, nor did they assist in the sacrifice to the dead or the gods. On the evening before the sacrifice they took a bath.

Five days before the sacrifice a prince of the blood examined the sacrificial victims and pronounced them perfect. Two days before the sacrifice the animals were inspected again by the president of the Board of Rites.

Two days before the great ceremony the prayer offered to Heaven at the sacrifice was written on a tablet. Before dawn the reader of the sacrificial prayer brought a tablet on which the prayer was to be written to the emperor's Privy Council and handed it to the imperial secretaries. These officials placed the tablet in a purified room and wrote the prayer on it. The prayer was then deposited on a yellow table in the executive mansion. The grand secretary came to the table, examined the prayer and affixed the imperial name. The next day the prayer tablet was given to the one who read the prayer.

One day before the sacrifice from 11 p.m. to 1 a.m. the animals were killed and the blood was buried. On the same day the altar of Heaven was swept and the places were arranged for the tablet of Shangti on the north side of the highest terrace facing the south. The places for the tablets of T'ai Tsu (1616–26), Shih Tsu (1644–61), Shih Tsung (1723–35), Jen Tsung (1796–1820), Wen Tsung (1851–61), were arranged on the east side of the terrace and the places for the tablets of T'ai Tsung (1627–43), Sheng Tsu (1662–1722), Kao Tsung (1736–95), Hsüan Tsung (1821–50), Mu Tsung (1862–74), on the west side.

On the second terrace places were arranged for the tablets of the sun, moon, the seven stars of the dipper, the five planets, the twenty-eight constellations, the signs of the zodiac, the god of the clouds, the god of rain, the god of wind, and the god of thunder. The various receptacles for the offerings were put before the places of the tablets at the same time.

The time for the imperial cavalcade to go to the altar was fixed by the Imperial Board of Astronomy. It took place the day before the great sacrifice. The people were duly warned to keep off the road by which the procession passed. This procession was a magnificent affair, an epitome of the mythology and religious history of the Chinese people. The centre figure was the emperor. There were guards, musicians, marshals, flags with embroidered dragons, with the sun and moon, clouds, thunder, wind, rain, the banners of the twenty-eight constellations borne by twenty-eight men; there were the flags of the five planets, the flags of the five guardian mountains, the four rivers, the various constellations; there were flags for various birds; there were feathers and plumes, a revelry of colour and beauty. There were large red umbrellas with many folds.

After arrival the emperor examined the altar and the offerings and then retired into the palace of abstinence where he passed the night preparing himself for the great offering.

During the night the president of the Bureau of Sacrificial Offerings with his assistants lit the golden lamp and the candles, piled up the wood and put the ox on it and placed the offerings on the dishes before all the tablets. On the top terrace they placed a table with the prayer-tablet. On another table they put a blue piece of jade and twelve rolls of silk.

The emperor at the sacrifice occupied the south end of the second terrace. The top terrace was occupied by the one who read the prayer, those who offered incense, the silk rolls, cups, the bearers of the cushions on which the emperor knelt, and the censors who observed the ceremony. On the lowest terrace above the steps were the princes from the first to the third order. Below the steps were the princes of the fourth order. Below this terrace were the musical instruments with 180 musicians and 300 posturers and a host of minor officials to the fifth civil rank and the fourth military rank.

On the day of the sacrifice seven quarters before sunrise the prayer-tablet was placed on the altar. The president of the Board of Rites led the presidents of the Board of Sacrificial Worship to the tablets in order to invite the spirits to come into the tablets and partake of the offerings. The marshal of the Equipage Department placed the tablets into the niches prepared for them.

When this was done the emperor was led to his place on the altar and all the officials took their places.

The ceremony began by the emperor washing his hands. The pyre with the victim on it was kindled and the instruments struck up a hymn to invite the gods and spirits to partake of the sacrifice. . . .

. . . While the music was playing the emperor and his assistants at the sacrifice were led opposite the furnace to see the offerings burned up. The herald then announced the ceremony completed.

The music struck up the "Protecting Peace" as follows:—

For Heaven's great blessing I bring solemn offerings.
The flames of the sacrifice ascend and make announcement to Heaven.
Only the Holy One is able to receive the sacrifice.

VI

RICE-GODS AND BUDDHAS: RELIGION IN JAPAN

Japan is a narrow island nation, but few lands display a wider diversity of religion. The country of Mount Fuji and the rising sun has been called a "living laboratory of religion," and indeed it seems that almost every conceivable style of religious life has been found there. Moreover, virtually nothing from the past appears to be lost as new religious manifestations arise in the present. Within a few miles, one can see a Shinto shrine whose deity and rites reflect the world of archaic planters, a dim and numinous Buddhist temple redolent of medieval mysticism, a Christian church, and centers of several new, energetic religious movements derived from nineteenth or twentieth century revelations.

But certain unifying themes do run through this melange, so much in fact that Japanese religion, like Chinese, is from many points of view better seen as a single experience than as a collection of separate "isms."

One theme is shamanistic, charismatic leadership. From time immemorial certain people in Japan have gone into the mountains, or been overtaken by mediumistic trance, to attain super-normal power. Originally these practices were connected with the indigenous gods of the faith which came to be known as Shinto, "the Way of the Gods." To this day, particularly in northern Japan, shamanism is a part of folk religion.

But after the introduction of Buddhism in the sixth century A.D., soon enough shamanism intermingled with that faith in Japan as it had in Tibet and elsewhere. The prevailing forms of Buddhism in early medieval Japan, Shingon and Tendai, were deeply infused with esotericism as in the Himalayas. To become a Buddha was possible in this body, in this lifetime, through the mystical means of chanting, rites, and visualization techniques. In fact, the entire history of Buddhism in Japan coalesces around a few remarkable charismatic figures who were scarcely other than shamans in historical time working through the subtle philosophies of Buddhism, although their styles of Mahayana Buddhism differ greatly. One thinks of men like Kobo Daishi, Dengyo Daishi, Dogen, Honen, Shinran, and Nichiren.

Against this shamanistic background rests a second counterpuntal theme—community. Religious symbols in Japan (as everywhere) have been not only vehicles for the arduous individual spiritual quest, but also emblems of community and family identities, and this function has been immensely important in Japan. There personal identity has always been closely associated with group, whether it be the traditional clan or village, or modern sect or corporation. Groups offering religious identity have been of two types: the "natural" units of village and family sanctified by a traditional relation with a patronal Shinto god or Buddhist temple, and groups based on a self-chosen disciplic relation of individuals with a charismatic leader like the Buddhist saints or the modern founders of new religions.

A third theme, more subjective and harder to define, is a widespread Japanese feeling for the unity of religious experience beneath a wide diversity of forms, with a sense that ultimately religious forms are interchangeable. Exceptions exist of course: the Nichiren lineage in Buddhism has traditionally been more exclusivistic than others, and Japanese Christians have usually not felt able to see their faith as only on the same level as others. But by and large a peculiar sort of religious tolerance is characteristic of Japan. While Japan has frequently been very defensive of Japanese culture as over against foreign, internal pluralism within stylistic limitations honed by the culture as a whole are accepted gladly, and diversity is seen in a relativistic light. This attitude lies behind the fact that little of the religious past has entirely died out, and behind the comfortable symbiosis of Shinto, several strands of Mahayana Buddhism, and new religions. It explains why numerous Japanese do not feel it inappropriate to participate in several religions—even though modern Japan is actually a quite secular nation. It is probably reflected in the tendency of most Japanese not to talk much about religious belief, but to prefer indirect, poetic language.

Pluralism is the most striking theme of Japanese religion—a rich diversity within a small but densely populated and prosperous nation with a strong sense of separate identity.

SHINTO MYTHOLOGY

The oldest extant Japanese book is the Kojiki, *"Record of Ancient Things" (*A.D. *712), and shortly after it came the* Nihongi *or* Nihonshoki,

*"Records of Japan" (A.D. 720). Together these works are the fundamental
source for early Japanese mythology. Put down at the command of the
sovereign, they naturally emphasize the divine descent of the imperial
house and the major noble families associated with the court. But they
also exemplify the main themes of Shinto myth in general—the descent of
sky gods to marry earth goddesses, the agricultural year as a sacred cycle
culminating in the harvest festival, the emperor as a sacred king and
priest. In this passage from the Nihongi, we read the famous story of the
cave-hiding of Amaterasu, a goddess associated with the sun and ancestress of the imperial line. She was celebrating the Harvest Festival (note
the connection with the agricultural year), when her brother Susa no wo,
associated with storms, desecrated the rite. In anger the lovely goddess hid
in a cave, and had to be coaxed out by a conclave of the gods and a
sacred dance by a shamaness-goddess. The mirror mentioned is the one
later given by Amaterasu to her grandson on his descent to earth to found
the Japanese empire; it is still one of the imperial regalia and is said to
be enshrined at the Grand Shrine of Ise, the Shinto "National Cathedral." The story here presented unites several important Shinto themes
and undoubtedly is a ritual paradigm.*

From *Nihongi*

W.G. Aston

After this Sosa no wo no Mikoto's behaviour was exceedingly rude.
In what way? Ama-terasu no Oho-kami had made august rice-fields of
Heavenly narrow rice-fields and Heavenly long rice-fields. Then Sosa
no wo no Mikoto, when the seed was sown in spring, broke down the
divisions between the plots of rice, and in autumn let loose the Heavenly
piebald colts, and made them lie down in the midst of the rice-fields.
Again, when he saw that Ama-terasu no Oho-kami was about to celebrate
the feast of first-fruits, he secretly voided excrement in the New Palace.
Moreover, when he saw that Ama-terasu no Oho-kami was in her sacred
weaving hall, engaged in weaving the garments of the Gods, he flayed
a piebald colt of Heaven, and breaking a hole in the roof-tiles of the hall,
flung it in. Then Ama-terasu no Oho-kami started with alarm, and
wounded herself with the shuttle. Indignant at this, she straightway
entered the Rock-cave of Heaven, and having fastened the Rock-door,

W.G. Aston, trans., *Nihongi* (London: George Allen & Unwin, 1956), pp. 40–45.
First published 1896. Notes omitted. Reprinted by permission of the publisher and of
Charles E. Tuttle Co.

dwelt there in seclusion. Therefore constant darkness prevailed on all sides, and the alternation of night and day was unknown.

The the eighty myriads of Gods met on the bank of the Tranquil River of Heaven, and considered in what manner they should supplicate her. Accordingly Omohi-kane no Kami, with profound device and far-reaching thought, at length gathered long-singing birds of the Eternal Land and made them utter their prolonged cry to one another. Moreover he made Ta-jikara-wo no Kami to stand beside the Rock-door. Then Ame no Koyane no Mikoto, ancestor of the Nakatomi no Muraji, and Futo-dama no Mikoto, ancestor of the Imibe no Obito, dug up a five-hundred branched True Sakaki tree of the Heavenly Mt. Kagu. On its upper branches they hung an august five-hundred string of Yasaka jewels. On the middle branches they hung an eight-hand mirror.

One writing says Ma-futsu no Kagami.

On its lower branches they hung blue soft offerings and white soft offerings. Then they recited their liturgy together.

Moreover Ama no Uzume no Mikoto, ancestress of the Sarume no Kimi, took in her hand a spear wreathed with Eulalia grass, and standing before the door of the Rock-cave of Heaven, skilfully performed a mimic dance. She took, moreover, the true Sakaki tree of the Heavenly Mount Kagu, and made of it a head-dress, she took club-moss and made of it braces, she kindled fires, she placed a tub bottom upwards, and gave forth a divinely-inspired utterance.

Now Ama-terasu no Oho-kami heard this, and said:—"Since I have shut myself up in the Rock-cave, there ought surely to be continual night in the Central Land of fertile reed-plains. How then can Ama no Uzume no Mikoto be so jolly?" So with her august hand, she opened for a narrow space the Rock-door and peeped out. Then Ta-jikara-wo no Kami forthwith took Ama-terasu no Oho-kami by the hand, and led her out. Upon this the Gods Nakatomi no Kami and Imibe no Kami at once drew a limit by means of a bottom-tied rope (*also called a left-hand rope*) and begged her not to return again (into the cave).

MODERN SHINTO WORSHIP

Shinto in Japan is an aggregate of nearly a hundred thousand shrines—shrines large and small, shrines in the countryside, in nearly every village, in all the neighborhoods of towns and cities. The deities within them, whatever their names, are essentially finite guardians of the land around the shrine and the families that dwell on it. Ordinarily, the shrine has a still, solemn atmosphere, suitable for the private prayers of the passersby who continually pause for a moment before the fane with its porch rich in symbolic objects and the heavy closed doors behind which the deity, called a kami, *rests. But from time to time the shrine will be called into vibrant life by a festival or* matsuri. *Then the role of the shrine as the focus of traditional community is underscored. In the passage following, an American scholar describes one of the most conspicuous and important aspects of a festival—carrying the* mikoshi, *or palanquin bearing the* kami *or deity from the shrine through the streets of the city (Tokyo, in this case) around the shrine. This will be done after offerings and prayers have been solemnly presented by the priests in the shrine itself. The shift in mood from the sobriety of that part of the rite to the exuberance of the next is striking, but both parts suggest a divine variation from the pace of ordinary life.*

From *Carrying the Mikoshi: Further Field Notes on the Shrine Festival in Modern Tokyo*
A.W. Sadler

A festival is like a circus that has spilled out over a whole neighborhood; it brings with it the bitter-sweet feeling that no matter where you contrive to be, you are unavoidably missing most of the fun. A festival is a garden of delights, and part of the joy of it is knowing there is just too much joy abroad for any one person to absorb.

But the most conspicuous activity of the festival centers about the excitement of the street procession. For the great mass of people, it is the very heart of the festival. And for the priests, it is the emissary that transports the presence he guards at the sanctuary swiftly through the streets, to gather his people together and bring them to the sanctuary's domain.

As observers try to describe the exuberance of these street processions, the customary line that separates the sociologists from the poets becomes blurred. James Kirkup, for example, says of the festival of *Sanjasama* (in the Asakusa section of Tokyo): "The festive atmosphere takes most of its vigour and beauty from these parades of chanting youths, packed close together in dense masses of hot, sweating, naked humanity as they support on bare arms and shoulders the great weight of these

A.W. Sadler, "Carrying the Mikoshi: Further Field Notes on the Shrine Festival in Modern Tokyo," *Asian Folklore Studies* 31 (1972), pp. 89–93. Reprinted by permission of the author and *Asian Folklore Studies.*

black-lacquered palanquins with their rich ornamentation. The youths appear to be in a kind of trance of manly effort as they hoarsely chant their rhythmical cry of '*Washoi, washoi, washoi.*'[1]" And R. P. Dore writes: "All through the day relays of young men, well primed with rice wine and all wearing a cotton *yukata* of uniform pattern, their faces made up and a towel tied tightly round their foreheads, carried the heavy gilt god-cart on their shoulders, displaying their strength and virtuosity as they careened in a heaving rhythmically shouting mass from one side of the road to the other, narrowly missing trams and fences and deriving from their vociferous team action the exhilaration of a rugby scrum or of a bayonet charge.[2]" That is the exterior, the visible source of the excitement of the procession: the "trance of manly effort" of the young men carrying the *mikoshi*, the divine palanquin (the *Jinja Honcho*, the federated association of shrines, prefers that term) or (less elegantly) the "god-cart."

But there is also a less visible, an "interior" reason for excitement, better understood and remembered by the priest: "The essence of the procession . . . is the movement of the *kami* through the parish. This is accompanied by a symbolic transfer of the *kami* from the inner sanctuary to an ornate and gilded sacred palanquin (*mikoshi*), which becomes temporarily the abode of the *kami*.[3] This explanation was offered by a member of the faculty of Kokugakuin University, where young men are trained for the shrine priesthood: central to the procession, he says, and "in fact, the only reason for there being a procession, is the sacred palanquin. . . ."[4] Thanks to the *mikoshi*, the *kami* is able "to pass through the parish and bless the homes of the faithful."[5]

This "interior" reason for the excitement of the festival procession (this "theology" of the procession, I suppose we might say) is understood by the elders, as well as the priests; a recent traveler writes: "The palanquin advanced, now slowly, now quickly, lunging and swerving to right or left, or turning completely in its tracks, or sometimes spinning like a top. 'It goes where the gods want it to,' an old man explained to me."[6]

With the coming of autumn, the labyrinthine streets of old Tokyo are noisy with these processions. One simply ventures out onto the streets on a Saturday afternoon or Sunday, and the sound of distant drums and shouting is in the air. When I arrived in Tokyo some years ago (in Sep-

[1] James Kirkup, *Tokyo* (London, 1966), p. 83.

[2] R. P. Dore, *City Life in Japan: A Study of a Tokyo Ward* (Berkeley, 1965), p. 251.

[3] Ono Sokyo, *Shinto: The Kami Way* (Rutland and Tokyo, 1962), p. 68.

[4] *ibid.*, p. 69.

[5] *ibid.*, p. 70.

[6] Fosco Maraini, *The Island of the Fisherwomen* (New York, 1962), p. 85.

tember, as it happened), I had barely found my family a place to live and begun the unpacking, when we heard a rhythmic drumbeat, and went up to the roof to see what was going on. In the street below, a procession appeared, and we quickly went down to join them. There we encountered a long straggling procession of fifty or more small children, the little girls in bright, pretty *yukata*, and the little boys in Western-style short pants and summer shirts. They were pulling on long ropes, drawing a small cart with a large drum on it. On this little wagon were four boys, who took turns beating the drum, as the rest of the children (more girls than boys) pulled the drum-cart along the street, carefully watched by a young policeman in a snappy white cap, a scattering of easy-going local merchants in loose-fitting *happi* coats over equally loose-fitting *zubon-shita* (long white cotton undershorts), and assorted young mothers with babies strapped to their backs. Atop the drum, his majestic wings arched upward as though ready for flight, his broad tail feathers fanned out in splendid display, perched the golden phoenix. He had the grandeur of an eagle, the pomp of a peacock, the bravado of a rooster, and is the delight of Jungians who see him as an archetypal reminder of "the 'phoenix' which we all keep within ourselves, enabling us to live out every moment and to overcome each and every partial death. . . ," a symbol of "the regeneration of universal life."[7] The street procession, as we shall see, is at one of its levels a celebration of male youth, of young manhood, and the phoenix is an apt mascot for the energetic lads beating the drum. These particular drummer boys employed two rhythmic patterns, one of which was *DON DON chin chin chin* (where *DON* indicates a resounding thump made by striking the drum hard in the center, and *chin* indicates a clacking blow that is made by striking the drum at the rim, in both cases with the drum stick; capital letters are used to indicate the louder sound, lower case the quieter). The alternate pattern, which follows, is *DON DON DON chin chin*; so the whole pattern sounds something like this: *DON DON chin chin chin DON DON DON chin chin DON DON chin chin chin DON DON DON*—and so on.

---

[7] J. E. Circlot, *A Dictionary of Symbols* (New York, 1962), p. 242. See also C. G. Jung, *The Archetypes and the Collective Unconscious* (London, 1959), pp. 375–376. Sigmund Freud, somewhat less complicatedly, suggests that "probably the earliest significance of the phoenix was that of the revivified penis after its state of flaccidity . . . " (*Collected Papers*, vol. V, London 1950: "Acquisition of Power over Fire" 1932, p. 292). The Japanese for phoenix is *hô-ô*. Its mythology came to Japan from China, along with that of the dragon, the *kirin* (the camelopard or fiery horse) and others. As to what its presence on the *mikoshi* means, I found a variety of opinions. One man told me it is an omen of a prosperous year. Another told me he was quite sure it was "the bird that lighted atop the Emperor Jimmu's bow to guide his way in battle. It was a golden bird, and its radiance blinded his enemies, and so they were defeated. That is what we were taught in school, in my day (before the Pacific War)." He was confusing it with the *Yata-garasu* of mythology, which was a crow sent by the sun goddess. Still another man told me: "It is a happy bird, like the stork."

Over the drumbeat we now heard shouts. The drum cart (called *dashi*) simply announces what is to come, it prepares the way for the *mikoshi*. Pulling the *dashi* is primarily the work of the girls, but beating the drum and carrying the *mikoshi* are male privileges. And here they came, fifteen boys all dressed in short checkerboard jackets, carrying a glittering *mikoshi*, and chanting with great gusto: *hai-za HAI-ZA hai-za HAI-ZA*. . . The *mikoshi* (W. G. Aston called it the "carriage" of the God,[8] because it is a means of carrying the *kami* to his parishioners) resembles a very ornate miniature temple, black lacquered and encrusted with golden ornaments and trimmings, some of which hang loose and jingle as the *mikoshi* is jostled about. It is draped with a red silk cord, and surmounted by another, even more majestic phoenix, in the same attitude as the one on the path-clearing drum. This ornate portable temple is mounted on two large beams that extend lengthwise, out beyond the base and two shorter beams tied or otherwise fixed laterally across the two main beams. The *mikoshi* is thus carried ark-of-the-covenant style, with the boys on the left side calling out *"HAI-ZA!"*, jogging to a little dance step, left on *HAI*, right on *ZA*, as the boys on the other side chant the response, *"hai-za!"* This chant is in effect a simple work chant, for the *mikoshi* is heavy, and the work of carting it and hoisting it goes easier if the whole *mikoshi* team can move with a single movement, and with a certain *esprit*. Sometimes (as in this case) the boys are very young and inexperienced, and so are led by a young adult (who often turns out to be the school's track coach) who at times puts his shoulder to the *mikoshi* alongside the others, and at times runs ahead of the *mikoshi*, jogging backwards, to give them direction and encouragement. He keeps his police whistle in his mouth, and toots out the pace, so that with every *HAI-ZA hai-za HAI-ZA* you hear a *tweet tweet* (rest, rest) *tweet tweet*. Other guides will be on hand as well: merchants in *happi* coats, one carrying a pair of saw-horses on which to rest the *mikoshi* from time to time, policemen in white pith helmets, another schoolteacher keeping up on his bicycle.

The atmosphere about the procession is all informality and congeniality. People are relaxed, enjoying their children's fun and their own, getting in touch again with their own youthful memories, and warmly cordial to neighbors and strangers. At festival time, there are in fact no strangers. As I made my way through the fall festival season that year, I would begin my Friday evening or Saturday morning taking the streetcar at the corner, in any direction, and getting off at the first sign of a neighborhood festival (clusters of girls in their best *kimono*, paper flowers over every garden gate, the sound of a distant drum), usually just a few stops from home. I carried a camera (one doesn't like to be too conspicuous),

[8] W. G. Ashton, *Shinto: The Way of the Gods* (London, 1905), p. 222.

a small tape recorder, and a roomy camera bag without which my work would have been difficult indeed. As I followed this or that *mikoshi* team or *dashi* procession about, neighborhood residents and shop keepers (the "downtown" people, Tokyo's salt-of-the-earth) would hand me pears, mandarin oranges (*mikan*), box lunches (*obento*) of *sekihan* (festival rice), O-Inari-san (the fox's favorite), assorted *sushi*, and an occasional small bottle of *sake*, complete with a plastic cup. I would stuff my pockets, and then the camera bag, munch what I could as I went, but soon I would have to return home to unload, and then set out to find my way back, often happening upon the wrong *mikoshi* team, and finding myself at an entirely different festival! Sometimes I was with my family, and we would meet some proud parents along the procession route, who would invite us to their home for green tea and bean-paste sweets. One such introduced himself as a radio announcer, whose four-year-old son had just carried the *mikoshi* (the very smallest one) for the very first time. A prouder father cannot be imagined. He called his son "Mr. Taihe." He said that he himself never visits the neighborhood shrine, and suggested that he was really too sophisticated a man, and too enlightened, to want to have much to do with the shrine faith. But carrying the *mikoshi* was obviously a different matter. His wife refilled our cups, and we discussed the severe tremors of the night before (he called earthquakes "earth aches," a phrase that still haunts me). Then shouts of *"hai-za!"* greeted our ears, and we were off again, following another procession, and meeting new friends.

SHINGON BUDDHISM

This is a passage by Kukai or Kobo Daishi (773–835), the founder in Japan of Shingon, a form of Buddhism related to the Vajrayana of Tibet. It is centered on the use of mystic rites and meditation to attain the Diamond Nature—that is, become a Buddha—in this life. The Dharmakaya means the Buddha-nature as the essence of the universe. The Three Mysteries mean mantras or chanted sacred words, mudras or sacred gestures made with the hands, and evocational meditation. Together these make the body and mind a unity expressing buddahood. Mahavairocana, the Vairocana of the Tibetan Book of the Dead, represents the Dharmakaya itself personified. One can catch in a passage like this the flavor of this mystical and profound style of Buddhism.

From *Kukai: Major Works*

Yoshito S. Hakeda

ATTAINING ENLIGHTENMENT IN THIS VERY EXISTENCE

QUESTION: In sutras and shastras it is explained that after three aeons one can attain enlightenment. Is there evidence for the assertion that one can attain enlightenment in this very existence?

ANSWER: The Tathagata has explained it in the Esoteric Buddhist texts.

QUESTION: How is it explained?

ANSWER: It is said in the *Vajrasekhara Sutra* that "He who practices this samadhi can immediately realize the enlightenment of the Buddha."[1] Also: "If the sentient beings who have come across this teaching practice it diligently four times day and night, they will realize the stage of joy in this life and perfect enlightenment in their subsequent sixteen lives."[2]

REMARKS: "This teaching" in the foregoing quotation refers to the king of teachings, the teaching of samadhi realized by the Dharmakaya Buddha himself. "The stage of joy" is not the first stage of Bodhisattvahood as defined in the Esoteric Buddhist teachings, but the first stage of Buddhahood of our Buddha Vehicle, the details of which are explained in the chapter discussing stages.[3] By "sixteen lives" is meant that one is to realize the attainments of the sixteen great Bodhisattvas,[4] the

Yoshito S. Hakeda, *Kukai: Major Works* (New York and London: Columbia University Press, 1972), pp. 225–27, 233–34. Some notes omitted. Reprinted by permission of the publisher.

[1] *Chin-kang-ting (vajrasekhara) i-tzu-ting-lun-wang-yü-ch'ieh i-kuei.* After the quotation there is a parenthetic comment which reads, "This samadhi is the samadhi of Mahāvairocana Buddha in the form of a universal monarch, represented by a seed mantra [*bhrūm*]."

[2] *Chin-kang-ting-yü-ch'ieh-san-mo-ti-fa.*

[3] Kūkai seems to be referring to the discussion of the ten stages of the development of the religious mind in the first chapter of the *Mahāvairocana Sutra.*

[4] Kūkai interprets "sixteen lives" as realizing the samadhi of the sixteen Bodhisattvas surrounding the Four Buddhas in the inner circle of the Diamond Mandala, not as repeating the cycle of birth and death sixteen times.

details of which are also explained in the chapter discussing the stages.[5]

Again it is said: "If a man disciplines himself according to this superior doctrine, he will be able to attain in this life unsurpassed enlightenment."[6] Furthermore: "It should be known that he himself turns into the Diamond Realm; since he becomes identical with the Diamond, he is firm and indestructible. An awareness will emerge that he is of the Diamond Body."[7] The *Mahāvairocana Sutra* states: "Without forsaking his body, he obtains supernatural power, wanders on the ground of great space, and perfects the Mystery of Body." Also: "If he wishes to gain the perfection of religious discipline in his lifetime, he must select a certain method of meditation that suits his inclinations and concentrate on it. For this, he must personally receive instruction in mantra recitation from an authentic master. If he observes the mantras and masters yoga, he will gain perfection."

REMARKS: "The perfection of religious discipline" mentioned in the sutra refers to the perfection of yoga which uses recitation of and meditation on mantras and to the perfection of yoga of the Dharmakaya Buddha. "The ground of great space" is the Dharmakaya Buddha. He is analogous to great space; he is eternal, being unobstructed, and embraces in himself all phenomena. That is why he is compared to great space. Grounded on him, all things exist; therefore, the term "ground" is used. The term "Mystery of Body" is introduced because the Three Mysteries of the Dharmakaya Buddha are imperceptible, even by the bodhisattvas in the Ten Stages of Bodhisattvahood, let alone by other bodhisattvas lower than they.

In the *Aspiration to Enlightenment* of Nāgārjuna it is explained: "It is through the teaching of Mantrayāna that we can attain enlightenment in this very existence; this teaching explains the way of samadhi which is either neglected or totally ignored in other teachings."

REMARKS: By "samadhi" in this quotation is meant the samadhi realized by the Dharmakaya Buddha himself. The "other teaching" designate the Esoteric Buddhist teachings expounded by the Buddha [Shakyamuni] for the sake of saving others.

It is also said: "If, seeking after the Buddha Wisdom, a man penetrates into the enlightenment mind (*bodhicitta*), he will quickly realize great Buddhahood in the very body given him by his parents." This doctrinal evidence establishes the assertion.

QUESTION: How do you analyze the meaning of the words [attaining enlightenment in this very existence] given in these sutras and shastras?

---

[5]This reference is ambiguous. Kūkai may well be referring to the section on the emergence of the sixteen Bodhisattvas of the Diamond Mandala in the Mind of Mahāvairocana while in samadhi. Cf. *Fen-pieh-sheng-wei ching.*

[6]*Kuan-chih i-kuei.*

[7]*Chin-kang-ting-yü-ch'ieh-san-mo-ti-fa.*

A summary in verse:

The Six Great Elements are interfused and are in a state of eternal harmony;

The Four Mandalas are inseparably related to one another:

When the grace of the Three Mysteries is retained, [our inborn three mysteries will] quickly be manifested.

Infinitely interrelated like the meshes of Indra's net are those which we call existences.

There is the One who is naturally equipped with all-embracing wisdom.

More numerous than particles of sand are those who have the King of Mind and the consciousnesses;

Each of them is endowed with the Fivefold Wisdom, with infinite wisdom.

All beings can truly attain enlightenment because of the force of mirrorlike wisdom. . . .

. . . Concerning the line "There is the One who is naturally equipped with all-embracing wisdom," in the *Mahāvairocana Sutra* it is said: "I am the origin of all. I am called the One on whom the world depends. My teachings are peerless. I am in the state of quiescence, and there are none who surpass me." "I" in the quotation refers to Mahāvairocana, and "all," to innumerable existences. "The origin" means the primary one who realized naturally from the very beginning all the states of being characterized by the great freedom as suggested above. The Dharmakaya of the Tathagatas and the essential nature of sentient beings are identical; both are in possession of the principle of primordial quiescence. Yet, sentient beings are unaware of this and remain ignorant. The Buddha preaches this message and causes sentient beings to awaken to enlightenment. . . . Each of the Buddhas [actual or potential Buddhas, that is, all sentient beings] is endowed with the Fivefold Wisdom, with the Thirty-sevenfold Wisdom,[8] with infinite wisdom. This meaning is expressed in the following two lines ["More numerous than particles of sand are those who have the King of Mind and the consciousness;/Each of them is endowed with the Fivefold Wisdom, with infinite wisdom"]. . . . "The King of Mind" is the Wisdom that perceives the essential nature of the World of Dharma, and "consciousness" is a collective name for the manifold levels of consciousness. . . .[9]

[8]The Thirty-sevenfold Wisdom stands for the Thirty-seven Buddhas and Bodhisattvas in the inner circle of the Diamond Mandala, of which the center is Mahāvairocana. Since the thirty-six deities represent aspects of Mahāvairocana, the Thirty-sevenfold Wisdom is a synonym for the Fivefold Wisdom and for infinite wisdom, which represent the totality and the parts of the wisdom of Mahāvairocana.

[9]The Wisdom that perceives the essential nature of the World of Dharma corresponds to Pure Consciousness (*amala-vijñāna*), and consciousnesses, to the eightfold consciousness (*ālaya*-consciousness, ego-consciousness, etc.).

The last line ["All beings can truly attain enlightenment because of the force of mirrorlike wisdom"] gives the reason why [one can attain enlightenment here and now]. The reason why all the Buddhas are said to have realized enlightenment is that their mirrorlike mind functions like a bright mirror set on a high stand, reflecting all images. The faultless, bright Mind-mirror [of Mahāvairocana], being placed on the summit of the World of Dharma, illumines calmly all beings without any distortion or error. Which Buddha [sentient being with Buddha nature] does not possess such perfect, mirrorlike wisdom? It is therefore said in the last line: "All beings can truly attain enlightenment because of the force of mirrorlike wisdom."

PURE LAND BUDDHISM

The following passage is from the Tannisho, *a compilation of the "Pure Land" teachings of Shinran (1173–1263) by his disciples. Pure Land is a Buddhist path which depends not upon one's efforts in meditation and leading a holy life, but upon the promise attributed to Amida (Amita) Buddha (who amounts to a personification of the Buddhahood in all things) that all who call upon his name will be saved in his Western Paradise. This is the Vow of Amida; the method of expressing this faith is to say the* Nembutsu, *"Namu Amida Butsu" or "Hail Amida Buddha." For Pure Land Buddhists, the simple trust implicit in this act is at the heart of the negation of egotism all Buddhism requires.*

Shinran was the most radical of the Pure Land Buddhists. He saw trust in the Vow of Amida as an existential choice he made after realizing the self-deception and futility inherent in the "Path of Sages"—the way of trying to be saved through one's own efforts. The key to the meaning of trust in Amida was its utter simplicity and the equality of all people before it.

From *The Shinshu Seiten:*
The Holy Scripture of Shinshu

"The moment faith gets established within us that we enjoy birth in the Pure Land by the inconceivably great power of the Vow of Amita

The Shinshu Seiten: The Holy Scripture of Shinshu (Honolulu: Honpa Hongwanji Mission of Hawaii, 1955), pp. 263–68. Reprinted by permission of the publisher.

Buddha and the moment a wish to say the Nembutsu arises in us, that moment we are embraced eternally in His hand. The Vow of Amita Buddha makes no choice as to whether we are old or young, good or evil. Faith is all paramount. This we should know. The reason thereof is that the aim of the Vow is to save those who are lost in the mire of sins and whose illusions and passions burn their self. This being the case, in order to believe in the Vow, no other virtues are needed of us, because there can be no virtues that can surpass the Nembutsu; no fear need we entertain in regard to our sins, because no sins can hinder the Way of the Vow of Amita Buddha." So was the word of our Master.   (1)

"All of you are come traveling over ten provinces, not even caring about the safety of your own lives. And your desire is but to learn from me the Way to the Pure Land. But should you be cherishing in your mind a loving thought that I must know Ways other than the Nembutsu that can lead us to the Pure Land or that I must be highly versed in matters of scriptures, you are extremely misled in your conception. Should this be the case, you should go to Nara or Mount Hiei, where you will find many a learned scholar. These scholars you may call upon and ask of them in detail the Way that will take you to the Pure Land. As for me Shinran, I but trust in the word of my good master by whom I was told that only through the Nembutsu we get embraced by Amita Buddha. There is no other thought. Whether the Nembutsu be truly the seed to lead me to the Pure Land or whether it be the karmic seed that will carry me down to hell, I wholly know nothing. Be it that I were cheated by Honen Shonin and be it that I were to go to hell by saying the Nembutsu, there is nothing in me to be sorry about. The reason is that there could well be a ground for me to be sorry about and to say I was cheated, if I, being able to practice the Ways other than the Nembutsu and thereby becoming the Buddha, were to go to hell by saying it. All practices are beyond me: so that there can be ahead of me no other course than that which will lead me to hell. If it is that the Vow of Amita Buddha was true, the sermons of Shakyamuni Buddha could not have been untrue. If it is that the teaching of Shakyamuni Buddha was true, the expositions of the venerable Shan-tao could not have been untrue. If it is that the expositions of the venerable Shan-tao were true, how could it be that what Honen Shonin said was untrue? If it is that what Honen Shonin said was true, may I not say that what I, Shinran, say is also not untrue? After all, what concerns my humble faith is this. Beyond this it is entirely up to you whether you take up the Nembutsu and put faith in it or cast it off." So was the word of our Master.   (2)

" 'Even the virtuous get born in the Pure Land: why not we who are sin-ridden?' Against this, people always say: 'Even the sin-ridden get born in the Pure Land: why not the virtuous?' This at first sight seems to be very well, but it goes against the purport of the Vow, the Way of the Other-Power. The reason thereof is that those who rely upon good, the good practiced by the Self-Power, lack that singleness of faith with which to trust upon the Other-Power. This does not go in accord with the purport of the Vow of Amita Buddha. But when one casts off the mind of the Self-Power and puts full trust upon the Other-Power, such a one will be born in the true Recompensed Land. We are wholly bound up by illusion. As there was no hope before us, no matter what virtues we practiced, to depart from birth and death, Amita Buddha had pity on us and took His vow, the aim of which was to enable us the sin-ridden to become Buddhas. Therefore the sinful who put sole reliance upon the Other-Power are the right cause for the vow to be taken for our being born in the Pure Land. Hence 'Even the virtuous get born in the Pure Land: why not, all the more, those of us who are sin-ridden?' " So was the word of our Master.   (3)

"In compassion, a difference exists between that of the Path of Sages and that of the Pure Land. The compassion talked about in the Path of Sages is to take pity on, to sympathize with, and to nurture others. But it is extremely rare that we can truly save others as we will. The compassion talked about in the Pure Land School is to say the Nembutsu, to become a Buddha quickly, and with the great compassionate heart of an Enlightened One to save beings just as we will. We can have in this life as much pitying heart as we will, but thorough salvation, as we may well know, is not possible. This will say that any compassion like this cannot persist. So the Nembutsu is the only great compassion that passes to the end." So was the word of our Master.   (4)

"I, Shinran, have up to now not once yet said the Nembutsu from any filial piety toward father or mother. The reason thereof is that all are fathers, mothers, brothers, and sisters in the course of generations and lives. We can save all when we become enlightened in the life to come. If it were that the Nembutsu is the good we can practice by our own power, we may well save our father and mother by transferring its merit. Only when we cast off the Self-Power and get enlightened as quick as possible, we may well save, with the miraculous powers we may then be possessing, those with whom we are related, be it where they live, there suffering the result of their past karma—be it that they are in the *Six Realms* or *Four Lives*." So was the word of our Master.   (5)

"It is extremely hard to understand that disputes should go among those who take exclusively to the path of the Nembutsu and that they should be saying whom the disciples should belong to. I, Shinran, have no disciples to call as mine own. The reason is that we may well call one our own, if it is that we make one say the Nembutsu by our own power. It is because of Amita Buddha and because His light nurtures us that the Nembutsu comes to our lips. If we are to call one who has thus come to say the Nembutsu our own disciple, no act can be more self-presuming than this. We meet or part just as we are so made by our own karma. Against this, what is difficult to understand is that words should go that birth in the Pure Land is not possible if one acts against and leaves the teacher and say the Nembutsu following other persons. Will this say that they take credit to themselves for the faith given one by Amita Buddha? I repeatedly say such could never be. If faith buds as it ought to bud, we may well come to feel grateful for what we owe the Buddha and also our own teacher." So was the word of our Master. (6)

"The Nembutsu is an Unhindered Single Way. The reason is that even the gods of heaven and earth get overawed and that they revere one who takes the path of faith. The maras and heathen stand not in the way. No sins can feel the karma effect. Even all virtues cannot overtake." So was the word of our Master. (7)

"The Nembutsu is neither practice nor virtue to one who practices it. As it is not practiced through one's own will or power, it is no practice; as it is no virtue perfected by one's own will or power, it is no virtue. It solely arises from the Other-Power and has nothing to do with the Self-Power. Hence no practice and no virtue to one who practices it." So was the word of our Master. (8)

"Although I say the Nembutsu, a welling joy is hard to come. No desire hastens me to the Pure Land. How might I accept this?" To this his word was: "I, Shinran, too had this doubt with me. And I find you, Yuiembo, too have the same doubt with you. But be assured. In as much as no thought wells up in you for what you ought really to be glad at without bound, your birth in the Pure Land is so much sure. It is the illusions that suppress our minds that will feel glad. But all this the Buddha was well aware of on beforehand. Therefore He would call us the illusion-clad common mortals. Because of this, the all-compassionate Vow of Amita Buddha had to be vowed for beings such as we are. As I take things in this light, I feel all the more hopeful. And it is also because of this illusion that thought does not hasten us for birth in the Pure Land and that apprehension of death takes us to lonesome channels as we feel even a little bit unwell. Strong indeed is this fire of illusion that burns us! Because of this it is all so hard to throw away this time-old home of suffering wherein we have been repeating birth and death for so long and because of this no yearnings arise in us for birth in the Pure Land of Rest and Happiness where we are not yet born. But howsoever unwilling we might be to depart from this life, when the karmic seed to be in this mundane world is gone and when power is all out of us, we are sure to be born in His land. His is the mercy that especially is directed toward those whose minds feel no yearnings for early birth. In as much as this is so, His Great Compassionate Heart is all the more to be relied upon and you may be rest assured that your birth in the Pure Land is all the more an established fact. Should it be that an overwhelming happiness arises in you and should it be that you feel for early birth in the Pure Land, you might well want to know if you are not lacking in illusion." So was the word of our Master. (9)

"In the Nembutsu non-reason is reason, because it stands wholly above praise, explanation, or comprehension." So was the word of our Master. (10)

ZEN

The form of Japanese Buddhism best known outside Japan is undoubtedly Zen. The Japanese version of the Chinese Ch'an, it teaches enlightenment through meditation and realizing the secondary nature of words and concepts. This passage is from the autobiographical writings of Hakuin (1685–1768), a great master of the Rinzai school of Zen; he put its system of koans *in the modern form. The* koan *is a riddlelike question and answer whose meaning—or meaningful lack of meaning— a student must demonstrate to his master.* Mu *means nothingness or emptiness, in the Mahayana sense of the entire universe being "empty," and only a set of interrelated reflections without separate existence, a hall of mirrors or the inside of a soap bubble.*

From *The Zen Master Hakuin: Selected Writings*
Philip B. Yampolsky

The spring of my twenty-fourth year found me in the monk's quarters of the Eigan-ji[1] in Echigo, pursuing my strenuous studies. Night and day I did not sleep; I forgot both to eat and rest. Suddenly a great doubt manifested itself before me. It was as though I were frozen solid in the midst of an ice sheet extending tens of thousands of miles. A purity filled my breast and I could neither go forward nor retreat. To all intents and purposes I was out of my mind and the *Mu* alone remained. Although I sat in the Lecture Hall and listened to the Master's lecture, it was as though I were hearing a discussion from a distance outside the hall. At times it felt as though I were floating through the air.

This state lasted for several days. Then I chanced to hear the sound of the temple bell and I was suddenly transformed. It was as if a sheet of ice had been smashed or a jade tower had fallen with a crash. Suddenly I returned to my senses. I felt then that I had achieved the status of Yen-t'ou, who through the three periods of time encountered not the slightest loss [although he had been murdered by bandits]. All my

Philip B. Yampolsky, trans., *The Zen Master Hakuin: Selected Writings* (New York and London: Columbia University Press, 1971), pp. 118–23. Notes slightly abridged. Reprinted by permission of the publisher.

[1]Temple located at Takada in present-day Niigata Perfecture.

former doubts vanished as though ice had melted away. In a loud voice I called: "Wonderful, wonderful. There is no cycle of birth and death through which one must pass. There is no enlightenment one must seek. The seventeen hundred koans handed down from the past have not the slightest value whatsoever." My pride soared up like a majestic mountain, my arrogance surged forward like the tide. Smugly I thought to myself: "In the past two or three hundred years no one could have accomplished such a marvelous breakthrough as this."

Shouldering my glorious enlightenment, I set out at once for Shinano. Calling on Master Shōju,[2] I told of my experience and presented him with a verse. The Master, holding my verse up in his left hand, said to me: "This verse is what you have learned from study. Now show me what your intuition has to say," and he held out his right hand.

I replied: "If there were something intuitive that I could show you, I'd vomit it out," and I made a gagging sound.

The Master said: "How do you understand Chao-chou's *Mu?*"

I replied: "What sort of place does *Mu* have that one can attach arms and legs to it?"

The Master twisted my nose with his fingers and said: "Here's someplace to attach arms and legs." I was nonplussed and the Master gave a hearty laugh. "You poor hole-dwelling devil!" he cried. I paid him no attention and he continued: "Do you think somehow that you have sufficient understanding?"

I answered: "What do you think is missing?"

Then the Master began to discuss the koan that tells of Nanch'üan's death.[3] I clapped my hands over my ears and started out of the room. The Master called after me: "Hey, monk!" and when I turned to him he added: "You poor hole-dwelling devil!" From then on, almost every time he saw me, the Master called me a "poor hole-dwelling devil."

One evening the Master sat cooling himself on the veranda. Again I brought him a verse I had written. "Delusions and fancies," the Master said. I shouted his words back at him in a loud voice, whereupon the Master seized me and rained twenty or thirty blows with his fists on me, and then pushed me off the veranda.

This was on the fourth day of the fifth month after a long spell of rain. I lay stretched out in the mud as though dead, scarcely breathing and almost unconscious. I could not move; meanwhile the Master sat on the veranda roaring with laughter. After a short while I regained consciousness, got up, and bowed to the Master. My body was bathed in perspiration. The Master called out to me in a loud voice: "You poor hole-dwelling devil!"

After this I devoted myself to an intensive study of the koan on

[2]At the Shōju-an in Iiyama, present-day Nagano Prefecture.

[3]This koan has been mentioned before. It is given in abbreviated form at the end of this section of the text.

the death of Nan-ch'üan, not pausing to sleep or eat. One day I had a kind of awakening and went to the Master's room to test my understanding, but he would not approve it. All he did was call me a "poor hole-dwelling devil."

I began to think that I had better leave and go somewhere else. One day when I had gone to town to beg for food I encountered a madman who tried to beat me with a broom. Unexpectedly I found that I had penetrated the koan on the death of Nan-ch'üan. Then the other koans that had puzzled me, Su-shan's Memorial Tower and Ta-hui's verse on the Roundness of the Lotus Leaf[4] fell into place of themselves and I penetrated them all. After I returned to the temple I spoke of the understanding I had gained. The Master neither approved nor denied what I said, but only laughed pleasantly. But from this time on he stopped calling me a "poor hole-dwelling devil." Later I experienced enlightenment two or three times, accompanied by a great feeling of joy. At times there are words to express such experiences, but to my regret at other times there are none. It was as though I were walking about in the shadow cast by a lantern. I returned then and attended on my old teacher Nyoka,[5] who had fallen ill.

One day I read in the verse given by Hsi-keng to his disciple Nampo as they were parting, the passage: "As we go to part a tall bamboo stands by the gate; its leaves stir the clear breeze for you in farewell."[6] I was overcome with a great joy, as though a dark path had suddenly been illumined. Unconsciously I cried aloud: "Today for the first time I have entered into the *samādhi* of words." I arose and bowed in reverence.

After this I set out on a pilgrimage. One day when I was passing through southern Ise I ran into a downpour and the waters reached to my knees. Suddenly I gained an even deeper understanding of the verse on the Roundness of the Lotus Leaf by Ta-hui. I was unable to contain my joy. I lost all awareness of my body, fell headlong into the waters, and forgot completely to get up again. My bundles and clothing were soaked through. Fortunately a passer-by, seeing my predicament, helped me to get up. I roared with laughter and everyone there thought I was mad. That winter, when I was sitting at night in the monk's hall at Shinoda in Izumi,[7] I gained an enlightenment from the sound of snow

---

[4]Su-shan's Memorial Tower has appeared before. Ta-hui's verse on the Roundness of the Lotus Leaf is to be found in *Ta-hui P'u-chüeh ch'an-shih yü-lu*. It begins: "The lotus leaf is round, round as a mirror; the arrowroot is pointed, pointed as an awl." It is not found in Chinese koan collections and was apparently first used in Japan. See Akizuki Ryūmin, *Kōan* (Tokyo, 1965), p. 104.

[5]Nyoka is apparently another name of Sokudō (d. 1712) who resided at the Daishō-ji in Numazu. Hakuin had studied with him shortly after he became a monk.

[6]Hsi-keng (Hsü-t'ang Chih-yü) was the teacher of Nampo Jōmyō (Daiō Kokushi). Both have been mentioned before. These lines are found as part of a verse in *Hsü-t'ang ho-shang yü-lu*. They are, however, not addressed to Nampo, but to three monks who are off on a visit to another temple.

[7]The Inryō-ji at Shinoda in present-day Osaka Prefecture.

falling. The next year, while practicing walking meditation at the monk's hall of the Reishō-in in Mino,[8] I suddenly had an enlightenment experience greater than any I had had before, and was overcome by a great surge of joy.

I came to this dilapidated temple[9] when I was thirty-two. One night in a dream my mother came and presented me with a purple robe made of silk. When I lifted it, both sleeves seemed very heavy, and on examining them I found an old mirror, five or six inches in diameter, in each sleeve. The reflection from the mirror in the right sleeve penetrated to my heart and vital organs. My own mind, mountains and rivers, the great earth seemed serene and bottomless. The mirror in the left sleeve, however, gave off no reflection whatsoever. Its surface was like that of a new pan that had yet to be touched by flames. But suddenly I became aware that the luster of the mirror from the left sleeve was innumerable times brighter than the other. After this, when I looked at all things, it was as though I were seeing my own face. For the first time I understood the meaning of the saying. "The Tathāgata sees the Buddha-nature within his eye."

Later I happened to read the *Pi-yen lu* again, and my understanding of it differed completely from what it had been before. One night, some time after, I took up the *Lotus Sūtra*. Suddenly I penetrated to the perfect, true, ultimate meaning of the *Lotus*. The doubts I had held initially were destroyed and I became aware that the understanding I had obtained up to then was greatly in error. Unconsciously I uttered a great cry and burst into tears.

I wish that everyone would realize that studying Zen under a teacher is not such a simple matter after all. Although I am old and dissipated, and have nothing of which I can be proud, I am aware that at least I have not spent forty years in vain. Was it not for this reason that Chang Wu, when he was in Yang-chou, let go of his gold and engaged in his painful struggles [toward success]? As in the example I gave you, if you shoulder the one-sided understanding you have gained and spend your whole life vainly polishing and purifying it, how are you any different from Chang Lu, who guarded his piece of gold throughout his life, starving himself and bringing only harm to his body?

In India such a person is called a poor son of a rich man, [a follower] of the Two Vehicles.[10] In China he is spoken of as belonging to the group that practices the heretical silent-illumination Zen. None of these knows the dignity of the bodhisattva, nor does he reach the understanding that illuminates the cause for entrance to a Buddha land.

[8]The Reishō-in at Iwasaki, Yamagata-gun, in present-day Gifu Prefecture.

[9]The Shōin-ji, Hakuin's temple at Hara, in present-day Shizuoka Prefecture.

[10]"The Two Vehicles" refers here to the two kinds of Hinayana practitioners, the *śrāvaka* and the *Pratyeka-buddha*. The *śrāvaka* is working toward or has gained Nirvana in Hinayana terms only. The *Pratyeka-buddha* has gained enlightenment through his own efforts, but gives no thought to aiding others.

Nowadays people go about carrying on their shoulders a single empty principle and with it "understand the Buddha, understand the Patriarchs, understand the old koans." Then they all say: "Like the stick, like the *dhāranī*, like the *katsu*."[11] How laughable this is! Exert yourselves, students, for the Buddha Way is deep and far. Let everyone know that the farther you enter the sea the deeper it becomes and the higher you climb a mountain the taller it gets.

If you wish to test the validity of your own powers, you must first study the koan on the death of Nan-ch'üan.[12]

A long time ago San-sheng had the head monk Hsiu go to the Zen Master Tsen of Ch'ang-sha and ask him: "What happened to Nan-ch'üan after he passed away?"

Ch'ang-sha replied: "When Shih-t'ou became a novice monk he was seen by the Sixth Patriarch."

Hsiu replied: "I didn't ask you about when Shih-t'ou became a novice monk; I asked you what happened to Nan-ch'üan after he passed away."

Ch'ang-sha replied: "If I were you I would let Nan-ch'üan worry about it himself."

Hsiu replied: "Even though you had a thousand-foot winter pine, there is no bamboo shoot to rise above its branches."

Ch'ang-sha had nothing to say. Hsiu returned and told the story of his conversation to San-sheng. San-sheng unconsciously stuck out his tongue [in surprise] and said: "He has surpassed Lin-chi by seven paces."

If you are able to understand and make clear these words, then I will acknowledge that you have a certain degree of responsiveness to the teachings. Why is this so? If you speak to yourself while no one is around, you behave as meanly as a rat. What can anyone possibly prove [about your understanding]?

I may have been hitting a dangerous animal in the teeth three times. I join my palms together and say: "Let's leave it at that for today."

SACRED MOUNTAINS

A principal theme of popular religion in Japan is sacred mountains.
Rooted in the oldest levels of folk religion, this theme runs through both

[11]This passage is unclear. Presumably these people, who bear a single empty principle on their shoulders, and claim to understand the Buddha, Patriarchs, and koans, equate the stick with the Buddha, the *dhāranī* with the koans, and the shout (*katsu*) with the Patriarchs.

[12]This koan has been mentioned before. The story appears in *Ching-te ch'uan-teng lu*. Hakuin's version varies from the original and is somewhat abbreviated. Of the people who appear in the story below, we have seen Nan-ch'üan, Ch'ang-sha, Shih-t'ou and Lin-chi before. San-sheng Hui-jan (Sanshō E'nen, n.d.) was a disciple of Lin-chi. The head monk Hsiu is not identified. The Sixth Patriarch is Hui-neng (Enō, d. 713).

Shinto and Buddhism, and illustrates one of their many points of convergence in traditional society. This unity was especially apparent in the activity of the religious adepts called yamabushi, *mountain priests, who followed the spiritual path called Shugendo.* Yamabushi *go into the mountains, practice mystic austerities, initiate novices, and then return to the countryside to heal, divine, and guide pilgrims. Mt. Gassan and Mt. Haguro in the north of Japan are very important in this tradition. Notice in the passage below how the mountain tradition is permeated with symbolism of the esoteric Buddhist tradition regarding the Womb and Diamond (phenomenal and absolute) aspects of the Buddha-nature and of Vairocana, motifs first transmitted by Shingon.*

From *Folk Religion in Japan: Continuity and Change*
Ichiro Hori

MOUNTS GASSAN AND HAGURO AS DIVINE MOTHERS

As noted earlier, many of the mountains in Japan became centers of the activities of Shugen-dō. Chief among these is Mount Gassan, the most prominent among the three sacred mountains in Dewa, or present-day Yamagata prefecture (Dewa-San-zan), where the mountain ascetics of both the Haguro and Yudono sects practice religious austerities. Mount Gassan (literally, "Mount Moon") is worshipped by the farmers of the vicinity as an agricultural deity (Nō-gami) and as the resting place of ancestors or spirits of the dead. Special Shugen-dō annual rites are performed on Mount Gassan for the four seasons: Entering the Spring Peak (Haru-no-mine), Entering the Summer Peak (Natsu-no-mine), Entering the Autumn Peak (Aki-no-mine), and Entering the Winter Peak (Fuyu-no-mine). The autumn peak is of special interest because it features rituals that include the initiatory austerities for the novices of Shugen-dō.

The main rites of the autumn peak begin with the mystery of entering the Great Womb Store (*garbha-hukshi* or *taizō-kai*), symbolized by the special hat and sacred wooden box (*oi*) on the back of the leading mountain ascetic (*dai-sendatsu*, "great [or. chief] leader") and by the ritual act of throwing down the symbolic and decorative pillar (*bonden*) in front of the main Buddha hall of Shugen-dō seminaries in Tōge-mura

Ichiro Hori, *Folk Religion in Japan: Continuity and Change* (Chicago: University of Chicago Press, 1968), pp. 170–74. Notes omitted. Reprinted by permission of the publisher. Copyright 1968 by the University of Chicago.

on Mount Haguro. These symbols and rituals are explained by the fact that all the novices, together with the leading mountain ascetic, symbolically die and enter the womb of the Great Mother, Dai-nichi-nyorai (Great Sun Buddha Mahavairocana) or enter the underworld. The religious austerities and rituals continue for about ten days at the end of August, though they are now extremely shortened and simplified from their original forms. The series of rituals and austerities is divided into three periods: severe ordeals; taboos of food, speech, and sleeping; and the *dhûta* (*zuda* in Japanese) practices. Symbolically, the novices pass through the six stages of Buddhist Hell (Jigoku), Inferno of Starvation (Gaki), the Realm of Beasts (Chikushō), the World of Asûras (Shura), the World of Humans (Ningen), and Heaven (Tenjō) into the Great Womb Store. At each step of the three periods, several mysteries and *dhûta* practices are performed. It is noteworthy that the main hall of the Kōtaku-ji temple on top of Mount Haguro, in which the novices lead a secluded life, is decorated with symbols of the Great Mother's womb. Hanging from the ceiling in the center of the hall are red and white pieces of cloth about one meter long about which twisted hemp threads are wrapped. These pieces of cloth are said to symbolize the Great Mother's blood vessels, and the hemp threads symbolize her bones. Because the religious austerities of the Autumn Peak are those of the Great Womb Store, or of pilgrimages into the Great Mother's womb, the *dhûta* practices are usually performed at the rapids, streams, or waterfalls which flow down from the mountaintop. The novices as well as the leader wear white robes, different from the normal mountain ascetic's robes of yellowish brown. The white robe corresponds to that of the deceased and the mourner. At the end of the series of initiatory rituals, each novice is led to the most sacred valley, Moto-haguro ("Original Haguro"). He makes his final confession here and purifies himself by the sacred waterfall. Then, novices go to the top of Mount Haguro and crouch together in front of the main shrine of Hagurogongen. At the signal of a loud cry by the leader, the novices spring up suddenly, shout loudly, and run downhill to the main seminary in Tōge-mura at midslope. The shout is called the first cry of a child at birth (*ubu-goe*). Finally, the novices must jump over the sacred fire in front of the main seminary and the main Buddha hall, where the first mystery was performed. After this, the novices are believed to be reborn as new mountain ascetics from the Great Womb Store and have conferred upon them certificates giving the mountain ascetics new names, degrees, and secret knowledge of Shugen-dō.

RICE RITUALS

Japanese folk religion in agricultural communities typically centers around the planting, transplanting, and harvesting of rice. The arduous and crucial labors of each stage are alleviated by song, dance, and rites, which incorporate them into a cosmic pattern and engage the help of deities whose special interest is in farming. The following passage brings this world of traditional agricultural religion to life.

From *Seasonal Rituals Connected with Rice Culture*

Toshijiro Hirayama

The ritual held at the beginning of the transplantation is called by an old word, *sa-ori*. *Sa* seems to mean the deity of the rice field, *ori* being "to descend." Consequently, the word means the day on which the people invite the rice-field deity down from the mountain. This connection is also seen in the words Sa-tsuki and *sa-otome;* Sa-tsuki is the name of the month (tsuki) in which the rice transplantation is done and *sa-otome* refers to the maiden (*otome*) who transplants the rice seedlings. The sa-ori ritual is also called *sa-biraki* and *wasa-ue*, both signifying the onset of transplanting. These words suggest the idea that the deity descends and the people initiate the transplanting. In the eastern part of Japan, sa-ori takes place on the thirty-third day after minakuchi matsuri (when the taboo against touching the seedlings ends), and farmers once transplanted all their rice on this day, simply for the sake of formality. The prevalent practice for the ritual of sa-ori, however, is to transplant three plants or bundles of rice seedlings on a certain day in April of the lunar calendar. The remainder of the rice seedlings is transplanted whenever the season is suitable. As on the minakuchi matsuri, people sometimes erect a chestnut-tree branch in the rice field and decoate it with the flowers of the season. Nowadays, in many parts of Japan, these seedlings are regarded as offerings to the deity, but the erected tree branch would originally have been a symbol of the divine presence.

There are many local names for the ritual which is held at the end of the transplantation. *Sanobori* and *sanaburi* are representative names among many for this ritual signifying that *sa*, the deity, goes back to the mountain. In this ritual, the villagers also decorate or consecrate the seedlings of rice as they do in sa-ori. The ritual is usually held before the standing altar within a house, and the people who have joined in the transplanting are invited to a congratulatory feast. The sa-otome are given seats of honor at this banquet, because these women have played an important role in ta-ue. According to one explanation, this practice

Toshijiro Hirayama, "Seasonal Rituals Connected with Rice Culture," in Richard M. Dorson, ed , *Studies in Japanese Folklore* (Bloomington: Indiana University Press, 1963), pp. 66–73. Reprinted by permission of the publisher.

is based on an old idea which makes the fecundity of a woman parallel with the richness of the soil—as is indicated by the former custom of a priestess' presiding over the rice-planting ritual. Following the ritual of sanobori, several days of self-confinement were formerly observed by the workers, but at the present time this period is used for rest and recreation.

The twofold character of this custom is of particular interest. One ritual is held by each household at the close of transplantation; the other is held by the whole village on an appointed day. In some districts, both rituals are held on the same day, while in other districts only one or the other is observed. And in still other places the ritual is not to be found at all. If we look at their geographical distribution, we find that the areas in which the sanobori ritual is held only once by a whole village encircle the places where it is held twice. From this fact we may be able to reconstruct historically the bifurcation of the ritual. The reason why these two forms of sanobori split off from the original single form honoring the departure of the rice-field deity becomes clear from the history of the village labor organizations. Up to recent times, the small farmers in certain villages took part only in the sanobori held by their stem family. When the small families subordinate to or branching out from the stem family became independent, the custom of holding sanobori at each home was instigated, and so brought a change in the nature of the village sanobori. Although in some villages the home and the village sanobori have been celebrated on the same day, their functions differ; the main purpose of the ritual at home is to send off the deity suitably by providing a congratulatory feast, whereas in the village shrine festivals, the people pray to their tutelary deity for a rich crop and for protection against harmful insects, and they enjoy the holiday together. Thus the two forms of sanobori have become quite distinct.

After the transplantation of the rice seedlings is completed, the farmers turn their energies to eradicating the weeds that spring up in the rice fields during the summertime. This is very toilsome labor and needs to be repeated two or three times. Along with this work they attempt with great effort to keep the water in the rice field standing at the appropriate level, and they conduct rituals and utter spells to protect the rice plants from injurious insects and from the strong wind.

When the water supply becomes insufficient, the farmers pray for rainfall in a widely observed ritual known as *ama-goi* (praying for rain). In ama-goi the villagers may gather at the shrine and pray for rain all night through, or they may kindle a large fire on the mountain or take some water believed to be endowed with a spiritual power and wait in their own houses for rain. Again, they may dedicate dances to please the deity of water, or even commit deeds to offend him and so precipitate a rainfall. If the rain continues to fall day after day and the people fear damage to the rice plants, a ritual is staged to pray for fair weather.

In former days, the curse of an evil spirit was believed to be responsible for the appearance of insects harmful to the rice plants. The belief that the spirits of people who die bearing grudges can cause epidemics is seen in documents of the seventeenth century, which liken the malignancy of noxious insects to the dreadful power of evil spirits. In the nocturnal ritual to drive away the insects, the villagers make a straw doll which they carry about and cast away at the border of the village, while a row of people with glowing torches in their hands parade through the streets loudly reciting a spell.

The first of September (two hundred and one days from the beginning of spring) the people believe to be an evil day. Since plants suffer much damage from strong winds, the people ask the priests of the shrines and the monks of the temple to pray and to hold a ritual to placate the deity of the wind. In some districts at this season the farmers go out into the rice field and speak words of praise to the rice plants to precipitate their sound growth and utter a spell to hasten the budding of the ears.

The last stage in the series of rituals connected with rice cultivation comes with the autumn harvest rites. There are two rituals on this occasion, one at the beginning and the other at the end of the harvest. The autumn festivals were once the joint activity of all the members of the village, but now an autumn festival is held at the shrine, and the original rites are usually conducted in each house.

The ritual held at the beginning of the harvest is called *ho-kake* The farmers reap a small portion of the rice ears (*ho*) before the real harvest to hang (*kake-ru*) in front of the deity, and offer parched rice taken from the new crop. The date of the ritual differs from place to place. In some districts it is held on August first, or at the time of the wind-placating ritual, while in others it occurs on shanichi in autumn. In some places the farmers hold the ritual on the very first day on which they actually reap the rice plants. The deity to be served should have originally been the deity of the rice field, since this is a day of thanksgiving for the rice crop. According to present-day customs, however, the first crop is offered not only to this deity but also at the shrine of the mountain deity, at the shrine of the village tutelary deity, at the family altar, and at the tomb of the ancestors. There is a fairly general trend for the deity of the rice field to be syncretized with such tutelary deities and also with the ancestral deities, all of whom are worshiped in a similar manner.

Kariage matsuri (finishing-of-the-harvest festival) is held when the harvest is over. Since Japan consists of islands which range a considerable distance from the south to the north, the climate varies, and consequently this ritual has come to be held roughly at three different times according to latitude. People in the Tohoku area call the days to which the number nine is attached *san-ku-nichi,* and they choose one of these three days as the day of the ritual. Usually they choose the twenty-ninth. In the Kanto area, they hold the ritual on the tenth of October and call it *tōkan-ya* or *jū-ya* (the night of the tenth). In the Kansai area and in the western parts of Japan, they call the day of the wild boar, in October, I-no-ko (Child of the Wild Boar). The ritual is held on that day, and rice cakes shaped like piglets are eaten. Kariage matsuri in Kyushu is held still later, on the day of the ox in November, and is called *Shimo-tsuki matsuri* (November festival).

The ritual that comes at the end of the harvest seems to have been initially held in front of the *nio,* a heap made of the reaped rice plants. The vestige of this old custom can be recognized even today. In some districts the farmers make shelves on which to hang and dry the sheaves of rice plants. However, in many instances they hold this ritual inside the house rather than outside by the rice field. They take away the *kagashi* (scarecrow), which has threatened the birds all summer long in the rice field and erect it at a corner of the house to worship it there. This practice can be seen in the ritual of tōkan-ya in Nagano prefecture, where the kagashi is regarded as the symbol of the deity of the rice field. The ritual of consecrating or offering up the sickle used in reaping the rice plants is also widespread. O-ushi-sama in Kyūshū is now associated with Daikoku, an agricultural deity, and is worshiped on the day of *ushi,* the ox. To serve this deity, they reap the rice plants that have been left unreaped for this day, take them home, and offer them at an altar made of a mortar. Never do the people forget to include the rice cakes (*mochi*) made from newly harvested rice, along with some vegetable, in the offerings of this ritual. In most cases, these rice cakes are covered with red beans. In an old form of celebrating I-ni-ko matsuri, they put *bota-mochi* (rice-cake dumplings covered with sweet bean paste) in a one-*sho* measuring cup and offer it up before a mortar. This custom is also observed at Ushi matsuri. These rice cakes might once have been eaten by the people who had joined the ritual. Now that the ritual has come to be held at each house, families present these rice cakes to each other.

The Shimo-tsuki matsuri and the Ushi matsuri in Kyūshū are held long after the end of the actual harvest. The twenty-third of November in the lunar calendar is the proper day for these festivals, which are linked with many differing traditions; among these festivals there are some which resemble the ritual connected with rice culture and others in which the villagers worship their ancestor spirits. This is now the date of our national holiday, Kinrō Kansha no Hi (Labor Thanksgiving Day), the direct antecedent of which is the harvest ritual held at the imperial court.

Originally the people stored the reaped rice plants for a long time just as they were harvested; but from the Middle Ages on they hastened to thresh them and to put the unhusked or unpolished rice in bags made of rice straw, since these bags of rice were the required form of tax payment. Consequently, the *niwa shigoto* (the work done in the yard) such as threshing and husking rice, came to be included in the labor of the harvest season. At the end of each of these processes the farmers individually celebrate with a feast.

NICHIREN SHOSHU

A very important wing of Buddhism in Japan is Nichiren Shoshu, the "true teaching" Nichiren Daishonin ("Saint Nichiren," 1222–82). Nichiren, one of the mighty charismatic spiritual leaders of Japan, taught that the Lotus Sutra is the supreme expression of Buddhism, that its teaching unites all levels of reality and all areas of human experience, and that one can bring himself into its power and that of the universe by chanting six syllables addressed to it, "Nam Myoho Renge Kyo." Nichiren practice is said to bring both material and spiritual benefits, and is seen as the inauguration of a new civilization for a new age beginning in Japan. Therefore this tradition emphasized the conversion of the entire nation as most important.

Nichiren Buddhism experienced a tremendous resurgence in Japan after the Second World War through the lay organization Soka Gakkai, which is affiliated with it as an evangelizing movement. Soka Gakkai was started in the 1930s by Tsunesaburo Makiguchi, an educator who taught that the traditional triad of supreme values, truth, goodness, and beauty, should be replaced by goodness, beauty, and gain, since what benefits humankind is of more value than abstract truth. He saw Nichiren practice as the best way to honor goodness and beauty and to realize human benefit. Under the leadership of Josei Toda in the 1950s, Soka Gakkai and because of it Nichiren Shoshu was said to be the fastest-growing religion in the world. The following passage is from a book by Daisaki Ikeda, who became president of Soka Gakkai after Toda's death in 1958. Describing a meeting held in 1946, shortly after the end of the war, it well captures the spiritual vacuum of that era in Japan and shows how Nichiren Buddhism, as interpreted by Soka Gakkai, was able to flourish by giving very ordinary, war-weary people new hope and a sense of personal importance. The Gohonzon is a diagram used in Nichiren Buddhism as a focus of worship; it has transcribed on it the principal Buddhas and bodhisattvas named in the Lotus Sutra.

From *The Human Revolution*

Daisaku Ikeda

The lecture on the Lotus Sutra began promptly at 2:00 P.M., on September 22, in the tatami-floored sewing classroom of the village ele-

Daisaku Ikeda, *The Human Revolution*, Vol. 1 (New York and Tokyo: John Weatherhill, 1972), pp. 145–50. Reprinted by permission of the publisher. Copyright 1965, 1966, 1972 by Daisaku Ikeda.

mentary school. There were eighty people in the audience. By way of an opening address, Kyuichiro Masuda made a few remarks. Standing tall and erect among the people seated on the floor, he said that he deplored the ruination of Japan and that the only way to save the country and her people was through faith in the teachings of Nichiren. His impassioned tone at once surprised and interested his audience, some of whom had been nonchalantly chatting or smoking. But his speech was brief, and after a slight pause he presented the speakers for the day. There was scattered applause. Konishi was first, with the topic "Recognition and Evaluation." He introduced himself by saying that though born the son of a farmer he had, by some strange quirk of fate, become a teacher. He went on:

"We are often asked what the purpose of life is. Scholars and academicians say that its purpose is the pursuit of truth, by which they probably mean such things as the discovery that the earth revolves around the sun. But many others ask: 'What practical value does such knowledge have?' This question implies that human beings are always seeking value and that abstract truths in themselves are valueless.

"The purpose of life is the pursuit of happiness, or the quest for value. Recognition and evaluation are often confused because we tend to equate truth and value. The first person to point out the mistake in this approach and to establish a philosophical system of value was the late Tsunesaburo Makiguchi, the first president of our society. He made it clear that things assume true value only when they come into contact with or make an impact upon our daily lives and sensory perceptions. However, he also cautioned us against attempting to evaluate things without recognizing or understanding them fully. Correct evaluation, in other words, depends on correct recognition. I have brought up this topic in order to prepare you for the discussion of the teachings of Nichiren Daishonin, which my colleague Josei Toda will present later."

After Konishi left the platform, Hisao Seki rose to speak: "Continuing the train of thought begun by my colleague, I should like to say first that human happiness depends on both the amount and the nature of the value we create. Kant says that the supreme values are truth, goodness, and beauty; but our teacher Mr. Makiguchi showed that this conception is mistaken. Since it can be recognized but cannot be created, truth has no independent value. Mr. Makiguchi's revolutionary system established goodness, beauty, and gain as the three greatest values of human life. He further taught that values arise only in man's subjective relations with his environment. For example, knowing how to produce rice is a good thing, but it will not ease the pangs of hunger as the rice itself can.

"Mr. Makiguchi also taught us that three negative values exist as well. These are ugliness, evil, and loss. The positive values make life happy; the negative ones make it wretched. Values arise only in relationships between man and his exterior environment. For that reason, a life manifesting the positive values indicates harmony with the outer world. Conversely, a life marked by the negative values is one of discord with its surroundings. The kind of life a person leads, then, becomes the most important issue. This is where religion enters the picture because the fundamental purpose and problem of religion is the exploration of the mystery of human life.

"Now there are both true and false religions, and it goes without saying that selection of religion determines human destiny because only a true religion can bring happiness. Nichiren Daishonin declared that false religions lie at the root of all misfortune and that this principle applies to all men, all families, all nations. Japan's defeat in World War II and her postwar misfortunes stem directly from the false nature of Shinto.

"The staggering task of reconstruction, which we face right now, can only be accomplished successfully if we take into account the fundamental problems of human life. Only faith in a true religion can help us solve these problems. Our colleague Miss Kiyohara will explain what true religion is and how we can practice it when she speaks next on the topic 'Purification of Life.' "

The audience applauded politely when Seki left the platform. When the small and unprepossessing Miss Kiyohara began her talk, the villagers were puzzled to find a woman in the speaker's place. Many of the women in the audience exchanged suspicious and disapproving glances. Nevertheless, Miss Kiyohara began:

"I am nervous, and what is more, I am not a good speaker. But I will begin my remarks by stating my conclusion, so there will be no misunderstanding when I finish."

She smiled, and the audience muffled its laughter.

"We can only attain happiness if we lead pure lives." As she overcame her initial stage fright and began to deal with a subject about which she felt very deeply, Miss Kiyohara gained confidence. Her assurance was reflected in her voice and manner.

"True purification can only be the result of faith, and faith can only grow from practice and experience, because it is much more than a mere idea. Only the practice of true faith can purify human life, but what is true religion?"

At this point she gave a brief history of Buddhism. She pointed out the supremacy of the Lotus Sutra in the hierarchy of the teachings of Sakyamuni, the historical Buddha. She then went on to outline the state of Buddhism in the final, decadent Latter Day of the Law and talked about the teachings of Nichiren and the importance of Nam-myoho-renge-kyo, the prevailing article of faith in that period.

"Many people today labor under the misconception that only the teachings of Sakyamuni embody the true Buddhism. For them, real faith is dead. They rely on faith only at times of funerals and memorial services. They don't even try to understand the Mystic Law of Nichiren Daishonin. Modern man's greatest misfortune is his refusal to understand the meanings of the true Law. As there are no two suns in the heaven, so there is only one true Buddhism, the Three Great Secret Laws of Nichiren Shoshu, the one orthodox sect that has preserved the true essence of Buddhism that it inherited almost seven centuries ago.

"Once I was a bitterly unhappy, disillusioned woman—perhaps more so than any of you—but today I am joyful because of my faith. And I will remain happy as long as I live. Each of us can achieve the purification of life that brings joy if we have faith in the Gohonzon, which is the essence of Buddhism."

Although Miss Kiyohara's obvious devotion to her faith won applause from many, there were still some skeptical faces when she left the platform.

The next person to speaks was Mrs. Take Sakata, a chubby, middle-aged housewife, who walked timidly to the platform and bowed deeply to the audience. Sensing her shyness, Toda applauded warmly to encourage her; the others followed suit. But after a faltering start, Mrs. Sakata fell silent in embarrassment and fright. "Easy does it," whispered Toda. Taking heart, she began again:

"I would like to tell you about my experiences. My family ran a small steel plant. During the war we made munitions. When I was converted to Nichiren Shoshu, my whole family opposed it violently. My husband even threatened to divorce me. I was an orphan and had been unhappy all my life, but my new faith gave me peace and happiness. At home I had no one to talk to about it. I suffered all kinds of hardships and mental persecution, but I clung to my faith. Then, in one year, eight of the people who had been against my conversion died, miserable and impoverished. When my maid saw the terrible consequences of making fun of the true Buddhism she became frightened. She too was soon converted to the faith, but not my husband. He continued to oppose my religion, but his life gradually took a turn for the worse until he became very unhappy. I wanted to save him and our marriage, so I prayed sincerely for him. But I had to do so in silence. Finally, in June, 1942, my husband saw the light and accepted Nichiren Shoshu. I was so overcome with joy that I wept before the Gohonzon. That was the most unforgettable day of my life."

Mrs. Sakata paused to dab her eyes with a handkerchief; the villagers were clearly moved by this woman's simple story of suffering and triumphant faith. She continued:

"I'm no speaker, but I will do the best I can. As I had expected, after my husband accepted the faith, our factory began to prosper. Soon, the air raids began. Bombs often fell on our neighborhood and turned everything into a sea of flames. Still, we all knelt and prayed before the Gohonzon, and sometimes when it was too dangerous to stay at home, we sought shelter somewhere else but we always took our Gohonzon with us. I was easily upset and frightened before, but during that whole awful period my faith gave me courage to organize my own family and to become a leader in the neighborhood. All our neighbors came to count on me. We fought the fires together, and there were many of them. In fact, by the end of the war, Kamata, where I live, was reduced to a charred ruin. But our house and six neighboring houses escaped unharmed. In all that burned area, only our few houses stood. And it was all thanks to the Gohonzon.

"Not only that, but after the war our factory continued to do well. We used our house for discussions among believers in Nichiren Shoshu. Now I know in my heart that the Gohonzon protects us wherever we are and whatever happens. I believe that all people who do not have the Gohonzon to rely on are very unfortunate."

With a quick bow, the timid Mrs. Sakata left the platform, but the audience responded with great warmth. Obviously they believed the artless sincerity of her story and the wisdom she had acquired through unpretentious devotion and daily faith. She did not theorize; she spoke in terms of everyday experiences. This is the kind of thing that truly moves people.

Toda saw that human experiences are the most powerful tool for converting people to the faith. Theories, learned arguments, and doctrines interest bookish people, but not the masses. He began to understand that it was a mistake to use too much sophisticated dogma in speeches to audiences of uninitiated people. The beneficial power of the Gohonzon cannot be understood by means of theory alone; it must be grasped through the actual practice of faith and through experience. Similarly, faith in the teachings of Nichiren is, above all, a real experience, not an empty theory. The universal propagation of true Buddhism can be effected only if the masses see the everyday grace of Nichiren's teaching. Toda felt keenly that it was time to modify the society's methods of winning members.

WORLD MESSIANITY

The period since the Second World War has seen the rapid growth of a number of "New Religions" besides Soka Gakkai. The Church of World Messianity can be taken as an example. It was established by Mokichi Okada (called Meishu-sama; 1882–1955) after a series of supernatural occurrences, one of which was when he was inspired to recite a prayer he said was the oldest in the world as he stood atop an ancient sacred mountain. This exemplifies links with the primordial shamanistic tradition. The chief sacred rite of World Messianity is Johrei, the impartation of Divine Light through a gesture of holding up the cupped hand in blessing. This practice is believed to augment the coming of a new and better age. The idea of a coming new age (a recurrent theme in Japanese religion, especially the New Religions) is important in World Messianity. Today it suggests response to the rapid changes of modernization implicit in many of the New Religions, with their indication that all this is but prelude to even greater and more wonderful changes. The following passage, by Meishu-sama himself, expounds this expectation and the place the Divine Light given by Johrei has in its preparation.

From *Teachings of Meishu-sama*

We stand today at the turning point between the old order and the new, a big, worldwide transitional period. Such a great change has never before been experienced by humanity. It is entirely unprecedented.

What will the new civilization which takes the place of the old be like? Of course, with man's limited intellect we cannot grasp even the slightest idea of it. But what *can* it be like, and who is going to take charge of such a task as the creation of a new civilization? The time will come at last when all the people of the world will have to admit the existence of God—believers and non-believers alike.

God, the Creator of the Universe, the Absolute Being, has been worshiped by many races under many names, such as Jehovah, Allah, Heavenly Father, the Limitless. During the Age of Night man could not receive direct benefits from Him no matter how ardently he worshiped, for his connection with God was across a veil of clouds, in a manner of speaking.

It is the final Plan of God to establish an ideal world where truth, virtue, and beauty are manifested in complete balance. This can be accomplished only when all the necessary conditions are fulfilled. This is why God has waited for the right time, and now is that time. It is urgent for humanity to realize this and to accomplish the spiritual revolution of its inner self.

However high our ideal for the New Age might be, as long as the level of material civilization was still primitive the state of the world could not be clear. While different races or nations lived in completely different ways, with little understanding of each other and little or no transportation facilities, the unification of thought was impossible.

There are many signs in our present civilization, however, which prove the approach of the New Age. The progress of material civilization itself is a sign of the coming of the ideal world.

Now that the time is at hand for the creation of the new civilization, it is necessary for humanity to be informed of the grand Plan. God does

Teachings of Meishu-sama, Vol. 2 (Atami, Japan: Church of World Messianity, 1968), pp. 10–12, 19–21. Reprinted by permission of the Church of World Messianity.

this work through the instrument of physical man. Here is the significance of the birth of World Messianity. God has revealed His Plan and the Church of World Messianity is working according to His Order to teach the truth for the New Age.

Some of the things in the old order which God deems of use for the New Age He will save. Those which require changing He will change through His great Love. Everything other than these, sad as it may be, must be removed. This is the action which has been termed the Last Judgment. It will be a wonderful as well as a cataclysmic event.

Now that the world is standing on the verge of this critical change, it is most important for man to qualify himself to survive, in order to become a resident in the new world.

When individuals join the Divine Light Program and become channels of the Divine Light, they are endowed with a healing power. Miracles are daily being experienced through our members. What wonderful, divine blessings all are receiving! The teachings of the church help members to reach a better understanding of the secrets of life and to awaken to Truth.

Each member's daily living is improved through the understanding and help of the Divine Light. He becomes happier and is able to face the future with firm conviction and a great sense of well-being and security, for he knows what is to come. . . .

. . . Such words as radial energy and radioactivity are now included in the average vocabulary. They came into focus with the discovery of radium and became a part of our everyday language with the development of atomic fission. Now, many other elements have been discovered and are being used in the development of science. These elements— uranium, thorium, plutonium, etc.—will no doubt be applied in many new fields in future, contributing in larger and larger measure to the welfare of mankind.

There is something, however, that surpasses mineral radiation in every way. I call it Divine Spiritual Radiation. When applied to human problems, it produces wonderful results. Unlike mineral radiation, which must come from earth elements, the Divine Spiritual Radiation comes from Universal Life Energy. It is without limitation and is transmitted through the human body. It contains particles which are more minute and of a higher vibratory rate than that of mineral radiations.

The Divine Spiritual Radiation can be activated by following a specific method, which I call Johrei. One of its most outstanding characteristics is that it is effective only when the motive for using it is virtuous, just and beneficial to humanity.

The divine blessings which have been granted to the devotees of various religions through the ages have been due to this Divine Light. Compared to the Radiation channeled through Johrei, however, that which God sent in the past was considerably weaker, because the time was premature.

Divine Radiation, or the Divine Light, when channeled to the spiritual body of an individual dispels clouds on the spiritual body and raises the spiritual vibration, thereby causing reactions in the spiritual, mental, and physical bodies. When clouds are dispelled the spirit is uplifted and the divine nature unfolds itself more and more, causing the finest spiritual qualities of the individual to come to the fore. Mind is properly focused, relieving it from confusion.

This is why Johrei has proved highly effective when used on mental disorders of many types. When clouds are dispelled from the spiritual body, toxins in the physical body dissolve and are eliminated to a large extent. Pain or discomfort felt by the individual is part of the purifying process and Johrei accelerates this process, bringing it to an end more quickly than it would terminate otherwise.

The use of Divine Spiritual Radiation is not limited to human beings. Many plants which have become weakened from insect blights, extremes of weather or other destructive forces have been revived through Johrei, and the quality of the soil itself has been improved. When the seeds and the soil have become sufficiently purified, a considerable improvement is seen in the quality and quantity of crops too.

It might seem such a great power would be available only to a select few individuals, but this is not so. Any individual, when properly prepared, can channel the Divine Light. The intensity may differ according to the level of individual awareness, but it is possible for any member to channel it effectively.

VII

GODS OF GROVE AND GLORY:
RELIGIONS OF
ANCIENT EUROPE
AND THE NEAR EAST

From several points of view, the seven cultures brought together in this chapter should not be brought together at all. From the beginnings of Sumeria and Egypt to the end of pagan Germanic religion in Iceland, around 1000 A.D., lie not only some five thousand miles but also some five thousand years. That is twice the span of as ancient a faith as Buddhism and more than twice the age of Christianity. If these religious traditions are not synchronous, neither do they derive from any common national, cultural, or language background. Indeed the contrasts between them are often more significant than the parallels.

Yet there are common motifs in these cultures and their religions. However great their time span, they all reflect a particular stage in human development, one that occurred at different times in different societies. That is the stage of the slow emergence of prehistoric peoples —hunters or primitive agriculturists—into larger agricultural societies, gradually developing the cosmopolitanism wrought by extensive trade, writing (which leads to keeping records and, therefore, to some sense of history), and sophisticated political systems—whether the city-states of Greece and early Rome, the tribal kingdoms of the north, or the great empires toward which ancient agricultural societies tend. For imperial rule is relatively easy to establish and relatively beneficial in a society of sendentary agriculturalists requiring security from marauders, stable trade conditions, large-scale hydraulic works, and hub cities in which surplus populations can find employment.

This stage has several common, although not universal, religious characteristics. First, numerous motifs of primitive religion, especially those of primitive agriculture, remain, although sometimes with diminishing force—sacrifice, the seasonal cycle with spring and harvest festivals, the high god as a remote figure, the soul's career after death, and elements of shamanism. Two other motifs often found in primitive religion are likely to grow in importance—polytheism and sacred kingship. Polytheism is strengthened and made more complex initially by the coming together of many peoples, each contributing personal gods to a melting-pot spiritual culture; by the growing division of labor wanting divine paradigms for numerous tasks; and by the elaboration of bureaucratic imperial courts calling for heavenly counterparts. Sacred kingship is obviously related to the growth of ancient empires and to the complete economic dominance of agriculture in them—the rituals of sacred priest-kings typically are designed to reflect the seasonal cycle and increase fertility.

More than anything else, these two motifs set the tone of religion in this centuries-long era. Polytheism is not just a quantitative matter, but also qualitative—it represents an acute spiritual sense of nature as rich, varied, full of a diversity of often competing yet always wondrous finite powers. Sacred kingship is not only a system of government, but suggests a total view of society as stable, organic, and cooperating explicitly with both the earth and the gods.

But the religions of those days did not last; the stable cosmos they envisioned turned out, at least on the historical level, to be mutable. They were all replaced by monotheisms, Christianity or Islam, which cast the gods out of heaven and shrine (even if they often returned as saints or angels), and little by little desacralized the kings. An exception is Zoroastrianism, which was already monotheistic, although not without strong polytheistic strands. Of it a remnant survives, as we have seen in Chapter I.

This change is anticipated in a theme that runs through the later spiritual culture of these societies especially, a yearning for one God supreme over the many gods and kings alike. This quest was abetted by the waxing influence of Zoroastrianism, Judaism, Christianity, and Islam. But the archaic cultures, though replaced by the latter two, live on in written memory with a special glow of their own.

EGYPTIAN RELIGION

The religion of ancient Egypt was a confusing whirl of gods and rites and theologies; constant themes were the regular rise and fall of the Nile, the sovereignty of pharaoh as sacred king, and the agricultural and fertility basis of many of the most important ceremonies. Equally important was the well-known mortuary cult, designed to give first the pharaoh, and finally all people, a joyful immortality. In this passage, a modern scholar describes clearly some of the major themes of Egyptian religion.

From *Ancient Myth and Modern Man*

Gerald A. Larue

Egyptian mythology abounds in gods: more than eighty are known by name, and in numerous instances their functions and identities overlap. Each of the forty-two *nomes* or provinces which were to combine to form the united kingdoms of Upper and Lower Egypt had its own official god. Sometimes the same god or goddess was important in more than one district. Battles between the nomes were simultaneously struggles between the representative deities; when one district was absorbed by another, the god of the conquered area was ·taken into the pantheon of the victor. After Egypt was united, and specific areas emerged from time to time as national cult centers, the chief god or goddess of the particular locale would assume cosmic dimensions and qualities that may have belonged to the god whose status he or she had preempted.

Because local gods had been conceived in a variety of human, animal, and insect forms or combinations of these, the manifestations of divinity during the long period of the united nation were many and varied. A single god might assume many different forms. There developed in Egypt a lack of dogmatism and an open toleration of contradictions. There was no "basic truth," no structured dogma or sacred scripture, no fundamental creed, but rather a variety of unharmonized beliefs that led away from systematized theology. Parallels constituted no problem, but were treated as similar but individual aspects of whatever "reality" might be.

The concept of divinity was fluid. Kings could be gods. At the cult center at Heliopolis, a myth explained that the sun god, Ra, selected the wife of the high priest and, assuming the identity of her husband, copulated with her to produce three sons who were to become the first three pharaohs of the First Dynasty. From that point on, all pharaohs were accepted as sons of Ra. Later, viziers and wise men were believed to be able to become gods after death, a belief which engendered an extensive mortuary religion, originally formulated for the king but extended to queens and nobles.

The fluidity of Egyptian religious thought evoked creative, imaginative mythic patterns. No doubt many Egyptians accepted symbolic animals and human representations of the gods literally, but the sophis-

Gerald A. Larue, *Ancient Myth and Modern Man* (Englewood Cliffs, N.J.: Prentice-Hall, Inc., 1975), pp. 26–28. Reprinted by permission of the publisher.

ticated worshiper, whose beliefs we are slowly coming to understand, recognized in the symbols qualities of the divinity with which certain animals were believed to be endowed. There was a sacred oneness in life. As Henri Frankfort has pointed out, the Egyptian saw the universe "suffused with life" and human life "integrated with the life of nature."

Egyptian mythology centered in two natural phenomena: the Nile river and the sun. Territorially, Egypt was simply the narrow strip of rich black land that bordered the Nile. Here life could be sustained. Soil fertility depended on the rise of the Nile, which began each year when the Dog Star, Sothis (Sirius), appeared on the horizon just before sunrise (July 19). The Nile, fed by rains and melting snow in the head-waters at the Equator, carried down humus and minerals essential for replenishing the soil. Its alluvium-bearing waters were channeled into fields along the Nile and captured by small dams for use later in the season. The earliest literature describes the Nile as flowing from the phallus of Osiris, who as a fertility god was at one time depicted as the fructiferous earth. The sun, which shines on Egypt from an almost always cloudless sky, was recognized as the other life-sustaining force. Manifestations of the sun god ranged from the eye of the falcon to the sun-disc Aton, espoused as the sole acceptable representation by King Akhenaton in the fourteenth century B.C. In the morning, the sun was Khephri, the scarab or dung beetle that rolled the dung ball (the sun) with its hind legs toward the zenith of the heavens. At noon, the sun was Re or Ra, the vigorous young god of Heliopolis. By evening, the sun became an old man, Atum. Or again, in the morning he was born anew as a golden calf from the celestial cow, or as a child of the celestial woman who swallowed him again in the evening. No matter what the manifestation, the sun was the most important factor in Egyptian mythology.

Egyptian mythologies taught that the cosmos, with Egypt and the Nile valley at its center, had emerged from the primeval surfaceless waters, the all-encompassing abyss called Nun. Nun was without form, and void, and complete darkness permeated the deep. The cosmos was a hollowed-out chamber within the waters, protected from their intrusion from below by the earth and from above by the sky. The sky, a hemisphere above the earth, was depicted variously as a cow held up by four legs, as an arched female figure supported by its extended arms and legs, or as a shell supported by mountains or by four posts at the cardinal points. In the beginning, the sun, described sometimes as self-created and sometimes as the child of the sky-goddess, pushed back the abysmal darkness, just as each day the sun's rays push back the darkness of the night. During the night hours, the sun fought its way back through the darkness of the underworld to rise again over Egypt and the world.

Creation itself, attributed to several deities by their respective cult centers, occurred because of some form of sexual activity or through word, which was interpreted as the projection of thought.

THE BABYLONIAN ACCOUNT
OF THE FLOOD

In the Valley of the Two Rivers—modern Iraq—the gods were less predictable than those of the Nile, even as the Tigris and Euphrates were less steady than the river of the pharaohs. The ancient Babylonians were not unfamiliar with both skepticism and anxiety before their deities. But out of such painful stirrings can flow profound literature, and so it was in the land once thought to be the site of the Garden of Eden.

The greatest work from ancient Babylon was the epic of Gilgamesh, based on a myth of the earlier Sumerians. This story tells of the adventures of a hero who sought unsuccessfully for the secret of immortality—that prize was reserved for the gods alone, with two exceptions. Gilgamesh found his way to the home of an ancient sailor, Utnapishtim, and his wife. These two had been given the unique boon of deathlessness after a remarkable adventure long before when certain of the gods tried to destroy mankind by flood. In this passage, we read Utnapishtim's narration to Gilgamesh of that event. Several Babylonian gods are named: Anu, the supreme lord; Enlil, often angry at humankind; Ea, often helpful to humans; and Ishtar, the passionate but compassionate goddess of love. Parallels are evident between this story and the tale of the flood involving Noah in the Book of Genesis.

From *The Epic of Gilgamesh*
N.K. Sanders

THE STORY OF THE FLOOD

'You know the city Shurrupak, it stands on the banks of Euphrates? That city grew old and the gods that were in it were old. There was Anu, lord of the firmament, their father, and warrior Enlil their counsellor, Ninurta the helper, and Ennugi watcher over canals; and with them also

N.K. Sanders, trans., *The Epic of Gilgamesh* (New York: Penguin Books, Inc., 1964), pp. 105–10. Reprinted by permission of Penguin Books Ltd.

was Ea. In those days the world teemed, the people multiplied, the world bellowed like a wild bull, and the great god was aroused by the clamour. Enlil heard the clamour and he said to the gods in council, "The uproar of mankind is intolerable and sleep is no longer possible by reason of the babel." So the gods in their hearts were moved to let loose the deluge; but my lord Ea warned me in a dream. He whispered their words to my house of reeds, "Reed-house, reed-house! Wall, O wall, hearken reed-house, wall reflect; O man of Shurrupak, son of Ubara-Tutu; tear down your house and build a boat, abandon possessions and look for life, despise worldly goods and save your soul alive. Tear down your house, I say, and build a boat. These are the measurements of the barque as you shall build her: let her beam equal her length, let her deck be roofed like the vault that covers the abyss; then take up into the boat the seed of all living creatures."

'When I had understood I said to my lord, "Behold, what you have commanded I will honour and perform, but how shall I answer the people, the city, the elders?" Then Ea opened his mouth and said to me, his servant, "Tell them this: I have learnt that Enlil is wrathful against me, I dare no longer walk in his land nor live in his city; I will go down to the Gulf to dwell with Ea my lord. But on you he will rain down abundance, rare fish and shy wild-fowl, a rich harvest-tide. In the evening the rider of the storm will bring you wheat in torrents."

'In the first light of dawn all my household gathered round me, the children brought pitch and the men whatever was necessary. On the fifth day I laid the keel and the ribs, then I made fast the planking. The ground-space was one acre, each side of the deck measured one hundred and twenty cubits, making a square. I built six decks below, seven in all, I divided them into nine sections with bulkheads between. I drove in wedges where needed, I saw to the punt-poles, and laid in supplies. The carriers brought oil in baskets, I poured pitch into the furnace and asphalt and oil; more oil was consumed in caulking, and more again the master of the boat took into his stores. I slaughtered bullocks for the people and every day I killed sheep. I gave the ship-wrights wine to drink as though it were river water, raw wine and red wine and oil and white wine. There was feasting then as there is at the time of the New Year's festival; I myself anointed my head. On the seventh day the boat was complete.

'Then was the launching full of difficulty; there was shifting of ballast above and below till two thirds was submerged. I loaded into her all that I had of gold and of living things, my family, my kin, the beasts of the field both wild and tame, and all the craftsmen. I sent them on board, for the time that Shamash had ordained was already fulfilled when he said, "In the evening, when the rider of the storm sends down the destroying rain, enter the boat and batten her down." The time was fulfilled, the evening came, the rider of the storm sent down the rain. I looked out at the weather and it was terrible, so I too boarded the boat and battened her down. All was now complete, the battening and the caulking; so I handed the tiller to Puzur-Amurri the steersman, with the navigation and the care of the whole boat.

'With the first light of dawn a black cloud came from the horizon; it thundered within where Adad, lord of the storm was riding. In front over hill and plain Shullat and Hanish, heralds of the storm, led on. Then the gods of the abyss rose up; Nergal pulled out the dams of the nether waters, Ninurta the war-lord threw down the dykes, and the seven judges of hell, the Annunaki, raised their torches, lighting the land with their livid flame. A stupor of despair went up to heaven when the god of the storm turned daylight to darkness, when he smashed the land like a cup. One whole day the tempest raged gathering fury as it went, it poured over the people like the tides of battle; a man could not see his brother nor the people be seen from heaven. Even the gods were terrified at the flood, they fled to the highest heaven, the firmament of Anu; they crouched against the walls, cowering like curs. Then Ishtar the sweet-voiced Queen of Heaven cried out like a woman in travail: "Alas the days of old are turned to dust because I commanded evil; why did I command this evil in the council of all the gods? I commanded wars to destroy the people, but are they not my people, for I brought them forth? Now like the spawn of fish they float in the ocean." The great gods of heaven and of hell wept, they covered their mouths.

'For six days and six nights the winds blew, torrent and tempest and flood overwhelmed the world, tempest and flood raged together like warring hosts. When the seventh day dawned the storm from the south subsided, the sea grew calm, the flood was stilled; I looked at the face of the world and there was silence, all mankind was turned to clay. The surface of the sea stretched as flat as a roof-top; I opened a hatch and the light fell on my face. Then I bowed low, I sat down and I wept, the tears streamed down my face, for on every side was the waste of water. I looked for land in vain, but fourteen leagues distant there appeared a mountain, and there the boat grounded; on the mountain of Nisir the boat held fast, she held fast and did not budge. One day she held, and a second day on the mountain of Nisir she held fast and did not budge. A third day, and a fourth day she held fast on the mountain and did not budge; a fifth day and a sixth day she held fast on the mountain. When the seventh day dawned I loosed a dove and let her go. She flew away, but finding no resting-place she returned. Then I loosed a swallow, and she flew away but finding no resting-place she returned. I loosed a raven, she saw that the waters had retreated, she ate, she flew around, she cawed, and she did not come back. Then I threw everything open to the four winds, I made a sacrifice and poured out a libation on the mountain top. Seven and again seven cauldrons I set up on their stands, I heaped up wood and cane and cedar and myrtle. When the gods smelled the sweet savour, they gathered like flies over the sacrifice. Then, at last, Ishtar also came, she lifted her necklace with the jewels of heaven that once Anu had made to please her. "O you gods here present, by the lapis lazuli round my neck I shall remember these days as I remember the jewels of my throat; these last days I shall not forget. Let all the gods gather round the sacrifice, except Enlil. He shall not approach this offering, for without reflection he brought the flood; he consigned my people to destruction."

'When Enlil had come, when he saw the boat, he was wrath and swelled with anger at the gods, the host of heaven, "Has any of these mortals escaped? Not one was to have survived the destruction." Then the god of the wells and canals Ninurta opened his mouth and said to the warrior Enlil, "Who is there of the gods that can devise without Ea? It is Ea alone who knows all things." Then Ea opened his mouth and spoke to warrior Enlil, "Wisest of gods, hero Enlil, how could you so senselessly bring down the flood?

> Lay upon the sinner his sin,
> Lay upon the transgressor his transgression,
> Punish him a little when he breaks loose,
> Do not drive him too hard or he perishes;
> Would that a lion had ravaged mankind
> Rather than the flood,
> Would that a wolf had ravaged mankind
> Rather than the flood,
> Would that famine had wasted the world
> Rather than the flood,
> Would that pestilence had wasted mankind
> Rather than the flood.

It was not I that revealed the secret of the gods; the wise man learned it in a dream. Now take your counsel what shall be done with him."

'Then Enlil went up into the boat, he took me by the hand and my wife and made us enter the boat and kneel down on either side, he standing between us. He touched our foreheads to bless us saying, "In time past Utnapishtim was a mortal man; henceforth he and his wife shall live in the distance at the mouth of the rivers." Thus it was that the gods took me and placed me here to live in the distance, at the mouth of the rivers.'

THE POEMS OF ZOROASTER

These verses are among those attributed to Zoroaster himself. They are not easy to follow, and so the commentary by the modern translator is included. But these lines do express several of the main themes of Zoroaster's teaching: the dualism of good and evil spiritual forces warring for the world, the necessity of people to make a choice between them, the

*ultimate eschatological promise of a fair world for those who have made
the right choices. The personified virtues—Dominion, Good Mind, Righteousness, and so forth—are mighty but rather mysterious beings who occur
in Zoroaster's discourse. They are apparently personified attributes or
archangels of the Wise Lord, Ahura Mazda. The "false gods," or daivas,
have given us our word "devil."*

From *The Hymns of Zarathustra*

Jacques Duchesne-Guillemin

1

Now will I speak to those who will hear
Of the things which the initiate should remember:
The praises and prayer of the Good Mind to the Lord
And the joy which he shall see in the light who has remembered
   them well.

2

Hear with your ears that which is the sovereign good;
With a clear mind look upon the two sides
Between which each man must choose for himself,
Watchful beforehand that the great test may be accomplished in our
   favour.

3

Now at the beginning the twin spirits have declared their nature,
The better and the evil,
In thought and word and deed. And between the two
The wise ones choose well, not so the foolish.

4

And when these two spirits came together,
In the beginning they established life and non-life,
And that at the last the worst existence should be for the wicked,
But for the righteous one the Best Mind.

Jacques Duchesne-Guillemin, *The Hymns of Zarathustra* (Boston: The Beacon
Press, Inc., 1963), pp. 103–7. Reprinted by permission of John Murray, Ltd.

5

Of these two spirits, the evil one chose to do the worst things;
But the Most Holy Spirit, clothed in the most steadfast heavens,
Joined himself unto Righteousness;
And thus did all those who delight to please the Wise Lord
    by honest deeds.

6

Between the two, the false gods also did not choose rightly,
For while they pondered they were beset by error,
So that they chose the Worst Mind.
Then did they hasten to join themselves unto Fury,
That they might by it deprave the existence of man.

7

And to him came Devotion, together with Dominion, Good
    Mind and Righteousness:
She gave endurance of body and the breath of life,
That he may be thine apart from them,
As the first by the retributions through the metal.

8

And when their punishment shall come to these sinners,
Then, O Wise One, shall thy Dominion, with the Good Mind,
Be granted to those who have delivered Evil into the hands of
    Righteousness, O Lord!

9

And may we be those that renew this existence!
O Wise One, and you other Lords, and Righteousness, bring
    your alliance,
That thoughts may gather where wisdom is faint.

10

Then shall Evil cease to flourish,
While those who have acquired good fame
Shall reap the promised reward
In the blessed dwelling of the Good Mind, of the Wise One,
    and of Righteousness.

11

If you, O men, understand the commandments which the Wise
    One has given,
Well-being and suffering—long torment for the wicked and
    salvation for the righteous—
All shall hereafter be for the best.

In the body of the hymn the account of the choice occupies stanzas 3 to 6 and half of the seventh, and the eschatology the rest of the poem, except the eleventh and final stanza.

Stanza 3 assumes the two twin Spirits at the origin, one good, the other evil, in thought, speech, and deed, between whom, or in imitation of whom, man's choice must be made: the good choice of the wise and the bad choice of the others. (Here appears the "human triad" thought-speech-action, characteristic of this religion, which does not limit its horizon to actions only, or to words only. Note also the coincidence between intelligence and good.)

Stanza 4 describes the encounter between the two Spirits, who, as it were, divide the world between them, one establishing life, the other its opposite, and who apportion to the righteous and to the wicked their respective destinies. The cleavage is seen to widen: on one side good, intelligence, life; on the other, evil, foolishness, non-life. As to the two rewards, they do not at first appear to be of equally perfect symmetry: worst existence—Best Mind. But this is only appearance, for the *manah*, a term which we translate roughly as Mind, is almost synonymous with "principle of life."

Between these two domains the evil Spirit chooses the worse, the Most Holy Spirit joins itself to Righteousness (which is implicitly—for this goes without saying—on the side of the good). Then the choice of mankind took place: those who want to please the Wise Lord have imitated the Holy Spirit (5).

Next comes the turn of the *daivas* or false gods. Overtaken and possessed by error, by foolishness, they took the bad part, here described as the exact opposite of the Best Mind. At the same time they became the enemies of life and friends of the Fury which destroys the latter, violently set against man (6).

Against such enemies man had to have helpers: they were not only Righteousness and Good Mind, and Dominion, but also Devotion, whose part is specified. Devotion, who has already been seen to be invoked for strength, has given "lastingness of bodies and the breath of life" to allow man to endure and to survive until the final reward. At the time of this reward, which will take place by an ordeal by metal, man will be set apart from the false gods and their band of "non-living": he will be the first to be rewarded (7).

We come thus to the consideration of the final things. While the sinners will be punished, those who have fought against the wicked and delivered them "into the hands of Righteousness" will be rewarded: they shall have the Good Mind and the Dominion of the Lord.

Thus will this existence be renewed. May we, prays Zarathustra, by choosing with intelligence, with the help of the Entities, be the *agents* of this renewal. Clearly it is not a question of individual recompense, *undergone* after death. The event will be collective and will take place on earth, in this very life, which it will prolong by renewing it, by transforming it, for the righteous only.[1] The coming of the Kingdom of God, the establishment of a golden age, will correspond to the original choice, by which the "first existence" had begun. Evil will be conquered, while those who have acted well will be happy in the abode of the Triad (10).

The final stanza clearly repeats, in conclusion, the terms of the choice, which it is enough for mankind to understand well.

GREEK HYMNS

Something of the spirit of ancient Greece is caught in these hymns ascribed to the age of Homer and Hesiod (c. 800 B.C.) and probably composed by unknown poets between the eighth and sixth centuries B.C. They are addressed to certain of the best-known of the classic gods: Aphrodite, of love; Ares, of war; Artemis, the lone and virginal huntress; and mad frolicsome Dionysus, also called Bacchus. Dionysus is lover of music and mirth and giver of sweet song, but his rampages (as the myth here recounted illustrates) can run to excess. In their gods, and the rites that celebrated them, the Greeks expressed the many sides of their experience of life. Dionysus was patron of the maenads, crazed women who ran through the countryside slaying and devouring bulls, and of bucolic, boisterous harvest festivals. The more decorous sacrifices of the city temples, the famous shrines, and the initiatory mysteries of Eleusis all express other sides of Greek piety. But the stately tone of these hymns, even when describing the uninhibited sports of Dionysus, suggest the clarity and moderation of mind for which ancient Greece was famous.

Hesiod, The Homeric Hymns and Homerica
Huge G. Evelyn-White

TO APHRODITE

I will sing of stately Aphrodite, gold-crowned and beautiful, whose dominion is the walled cities of all sea-set Cyprus. There the moist breath

[1]The hopes of the first Christians spring to mind: "Verily I say unto you, that this generation shall not pass . . ."

Hugh G. Evelyn-White, *Hesiod, The Homeric Hymns and Homerica* (New York: G.P. Putnam's Sons, 1914), pp. 427–35. English text only. Reprinted by permission of the Harvard University Press and the Loeb Classical Library.

of the western wind wafted her over the waves of the loud-moaning sea in soft foam, and there the gold-filleted Hours welcomed her joyously. They clothed her with heavenly garments: on her head they put a fine, well-wrought crown of gold, and in her pierced ears they hung ornaments of orichale and precious gold, and adorned her with golden necklaces over her soft neck and snow-white breasts, jewels which the gold-filleted Hours wear themselves whenever they go to their father's house to join the lovely dances of the gods. And when they had fully decked her, they brought her to the gods, who welcomed her when they saw her, giving her their hands. Each one of them prayed that he might lead her home to be his wedded wife, so greatly were they amazed at the beauty of violet-crowned Cytherea.

Hail, sweetly-winning, coy-eyed goddess! Grant that I may gain the victory in this contest, and order you my song. And now I will remember you and another song also.

TO DIONYSUS

I will tell of Dionysus, the son of glorious Semele, how he appeared on a jutting headland by the shore of the fruitless sea, seeming like a stripling in the first flush of manhood: his rich, dark hair was waving about him, and on his strong shoulders he wore a purple robe. Presently there came swiftly over the sparkling sea Tyrsenian[1] pirates on a well-decked ship—a miserable doom led them on. When they saw him they made signs to one another and sprang out quickly, and seizing him straightway, put him on board their ship exultingly; for they thought him the son of heaven-nurtured kings. They sought to bind him with rude bonds, but the bonds would not hold him, and the withes fell far away from his hands and feet: and he sat with a smile in his dark eyes. Then the helmsman understood all and cried out at once to his fellows and said:

"Madmen! what god is this whom you have taken and bind, strong that he is? Not even the well-built ship can carry him. Surely this is either Zeus or Apollo who has the silver bow, or Poseidon, for he looks not like mortal men but like the gods who dwell on Olympus. Come, then, let us set him free upon the dark shore at once: do not lay hands on him, lest he grow angry and stir up dangerous winds and heavy squalls."

So said he: but the master chid him with taunting words: "Madman, mark the wind and help hoist sail on the ship: catch all the sheets. As for this fellow we men will see to him: I reckon he is bound for

---

[1]Probably not Etruscans, but the non-Hellenic peoples of Thrace and (according to Thucydides) of Lemnos and Athens. Cp. Herodotus i. 57; Thucydides iv. 109.

Egypt or for Cyprus or to the Hyperboreans or further still. But in the end he will speak out and tell us his friends and all his wealth and his brothers, now that providence has thrown him in our way."

When he had said this, he had mast and sail hoisted on the ship, and the wind filled the sail and the crew hauled taut the sheets on either side. But soon strange things were seen among them. First of all sweet, fragrant wine ran streaming throughout all the black ship and a heavenly smell arose, so that all the seamen were seized with amazement when they saw it. And all at once a vine spread out both ways along the top of the sail with many clusters hanging down from it, and a dark ivy-plant twined about the mast, blossoming with flowers, and with rich berries growing on it; and all the thole-pins were covered with garlands. When the pirates saw all this, then at last they bade the helmsman to put the ship to land. But the god changed into a dreadful lion there on the ship, in the bows, and roared loudly: amidships also he showed his wonders and created a shaggy bear which stood up ravening, while on the forepeak was the lion glaring fiercely with scowling brows. And so the sailors fled into the stern and crowded bemused about the right-minded helmsman, until suddenly the lion sprang upon the master and seized him; and when the sailors saw it they leapt out overboard one and all into the bright sea, escaping from a miserable fate, and were changed into dolphins. But on the helmsman Dionysus had mercy and held him back and made him altogether happy, saying to him:

"Take courage, good . . .; you have found favour with my heart. I am loud-crying Dionysus whom Cadmus' daughter Semele bare of union with Zeus."

Hail, child of fair-faced Semele! He who forgets you can in no wise order sweet song.

TO ARES

Ares, exceeding in strength, chariot-rider, golden-helmed, doughty in heart, shield-bearer, Saviour of cities, harnessed in bronze, strong of arm, unwearying, mighty with the spear, O defence of Olympus, father of warlike Victory, ally of Themis, stern governor of the rebellious, leader of righteous men, sceptred King of manliness, who whirl your fiery sphere among the planets in their sevenfold courses through the aether wherein your blazing steeds ever bear you above the third firmament of heaven; hear me, helper of men, giver of dauntless youth! Shed down a kindly ray from above upon my life, and strength of war, that I may be able to drive away bitter cowardice from my head and crush down the deceitful impulses of my soul. Restrain also the keen fury of my heart which provokes me to tread the ways of blood-curdling strife. Rather, O blessed one, give you me boldness to abide within the harmless laws of peace, avoiding strife and hatred and the violent fiends of death.

TO ARTEMIS

Muse, sing of Artemis, sister of the Far-shooter, the virgin who delights in arrows, who was fostered with Apollo. She waters her horses from Meles deep in reeds, and swiftly drives her all-golden chariot through Smyrna to vine-clad Claros where Apollo, god of the silver bow, sits waiting for the far-shooting goddess who delights in arrows.

And so hail to you, Artemis, in my song and to all goddesses as well. Of you first I sing and with you I begin; now that I have begun with you, I will turn to another song.

SIGNS AND WONDERS AT ROME

These lines by the great Roman historian Livy (59 B.C.–17 A.D.) relate events at a desperate moment in early Roman history, 217 B.C., when Hannibal was threatening Rome and the future seemed chancy indeed. As though reflecting this uncertainty about the settled order of things, strange wonders of nature were reported. In response, the Senate advised consulting the Sybilline Books, sacred writings containing words uttered long before by a prophetess in trance. At times of crisis, a message was obtained from the writings by a committee of the Senate through some unknown process of divination. On this occasion, certain religious offerings were made as indicated by the oracle, culminating in the great year-end festival called the Saturnalia. Apparently these measures worked, for Rome was saved.

From *Livy*

B.O. Foster

BOOK XXII

Spring was now drawing on, and accordingly Hannibal moved out of his winter encampment. He had tried before this to cross the Apen-

B.O. Foster, trans., *Livy,* Vol. V (New York: G.P. Putnam's Sons, 1929), pp. 199–205. English text only. Reprinted by permission of the Harvard University Press and the Loeb Classical Library.

nines, but had failed because of the intolerable cold. And the delay had been attended with the greatest danger and anxiety; for when the Gauls, whom the hope of spoil and pillage had excited to revolt, perceived that instead of harrying and plundering the fields of others, their own lands were the seat of war and were burdened with the winter quarters of both armies, they turned their hatred back again from the Romans upon Hannibal. But though their leaders laid many a plot against him, their treachery to one another saved him, for they gave him information of these conspiracies with the same inconstancy with which they had conspired. Moreover, changing now his dress and now his headgear, he protected himself against their plots by the uncertainty which this gave rise to. Still, the fear of such plots was another reason for quitting his winter quarters early.

About the same time, on the Ides of March, Gnaeus Servilius entered on his consulship at Rome. On his then referring the state of the nation to the senate for discussion, their anger at Gaius Flaminius was renewed. They had chosen two consuls, they said, but had only one; for what proper authority or right of auspices did Flaminius possess? Magistrates, they urged, carried with them this prerogative when they set out from home—from their own and the nation's hearth—after celebrating the Latin Festival, sacrificing on the Alban Mount and duly offering up their vows on the Capitol; but a private citizen could neither take the auspices with him, nor, if he had left Rome without them, receive them new from the beginning on foreign soil.

Men's fears were augmented by the prodigies reported simultaneously from many places: that in Sicily the javelins of several soldiers had taken fire, and that in Cardinia, as a horseman was making the round of the night-watch, the same thing had happened to the truncheon which he held in his hand; that many fires had blazed up on the shore; that two shields had sweated blood; that certain soldiers had been struck with lightning; that the sun's disk had seemed to be contracted; that glowing stones had fallen from the sky at Praeneste; that at Arpi bucklers had appeared in the sky and the sun had seemed to be fighting with the moon; that at Capena two moons had risen in the daytime; that the waters of Caere had flowed mixed with blood, and that bloodstains had appeared in the water that trickled from the spring of Hercules itself; that at Antium, when some men were reaping, bloody ears of corn had fallen into their basket; that at Falerii the sky had seemed to be rent as it were with a great fissure, and through the opening a bright light had shone; and that lots had shrunk and that one had fallen out without being touched, on which was written, "Mavors brandishes his spear;" that in Rome, about the same time, the statue of Mars on the Appian Way and the images of the wolves had sweated; that at Capua there had been the appearance of a sky on fire and of a moon that fell in the midst of a shower of rain. Afterwards less memorable prodigies were also given credence: that certain folk had found their goats to have got woolly fleeces; that a hen had changed into a cock and a cock into a hen.

When the consul had laid these reports before the senate exactly as they had come to him and had introduced into the House the men who vouched for their truth, he consulted the Fathers regarding their religious import. It was voted that these prodigies should be expiated, in part with greater, in part with lesser victims, and that a supplication should be held for three days at all the couches of the gods; as for the rest, when the decemvirs should have inspected the Books, such rites were to be observed as they should declare, in accordance with the sacred verses, to be pleasing to the gods. Being so admonished by the decemvirs, they decreed that the first gift should be made to Jupiter, a golden thunderbolt weighing fifty pounds; and that Juno and Minerva should be given offerings of silver; that Juno Regina on the Aventine and Juno Sospita at Lanuvium should receive a sacrifice of greater victims, and that the matrons, each contributing as much as she could afford, should make up a sum of money and carry it as a gift to Juno Regina on the Aventine and there celebrate a *lectisternium;* and that even the very freed-women should contribute money, in proportion to their abilities, for an offering to Feronia.

These measures being taken, the decemvirs sacrificed at Ardea in the market-place with the greater victims. Finally—the month was now December—victims were slain at the temple of Saturn in Rome and a *lectisternium* was ordered—this time senators administered the rite—and a public feast, and throughout the City for a day and a night "Saturnalia" was cried, and the people were bidden to keep that day as a holiday and observe it in perpetuity.

RELIGIONS OF THE ROMAN EMPIRE

As the Roman eagles went east and west, a vast multitude was brought together into one empire. People and ideas moved with relative ease about the Mediterranean world, and gods and cults from far and near settled in teeming Rome or the other great cities. The following passage gives something of the spiritual tone of this world. We see reference to Kybele the Great Mother, to Dionysus as Attis, to the Eleusinian mysteries. Note that now these cults are relatively detached from their place and community of origin to become free-floating experiences; note too the great emphasis on their power to grant personal salvation, for in a brutal and confusing world, personal salvation and faith in one God were what the hearts of many yearned for most.

From *Ancient Roman Religion*

H.J. Rose

This miscellaneous rabble of nominal Romans, mixed with resident foreigners, had lost its last semblance of political power under Tiberius, when the elections of magistrates were transferred to the Senate in A.D. 14. It still, however, could be troublesome if it rioted, so the standing governmental policy was to keep it in good humour; but little or nothing was done officially for its moral or educational improvement. It is therefore no wonder that non-Roman influences, good or bad, were rife.

One of these owed its beginnings to Sulla's campaigns in the Near East. His soldiers there came into contact with the goddess Ma (i.e. Mother) of Cappadocia, whose followers were even noisier than the Galli in their ritual. They were armed with swords and axes, with which, when wrought up into a frenzy by wild dancing attended by loud music, they cut themselves freely. They were supposed to be possessed by their goddess, and under that influence could prophecy; as one of them foretold that Sulla would win against Marius, his great rival, he favoured the cult and let it be introduced into Rome, where it continued after his death in 78 B.C., and the "people of the shrine" (*fanatici*), as the Romans called them, were a familiar sight and sound in the City under the early Empire. The goddess herself was identified, owing presumably to the warlike appearance of her followers, with Bellona, the Roman war-goddess, associated with Mars, and so was commonly called by that name in Latin. She was, it would seem, no very formidable rival to the Great Mother, being indeed too much like her to constitute a counter-influence.

Kybelê's rites continued to increase in popularity, and were enlarged by two different kinds of ceremonial, the one savage and revolting, the other containing at least the germs of a lofty religion. The former, which can be traced back to the second century of our era, though its ultimate origins are obscure, was the notorious *taurobolium*. The word is Greek, like many of the technicalities of all these cults, for Greek, in forms more or less corrupt and degenerate, was the lingua franca of the Near East by that time, few of the native languages ever having more than a local popularity, for few of them had any literature at all, and a language not commonly written will not spread far beyond its native

H.J. Rose, *Ancient Roman Religion* (London: Hutchinson's University Library, 1948), pp. 128–31. Reprinted by permission of Hutchinson Publishing Group Ltd.

place. In Greece itself, none of these religions had much vogue.[1] *Tauro-bolium*, then, means properly the shooting of the bull (by means of arrows or other missiles), which indicates that the practice began somewhere in a district containing wild cattle. A bull was stood over a grating which covered a pit, and there killed with a hunting-spear. The person for whose benefit the rite was performed was in the pit, and received the blood from the slaughtered beast all over his body. He then emerged and the congregation bowed in veneration before him, for he was, as inscriptions assure us, "reborn for ever," although others, more modestly, limit the "new birth" to twenty years. In some cases a ram was substituted for the bull, but the effect was the same; the man thus reborn was or became in either case a priest of the Great Mother, at least normally. It is fairly clear that the originators of the rite meant to acquire, by the blood of the sacred animal, perhaps an avatar of some god, something of his divine power and nature. The worshippers of Kybelê do not seem to have had so clear-cut a belief, though they held the ceremony to be very efficacious, and one of their most interesting inscriptions indicates that they somehow attached moral attributes to their savage performance, which they expressed in language derived ultimately from the Zoroastrian scriptures, the Gathas.

The other development was a comparatively spiritual and exalted cult of Attis. We have already seen that his worshippers were on occasion addressed as "initiates," and that they celebrated his death and resurrection with pious zeal. It will be remembered, also, that they were invited to base their own hopes of "salvation after their toils" upon the deliverance from the death of their god. It would seem, therefore, that they were in some measure identified with him, a not uncommon phenomenon in cults, not so much of the classical world proper, as of those regions lying just east of it. The best-known form of the belief, which reached Greece at a fairly early date, perhaps the seventh century B.C., was that a worthy worshipper of Dionysus could gain, under certain circumstances, such identification with the god as to be called by his characteristic epithet, Bakchos. But it is likewise the central feature of the worships we are now discussing, which generally are known collectively as the mystery-cults. It seems likely that anyone who had undergone the *taurobolium* was "reborn," not as a human being but as Attis; and apart from this unpleasing method of attaining permanent or temporary deity, we have a fragment of the ritual of a more sober cult. One of the Christian controversialists to whom we owe not a little knowledge of the later forms of paganism, Firmicus Maternus, who preached against what had once been his own religion or one like it with all the zeal of a convert, says in his interesting tract, *On the Error of Profane* (i.e., non-Christian) *Cults*, that the pagans had certain passwords, the result of "the devil's

[1]See Rose, *Ancient Greek Religion,* p. 129.

teaching," and that one of them, which he gives both in the original Greek and in a free Latin translation, ran:

> I have eaten from the timbrel; I have drunk from the cymbal; I am become an initiate of Attis.

He then proceeds to thunder against it with all the force of his rhetorical powers and explain how much better is the Christian Eucharist. To those who look at such things calmly, away from the atmosphere of religious controversies now long dead, it is an interesting formula, for it bears a resemblance which can hardly be accidental to one adduced by St. Clement of Alexandria as belonging to the Eleusinian Mysteries.

> I fasted; I drank the *kykeon*; I took from the sacred chest; I wrought therewith and put it in the basket, and from the basket into the chest.

The *kykeon* was a ritual drink containing water, meal and some other ingredients. Clement also knows a fuller version of the formula concerning Attis, in which the initiate mentions two more sacral actions, carrying a vessel called a *kernos,* of very ancient fashion and used in other mystic rites as well, and entrance into the *pastos* or marriage-chamber. Naturally, these formulae are not explicit; they do not, for instance, tell us what the Eleusinian initiate took from the chest nor what he "wrought" with it, nor why the votary of Attis carried the *kernos,* what the marriage-chamber was nor what he did in it. His co-religionists would know, and the profane were meant to be left uninformed. But from what we know or can guess concerning rites of this kind, we are left with some information. The devotee of Attis ate and drank from sacred utensils, musical instruments of oriental types used in the service of their deity. He thus partook of a sacred feast, the food and drink being charged with the holiness of the god. At some time during the ritual, whether the occasion to which the password refers or not, the initiate drank milk, and as that is the food of babies, it was interpreted by some at least as a symbol of rebirth. There exists a late but interesting treatise by one Sallustius, probably that Sallustius who was a friend of Julian the Apostate, Emperor 361–363 A.D. and would-be restorer of paganism, which explains it so, and furthermore, finds in the whole series of rites, from the cutting of the pine-tree onwards, a deep allegory of the return of the human soul from its present unworthy environment to the company of the gods whence it sprang. Sallustius is far from being an original thinker, and it may be taken as certain that his interpretations were those of many pious followers of this or similar religions. Thus we find that out of a cult originally grotesque, revolting and founded upon notions belonging to a barbarous stage of human development, there could arise, with the admixture of a little Greek philosophy, a faith anything but degraded, though hampered with the need for explaining away many features of ritual which no Westerner would welcome save under the influence of a conviction that in these barbarian practices there lurked ancient wisdom and a system both metaphysical and ethical which was worthy of admiration and adoption.

CELTIC RELIGION

Before and during the days of the Roman Empire, the Celtic peoples were the inhabitants of much of western Europe; their distinctive language and culture still survives, sometimes tenuously, in the "Celtic fringe" of Europe—Brittany, Cornwall, Wales, Ireland, and Scotland. This passage by two modern scholars tells of one of the most striking motifs of Celtic religion, the vivid sense of the sacred meaning of the turning of the seasons. Observe the rich interaction between our world and the world of the fairies, probably originally Celtic gods or spirits of the departed. Note also the background of many of our holidays, such as Halloween and May Day, in Celtic lore, reinforced in England by Anglo-Saxon and Christian parallels.

From *Celtic Heritage*
Alwyn Rees and Brinley Rees

The dividing lines between the contrasting periods of time are haunted by a mysterious power which has a propensity both for good and for evil. Certain acts were forbidden at sunrise and at sunset because these were moments of danger; on the other hand, morning dew and morning water had a particular virtue, and cures could be effected by remedies sought at sunset. This supernatural power breaks through in a most ominous way on November Eve and May Eve, the joints between the two great seasons of the year. These two Eves (together with Midsummer's Eve) were known as 'spirit nights' in Wales, and throughout the Celtic lands chaos was as it were let loose at these two junctures, fairies were unusually active, witches worked their charms, and the future was foreshadowed by omens of all kinds. The customs of both Eves have features characteristic of New Year celebrations generally; for example, the prac-

Alwyn Rees and Brinley Rees, *Celtic Heritage* (London: Thames and Hudson, 1973), pp. 89–93. Notes omitted. Reprinted by permission of the publisher. Copyright 1961 by Alwyn and Brinley Rees.

tice of divinations and the re-lighting of household fires from a ceremonial bonfire. But in atmosphere the two festivals differed fundamentally in that they epitomized the contrasting seasons which they inaugurated.

Hallowe'en, the Calends of winter, was a solemn and weird festival. The *sid*-mounds were open on this '*púca*' night, and their inhabitants were abroad in a more real sense than on any other night. The souls of the dead returned and became visible. In Ireland, until recently, people did not leave the house on this night unless obliged to do so, and if they did they kept clear of churchyards. They should not look behind when they heard footsteps, for it was the dead that were on their tracks. In Wales it was said that there was a phantom on every stile. Food, called *bwyd cennad y meirw*, was left out-of-doors to propitiate the wandering dead, doors were left unbolted, and special care was taken before going to bed to prepare the hearth for the visit of dead relatives.

In Scotland, it was a 'night of mischief and confusion,' and its eeriness was intensified by the impersonation of spirits of the dead by young men who went about with masked, veiled or blackened faces, and dressed in white or in disguises of straw. The boundary between the living and the dead was thus obliterated, and so was the separation of the sexes, for boys wore the clothing of girls and sometimes girls disguised themselves as boys. The general disorder was further intensified by mischievous pranks. Ploughs, carts, gates, and other belongings were borne away and thrown into ditches and ponds; horses were led away and left in other people's fields. The peace of the household itself was disturbed: the door was bombarded with cabbages pulled at random from gardens, the chimney was blocked with turf, and smoke was blown in through keyholes.

An extraordinarily wide variety of divinations were practised on Winter's Eve to discover who would die during the course of the year, who would marry, and who the future partner would be. In Wales, anyone bold enough to wait in the church porch until midnight might hear a voice calling out the names of those who were to die during the year—but he ran the risk of hearing his own name among those of the doomed. Marriage divinations were a particular feature of this Eve, but even in these death lurked round the corner; there was always the danger of seeing a coffin instead of the face of the future partner. Hazel-nuts and apples, the fruits of two trees with rich otherworld associations, figured prominently in many of the divinatory pastimes.

A period of disorder in between the old year and the new is a common feature of New Year rituals in many lands, but it is soon followed by the re-creation of an orderly world which lasts for another year. At Hallowe'en the elimination of boundaries, between the dead and the living, between the sexes, between one man's property and another's and, in divinations, between the present and future, all symbolize the return of chaos. It is noteworthy that the 'day with a night' which the Mac Óc, in the foregoing story, equated with the whole of time, were those of Samain. This day partakes of the nature of eternity. But, bonfires apart, the positive side of the ritual is not evident in the surviving customs. What Hallowe'en inaugurates is winter, and much of the uncanniness of the night, when man seems powerless in the hands of fate, will prevail until the dawn of another summer.

Summer's Eve, on the other hand, has a positive as well as a negative aspect. Fairies can work mischief and witches can bring misfortune by stealing the year's profit from cattle and from wells, but the dangers of the night are different from the awful imminence of death experienced at Allhallowtide. This world is no longer swamped by the world beyond; one's *luck* in the ensuing year may be in the balance, but one is not brought face to face with an unalterable destiny. And effective measures can be taken to ward off evil. One can keep watch to prevent witches from stealing the first milk and from skimming the well on May morn, and other precautions against the dangers of witchcraft can be taken by refusing to give away fire, water, and food. Branches of the rowan-tree, placed over the doors of house and byre, will keep away witches and fairies alike. Whereas folklore has little to say about what one should do on the first *day* of November, the perils of May Eve are but a prelude to the joys of the first summer's day: a climb up a hill to see the sunrise, washing in the morning dew, drinking from the well before sunrise, the gathering of leaves and flowers and the wearing of greenery instead of the straw of winter. It was the dawn of a new and orderly day, the sun rose early and so should men, and the ritual niggardliness and guarding of property on this day is in marked contrast to the free giving to the living and the dead, and the liberties taken with other people's belongings, on Hallowe'en.

While the twofold structure was basic to the Celtic conception of time, other patterns, such as the fourfold division of the day into morning, afternoon, evening, and night, of the moon into quarters, and of the year into spring, summer, autumn, and winter, all had a meaning beyond the purely temporal one. And the moments at which the divisions joined partook in some degree of the significance attached to the great turning-points of the year. Midday and midnight, like sunrise and sunset, were moments when the veil between this world and the unseen world was very thin. Fairy funerals were to be seen at noon, and it was an auspicious moment for banishing fairy 'changelings.' Midnight was the 'witching hour,' fairies and phantoms became visible, and to visit a churchyard at this hour was a challenge to be reckoned with.

St Bridgid's Night (The Eve of the First of February) divided the winter half of the year into winter and spring; *Lugnasad* (Lammas, 1st August) divided the summer half into summer and autumn. St Brigid's Day, *Imbolc*, is the old festival of spring, and the Eve is still observed in Ireland with various rituals and divinations. Spring activities are over by the time May gives the trees their 'green livery.' Summer ends in July, and Lugnasad, the first day of autumn, was a festival of first-fruits which used to rival Beltaine and Samain in importance. By Samain all the crops had been gathered in. Fruit left on the trees after this date was contaminated by the *púca*. Thus the main divisions of the Celtic year were related to the annual round of agricultural life rather than to the movements of the sun, though it is clear from the Coligny Calendar and from folklore that the solstices and equinoxes were also observed.

In Scotland, Quarter-Days still fall in November, February, May and August, but various changes in the calendar during the course of the centuries have resulted in minor displacements, so that the actual dates are now November 11th, February 2nd, May 15th and August 1st. They are known as 'Witches' Days,' and fairies hold revels and raid helpless human beings on their Eves. It is said that the fairies remove to different dwellings at the beginnings of each quarter. Lending is unlucky as it is on May Day, rowan crosses are used as a protection against supernatural dangers, and divinations are practised. Changelings can be got rid of on Quarter Days as they can at noon time, but it is unlucky to 'straddle' the beginning of a quarter—for example, by proclaiming a marriage at the end of one quarter and solemnizing it at the beginning of the next.

The turning-points in time have a paradoxical quality everywhere. In one sense they do not exist; in another sense they epitomize the whole of existence. Their significance may be compared with that of the 'Twelve Days of Christmas' each of which prognosticates the weather of the corresponding month in the New Year. These twelve days were marked by mumming, buffoonery, license, mock-mayors, witchcraft, and other signs of chaos. In Scotland, no court had any power during these days, and in Ireland those who died went to heaven without having to face Purgatory and Judgement. In Wales they were called omen days (*coel-ddyddiau*) and in Brittany 'over-days' (*gourdeziou*). It has been suggested that a period of twelve days between two mid-winter festivals in the Coligny Calendar had a similar significance. Furthermore, the thirty days of the intercalary month which precedes each half-cycle in this calendar bear the names of the thirty months in a half-cycle. The intercalary month is thus a microcosm of a half-cycle, though it has recently been argued that it is a recapitulation of the half-cycle which precedes it rather than a prefiguration of the ensuing one.

THE DRUIDS

This is an account by Julius Caesar of the celebrated Druid priests and Celtic religion as he encountered it in his conquest of Gaul (modern France). The passage presents a colorful firsthand picture. It should not, however, be taken as entirely accurate; Caesar was a busy general, not a scholar, and he was fighting against the Celtic Gauls. Few are inclined to describe in flattering terms those against whom they are making war. In any case, the matters discussed probably apply only to the aristocratic

classes. But Caesar's account provides an instructive contrast to the pre-
vious passage; we note how different the tone of the same culture can
appear to observers very far removed from each other in time and temper.
Caesar, like most Latin writers, gave each Celtic deity the name of the
Roman god he thought most corresponded to it; the Celtic names of these
gods would, of course, have been different.

From *Caesar: The Gallic War*
H. J. Edwards

Throughout Gaul there are two classes of persons of definite account and dignity. As for the common folk, they are treated almost as slaves, venturing naught of themselves, never taken into counsel. The more part of them, oppressed as they are either by debt, or by the heavy weight of tribute, or by the wrongdoing of the more powerful men, commit themselves in slavery to the nobles, who have, in fact, the same rights over them as masters over slaves. Of the two classes above mentioned one consists of Druids, the other of knights. The former are concerned with divine worship, the due performance of sacrifices, public and private, and the interpretation of ritual questions: a great number of young men gather about them for the sake of instruction and hold them in great honour. In fact, it is they who decide in almost all disputes, public and private; and if any crime has been committed, or murder done, or there is any dispute about succession or boundaries, they also decide it, determining rewards and penalties: if any person or people does not abide by their decision, they ban such from sacrifice, which is their heaviest penalty. Those that are so banned are reckoned as impious and criminal; all men move out of their path and shun their approach and conversation, for fear they may get some harm from their contact, and no justice is done if they seek it, no distinction falls to their share. Of all these Druids one is chief, who has the highest authority among them. At his death, either any other that is preeminent in position succeeds, or, if there be several of equal standing, they strive for the primacy by the vote of the Druids, or sometimes even with armed force. These Druids, at a certain time of the year, meet within the borders of the Carnutes, whose territory is reckoned as the centre of all Gaul, and sit in conclave in a consecrated spot. Thither assemble from every side all that have disputes, and they obey the deci-

Reprinted by permission of the publishers and the Loeb Classical Library from *Caesar: The Gallic War,* trans. by H. J. Edwards (Cambridge, Massachusetts: Harvard University Press, 1946), pp. 535–45. English text only.

sions and judgments of the Druids. It is believed that their rule of life was discovered in Britain and transferred thence to Gaul; and to-day those who would study the subject more accurately journey, as a rule, to Britain to learn it.

The Druids usually hold aloof from war, and do not pay war-taxes with the rest; they are excused from military service and exempt from all liabilities. Tempted by these great rewards, many young men assemble of their own motion to receive their training; many are sent by parents and relatives. Report says that in the schools of the Druids they learn by heart a great number of verses, and therefore some persons remain twenty years under training. And they do not think it proper to commit these utterances to writing, although in almost all other matters, and in their public and private accounts, they make use of Greek letters. I believe that they have adopted the practice for two reasons—that they do not wish the rule to become common property, nor those who learn the rule to rely on writing and so neglect the cultivation of the memory; and, in fact, it does usually happen that the assistance of writing tends to relax the diligence of the student and the action of the memory. The cardinal doctrine which they seek to teach is that souls do not die, but after death pass from one to another; and this belief, as the fear of death is thereby cast aside, they hold to be the greatest incentive to valour. Besides this, they have many discussions as touching the stars and their movement, the size of the universe and of the earth, the order of nature, the strength and the powers of the immortal gods, and hand down their lore to the young men.

The other class are the knights. These, when there is occasion, upon the incidence of a war—and before Caesar's coming this would happen well-nigh every year, in the sense that they would either be making wanton attacks themselves or repelling such—are all engaged therein; and according to the importance of each of them in birth and resources, so is the number of liegemen[1] and dependents that he has about him. This is the one form of influence and power known to them.

The whole nation of the Gauls is greatly devoted to ritual observances, and for that reason those who are smitten with the more grievous maladies and who are engaged in the perils of battle either sacrifice human victims or vow so to do, employing the Druids as ministers for such sacrifices. They believe, in effect, that, unless for a man's life a man's life be paid, the majesty of the immortal gods may not be appeased; and in public, as in private, life they observe an ordinance of sacrifices of the same kind. Others use figures of immense size, whose limbs, woven out of twigs, they fill with living men and set on fire, and the men perish in a sheet of flame. They believe that the execution of those who have been caught in the act of theft or robbery or some crime is more pleasing to

[1] *Soldurii* among the Aquitani (III. 22); both stand in a somewhat higher relation to their lords than the *clientes*.

the immortal gods; but when the supply of such fails they resort to the execution even of the innocent.

Among the gods, they most worship Mercury. There are numerous images of him; they declare him the inventor of all arts, the guide for every road and journey, and they deem him to have the greatest influence for all money-making and traffic. After him they set Apollo, Mars, Jupiter, and Minerva. Of these deities they have almost the same idea as all other nations: Apollo drives away diseases, Minerva supplies the first principles of arts and crafts, Jupiter holds the empire of heaven, Mars controls wars. To Mars, when they have determined on a decisive battle, they dedicate as a rule whatever spoil they may take. After a victory they sacrifice such living things as they have taken, and all the other effects they gather into one place. In many states heaps of such objects are to be seen piled up in hallowed spots, and it has not often happened that a man, in defiance of religious scruple, has dared to conceal such spoils in his house or to remove them from their place, and the most grievous punishment, with torture, is ordained for such an offence.

The Gauls affirm that they are all descended from a common father, Dis, and say that this is the tradition of the Druids. For that reason they determine all periods of time by the number, not of days, but of nights, and in their observance of birthdays and the beginnings of months and years day follows night. In the other ordinances of life the main difference between them and the rest of mankind is that they do not allow their own sons to approach them openly until they have grown to an age when they can bear the burden of military service, and they count it a disgrace for a son who is still in his boyhood to take his place publicly in the presence of his father.[2]

The men, after making due reckoning, take from their own goods a a sum of money equal to the dowry they have received from their wives and place it with the dowry. Of each such sum account is kept between them and the profits saved; whichever of the two survives receives the portion of both together with the profits of past years. Men have the power of life and death over their wives, as over their children; and when the father of a house, who is of distinguished birth, has died, his relatives assemble, and if there be anything suspicious about his death they make inquisition of his wives as they would of slaves, and if discovery is made they put them to death with fire and all manner of excruciating tortures. Their funerals, considering the civilization of Gaul, are magnificent and expensive. They cast into the fire everything, even living creatures, which they believe to have been dear to the departed during life, and but a short time before the present age, only a generation since, slaves and dependents known to have been beloved by their lords used to be burnt with them at the conclusion of the funeral formalities.

---

[2]When the father appeared *in publico, i.e.* as a warrior, he was disgraced (probably a survival of *taboo*) if a son, not yet a warrior also, appeared in his presence.

THE NORTHERN ACCOUNT OF THE
END OF THE WORLD

The Elder Edda, written in Iceland in the thirteenth century A.D.
*but containing some much older material, is the great verse narrative of
the rise and fall of the gods of the northern peoples of pre-Christian Europe. These people are the main ancestors of the modern Germans, English, Dutch, and Scandinavians. Their faith seems to have been relatively
simple in practice. While there were massive sacrifices and festivals, especially connected with kingship and fertility, piety was basically a personal
relation between a farmer or a Viking warrior and the favorite god whose
rude shrine was at the back of his fields or whose charm he carried. But
if the worship was simple (although often bloody), the richness of the
myths the bards told around the fires in the great halls of the north more
than compensated. Here we see an account, allegedly from a sibyl or
prophetess, of the destruction of this world and the making of a better,
from the moment the nightmarish dog Garm barks and the world-tree
Yggdrasil shakes and the gods of Valhalla (the Aesir) begin their final
battle to settle old accounts, to the arising from the flames and ashes of
a new and better earth ruled by the peaceful god Balder. It is possible
that some Christian influence is reflected in this version of the eschatological myth.*

From *Poems of the Vikings: The Elder Edda*

Patricia Terry

Garm bays loudly   from Gnipa Cave;
his rope will break   and he will run free.
Many spells I know,   and I can see
the doom that awaits   the almighty gods.

Brothers will die,   slain by their brothers,
incest will break   kinship's bonds;
woe to the world then,   wedded to whoredom,

battle-axe and sword rule,   split shields asunder,
storm-cleft age of wolves   until the world goes down,
only hatred   in the hearts of men.

Mim's sons play;   now fate will summon
from its long sleep   the Gjallarhorn:[1]
Heimdal's horn   clamors to heaven.
dead Mim's head[2] speaks   tidings to Odin.

Lofty Yggdrasil,[3]   the Ash Tree, trembles,
ancient wood groaning;   the giant goes free.

How fare the Aesir?   How do the Elves fare?
Jotunheim groans,   the gods meet in council,
at the stone doorways   of deep stone dwellings
dwarfs are moaning.   Seek you wisdom still?

Garm bays loudly   from Gnipa Cave,
his rope will break,   and he will run free.

Westward drives the giant,   Hrym, his shield high;
the world girding Serpent   rises from the water,
lashing at the waves;   the bright-beaked eagle
rends corpses, screaming;   Naglfar sails free.

Southward the ship sails;[4]   ruin by fire,
fiends led by Loki,   flies across the sea,
monstrous companions   to his wolf brood;
Byleist's brother,   Loki, leads them.

Surt fares northward,   lord of the fire-giants;
his sword of flame   gleams like the sun;
crashing rocks drag   demons to their doom;
men find the way to Hel   as the sky splits open.

The second sorrow   comes to Odin's wife:[5]
Odin goes forth   to fight the Wolf.
Frey, Beli's slayer,   battles with Surt;
thus will Freyja's   loved one fall.

Garm bays loudly   from Gnipa Cave;
his rope will break   and he will run free.

---

[1]*Gjallarhorn.* The horn buried under the Ash tree.

[2]*dead Mim's head.* Another explanation of Odin's wisdom. With herbs and charms Odin preserved Mimir's head, cut off by the Vanir, and received wise counsel from it.

[3]*Lofty Yggdrasil.* Neckel adds two more lines here, as in stanza 48.

[4]*Southward the ship sails.* As in Boer.

[5]*comes to Odin's wife.* Frigg, or Hlin, the goddess of love. Her first sorrow was Balder's death.

Odin's son Vithar   goes to fight the Wolf;
then in the heart   of the carrion beast,
Loki's foul son,   stands Vithar's sword.
So is the god   Odin avenged.

Far-famed Thor,[6]   the son of Earth,
the son of Odin,   battles with the Snake.
Nine steps beyond   the serpent's fury
Hlodin's son   still walks in pride.

Dark is the sun,   the Earth sinks below the sea,
no bright star now   shines from the heavens;
only smoke   and menacing fires
leap to the skies   in lordly flame.[7]

I see rising   a second time
out of the waters   the Earth, green once more;
an eagle flies   over rushing waterfalls,
hunting for fish   from the craggy heights.

The Aesir meet   in Idavelli;
they speak together   about the Serpent,
looking again   at days long past,
remembering Odin's   ancient runes.

In later times   a wondrous treasure,
chessmen of gold,   will be found in the grass
where the Aesir had left them   ages ago.

Barren fields   will bear again,
woes will be cured   when Balder comes:
Hod and Balder   will live in Odin's hall,
home of the war-gods.   Seek you wisdom still?

From bloody twigs   Hoenir tells the future;
the sons of Ve and Vili   dwell in the sky,
home of the wide winds.   Seek you wisdom still?

The mighty one[8] comes down   on the day of doom,
that powerful lord   who rules over all.

---

[6]*Far-famed Thor.* The following lines have been omitted from this stanza:

> He strikes in wrath Midgard's protector;
> now will all men leave their homes.

It is uncertain whether "Midgard's protector" (Thor) is nominative or accusative here and the following line, although defensible, is unconvincing. Thor killed the Snake, but died of its venom.

[7]*. . . in lordly flame.* Stanza 53 occurs again after this line. It is obviously misplaced, and has been deleted here.

[8]*the mighty one.* This stanza is sometimes considered a reference to Christ.

I see a hall   fairer than the sun,
thatched with gold;   it stands at Gimli.
There shall deserving   people dwell
to the end of time   and enjoy their happiness.

There comes the dark   dragon flying,
flashing upward   from Nidafells;
on wide swift wings   it soars above the Earth
carrying dead bodies.   Now it will sink down.[9]

THE VANIR

This passage by a leading modern scholar gives insight into another side of northern religion from that of the warlike Aesir whose Valhalla was first built and then destroyed—the side of the peaceful Vanir, gods of fertility whose concerns were love and rich fields. The two great orders of gods of the North were often at war with each other. Indeed it was the crimes of that conflict that brought on the doom of this world described in the previous passage. But actually the two orders personify the ideals of two great classes within northern society, or at least (if some persons participated in both roles) the two modes of human life they well knew: the way of the aristocratic warrior and the way of the farmer.

From *Gods and Myths of Northern Europe*
H.R. Ellis Davidson

The deities known as the Vanir are not easy to define in the northern myths, because of the many divine or semi-divine figures who emerge at different points, and whose relationships to one another are complex in the extreme. Yet in some ways they form a clear-cut and convincing group, because we can see the main characteristics of fertility gods and goddesses from other civilizations and other regions of the world repeated once again in the figures of Freyr and Freyja and their

[9]*Now it will sink down.* That is, disappear in the new order. Another interpretation has it that the sibyl sinks down at the end of her prophecy.

H.R. Ellis Davidson, *Gods and Myths of Northern Europe* (Baltimore: Penguin Books, 1964), pp. 124–27. Reprinted by permission of Penguin Books Ltd.

following. The fertility pattern is a definite one, easy to recognize, and the northern myths which have to do with the Vanir fall into the accustomed forms.

Snorri saw the Aesir and the Vanir as two powerful companies of gods, able to wage war against one another; yet the only names of male deities of the Vanir which are given in his account are Njord and Freyr, who were given as hostages to the Aesir when the war was over. Who were the rest of the company of the fighting Vanir? The most likely answer seems to be the vast assembly of gods of fertility from many different localities, of which a few names like Ing, Scyld, and Frodi have come down to us, while many more are utterly forgotten. Freyr, the fertility god of the Swedes in the eleventh century, and chief deity after Thor in Uppsala when Adam of Bremen was writing, has become the prototype of the male god of fertility in the literature, but behind him there must have been a vast host representing the givers of peace and plenty to many tribes and families throughout the northern world. Freyr's name is really a title, meaning 'lord,' while Freyja meant 'lady.' Perhaps in the lord and lady of the May Day festivities we are seeing their final manifestation, a last glimpse of the fertility powers, humbled from their once high estate. Similarly, Frodi's name is an adjective, describing him as 'the fruitful one,' and the list of kings called Frodi in Saxo implies that it was a title which many men bore in turn. The male god must not only have appeared in many different localities, but also have been represented by many different men, priests or priest-kings, who impersonated him; although he was also depicted in temples and appeared in the myths in his own right as the great god of the Vanir, the God of the World, giver of peace and plenty.

In some way the deities of the Vanir are the closest of all the heathen deities to mankind. We have the line of kings, taking it in turn to rule the land and acting as the givers of prosperity if the Vanir favoured them and abode with them. We have the seeresses, a link between men and the Vanir, sometimes possibly appearing in the very guise of Frigg and Freyja, coming right into men's homes as the Mothers, or the *Parcae* or the Givers, to convey the blessings of the goddesses. The Vanir were amoral, in the sense that their province was not to distinguish between good and evil, to bring men the ideals of justice, or to teach them loyalty to one another. They were there to give men the power that created new life and brought increase into the fields, among the animals, and in the home. They brought also the power to link men with the unseen world. Beside the fruits of the earth and the baby in the cradle, their gifts to men included the wise counsels granted through divination, when the god spoke through a human mouth. They offered also the collective excitement of the ceremonies when the god revealed his power to men and women gathering to worship him and the goddesses.

The gift of life brought by the Vanir was a mysterious and impalpable one, but it was essential to men. Without it, good fortune and victory and prudent rule were worthless and empty things, for if the crops failed and children died or there was no quickening in the womb, the community was doomed and without hope. Every pagan settlement has thus paid some service to the fertility powers, who possessed the ultimate say as to its future, and the people of the north were no exception. If the grudging soil of the northern lands and the bitter winters and long nights prevented the glorification of the Vanir which might have come with a warmer, more fertile setting, the gift of life which they offered was the more precious because of the precarious conditions in the world that waited to receive it.

To get into touch with these life-giving deities might necessitate strange, even revolting ceremonies. Orgies have always formed part of the fertility cults, and the reason is given by Eliade;[1]

> The awakening of an orgy may be compared with the appearance of the green shoots in the field; a new life is beginning, and the orgy has filled men with substance and with energy for that life. And further, by bringing back the mythical chaos that existed before the creation, the orgy makes it possible for creation to be repeated.

Thus the religion of the Vanir was bound to include orgies, ecstasies, and sacrificial rites. In these, and in the turning to the earth and the dead, whose blessing would help to bring the harvest, it can be seen that the Vanir were the rivals of Odin, god of ecstasy and of the dead. It is hardly surprising that the idea of rivalry between the two cults is sometimes implied in the myths, and is symbolized by the tradition of a war between the Aesir and the Vanir. The Vanir also protected men in battle, and they were the gods of royal houses, worshipped for a long period by the Swedish kings who wore the boar image, and who were believed to be informed for a while by the spirit of the Vanir who possessed them. There seem to have been many who worshipped them with fervour and devotion, finding their cult nearer, more rewarding and comforting than that of the sky god or the wilful god of war. The friendship of the Vanir had none of the treacherous, sliding quality of Odin's favours, and it extended, like his, beyond the grave.

The worshippers of the Vanir were very conscious of the earth, and remembered and venerated the dead ancestors who rested within it. The distant kingdom of the sky was not their concern, although behind the legends of the peace kings the idea of a departure to a land beyond the sea is held out as a promise to men. Indeed there was always a close link between the Vanir and the depths of the earth and sea. The chthonic element is present in their worship, and is emphasized in the myths. The Vanir male gods looked for brides among the giantesses, and

[1]*Patterns in Comparative Religion*, London, 1958, p. 359.

Freyr himself looked down into the underworld to find the radiant maiden Gerd to whom he gave his love. The spirits of land and sea are ranged behind the Vanir, and it was they who assisted the seeress in her journeys to the 'other world' and helped her to win hidden knowledge. Behind the goddesses of the Vanir is the conception of the Earth Mother, the Great Goddess who gives shelter to us all.

VIII

WANDERERS OF GOD:
THE STORY OF JUDAISM

The Jewish faith today has far fewer adherents than any other major religion; its numbers were nearly halved in the twentieth century by the horrible genocide its people suffered under Hitler. But Judaism is fully entitled to its place among the major religious traditions for two reasons: first, the history, culture, and thought of both ancient and modern Judaism are as rich a part of the human heritage as any other faith, and second, if Judaism itself is not large in numbers, two great faiths that together embrace almost half the human race—Christianity and Islam—stem from ancient Judaism and see themselves as perpetuations of its teaching lineage and fulfillments of its hope. Neither can be well understood without some knowledge of Judaism.

What is Judaism? It it four things: a People, a Book, a Way of Life, and a Hope grounded in faith.

The People began some four thousand years ago as a wandering desert tribe, probably on the fringes of the great civilization of the Valley of the Two Rivers. The tradition says that one of them, Abraham, was called by God to go to a promised land, and that God said that from his seed would come a mighty nation. At that point begins what is most distinctive in Judaism and the faiths derivative from it—monotheism, faith in one God who is personal, who has particular purposes to which he calls people, and who acts through historical events to advance his ends. But Abraham's grandson Jacob (Israel) went down to Egypt, and his descendants became slaves.

Centuries later, slavery ended with the exodus out of Egypt under Moses. This was a decisive turning point and the real beginning of Judaism, for we are told that passing out from Egypt to the land promised anew, they halted at Mount Sinai. Here, the tradition says, God gave these people the Law—a set of provisions for a way of life to be followed in the promised land. It included the Ten Commandments, rules about diet, rules for the treatment of servants and animals, rules about festivals and the performance of ritual sacrifices.

That is the beginning of the Book, which opens with the account of the creation in Genesis, proceeds to relate the stories of Abraham and Moses, gives the Law, and presents a medley of later history, literature, and the words of the men called prophets, who spoke words from God to admonish and to give hope. This is the Book called the Old Testament by Christians. It is the sacred scriptures of Judaism, and for Jews its most important sections are the first five books, the "Books of Moses," in which the Law is found.

The Book and the People, then, develop together. The Book shapes the life of the People, making it more distinctive as they become a people separated from others by their keeping of the Law. Practices ranging from circumcision to a distinctive diet to a powerful code of justice make it hard for them to intermarry or even adopt the customs of others, so their identity is kept. By portraying the great events of their history as special works of God, the Book creates the People through giving them a common heritage as a folk with a unique relationship to God. Indeed, a fundamental message is that they have a special destiny essential to the working out of God's plans, but a destiny with both its glorious and difficult sides—to them may be allotted both more honor and more suffering than others.

The Way of Life derives from this heritage of Book and sense of Peoplehood. It began to acquire its modern shape in the days of the Roman Empire, especially after the destruction of the temple in Jerusalem in 70 A.D. Thereafter, most of the Jewish people were dispersed to many lands. Their local places of worship, the synagogues, replaced the temple with its sacrifices as the public spiritual centers of Judaism. The following of the Law fell into well-defined patterns through the interpretive work of learned rabbis. Jewish life centered—as it still does—around Sabbath, family, customary observances, and deep study. For some, it was enriched by the profound mystical philosophy called Kabbalah and by the more effusive devotional mysticism of Hasidism. More recently, it has been affected by those who have favored the updating of Jewish practice and a rich interaction between Judaism and surrounding culture.

Behind all this lies Judaism as a Hope grounded in faith. That is suggested by the forward-looking tone of its classical literature, so often concerned with future promises within historical time, whether promises of reaching the promised land or of return to it. This note is different from that of religious literature concerned instead with mystical or salvationist release from our time and our world. For Jews, hope makes their suffering in this world bearable, and their joy all the greater. The nature of the Jewish hope is interpreted in various ways. But whether it is hope for divine intervention in the world to rectify the evils of history, or hope for a better world in the future through the labors of men and women of goodwill, it is a hope born out of suffering and endurance, and grounded in faith based on God's past works and words.

THE SCRIPTURES

Here are four passages from the Bible representing four types of biblical literature. The first, from Deuteronomy, Chapter 7, presents Moses speaking to the people of Israel beyond the Jordan before they entered the promised land. It vividly suggests the concept of the chosen people, validated by the mighty works in history that God had done for them, and the moral obligation this awesome privilege entailed.

The second passage, from I Kings, Chapter 21, shows one of the first and greatest prophets, Elijah, confronting the unworthy king Ahab and his wife Jezebel in a matter of simple justice. It suggests the kind of concrete situations in which the work of God through the Law and the People is continued.

The third passage, Psalm 104 (103 in the Hebrew Bible and some Roman Catholic versions), is a splendid example of ancient Hebrew poetry. It extols the majesty of God through his creation.

The fourth passage, Isaiah, Chapters 60 and 65: 17–15, evokes the hope of Israel in its highest moments. Written in expectation of the return of the Jewish people from captivity in Babylon, these lines go beyond that historical situation as they seem to sing of every kind of human triumph, even victory over bondage to the tear-stained earth itself in the hope of a new and radiant heaven and earth.

From *The Revised Standard Version of the Bible*

DEUTERONOMY   7

"When the LORD your God brings you into the land which you are entering to take possession of it, and clears away many nations before

The Revised Standard Version of the Bible (New York: Thomas Nelson and Son), pp. 191–93, 381–83, 631–33, 773–75, 779–80 of the Old Testament). Copyright 1946, 1952, 1971, 1973 by the National Council of the Churches of Christ in the U.S.A., and reprinted with its permission.

you, the Hittites, the Gir'gashites, the Amorites, the Canaanites, the Per'iz-
zites, the Hivites, and the Jeb'usites, seven nations greater and mightier
than yourself, ²and when the LORD your God gives them over to you,
and you defeat them; then you must utterly destroy them; you shall make
no covenant with them, and show no mercy to them. ³You shall not make
marriages with them, giving your daughters to their sons or taking their
daughters for your sons. ⁴For they would turn away your sons from following me, to serve other gods; then the anger of the LORD would be
kindled against you, and he would destroy you quickly. ⁵But thus shall
you deal with them: you shall break down their altars, and dash in pieces
their pillars, and hew down their Ashe'rim, and burn their graven images
with fire.

⁶"For you are a people holy to the LORD your God; the LORD your
God has chosen you to be a people for his own possession, out of all the
peoples that are on the face of the earth. ⁷It was not because you were
more in number than any other people that the LORD set his love upon
you and chose you, for you were the fewest of all peoples; ⁸but it is because the LORD loves you, and is keeping the oath which he swore to your
fathers, that the LORD has brought you out with a mighty hand, and redeemed you from the house of bondage, from the hand of Pharaoh king
of Egypt. ⁹Know therefore that the LORD your God is God, the faithful
God who keeps covenant and steadfast love with those who love him and
keep his commandments, to a thousand generations, ¹⁰and requites to
their face those who hate him, by destroying them; he will not be slack
with him who hates him, he will requite him to his face. ¹¹You shall therefore be careful to do the commandment, and the statutes, and the ordinances, which I command you this day.

¹²"And because you hearken to these ordinances, and keep and do
them, the LORD your God will keep with you the covenant and steadfast
love which he swore to your fathers to keep; ¹³he will love you, bless you,
and multiply you; he will also bless the fruit of your body and the fruit
of your ground, your grain and your wine and your oil, the increase of
your cattle and the young of your flock, in the land which he swore to
your fathers to give you. ¹⁴You shall be blessed above all peoples; there
shall not be male or female barren among you, or among your cattle.
¹⁵And the LORD will take away from you all sickness; and none of the evil
diseases of Egypt, which you knew, will he inflict upon you, but he will
lay them upon all who hate you. ¹⁶And you shall destroy all the peoples
that the LORD your God will give over to you, your eye shall not pity
them; neither shall you serve their gods, for that would be a snare to you.

¹⁷"If you say in your heart, 'These nations are greater than I; how
can I dispossess them?' ¹⁸you shall not be afraid of them, but you shall
remember what the LORD your God did to Pharaoh and to all Egypt, ¹⁹the
great trials which your eyes saw, the signs, the wonders, the mighty hand,
and the outstretched arm, by which the LORD your God brought you out;
so will the LORD your God do to all the peoples of whom you are afraid.

²⁰Moreover the LORD your God will send hornets among them, until those who are left and hide themselves from you are destroyed. ²¹You shall not be in dread of them; for the LORD your God is in the midst of you, a great and terrible God. ²²The LORD your God will clear away these nations before you little by little; you may not make an end of them at once, lest the wild beasts grow too numerous for you. ²³But the LORD your God will give them over to you, and throw them into great confusion, until they are destroyed. ²⁴And he will give their kings into your hand, and you shall make their name perish from under heaven; not a man shall be able to stand against you, until you have destroyed them. ²⁵ The graven images of their gods you shall burn with fire; you shall not covet the silver or the gold that is on them, or take it for yourselves, lest you be ensnared by it; for it is an abomination to the LORD your God. ²⁶And you shall not bring an abominable thing into your house, and become accursed like it; you shall utterly detest and abhor it; for it is an accursed thing.

I KINGS   21

¹Now Naboth the Jez′reelite had a vineyard in Jezreel, beside the palace of Ahab king of Samar′ia. ²And after this Ahab said to Naboth, "Give me your vineyard, that I may have it for a vegetable garden, because it is near my house; and I will give you a better vineyard for it; or, if seems good to you, I will give you its value in money." ³But Naboth said to Ahab, "The LORD forbid that I should give you the inheritance of my fathers." ⁴And Ahab went into his house vexed and sullen because of what Naboth the Jez′reelite had said to him; for he had said, "I will not give you the inheritance of my fathers." And he lay down on his bed, and turned away his face, and would eat no food.

⁵But Jez′ebel his wife came to him, and said to him, "Why is your spirit so vexed that you eat no food?" ⁶And he said to her, "Because I spoke to Naboth the Jez′reelite, and said to him, 'Give me your vineyard for money; or else, if it please you, I will give you another vineyard for it'; and he answered, 'I will not give you my vineyard.' " ⁷And Jez′ebel his wife said to him, "Do you now govern Israel? Arise, and eat bread, and let your heart be cheerful; I will give you the vineyard of Naboth the Jez′reelite."

⁸So she wrote letters in Ahab's name and sealed them with his seal, and she sent the letters to the elders and the nobles who dwelt with Naboth in his city. ⁹And she wrote in the letters, "Proclaim a fast, and set Naboth on high among the people; ¹⁰and set two base fellows opposite him, and let them bring a charge against him, saying, 'You have cursed God and the king.' Then take him out, and stone him to death." ¹¹And the men of his city, the elders and the nobles who dwelt in his city, did as Jez′ebel had sent word to them. As it was written in the letters which she

had sent to them, ¹²they proclaimed a fast, and set Naboth on high among the people. ¹³And the two base fellows came in and sat opposite him; and the base fellows brought a charge against Naboth, in the presence of the people, saying, "Naboth cursed God and the king." So they took him outside the city, and stoned him to death with stones. ¹⁴Then they sent to Jez'ebel, saying "Naboth has been stoned; he is dead."

¹⁵As soon as Jez'ebel heard that Naboth had been stoned and was dead, Jez'ebel said to Ahab, "Arise, take possession of the vineyard of Naboth the Jez'reelite, which he refused to give you for money; for Naboth is not alive, but dead." ¹⁶And as soon as Ahab heard that Naboth was dead, Ahab arose to go down to the vineyard of Naboth the Jez'reelite, to take possession of it.

¹⁷Then the word of the LORD came to Eli'jah the Tishbite, saying, ¹⁸"Arise, go down to meet Ahab king of Israel, who is in Samar'ia; behold, he is in the vineyard of Naboth, where he has gone to take possession. ¹⁹And you shall say to him, 'Thus says the LORD, "Have you killed, and also taken possession?" ' And you shall say to him, 'Thus says the LORD: "In the place where dogs licked up the blood of Naboth shall dogs lick your own blood." ' "

²⁰Ahab said to Eli'jah, "Have you found me, O my enemy?" He answered, "I have found you, because you have sold yourself to do what is evil in the sight of the LORD. ²¹Behold, I will bring evil upon you; I will utterly sweep you away, and will cut off from Ahab every male, bond or free, in Israel; ²²and I will make your house like the house of Jerobo'am the son of Nebat, and like the house of Ba'asha the son of Ahi'jah, for the anger to which you have provoked me, and because you have made Israel to sin. ²³And of Jez'ebel the LORD also said, 'The dogs shall eat Jez'ebel within the bounds of Jezreel.' ²⁴Any one belonging to Ahab who dies in the city the dogs shall eat; and any one of his who dies in the open country the birds of the air shall eat."

²⁵(There was none who sold himself to do what was evil in the sight of the LORD like Ahab, whom Jez'ebel his wife incited. ²⁶He did very abominably in going after idols, as the Amorites had done, whom the LORD cast out before the people of Israel).

²⁷And when Ahab heard those words, he rent his clothes, and put sackcloth upon his flesh, and fasted and lay in sackcloth, and went about dejectedly. ²⁸And the word of the LORD came to Eli'jah the Tishbite, saying, ²⁹"Have you seen how Ahab has humbled himself before me? Because he has humbled himself before me, I will not bring the evil in his days; but in his son's days I will bring the evil upon his house."

PSALMS 104

> Bless the LORD, O my soul!
> O LORD my God, thou art
>   very great!

Thou art clothed with honor and
    majesty,
2   who coverest thyself with light as
    with a garment,
who hast stretched out the heavens
    like a tent,
3   who hast laid the beams of thy
    chambers on the waters,
who makest the clouds thy chariot,
    who ridest on the wings of the
    wind,
4who makest the winds thy mes-
    engers,
    fire and flame thy ministers.

5Thou didst set the earth on its
    foundations,
    so that it should never be shaken.
6Thou didst cover it with the deep
    as with a garment;
    the waters stood above the moun-
    tains.
7At thy rebuke they fled;
    at the sound of thy thunder they
    took to flight.
8The mountains rose, the valleys
    sank down
    to the place which thou didst ap-
    point for them.
9Thou didst set a bound which they
    should not pass,
    so that they might not again
    cover the earth.

10Thou makest springs gush forth in
    the valleys;
    they flow between the hills,
11they give drink to every beast of the
    field;
    the wild asses quench their thirst.
12By them the birds of the air have
    their habitation;
    they sing among the branches.
13From thy lofty abode thou waterest
    the mountains;
    the earth is satisfied with the fruit
    of thy work.

14Thou dost cause the grass to grow

for the cattle,
and plants for man to cultivate,
that he may bring forth food from
the earth,
15 and wine to gladden the heart of
man,
oil to make his face shine,
and bread to strengthen man's
heart.
16The trees of the LORD are watered
abundantly,
the cedars of Lebanon which he
planted.
17In them the birds build their nests;
the stork has her home in the fir
trees.
18The high mountains are for the
wild goats;
the rocks are a refuge for the
badgers.
19Thou hast made the moon to mark
the seasons;
the sun knows its time for setting.
20Thou makest darkness, and it is
night,
when all the beasts of the forest
creep forth.
21The young lions roar for their prey
seeking their food from God.
22When the sun rises, they get them
away
and lie down in their dens.
23Man goes forth to his work
and to his labor until the evening.

24O LORD, how manifold are thy
works!
In wisdom hast thou made them
all;
the earth is full of thy creatures.
25Yonder is the sea, great and wide,
which teems with things innumerable,
living things both small and
great.
26There go the ships,
and Leviathan which thou didst
form to sport in it.

²⁷These all look to thee,
> to give them their food in due
> season.
²⁸When thou givest to them, they
> gather it up;
> when thou openest thy hand,
> they are filled with good
> things.
²⁹When thou hidest thy face, they
> are dismayed;
> when thou takest away their
> breath, they die
> and return to their dust.
³⁰When thou sendest forth thy
> Spirit, they are created;
> and thou renewest the face of
> the ground.

³¹May the glory of the LORD endure
> forever,
> may the LORD rejoice in his
> works,
³²who looks on the earth and it
> trembles,
> who touches the mountains and
> they smoke!
³³I will sing to the LORD as long as
> I live;
> I will sing praise to my God
> while I have being.
³⁴May my meditation be pleasing to
> him,
> for I rejoice in the LORD.
³⁵Let sinners be consumed from the
> earth,
> and let the wicked be no more!
> Bless the LORD, O my soul!
> Praise the LORD!

ISAIAH   60

> Arise, shine; for your light
> has come,
> and the glory of the LORD has
> risen upon you.
²For behold, darkness shall cover
> the earth,

and thick darkness the peoples;
but the LORD will arise upon you,
and his glory will be seen upon
you.
³And nations shall come to your
light,
and kings to the brightness of
your rising.

⁴Lift up your eyes round about, and
see;
they all gather together, they
come to you;
your sons shall come from far,
and your daughters shall be carried in the arms.
⁵Then you shall see and be radiant,
your heart shall thrill and rejoice;ᵃ
because the abundance of the sea
shall be turned to you,
the wealth of the nations shall
come to you.
⁶A multitude of camels shall cover
you,
the young camels of Mid'ian and
Ephah;
all those from Sheba shall come.
They shall bring gold and frankin-
cense,
and shall proclaim the praise of
the LORD.
⁷All the flocks of Kedar shall be
gathered to you,
the rams of Nebai'oth shall minister to you;
they shall come up with acceptance
on my altar,
and I will glorify my glorious
house.

⁸Who are these that fly like a cloud,
and like doves to their windows?
⁹For the coastlands shall wait for
me,

ᵃHeb *be enlarged*

the ships of Tarshish first,
to bring your sons from far,
their silver and gold with them,
for the name of the Lord your God,
and for the Holy One of Israel,
because he has glorified you.

10Foreigners shall build up your walls,
and their kings shall minister to
you;
for in my wrath I smote you,
but in my favor I have had mercy
on you.
11Your gates shall be open continually;
day and night they shall not be
shut;
that men may bring to you the
wealth of the nations,
with their kings led in procession.
12For the nation and kingdom
that will not serve you shall
perish;
those nations shall be utterly laid
waste.
13The glory of Lebanon shall come
to you,
the cypress, the plane, and the
pine,
to beautify the place of my sanctuary;
and I will make the place of my
feet glorious.
14The sons of those who oppressed
you
shall come bending low to you;
and all who despised you
shall bow down at your feet;
they shall call you the City of the
Lord,
the Zion of the Holy One of Israel.

15Whereas you have been forsaken
and hated,
with no one passing through,

I will make you majestic for ever,
a joy from age to age.
¹⁶You shall suck the milk of nations,
you shall suck the breast of kings:
and you shall know that I, the
Lord, am your Savior
and your Redeemer, the Mighty
One of Jacob.

¹⁷Instead of bronze I will bring gold,
and instead of iron I will bring
silver;
instead of wood, bronze,
instead of stones, iron.
I will make your overseers peace
and your taskmasters righteousness.
¹⁸Violence shall no more be heard in
your land,
devastation or destruction within
your borders;
you shall call your walls Salvation,
and your gates Praise.
¹⁹The sun shall be no more
your light by day,
nor for brightness shall the moon
give light to you by night;
but the Lord will be your everlasting light,
and your God will be your glory.
²⁰Your sun shall no more go down,
nor your moon withdraw itself;
for the Lord will be your everlasting light,
and your days of mourning shall
be ended.
²¹Your people shall all be righteous;
they shall possess the land for
ever,
the shoot of my planting, the work
of my hands,
that I might be glorified.
²²The least one shall become a clan,
and the smallest one a mighty
nation;
I am the Lord;
in its time I will hasten it.

ISAIAH 65

¹⁷"For behold, I create new heavens
and a new earth;
and the former things shall not be
remembered.
or come into mind.
¹⁸But be glad and rejoice for ever
in that which I create;
for behold, I create Jerusalem, a rejoicing,
and her people a joy.
¹⁹I will rejoice in Jerusalem,
and be glad in my people;
no more shall be heard in it the
sound of weeping
and the cry of distress.
²⁰No more shall there be in it
an infant that lives but a few
days,
or an old man who does not fill
out his days,
for the child shall die a hundred
years old,
and the sinner a hundred years
old shall be accursed.
²¹They shall build houses and inhabit
them;
they shall plant vineyards and eat
their fruit.
²²They shall not build and another
inhabit;
they shall not plant and another
eat;
for like the days of a tree shall the
days of my people be,
and my chosen shall long enjoy
the work of their hands.
²³They shall not labor in vain,
or bear children for calamity;
for they shall be the offspring of
the blessed of the Lord,
and their children with them.
²⁴Before they call I will answer,

while they are yet speaking I will
hear.
25The wolf and the lamb shall feed
together,
the lion shall eat straw like the
ox;
and dust shall be the serpent's
food.
They shall not hurt or destroy
in all my holy mountain,
says the LORD."

ANCIENT ISRAELITE RELIGION

*This passage, from a modern Jewish scholar, gives a picture of how
the ancient Jewish rites, which underlie both the scriptures and modern
Judaism, probably developed. Notice the importance of the transition
from herding to sedentary agriculture.*

From *The Story of Judaism*

Bernard J. Bamberger

At the earliest period when we can with certainty detach history
from legend and folklore, we find the Hebrews as a group of tribes but
recently settled in Palestine. Previously semi-nomads in the desert regions
to the south and east, they had forced their way into the country and
gained control of a large part of it. Many localities remained for a long
time in the hands of the earlier inhabitants.

Despite ties of common blood, language and culture, the tribes
had little sense of unity. There was no national government and there
was no central religious authority. Each tribe had its own holy places,
sacred objects, and priestly leaders.

Yet the religious cult of all the tribes was substantially the same.

Bernard J. Bamberger, *The Story of Judaism* (New York: The Union of American
Hebrew Congregations, 1964), pp. 7–10. Reprinted by permission of the publishers.
p. 343–45.

It was the worship of a deity called YHWH (probably pronounced Yahweh, though this is not quite certain).

The tribes also shared certain historic memories and traditions. They had not always worshipped Yhwh. Their fathers had "dwelt of old time beyond the River Euphrates . . . and they served other gods." The people also recalled living for a time in Egypt, where the ruling power oppressed them. They escaped under the leadership of a man named Moses; and it was he who formally inducted them into the religion of Yhwh. At Mount Sinai the people and God had become partners to a solemn covenant. Israel promised to give Him their exclusive and faithful worship and to obey the laws He imposed on them. Yhwh in turn undertook to guide, protect, and prosper them, and to bring them to a land "flowing with milk and honey." These traditions are so clearly attested in all our sources that we cannot doubt their historic truth. Especially do the covenant at Sinai and the compelling leadership of Moses influence the whole subsequent development of Judaism. The figure of Moses looms up magnificently through mists of popular fancy that blur its outlines. Generation after generation idealized him, and attributed to him not only the foundation of Judaism, but all the advances and elaborations which later ages produced. No other prophet, they believed, had ever risen or could rise to his level; his very face had shone with an unearthly radiance.

After we make due allowances for the adornments and exaggerations of legend, the greatness of Moses still remains clear. The Hebrew tribes had an extraordinary sense of a common destiny, of a dynamic role which they were to play in the economy of the world, and of a brotherhood which their tribal divisions could not efface. These convictions, on which the later development of Judaism was based, must have come to them from a greatly inspired and inspiring personality. If we knew nothing about Moses, we should have to assume that some such man existed.

We shall perhaps never succeed in distinguishing sharply between the Moses of history and the Moses of Jewish tradition. For this great figure became the symbol of Israel's highest idealism, the model teacher, leader, and good shepherd. His importance consists both in what he actually was and did, and in what later ages thought about him. In both senses, he has been for subsequent generations *Mosheh Rabbenu,* Moses our teacher.

How did the Hebrews worship God? The cult as we find it in the early Palestinian period includes two elements, already closely intertwined. Certain features reflect the life of the desert dwellers. There were few formal shrines: a bare rock at some central spot served as a sacrificial altar; heads of the clans acted as priests. One of the chief observances was the spring festival called *Pesach* (Passover); at this time the firstlings of the flocks were sacrificed to God.

But the wanderers from the desert soon gained a foothold in the fertile districts of Palestine and became farmers. Before long, their religious observances began to reflect the conditions of agricultural life. Three festivals in particular acquired an important place in the calendar of Israel. The beginning of the grain harvest (which in Palestine occurs in the spring) was marked by the Feast of *Matsos* (Unleavened Bread). It fell about the same time as the nomadic Passover, and the two were eventually combined into one observance. Seven weeks after Passover, the end of this first harvest period was celebrated by the Feast of *Shovuos* (Weeks). The vintage and fruit harvest, which marked the completion of the agricultural year, culminated in the Feast of *Sukos* (Tabernacles). In early times, the New Year Day, observed by rites of purification, was probably celebrated at the close of this autumn festival.

These holidays, celebrated at each village shrine by animal sacrifices and offerings of crops, by songs of thanksgiving and ritual dances, were not unlike the observances of other agricultural peoples, ancient and modern. It was something new, however, when the Israelites (from an early date) began to give their feasts an historical significance. The Pesach-Matsos festival was regarded as the anniversary of the deliverance from Egypt; the Feast of Tabernacles, as a memorial of Israel's desert wanderings. But the Feast of Weeks was not connected with the giving of the Torah at Sinai until post-Biblical times.

A unique feature of Israelite religion was the Sabbath. This institution must have arisen* after Israel entered the land; for under desert conditions, the shepherds must care for their animals every day. Sabbath observance was only possible after the Israelites had settled down as farmers. Some other Semite peoples, notably the Babylonians, had an observance which bore a similar name; but it was quite different in character. The Babylonian *Shapatum* was an unlucky day, on which certain official persons were forbidden to work (like "Friday the thirteenth"). Quite different was the Israelite Sabbath: it was a day of universal rest even for slaves and work-animals; and this rest was not a device to ward off evil fortune, but a commandment of God. Later on, the tremendous social and religious implications of the Sabbath were more fully developed; but this unique observance shows us how, even in its very early stages, the religion of Israel was already something new and distinctive.

It is true that in some ways the Yhwh-cult reminds us of other Near-Eastern religions. Its intent was to secure large flocks and plentiful crops, health, children, and victory. The chief means to these ends were offerings of animals and cereals to the Deity. Yhwh was thought to possess human form and feelings. Though all agreed that He had an exclusive claim to the worship of Israel, it was widely believed that other nations had gods just as (or almost as) real and useful to them.

Nevertheless, the differences that marked off Israel's religion from that of its neighbors are far more striking than the resemblances. In

---

*Or, at least, evolved fully.

these differences lay the seeds of sublime and revolutionary advances. First, Yhwh had no female consort. The cruder physical attributes ascribed by many peoples to their deities did not apply here; the gross sexual myths so common in ancient religion were never associated with the God of Israel.

But we can go further. The religion of Israel had no myths at all. Other peoples told not only of the loves and marriages of the gods, but of their battles with each other and with monsters and titans, of their banquets and festivities, of their rivalries and intrigues. All this was alien to the spirit of the Israelite religion. Yhwh was austere, apart, and subject to no mortal weaknesses.

Third, the Israelite cult was, generally speaking, imageless. In the earlier period, it is true, household gods and other objects of veneration were not entirely unknown; but the dominant trend, which grew stronger all the time, was to prohibit pictures or statues of the Deity. This helped enormously in educating the people up to a more lofty concept of God.

Again, most Semitic deities were thought to have a sort of family relationship to their worshippers. The god was therefore obligated to look out for his people, no matter how much they displeased him, as a father must still care for a disobedient child. But Yhwh became the God of Israel at a particular time and through a formal covenant. He and Israel had, so to speak, entered into a partnership on the basis of specific terms. Violation of this law would not only arouse God's wrath: it would dissolve the partnership. Thus the relation between God and Israel took on a fundamentally ethical character; Israel had Yhwh as its Protector only so long as it observed His Law.

Finally, the religion of Israel, even after the tribes had taken root firmly in Palestine, always retained something of its desert, pastoral tone. As civilization advanced, as increasing prosperity brought increasing social problems, as the multiplication of luxuries led to a weakening of moral fiber, the ancestral faith struck a wholesome note by recalling the stern simplicity of desert days.

Out of these unpretentious but significant beginnings the great structure of Judaism was destined to rise.

THE TEACHINGS OF PHILO

Much later, during the Hellenistic and Roman periods, Judaism came into close contact with the thought of other cultures, particularly the Greek. Some Jewish philosophers endeavored to reconcile the good they could see on both sides. They could feel the power of Plato's vision of the eternal as unchanging and of Aristotle's rational universe understandable through logic and scientific investigation. But they also appre-

ciated the heritage of their own people, with its biblical God more moral, personal, and purposive than the gods either of philosophers or of other nations. Therefore, they asked themselves how the vigorous, active Lord of scriptural history also could be understood as unchanging and rational, and how that history could be reconciled to the wisdom of that later Platonism, which emphasized the distinction of spirit (akin to the unchangeable God) and flesh, and said that knowledge and worship of God must be spiritual—not like the bloody and carnal sacrifices and the historical tumult of the scriptures.

The most important of attempts at reconciliation was that of Philo, a Jewish philosopher who lived in the first century in the Greek city of Alexandria. As in the following typical passage, he interpreted the scriptures allegorically or in terms of veiled meanings suggesting the work of the Logos or divine activity in the world and the response of mystic love for God by persons.

From *The Works of Philo Judaeus*
C.D. Yonge

A TREATISE ON THE UNCHANGEABLENESS OF GOD

I. "And after this," says Moses, "it came to pass that the angels of God went in unto the daughters of men, and they bore children unto them."* It is worth while, therefore, to consider what is meant by the expression, "And after this." It is therefore a reference to something that has been said before, for the purpose of explaining it more clearly; and a mention of the divine spirit has already been made, as he has already stated, that it is very difficult for it to remain throughout all ages in the soul, which is divisible into many parts, and which assumes many forms, and is clothed with a most heavy burden, namely its bulk of flesh; after this spirit, therefore, the angels of God go in unto the daughters of men. For as long as the pure rays of wisdom shine forth in the soul, by means of which the wise man sees God and his powers, no one of those who bring false news ever enters into the reason, but all such are kept at a distance outside of the sacred threshold.

But when the light of the intellect is dimmed and overshadowed, then the companions of darkness having become victorious, associate

C.D. Yonge, trans., *The Works of Philo Judaeus* (London: Henry G. Bohn, 1854), p. 343–45.
*Genesis vi. 2

themselves with the dissolute and effeminate passions which the prophet calls the daughters of men, and they bear children to them and not to God. For the appropriate progeny of God are the perfect virtues, but that offspring which is akin to the wicked, is unregulated wickedness. But learn thou, if thou wilt, O my mind, not to bear children to thyself, after the example of that perfect man Abraham, who offered up to God "The beloved and only legitimate offspring of his soul,"* the most conspicuous image of self-taught wisdom, by name Isaac; and who gave him up with all cheerfulness to be a necessary and fitting offering to God. "Having bound,"† as the scripture says, this new kind of victim, either because he, having once tasted of the divine inspiration, did not condescend any longer to tread on any mortal truth, or because he saw that the creature was unstable and moveable, while he recognised the unhesitating firmness existing in the living God, on whom he is said to have believed.‡

II. His disciple and successor was Hannah. The gift of the wisdom of God, for the interpretation of the name is her grace. For when she had become pregnant, having received the divine seed, and after she had completed the time of her labour, she brought forth, in the manner appointed by the arrangement of God, a son, whom she called Samuel; and the name Samuel being interpreted, means "appointed by God." She therefore having received him restores him to the giver; not looking upon anything as a good belonging to herself which is not divine grace. For in the first book of Kings,** she speaks in this manner: "I give him unto thee freely," the expression here used being equivalent to. "I give him unto thee whom thou hast given to me." According to that most sacred scripture of Moses, "My gifts and my offerings and my first fruits, ye shall observe to offer unto me,"†† For to what other being should one bring gifts of gratitude except to God? and what offerings can one bring unto him except of those things which have been given to us by him? For it is not possible for us to have an abundance of anything else.

And he has no need of any of those things which he enjoins men to offer unto him, but he bids us bring unto him the things which are his own, through the excess of his beneficence to our race. For we, studying to conduct ourselves with gratitude to him, and to show him all honours, should purify ourselves from sin, washing off all things that can stain our life in words, or appearance, or actions. For it is foolishness to imagine, that it is unlawful to enter into temples, unless a man has first washed his body and made that look bright, but that one may attempt to sacrifice and to pray with a mind still polluted and disordered. And yet temples are made of stone and timber, mere lifeless materials, and it is not possible for the body, if it is devoid of life by its own nature, to touch things devoid of life, without using ablutions and purifying ceremonies of holiness; and shall any one endure to approach God without being purified as to his soul, shall any one while

*Genesis XXII. 2   †Genesis XII. 9   ‡Genesis xv 6.   **Samuel i. 20.   ††Numbers xxviii. 2.

impure come near to the purest of all beings, and this too without having any intention of repenting? Let him, indeed who, in addition to having committed no new crimes, has also endeavoured to wash off his old misdeeds, come cheerfully before him; but let the man who is without any such preparation, and who is impure, keep aloof. For he will never escape the notice of him who can look into the recesses of the heart, and who walketh in its most secret places.

THE TALMUD

The Hebrew word Talmud means "study" or "learning," and refers to a collection of commentaries and interpretations of the Jewish scriptures compiled by rabbis in the first few centuries C.E. (A.D.). Actually two such collections exist, one made in Babylon and one in Palestine. The Talmud is commonly regarded as comprised of three parts: the Mishna, a collective of originally oral law supplementing and applying the biblical law; the Gemara, a running commentary on the Mishna; and some auxiliary essays. While basically a legal book, the Talmud provided its rabbinic authors with opportunity to expound on a variety of topics, from astrology to medicine, and above all to reveal something of the religious style of a devout life shaped by study of the law as the central religious act. It was this manner of spiritual life which characterized the transition of Judaism from its ancient life around temple and political nation to its later life as a dispersed minority in many places supremely engaged in the study and practice of the rabbinic law in synagogue and home. Without the work of the Talmudic rabbis, this transition might well have not been possible. The following passage, from a modern collection of excerpts from the rabbis of the Talmud, gives a taste of their teaching, in this case about the great task to which they had set themselves, the deep study of the law itself.

From *The Talmud: Selections*

H. Polano

THE LAW AND ITS STUDY

"The Lord created me as the beginning of his way" (Prov. 8:22). This means that God created the law before he created the world. Many sages have made their lives as black as the raven, that is, cruel to them-

H. Polano, *The Talmud: Selections* (London: Frederick Warne & Co., Inc., 1876), pp. 245–46.

selves as the raven is to her children, by means of continual study, day and night.

Rabbi Johanan said, "It is best to study by night, when all is quiet; as it is written, 'Shout forth praises in the night.' "

Reshbi Lakish said, "Study by day and by night; as it is written, 'Thou shalt meditate therein day and night.' "

Rabbi Chonan, of Zepora, said, "The study of the law may be compared to a huge heap of dust that is to be cleared away. The foolish man says, 'It is impossible that I should be able to remove this immense heap, I will not attempt it;' but the wise man says, 'I will remove a little to-day, some more to-morrow, and more the day after, and thus in time I shall have removed it all.'

"It is the same with studying the law. The indolent pupil says, 'It is impossible for me to study the Bible. Just think of it, fifty chapters in Genesis; sixty-six in Isaiah, one hundred and fifty Psalms, &c. I cannot do it;' but the industrious student says, 'I will study six chapters every day, and so in time I shall acquire the whole.' "

In Proverbs 24:7, we find this sentence: "Wisdom is too high for a fool."

"Rabbi Jochanan illustrates this verse with an apple depending from the ceiling. The foolish man says, 'I cannot reach the fruit, it is too high;' but the wise man says, 'It may be readily obtained by placing one step upon another until thy arm is brought within reach of it.' The foolish man says, 'Only a wise man can study the entire law;' but the wise man replies, 'It is not incumbent upon thee to acquire the whole.' "

Rabbi Levi illustrates this by a parable.

A man once hired two servants to fill a basket with water. One of them said, "Why should I continue this useless labour? I put the water in one side and it immediately leaks out of the other; what profit is it?"

The other workman, who was wise, replied, "We have the profit of the reward which we receive for our labour."

It is the same in studying the law. One man says, "What does it profit me to study the law when I must ever continue it or else forget what I have learned." But the other man replies, "God will reward us for the will which we display even though we do forget."

Rabbi Ze-irah has said that even a single letter in the law which we might deem of no importance, if wanting, would neutralise the whole law. In Deuteronomy 22:17, we read, "Neither shall he take to himself many wives, that his heart may turn away." Solomon transgressed this precept, and it is said by Rabbi Simon that the angels took note of his ill-doing and addressed the Deity: "Sovereign of the world, Solomon has made Thy law even as a law liable to change and diminution. Three precepts he has disregarded, namely, 'He shall not acquire for himself many horses;' 'neither shall he take to himself many wives;' 'nor shall he acquire to himself too much silver and gold.' " Then the Lord replied, "Solomon will perish from the earth; aye, and a hundred Solomons after him, and yet the smallest letter of the law shall not be dispensed with."

THE KABBALAH

One important wing of Jewish thought is the school of mysticism known as the Kabbalah. In some ways a continuation of the kind of Hellenistic Judaism characterized by Philo, it seeks—from out of finding hidden meanings in the narratives, words, and even letters of the Hebrew Bible—to erect a structure of intermediate divine attributes linking the God unchanging and unknowable in his essence, and the changing world. Kabbalism's greatest text is the Zohar, a book, although written in second-century Aramaic, believed by scholars to derive from the Jewish community of thirteenth-century Spain. Following is an account by a modern American rabbi of his experiences in learning something of the teaching of the Zohar from a twentieth-century representative of that tradition named Setzer, an elderly sage who lived very humbly in New York.

From 9½ Mystics: The Kabbala Today

Herbert Weiner

THE SEFIROT

By this time, I had acquired some information about the Zohar —for example, that it was really a group of books, including not only scriptural interpretations and legends but theosophic theology, mythical cosmogony, mystical psychology, and anthropology. According to the distinguished scholar, Gershom Scholem, most of the Zohar is written in an exalted style of Aramaic, the language spoken in second-century Palestine. Some of its books or tracts are terse and enigmatic; other portions flow like a novel, recording conversations carried on in the circle of disciples who followed Rabbi Simeon bar Yochai and his son Eliezer, as they wandered about second-century Palestine. Much of their discussion is carried on in a kind of code whereby terms like moon, sky, or Israel refer to the interrelationships of the *sefirot*.

The term *sefira* is first found in the *Sefer Yetzira*, a mystical text which Scholem believes was written between the third and sixth cen-

Herbert Weiner, 9½ Mystics: The Kabbala Today (New York: Holt, Rinehart and Winston, 1969), pp. 24–29.

turies. Here it is used to describe the ten elementary and primordial numbers, *sefirot,* as the book calls them, and the twenty-two letters of the Hebrew alphabet. These together represent the mysterious forces whose convergence has produced the various combinations observable throughout the whole of creation. They are the "thirty-two secret paths of wisdom: through which God has created all that exists."

The names, definitions, and characteristics of these *sefirot* undergo many changes in the history of the Kabbala, but throughout, the *tree of the sefirot* represents a dynamic, pulsating "world of divinity which underlies the world of our sense data and which is present and active in all that exists."

This subsurface reality is used by kabbalists to explain a problem, perhaps *the* problem of all medieval philosophy, the relationship between an all-perfect, all-knowing creator, and his finite creation. How can the perfect create something imperfect, such as our world? How can we say that an all-knowing God responds to prayer, reacts to injustice, is moved by the appeal of a broken heart? Does this not imply that God changes, and does not all change imply a lack? Indeed, how can finite minds say anything at all about the unknowable, undefinable "hidden root of all roots?" Kabbalists tried to resolve these problems by positing a dimension of reality mediating between the *ein sof,* the infinite source of all being and our own world.

The kabbalists believed that knowledge of the manner in which *sefirot* function could bring about a flow of *shefa,* life-sustaining grace, from the upper realms into our world. The *sefirot* themselves were arranged in various diagrams, the most popular of which began with an upper *sefira* called *keter,* or Crown, a level of reality quite beyond human perception. Indeed, so pure and undifferentiated was this *sefira* that it was altogether eliminated from some countings of the *sefirot.* The next lower level of this "tree" consisted of *chochma,* or wisdom, on the right and *bina,* understanding, on the left. Below them came *chesed,* grace, again on the right, and *gvurah,* strength, on the left. Below these and in the center was the *sefira* called *rachamim,* mercy, sometimes called *tiferet,* beauty. A final triad at the bottom consists of *hod,* glory, on the right, *netzach,* lastingness, on the left, and *yesod,* foundation, in the center.

The final level or *sefira* which is the recipient of all the *shefa* that flows from above, is called *malkut,* kingdom. Some diagrams have another *sefira* called *Daat,* knowledge, which is imagined as a kind of spine or center running through all the *sefirot.*

The human body is sometimes used to diagram the tree of the *sefirot.* The top of the head corresponds to crown; the head, heart, and spine to the upper triad; the upper limbs and body to the second level triad; the lower limbs and sexual organs to the final triad. At other times, the *sefirot* are pictured as concentric circles. Then the upper *sefirot* are closer to the inner core, while the lower *sefirot* are represented by the outer circles.

That the study of the Kabbala without an understanding of these

sefirot and their dynamics was impossible, I knew. On the other hand,
must confess that, when I began my studies with Setzer, all this termi
nology seemed to be more of a hindrance than a help to my goal. Wha
I really wanted to know was why and how the Kabbala or a book like the
Zohar had been able to feed the soul of earlier Jewish generations.

A FIRST LESSON

I had brought an old copy of the Zohar bound in worn leather with
rough green pages spotted by the wax of candles held by previous readers.
Setzer asked me to open the book to its Introduction. He spet a few
minutes reviewing the order of the ten *sefirot* and told me to read the
opening lines. My voice faltered through the first sentences of the Zohar,
while his hand tapped impatiently on the table:

> Rabbi Hizkiah opened his discourse with the text: "As a lily among thorns,
> etc." (Song of Songs, 2:2). "What," he said, "does the lily symbolize? It
> symbolizes the community of Israel. As the lily among thorns is tinged with
> red and white, so the community of Israel is visited now with justice and
> now with mercy; as the lily possesses thirteen leaves, so the community of
> Israel is vouchsafed thirteen categories of mercy which surround it on every
> side.

At this point, Setzer interrupted to point out some associative con-
notations of the terms I had just read. Red, I was told, is the color of
vigor, a characteristic of the *sefira gvurah,* strength; white is the color of
chesed, grace. Thirteen refers to the thirteen attributes of God mentioned
in the biblical phrase, "God is merciful and gracious, long-suffering and
abundant in goodness." The "third mention of Elohim" refers to the fact
that God is mentioned three times in the opening sentences of Genesis
before the divine fiat, "Let there be light."

But this type of association was given only passing attention by
Setzer; it was the sort of thing that one took for granted in a student
of the Zohar. So the Zohar was soon set aside while, in a mixture of
English, Hebrew, and Yiddish, Setzer pointed out that the book's central
concern was "the mystery of the creator and the creation, and the relationship between them." The mystery of an infinite God cannot, of course,
be fully fathomed by a finite mind, yet questions can be asked. To ask
"what?" already implies a certain degree of knowledge. To analyze the
nature of "what" is to reveal the existence of a nonmechanical personal
power and thus to replace the "what" with a "who." To go further into
the nature of "who" makes even this pronoun inadequate for the reality;
the "who" falls away, and there remains only a soundless question, more
akin to awe and inarticulate wonder, yet still implying a certain knowledge of the existence and nature of Something.

But how can we finite creatures know anything about that infinite
which is ultimately responsible for our existence?

The unspoken but necessary assumption, Setzer went on, is that in his creation a creator reveals something of his personality; touched by him, it must bear his stamp. The Zohar tries to proceed from speculation about the creation to speculation about God; similarly, it tries to analyze God's manner of creation by analyzing the creative process in nature and man. It is concerned with the tensions, antagonisms, and oppositions which necessarily precede any synthesis and creative unification. It probes the mystery of nothing becoming something by drawing analogies from the manner in which an immaterial thought or urge becomes materialized in words or even in flesh and blood.

In contemplating the subtleties of creativity, the Zohar turns to man in all his functions, physical as well as spiritual, for its analogue. The phrase from Job 19:26, "And I shall behold God out of my flesh," is one of the many biblical sentences used to prove that the body of man and its functions can provide a hint of the divine process. The Zohar sees nothing unspiritual about examining the human body, and particularly the sex act, as a paradigm of the hidden spiritual universe from which all existence draws its life. For that reason, the *sefirot* are sometimes compared to the various limbs of the human body. At other times, the world of the *sefirot* is visualized as a mystical organism with both feminine and masculine tendencies. Wisdom, the giving element, is thus labeled masculine and given the name *father*. Its opposite on the left side, understanding, is considered feminine because it is a receiver, and it is called *mother*. The next to last *sefira*, foundation, is also masculine, and associated with the male sex organ. The lower *sefira*, which receives the seed, is called both kingdom and *shekina*, the feminine presence of God. *Zivvug*, coupling, is a Hebrew term which can be applied to the sex act, as well as to the unifications of the *sefirot*. *Zivvug* is the goal of all the movements of the *sefirot* in the upper world. To be sure, the acts of unification are preceded in that world as in this by a dialectic of tensions between the polarities which evoke the flow of life-giving seed and prepare the receiver, but unification represents the fulfillmnt of the plan. What the Zohar is teaching, therefore, is that grace, life, or joy cannot flow through the inner worlds and permeate lower or external worlds until the proper couplings take place, the all-important principle that "what happens above depends upon what happens below."

"The perfection of the upper worlds waits upon the perfection of the lower worlds. . . . Adam and Eve must be turned face to face before the upper union is perfected." The total scheme is much more complicated; the practical meaning is always the same. The thoughts and acts of man in our world are invested with implications stretching far beyond the immediately visible scene. All acts of unification, including sexual acts, become not just symbols but instruments which enable the upper worlds to function.

The use of erotic imagery for spiritual symbolism is not, of course, unique to the Zohar; it is found in the prophets, the Song of Songs, and indeed, throughout the bible. In the Zohar, however, the eroticism is at times so daring and provocative as to make clearly understandable the law which requires a student of the Kabbala to be stabilized in his emotional and physical life by marriage and by a commitment to the revealed structure of the commandments. Setzer was a tactful teacher, not avoiding these erotic explanations, but communicating them always in a delicate multiallusional form which did not overemphasize their physical association. Nevertheless, there were passages where the old man did not offer an explanation, and I did not ask.

HASIDISM

A second great movement in Jewish spirituality is Hasidism, which began in eastern Europe with Baal Shem (1700–60). Hasidism combined orthodox practice with the sense of mysterious meanings beneath the surface suggested by the Zohar, *by which it was much influenced. But Hasidism was more popular and pietistic than earlier Kabbalism. By teaching the great worth of the faith and love and fervent feeling expressed through pious practice, Hasidism made religious reality more accessible to ordinary people. Above all, Hasidism exalted the role of gifted spiritual teachers, famous for the wise yet simple ways they expressed the deep insight that came out of their years of mystical study and experience. The following suggests something of the Hasidic world.*

From *Souls on Fire: Portraits and Legends of Hasidic Masters*
Elie Wiesel

"Only you, Lord, know why sometimes I rank myself ahead, and other times after, others," Rebbe Barukh of Medzebozh exclaimed one day.

A proud man, prone to fits of anger and depression, this grandson of the Baal Shem's, brought up by the Maggid of Mezeritch and educated

Elie Wiesel, *Souls on Fire: Portraits and Legends of Hasidic Masters* (New York: Random House, Inc., 1972), pp. 82–86. Reprinted by permission of the publisher and of Weidenfeld & Nicolson Ltd. Copyright by the author.

by Rebbe Pinhas of Koretz, claimed to be different from the other Hasidic Masters of his generation, and he was. He believed that everything was due him, for he saw himself as heir, not to his father, who went almost unnoticed, but to his grandfather. Did he truly believe that he alone was the Baal Shem's legitimate successor? Possibly. The fact is that to him every Rebbe was a potential rival and usurper. He declared himself superior to all of them.

This open arrogance could not fail to cause him trouble and provoke hostilities. His own brothers-in-law complained about his whims and frivolities and went so far as to denounce him to the Great Maggid. Whose grandson was to say later: "Rebbe Barukh of Medzebozh tried to ascend to heaven by stepping on the heads of other Tzaddikim."

He was forever dissatisfied, distrustful, suspicious; his grudges were universal in scope. Yet people forgave him his excessive language, his abrupt changes of mood. His visitors were blessed, even as he insulted them, even as he cursed them. To a child who had surprised him in a domestic quarrel, he said: "You don't understand; what you have just witnessed was a discussion between God and the Shekhina." Legend has absolved him. And more: it has granted him a place of honor. He is the only one to be called "Rebbe Reb" Barukh.

At the time of the Baal Shem's death he was only three, yet he remained obsessed by him. He wanted to resemble him, equal him. Sensing his failure, he often gave in to bleak anxiety and gloom. Though he fought as hard as he could, he was plagued by self-doubt. How was he to know whether the Hasidim's admiration was intended for him or his grandfather? To bring some diversion and cheer into his life, he retained the services of a famous jester: Hershele Ostropoler. This Hershele, devoted but brazenly impudent, became the only person to stand up to him and tell him the truth openly.

A story: One evening Hershele lights a candle. Reb Barukh reprimands him: the room is still too dark. The next evening Hershele lights a dozen candles. And Reb Barukh scolds him again: "Are you trying to blind me?"—"I don't understand you," says Hershele. "Yesterday you were angry with darkness, today you are annoyed with light . . ." Whereupon Reb Barukh bursts out laughing: "*You* want to teach *me* when and how I should unleash my wrath upon the world?"

"This world," he said, "is filled with light for whoever knows it, and covered with darkness for whoever loses his way. . . . As for myself, I live in it as a stranger. So does God. Thus our relationship is that of two strangers in a hostile land."

Another time: "Imagine two children playing hide-and-seek; one hides but the other does not look for him. God is hiding and man is not seeking. Imagine His distress.

"The greatest merit of the Prophet Elijah," he said, "is that when he fought the kings and crushed the idols, the people did not react as to a miracle but instead cried: God is our God."

Another time: "To obtain truth, man must pass forty-nine gates, each opening onto a new question. Only to arrive finally before the last gate, the last question, beyond which he could not live without faith."

He died at fifty-four. At his bedside, the Zohar was open at the page where there is mentioned a certain "wrath blessed from above and from below," and whose name is: Barukh.

Menahem-Mendl of Vitebsk was the only true disciple of the Maggid of Mezeritch to have met the Baal Shem; the Maggid himself had introduced him. Menahem-Mendl was eleven years old at the time and already known as a brilliant Talmudist.

Surrounded by his faithful, the Baal Shem looked at the boy searchingly and began to tell him a story that some of those present forgot immediately and whose hidden meaning eluded the others; only he, little Menahem-Mendl, remembered the tale in all its details and understood its significance: it was his life's story, from its first to its last day. The honors, the duties, the responsibilities, the illnesses, the disappointments, the journeys to the Holy Land: it was all there.

Later, whenever his health worried his friends, he would reassure them: "I still have one half, or one quarter, of the way to go."

This is how he became Rebbe:

The Maggid of Mezeritch, receiving a delegation of his followers from Vitebsk, entrusted them with his belt and cane. They were to be delivered to a certain Rebbe Menahem-Mendl, who lived in their town.

When the travelers returned home, they began looking for the fortunate man in their midst. In vain. There was no Rebbe Menahem-Mendl in Vitebsk. In their zeal to find him, they questioned even the passers-by on the streets. So doing, they came across a shabbily dressed woman, who told them: "I know one Mendl, only one, my son-in-law." They rushed to his house and without a word handed him the Maggid's cane and belt. Menahem-Mendl accepted them, and at that very moment his visitors realized that he had become another.

"My mission on earth," he said, "is to recognize the void—inside and outside me—and fill it."

Considerate, discreet, he was well liked by people of all backgrounds, and at all the courts. The Maggid publicly displayed his affection for him, appointing him to blow the shofar on Rosh Hashana. When Menahem-Mendl left for the Holy Land, the honor went to Levi-Yitzhak of Berditchev, who, overcome by emotion, clasped the shofar and fainted. "His predecessor, Menahem-Mendl, saw further and did not succumb to fear," the Maggid commented.

To friends expressing their admiration, he said: "Far from me the idea of rejecting your praise. I shall need it. And the day I shall face the heavenly tribunal, I shall request your appearance as my witnesses. Each of you will then justify my life by praising me, by stating what he thinks of me just as he does now. And I shall be happy, sure of having won my case. But then, at the last moment, one member of the court will ask me: "And you, Menahem-Mendl, what do *you* think of yourself? And I shall become humble and silent again."

"To fear punishment is nothing," he said. "What we must fear is sin."

Like all Hasidic Masters, he lived wholly in his expectation of the Messiah's coming. Mornings he would go to the window, look outside and sadly remark: "He has not yet come, for the world is still the same."

His most beautiful words: "Man is the language of God."

MAIMONIDES

Another strand of Jewish life is the liberal and rationalistic. It has emphasized Judaism as a reasonable way of life and faith, which can be expressed clearly and is compatible with all that is best in human nature. An early and great spokesman for this tradition (which can also be traced back to Hellenistic Judaism) was Moses Maimonides (1135–1204). Although he firmly believed in God and revelation, Maimonides, as we see in this passage about the Sabbath, was concerned to show persuasive reasons for the commandments and to expound them plainly for the average person. This statement can be compared with the later passage on the Sabbath by Rabbi Heschel.

From *The Guide to the Perplexed of Maimonides*

M. Friedlander

CHAPTER XXXI

It is perhaps clear why the laws concerning Sabbath are so severe, that their transgression is visited with death by stoning, and that the greatest of the prophets put a person to death for breaking the Sabbath.[1] The commandment of the Sabbath is the third[2] from the commandment

M. Friedlander, trans., *The Guide to the Perplexed of Maimonides*, Vol. II (London: Trubner & Co., 1885), pp. 159–60.

[1] Num. xv. *sqq.*

[2] The first and second commandments (Ex. xx. 2–6), counted by Maimonides as one, are in accordance with the Masora.

concerning the existence and the unity of God.[3] For the commandment
not to worship any other being is merely an explanation of the first. You
know already from what I have said,[4] that no opinions retain their vitality
except those which are confirmed, published, and by certain actions constantly revived among the people. Therefore we are told in the Law to
honour this day; in order to confirm thereby the principles of Creation
which will spread in the world, when all peoples keep Sabbath on the
same day. For when the question is asked, why this is done, the answer
is given: "For in six days the Lord hath made," &c. (Ex. xx. 11). Two different reasons are given for this commandment, because of two different
objects. In the Decalogue in Exodus, the following reason is given for
distinguishing the Sabbath: "For in six days," &c. But in Deuteronomy
(ch. v. 15) the reason is given; "And thou shalt remember that thou hast
been a slave in the land of Egypt,[5] &c., therefore the Lord thy God commanded thee," &c. This difference can easily be explained. In the former,
the cause of the honour and distinction of the day is given; comp. "Therefore the Lord hath blessed the day of the Sabbath and sanctified it" (Ex.
xx. 10), and the cause for this is, "For in six days," &c. But the fact that
God has given us the law of the Sabbath and commanded us to keep it,
is the consequence of our having been slaves; for then our work did not
depend on our will, nor could we choose the time for it; and we could
not rest. Thus God commanded us to abstain from work on the Sabbath,
and to rest, for two purposes; namely, 1. That we might confirm the true
theory, that of the Creation, which at once and clearly leads to the theory
of the existence of God. 2. That we might remember how kind God has
been in freeing us from the burden of the Egyptians.—The Sabbath is
therefore a double blessing: it gives us correct notions, and also promotes
the wellbeing of our bodies.

MOSES MENDELSSOHN

*The rationalist tradition was articulated more fully in the eight-
eenth century by Moses Mendelssohn (1729–86), a leader among those
Jews in western Europe who wished to share as Jews in the mainstream
of European culture, and show that their faith—which many like Mendelssohn certainly held deeply—was not vulnerable to the onslaughts against
traditional religion so characteristic of Enlightenment thought. The following excerpts from his writings illustrate Mendelssohn's view that Judaism is a way of life and an ethical ideal rather than a dogmatic or repres-
sive system.*

[3]Lit., the rejection of duality.
[4]This seems to be addressed especially to his pupil, and to refer to what Maimonides
told his pupil *vivâ voce*.
[5]In the original, "in Egypt."

From *Jerusalem and Other Jewish Writings* by *Moses Mendelssohn*

Alfred Jospe

A RELIGION WITHOUT DOGMA?

We have no doctrines that are contrary to reason. We added nothing to natural religion save commandments and statutes. But the fundamental tenets of our religion rest on the foundation of reason. They are in consonance with the results of free inquiry, without any conflict or contradiction.

From a letter to Elkan Herz,
July 23, 1771.

The sole purpose of the divine word was to single Israel out from among all other nations as God's special possession, to become holy unto Him before all other nations. With regard to the teachings of reason, however, there is no distinction between Israel and any other people.

Biur to Exodus 20.

Contemporary Judaism, like Judaism in earlier times, actually has no symbols of faith. Very few doctrines or tenets are prescribed for us. Maimonides counts thirteen of them, Albo only three; yet no one will accuse him [Albo] of heresy for that reason. We are free with regard to our doctrines. Where the opinions of the rabbis are divided, every Jew, whether uneducated or a scholar, is free to agree with the one or the other. *Elu v'elu divrei elohim chayim* ["these as well as those are the words of the living God"], say our rabbis wisely in such cases, even though this dictum is ridiculed by some who do not grasp its meaning and believe it denies the [validity of the] *principium contradictionis*. The Christians have now begun to realize how much bloodshed could have been avoided had they been guided by this saying at all times. The spirit of Judaism is conformity in deeds and freedom of thought in doctrinal matters—save for a few doctrines which are fundamental, on which all

Alfred Jospe, trans. and ed., *Jerusalem and Other Jewish Writings by Moses Mendelssohn* (New York: Schocken Books Inc., 1969), pp. 137–38, 148. Reprinted by permission of the publisher.

our teachers are in agreement and without which the Jewish religion simply could not exist.

From a letter to Abraham Nathan Wolf,
July 11, 1782.

ON THE MEANING OF THE LAW

Ritual Law as Unifying Bond

I realize that we do not agree on the necessity of ritual laws. They may have lost their significance and usefulness as script or sign language. But their necessity as a unifying bond of our people has not been lost. And this unifying bond will, I believe, have to be preserved in the plans of Providence as long as polytheism, anthropomorphism, and religious usurpation are rampant in the world. As long as these tormentors of reason are united against us, genuine theists must also create some kind of unifying bond among themselves lest the others gain the upper hand completely. But of what should this bond consist? Of principles and beliefs? We would then get articles of faith, symbols, doctrinal formulas —all shackling our reason. It is of acts that the bond must consist, and of meaningful acts at that—i.e., ceremonies. All our efforts should actually have only one goal: to eliminate the far-reaching abuses of the ceremonies and to endow them with genuine and real meaning.

From a letter to Herz Homberg,
September 22, 1783.

THE MEANING OF THE SABBATH

The most important ritual pivot of Judaism is the Sabbath. It is more important than the yearly festivals and High Holy Days, for only the Sabbath is sanctified in the creation narrative and represented in one of the Ten Commandments. The Jewish Sabbath is not just an occasion for going to temple or synagogue; the most basic traditional Sabbath rite, the Sabbath meal, is taken in the home with the family. The fundamental Sabbath observance, doing no work, characterizes the entire period, from sundown to sundown. The Sabbath is a deeply humanizing occasion, not only because it gives needed rest and change to human and beast, but because it suggests that there are other objects to human life than production of goods from the earth. For the devout Jew, it is even more—a joyous encounter with an entire other dimension of reality, an encounter as rapturous as that of bridegroom with bride. That attitude is well captured in this passage by a very distinguished modern rabbi who was something of a contemporary Jewish mystic. Rabbi Heschel continues with some significant words about Judaism as a religion centered on the Holy in time rather than space, a locus of the numinous well illustrated by the Sabbath itself.

From *The Earth Is the Lord's and the Sabbath*

Abraham Joshua Heschel

The Sabbath is a bride, and its celebration is like a wedding.

"We learn in the Midrash that the Sabbath is like unto a bride. Just as a bride when she comes to her groom is lovely, bedecked and perfumed, so the Sabbath comes to Israel lovely and perfumed, as it is written: *And on the Seventh Day He ceased from work and He rested* (Exodus 31:17), and immediately afterwards we read: *And He gave unto Moses kekalloto* [the word *kekalloto* means when he finished, but it may also mean] as his bride, to teach us that just as a bride is lovely and bedecked, so is the Sabbath lovely and bedecked; just as a groom is dressed in his finest garments, so is a man on the Sabbath day dressed in his finest garments; just as a man rejoices all the days of the wedding feast, so does man rejoice on the Sabbath; just as the groom does no work on his wedding day, so does a man abstain from work on the Sabbath day; and therefore the Sages and ancient Saints called the Sabbath a bride.

"There is a hint of this in the Sabbath prayers. In the Friday evening service we say *Thou hast sanctified the seventh day,* referring to the marriage of the bride to the groom (sanctification is the Hebrew word for marriage). In the morning prayer we say: *Moses rejoiced in the gift* [of the Sabbath] bestowed upon him which corresponds to the groom's rejoicing with the bride. In the additional prayer we make mention of *the two lambs, the fine flour for a meal offering, mingled with oil and the drink thereof* referring to the meat, the bread, the wine, and the oil used in the wedding banquet. [In the last hour of the day we say] *Thou art One* to parallel the consummation of the marriage by which the bride and groom are united." . . .

What is it that these epithets are trying to celebrate? It is time, of all phenomena the least tangible, the least material. When we celebrate

Abraham Joshua Heschel, *The Earth Is the Lord's and the Sabbath* (New York: Harper and Row, Publishers, 1966), pp. 9–10, 54–61. Citations from *The Sabbath*. Reprinted by permission of Farrar, Straus & Giroux, Inc. Copyright 1949, 1951, 1964 by the author. Notes omitted.

the Sabbath we adore precisely something we do not see. To name it queen, to call it bride is merely to allude to the fact that its spirit is a reality we meet rather than an empty span of time which we choose to set aside for comfort or recuperation.

Did the rabbis imagine that the Sabbath was an angel? a spiritual person? Religious thought cannot afford to associate closely with the powers of fantasy. Yet the metaphoric concept of the Sabbath held no danger of deification of the seventh day, of conceiving it to be an angel or a spiritual person. Nothing stands between God and man, not even a day.

The idea of the Sabbath as a queen or a bride did not represent a mental image, something that could be imagined. There was no picture in the mind that corresponded to the metaphor. Nor was it ever crystallized as a definite concept, from which logical consequences could be drawn, or raised to a dogma, an object of belief. The same Rabbi Hanina who celebrated the Sabbath as a queen preferred on another occasion to compare the Sabbath with a king.

It would be an oversimplification to assume that the ancient rabbis were trying to personify the Sabbath, to express an image which was in their minds. Between personifying time and calling it queen or bride the difference is as big as between presuming to count the exact sum of all beings and calling it universe. The rabbis did not believe that the seventh day was endowed with human features, with a figure or a face; their ideas did not result in either visible or verbal iconography. They rarely went beyond the venture of cherishing the endearing terms of queen or bride. This was not because of a dearth in imaginative power but because what they were eager to convey was more than what minds could visualize or words could say.

To most of us a person, a human being, seems to be a maximum of being, the ceiling of reality; we think that to personify is to glorify. Yet do not some of us realize at times that a person is no superlative, that to personify the spiritually real is to belittle it? A personification may be both a distortion and a depreciation. There are many persons in the world but only one Sabbath.

The idea of the Sabbath as a queen or a bride is not a personification of the Sabbath but an exemplification of a divine attribute, an illustration of God's need for human love; it does not represent a substance but the presence of God, His relationship to man.

Such metaphorical exemplification does not state a fact; it expresses a value, putting into words the preciousness of the Sabbath as Sabbath. Observance of the seventh day is more than a technique of fulfilling a commandment. The Sabbath is the presence of God in the world, open to the soul of man. It is possible for the soul to respond in affection, to enter into fellowship with the consecrated day.

The seventh day was full of both loveliness and majesty—an object of awe, attention and love. Friday eve, when the Sabbath is about to engross the world, the mind, the entire soul, and the tongue is tied with trembling and joy—what is there that one could say? To those who are not vulgarized, who guard their words from being tainted, queen, bride, signify majesty tempered with mercy and delicate innocence that is waiting for affection. . . .

. . . One of the most distinguished words in the Bible is the word *qadosh,* holy; a word which more than any other is representative of the mystery and majesty of the divine. Now what was the first holy object in the history of the world? Was it a mountain? Was it an altar?

It is, indeed, a unique occasion at which the distinguished word *qadosh* is used for the first time: in the Book of Genesis at the end of the story of creation. How extremely significant is the fact that it is applied to time: "And God blessed the seventh *day* and made it *holy.*" There is no reference in the record of creation to any object in space that would be endowed with the quality of holiness.

This is a radical departure from accustomed religious thinking. The mythical mind would expect that, after heaven and earth have been established, God would create a holy place—a holy mountain or a holy spring—whereup a sanctuary is to be established. Yet it seems as if to the Bible it is *holiness in time,* the Sabbath, which comes first.

When history began, there was only one holiness in the world, holiness in time. When at Sinai the word of God was about to be voiced, a call for holiness in *man* was proclaimed: "Thou shalt be unto me a holy people." It was only after the people had succumbed to the temptation of worshipping a thing, a golden calf, that the erection of a Tabernacle, of holiness in *space,* was commanded. The sanctity of time came first, the sanctity of man came second, and the sanctity of space last. Time was hallowed by God; space, the Tabernacle, was consecrated by Moses.

While the festivals celebrate events that happened in time, the date of the month assigned for each festival in the calendar is determined by the life in nature. Passover and the Feast of Booths, for example, coincide with the full moon, and the date of all festivals is a day in the month, and the month is a reflection of what goes on periodically in the realm of nature, since the Jewish month begins with the new moon, with the reappearance of the lunar crescent in the evening sky. In contrast, the Sabbath is entirely independent of the month and unrelated to the moon. Its date is not determined by any event in nature, such as the new moon, but by the act of creation. Thus the essence of the Sabbath is completely detached from the world of space.

The meaning of the Sabbath is to celebrate time rather than space. Six days a week we live under the tyranny of things of space; on the Sabbath we try to become attuned to *holiness in time.* It is a day on which we are called upon to share in what is eternal in time, to turn from the results of creation to the mystery of creation; from the world of creation to the creation of the world.

PURIM

This passage by a prominent American novelist describes one of the annual Jewish festivals. Purim, commemorating Queen Esther, is not as important as Passover or the solemn Yom Kippur, but it brings out that side of Jewish life which is full of fun and humor, and full of the kind of religious practices children find delightful and unforgettable. Significantly, this side of human life is integrated into the sacred round along with the more solemn.

From *This Is My God*
Herman Wouk

PURIM: THE FEAST OF ESTHER

Purim is the nearest thing Judaism has to a carnival. It is another full-moon celebration, falling on the fourteenth of Adar, usually in February or March. The origin of the holy day is in the Book of Esther. The occasion is, of course, the famous deliverance of the Persian Jews from their Hitler-like oppressor, Haman.

The keynote of Purim is riotous rejoicing. The Talmud gives leave to a worshipper to drink on this day until he cannot tell the difference between "Blessed be Mordecai" and "Cursed be Haman." To the credit of many otherwise non-observant Jews, they often do their best to comply. The most staid synagogue-goer will drink a formal little glass of whiskey. In Israel a public street festival not unlike Mardi Gras has sprung up, with the name *Ad'lo Yoda*, the Talmud words for "until he cannot tell the difference."

The day before Purim is the Fast of Esther, a sunrise-to-sundown abstention. At sundown the synagogues fill up. The marked difference between this and all other occasions of the Jewish year is the number of children on hand. Purim is Children's Night in the house of the Lord. It always has been, and the children sense their rights and exercise them.

Herman Wouk, *This Is My God* (New York: Doubleday & Company, 1959), pp. 96–99. Reprinted by permission of the publisher. Copyright 1959, 1970 by The Abe Wouk Foundation, Inc.

They carry flags and noisemakers, the traditional whirling rattles called "groggers," which can make a staggering racket. After the evening prayers the reading of the Book of Esther begins, solemnly enough, with the customary blessing over a scroll and the chanting of the opening verses in a special musical mode heard only on this holiday. The children are poised, waiting. The Reader chants through the first and second chapters and comes at last to the long-awaited sentence. "After these things, the king raised to power Haman the Agagite"—but nobody hears the last two words. The name "Haman" triggers off stamping, pounding, and a hurricane of groggers. The Reader waits patiently. The din dies. He chants on, and soon strikes another "Haman." Bedlam breaks loose again. This continues, and since Haman is now a chief figure in the story, the noisy outbursts come pretty frequently. The children, far from getting tired or bored, warm to the work. They do it with sure mob instinct: poised silence during the reading, explosions on each "Haman." Passages occur where Haman's name crops up several times in a very short space. The children's assaults come like pistol shots. The Reader's patience wears thin and finally breaks. It is impossible to read with so many inter-ruptions. He gestures angrily at the children through the grogger storm and shoots a glance of appeal to the rabbi. This, of course, is what the children have been waiting for. The stag is down. Thereafter to the end it is a merciless battle between the Reader and the children. He tries to slur over the thick-falling "Hamans," they trip him every time with raucous salvos. He stumbles on to the final verse, exhausted, beaten, furi-ous, and all is disordered hilarity in the synagogue. It is perhaps not quite fair to make the Reader stand in for Haman on this evening, but that is approximately what happens.

I have described an old-fashioned Purim. The custom has immense vitality, and most American congregations, even Conservative and Re-form, are familiar with it to some extent. Those that are not are the poorer. All vital religions have such an interlude given to the comic spirit. Purim is ours.

On Purim Day the burlesque merrymaking continues. There is a very old tradition of mummery. Strolling players in former times acted the surefire drama year after year in the villages of Poland and Russia. Nowadays children dress up and enact the Purim Play at school. The note of parody invades the study halls of the pious. "Purim Torah" is a form of elaborate nonsense-learning carried on to this day, a tangle of wild jokes proving absurd laws by strict Talmudic method. The satire on sacred forms of Talmud study is extremely biting. In the modern yeshivas the Purim Play has evolved into a free-wheeling lampoon in music, rhymes, and skits. No personages, no situations are safe. The deans and rabbis themselves come in for burlesque which draws blood. Purim is a sort of safety valve which lets loose in humor and roistering all the pent irritations and pressures of the year. It is a wonderful time.

Beyond this gaiety, it carries four religious obligations: to hear the *Megillah* (the Scroll of Esther) read, to distribute largesse to the poor, to make a feast, and to exchange presents with neighbors and friends. This last institution is *Shalakh Manos,* the Sending of Gifts: things that can be eaten and drunk the same day.

Our forefathers made a great point of sending food on plates wrapped in cloths from house to house. Children ran the Shalakh Manos through the streets, collecting tips in sweets or wine. The custom was a source of excitement and nerve strain for housewives. The wrong amount or the wrong kind of Shalakh Manos sent to a touchy relative could give undying offense. The Purim feast, the *Suda,* began at noon and continued through the day. Families with crowds of guests ate huge repasts, and then ate the Shalakh Manos as it arrived. There was universal open house. Guests roved from one feast to the next. There was no poor Jew who was not everywhere welcome; no Jew rich or powerful enough to close his doors. The custom survives today in enclaves of the pious. Perhaps it is not wholly restorable in the United States, more is the pity. It is a long way from the lower east side in New York to the fashionable suburbs. Nor have we the overpowering sense of community that existed in the ghetto stockade. We are not a sealed-off settlement of inferior citizens, for which we can only thank Heaven. But we have lost some of the levelling camaraderie that prevails in a state of siege.

JUDAISM IN HITLER'S EUROPE

This true story pictures Jewish life in Holland under Nazi occupation, when Jews were being taken gradually to the dread camps in eastern Europe from which very few would return. At the time of this story enough remained to maintain family and synagogue life; in the end, of her family only the author, a child in school at the time, escaped arrest. Her account not only recalls those days but also gives a good picture of traditional Jewish family and synagogue life.

From *"Sabbath" in* Anthology of Holocaust Literature
Marga Minco

I looked down over my mother's book, over the finger with which she traced the lines to enable me to follow the prayers, down through

Marga Minco, "Sabbath," in Jacob Glatstein, Israel Knox, and Samuel Margoshes, eds., *Anthology of Holocaust Literature* (Philadelphia: The Jewish Publication Society of America, 1969), pp. 11–14. (Translated from the Dutch by Roy Edwards). Reprinted by permission of the publisher.

the lattice-work of the screen to where I saw my father standing wearing his prayer shawl. I could not help thinking of the synagogue at Breda. There Father had had a roomy pew all to himself. It had been just like a coach without wheels. To get out of it, he had to open a little round door and descend a few steps. The door squeaked, and when I heard it squeak I would look down.

Father would go to the center of the building. I would follow with my eyes his shining top hat and his ample prayer shawl, which floated out behind him a little as he walked. He would ascend the stairs of the *almemmor,* the dais in the middle of the synagogue from which the scrolls of the Law are read, and whither he was "summoned" to distribute blessings. Suddenly I would hear our names, between the half-chanted Hebrew texts. The names sounded very beautiful in Hebrew. And they were longer, because Father's name was always added to them. Then my mother would also look down through the grille and smile at Father. The other women in the gallery would nod to my mother, to show that they had heard, and want to see whether their husbands would give *them* a blessing, so that my mother would be able to nod to them in their turn. It was a custom in the Breda congregation.

But now I saw Father sitting somewhat toward the back, on a bench among other men. He was wearing an ordinary hat, and he remained where he was until the end of the service. It was a long service. Special prayers were said for Jews in the camps. Some women wept. In front of me one woman was sitting who blew her nose repeatedly, huddled behind her prayer book. She had on a reddish-brown *bandeau*—the wig worn by our married women—which had sagged backward a little under her hat.

My mother had laid her prayer book beside her on the seat. She was staring fixedly into space. I put my hand on her arm.

"It's very cold in Poland now," she whispered.

"Yes, but she was able to take warm clothes with her, wasn't she?" I said softly. "She had a rucksack lying ready."

Mother nodded. The cantor raised his voice in another prayer and we all stood up. Down below, someone had taken a Scroll from the Ark. The Scroll was covered with purple velvet, and there was a silver crown on it from which little bells hung. The Scroll was carried round the building. The bells tinkled. As the Scroll went past them the men kissed the tip of the velvet.

After a while, the final hymn burst forth. It is a cheerful melody, and I never ceased to be surprised by the rather exuberant way in which the congregation plunged into it. Singing, the men folded up their prayer shawls, and the women put on their coats. I saw my father carefully stowing his shawl away in the special bag intended for the purpose.

In front of the synagogue people waited for each other. They shook hands and wished each other "Good Sabbath." Father was already there when we came out. I remembered how I had hated having to walk home with the rest after Sabbath service, when I was a child. I was always frightened of running into children from my school.

Most of the people quickly dispersed over the square. Some went in the direction of Weesperstraat; others made for Waterlooplein. An acquaintance of my father asked us whether we cared to walk part of the way home with him along Nieuwe Amstelstraat.

"I've sent my wife and children into the country," he said. "At the moment it's better for them to be there than here."

"Why haven't you gone with them?" my mother asked.

"Oh, well," he said, "that's not in my line. I'll manage all right."

"Are you on your own at home now?" Mother asked him.

"No," he answered, "I'm staying with my sister. She's not doing anything about it either, for the time being."

"What could you do, actually?" asked my father.

"Well," said his friend, "you can shut the door behind you and disappear. But then, what are you going to live on?"

"Exactly," said my father. "You've got to live. You've got to have something to live on."

We were standing on the corner near the Amstel River. An ice-cold wind was blowing in our faces. My father's acquaintance shook hands all round. "I've got to go that way, to my sister's," he said. He crossed the bridge to Amstelstraat, a small, hunched figure, with the collar of his black overcoat right up round his ears and his hand on his hat.

We walked along beside the Amstel, and came to the bridge where it is joined by the Nieuwe Herengracht canal. We crossed the bridge, under the yellow board. The board bearing in black letters the German word *"Judenviertel."*

A couple of children with woollen scarves round their necks were hanging over the parapet, throwing bread to the seagulls. The birds, skimming low over the water, nimbly caught the scraps. A Black Maria drove down the other side of the canal. A woman pushed a window up and shouted something. The children dropped the rest of the bread on the ground and ran inside.

"Let's take the shortest way home," said my mother. We went along the canal.

"We'll be there in no time," said my father.

"You hear of more and more people going underground," I said.

"Yes," said Father. "We'll have to see about finding something for you too."

"No," I said. "I'm not going alone."

"If we were still in Breda it'd be easier," my mother said. "There we should have had an address in a minute. Here we know nobody."

"There we might perhaps have been able to move in with the neighbors, just like that," I said.

"Oh, we could have gone anywhere we liked," said Mother. "We had friends everywhere."

"Here it costs a lot of money," said my father, "Where am I to get it from?"

"If only we knew more people. . . ." said Mother.

"Let's wait and see," said my father. "Perhaps it won't be necessary. And if it *isn't* necessary, there you sit, among strangers, and you're only a nuisance and a worry to them."

We were home once more. Father put the key in the lock. I glanced involuntarily up and down the street before I went inside.

In the living room the stove was burning and the table was set. Mother had done that before we left. Father went to wash his hands. Then he came and stood with us at the table, took the embroidered cloth from the Sabbath bread, broke the crust off it, and divided it into three pieces while praying. He dipped the bread in salt. I muttered grace, and ate the salted crust.

"That's right," said my father, and sat down.

IX

FREEDOM IN THE CROSS: THE MANY FACES OF CHRISTIANITY

Few religious traditions display the complex diversity of Christianity. Its cultural ambit, at least, covers a fourth of the world's population and has deeply influenced perhaps half the world's known history. Its worship expression ranges from the gorgeous color of a Roman Catholic high mass or the Eastern Orthodox liturgy to the simplicity of a Quaker meeting, where worshippers sit in silence except as someone is moved to speak. In between are Protestant services that emphasize hymns and prayer and sermon—verbal expression—and the stately ceremonial worship of traditional Anglican (Episcopal) and Lutheran churches. One finds also a great collection of secondary sacred acts: pilgrimages to holy cities and shrines, prayer groups, private devotions with rosary or Bible. Christian history is a colorful procession of saints and evangelists, bishops and prophets, conservatives and reformers. Its adherents have ranged from the most rigid and rigorous affirmers of doctrine, to those for whom Christian meaning is always open to reinterpretation in light of current needs and knowledge. Christian social expression likewise has varied, from vast international institutions to national churches to denominations to tiny sects; it has included monastic orders and dropout communes, crusading armies and camp meetings.

All this diversity, however, traces back to a common historical moment: the life and ministry and death of Jesus in the first century, the Jesus who was called by his followers the Messiah or Christ. (The two words mean the same thing; they are Hebrew and Greek, respectively, for "The Anointed One," meaning the king later Judaism believed would be sent by God to restore the fortunes of Israel in the last days.) Jesus, a Jew, preached and worked for two or three years in the early thirties of the first century in Palestine. His fundamental message was that the Kingdom of God—the reign and power and glory of the Holy One of Israel—was at hand, about to break through in fullness and even now perceivable by those whose eyes and ears were open. Then, when still young and apparently only well started on his mission on behalf of the Kingdom, Jesus was arrested, and died cruelly on a wooden cross.

This was not the end of the story. Not long after the death, his followers reported that Jesus had been seen again. They said death had not held him, but that he had appeared to believers in the garden where his tomb was, or along a road, or while they were eating. The followers, above all Paul the great promoter of the new faith in Jesus in the middle years of the century, averred that his death had been a sacrifice necessary to bring in the Kingdom of which he spoke and cancel out the sins of men and women to make them able to share in it, and that his rising again was a triumph over death and sin in which others could share.

The early Christian church—the "ecclesia," or those "called out"—knew of ways for its members to participate in those mysteries. Its leaders preached about Jesus. Entry into the church was through the rite called baptism; the initiate was immersed in water and then rose out of it as a personal reenactment of the death and resurrection of Jesus Christ. The major form of worship was the Eucharist, or "Great Thanksgiving" (now also called the Lord's Supper, Holy Communion, Divine Liturgy, or Mass). It enacted again the meal that Jesus had shared with his disciples on the night before his death, when he had taken bread and said, "This is my body" and wine, saying, "This is my blood." At the service, the officiant took bread and wine, blessed them, broke the bread, and gave them to the faithful present. This was the universal principal act of Christian worship for the first fifteen hundred years of Christianity, and still is in many churches, although the form and ceremony surrounding it vary immensely.

As time went on and Christianity entered the Middle Ages, the church found a new role as the dominant religious institution in Europe. When the Middle Ages closed, further epochal changes occurred as the Reformation raised the cries of "Justification by faith" and "the Scriptures only." In much of northern Europe, new Protestant churches presented new faces to Christianity. It was now often a religion sober and plain in tone, stressing inward faith and services, mostly music and speaking, and expressed in national rather than international institutions. The former church continued on as Roman Catholicism in southern and central Europe and Ireland, and spread at about the same time to the vast new field of the Spanish, Portuguese, and French colonies in the New World. The Eastern Orthodox churches and related traditions, although weakened by the spread of Islam in the Near East, lived on in Russia and the Turkish-ruled Balkans.

Because of this history, Christianity always has been a faith in which forms have changed dynamically, and so it has been in the twentieth century. Tremendous changes in world society have affected Christianity from without, and new Christian movements such as Pentecostalism and the after-effects of the Second Vatican Council in Roman Catholicism from within. Christianity remains among the most varied and lively of world religions.

THE NEW TESTAMENT

The scriptures telling about the life and early influence of Jesus are called the New Testament. The first four books of the New Testament are called the Gospels. They comprise the first three, often termed the Synoptic Gospels ("synoptic" means in Greek "seeing together") because they present, very roughly, parallel accounts of the life of Jesus; and the Fourth, the Gospel of St. John, which offers a somewhat different and often more philosophical version. After the Gospels comes the Book of Acts, describing the words and deeds of the Apostles—the first-generation leaders of the Christian church, that is, the disciples of Jesus, Paul, and their companions. Most of the remaining books of the New Testament are called epistles, letters written to early churches by apostles, mainly Paul.

Below is a passage from the Gospel of Luke, Chapter 10, giving something of the tone and intensity of Jesus' ministry of the Kingdom, including in context the famous parable of the Good Samaritan. (The point is that Samaritans were ordinarily disliked and considered highly unorthodox by the Jews of Judaea.) There is then a passage from St. John's Gospel, Chapter 13. The foot washing that seems to take the place of the Last Supper in the Synoptic Gospels suggests the distinctive character of John. The passage from the Book of Acts, Chapter 2, describes the coming of the Holy Spirit upon the disciples gathered on the Jewish feast of Pentecost (fifty days after the Passover) in an upper room; the chapter ends with an example of the earliest apostolic preaching and a description of the way of life of the early church. Finally, there is a passage from Romans 8 in a modern colloquial translation by the founder of a well-known Christian commune in Georgia. It gives an example of the theological teaching by which Paul and the early church understood the great change that Jesus Christ had made to them.

From *The Revised Standard Version of the Bible*

THE GOSPEL OF LUKE   10

After this the Lord appointed seventy others, and sent them on ahead of him, two by two, into every town and place where he himself was about to come. ²And he said to them, "The harvest is plentiful, but the laborers are few; pray therefore the Lord of the harvest to send out laborers into his harvest. ³Go your way; behold, I send you out as lambs in the midst of wolves. ⁴Carry no purse, no bag, no sandals; and salute no one on the road. ⁵Whatever house you enter, first say, 'Peace be to this house;' ⁶And if a son of peace is there, your peace shall rest upon him; but if not, it shall return to you. ⁷And remain in the same house, eating and drinking what they provide, for the laborer deserves his wages; do not go from house to house. ⁸Whenever you enter a town and they receive you, eat what is set before you; ⁹heal the sick in it and say to them, 'The kingdom of God has come near to you.' ¹⁰But whenever you enter a town and they do not receive you, go into its streets and say, ¹¹'Even the dust of your town that clings to our feet, we wipe off against you; nevertheless know this, that the kingdom of God has come near.' ¹²I tell you, it shall be more tolerable on that day for Sodom than for that town.

13 "Woe to you, Chora'zin! woe to you, Beth-sa'ida! for if the mighty works done in you had been done in Tyre and Sidon, they would have repented long ago, sitting in sackcloth and ashes. ¹⁴But it shall be more tolerable in the judgment for Tyre and Sidon than for you. ¹⁵And you, Ca-per'na-um, will you be exalted to heaven? You shall be brought down to Hades.

16 "He who hears you hears me, and he who rejects you rejects me, and he who rejects me rejects him who sent me."

17 The seventy returned with joy, saying, "Lord, even the demons are subject to us in your name!" ¹⁸And he said to them, "I saw Satan fall like lightning from heaven. ¹⁹Behold, I have given you authority to tread upon serpents and scorpions, and over all the power of the enemy; and nothing shall hurt you. ²⁰Nevertheless do not rejoice in this, that the spirits are subject to you; but rejoice that your names are written in heaven."

21 In that same hour he rejoiced in the Holy Spirit and said, "I thank thee, Father, Lord of heaven and earth, that thou hast hidden these things from the wise and understanding and revealed them to babes; yea, Father, for such was thy gracious will. 22All things have been delivered to me by my Father; and no one knows who the Son is except the Son and any one to whom the Son chooses to reveal him."

23 Then turning to the disciples he said privately, "Blessed are the eyes which see what you see! 24For I tell you that many prophets and kings desired to see what you see, and did not see it, and to hear what you hear, and did not hear it."

25 And behold, a lawyer stood up to put him to the test, saying, "Teacher, what shall I do to inherit eternal life?" 26He said to him, "What is written in the law? How do you read?" 27And he answered, "You shall love the Lord your God with all your heart, and with all your soul, and with all your strength, and with all your mind; and your neighbor as yourself." 28And he said to him, "You have answered right; do this, and you will live."

29 But he, desiring to justify himself, said to Jesus, "And who is my neighbor?" 30Jesus replied, "A man was going down from Jerusalem to Jericho, and he fell among robbers, who stripped him and beat him, and departed, leaving him half dead. 31Now by chance a priest was going down that road; and when he saw him he passed by on the other side. 32So likewise a Levite, when he came to the place and saw him, passed by on the other side. 33But a Samaritan, as he journeyed, came to where he was; and when he saw him, he had compassion, 34and went to him and bound up his wounds, pouring on oil and wine; then he set him on his own beast and brought him to an inn, and took care of him. 35And the next day he took out two denarii and gave them to the innkeeper, saying, 'Take care of him; and whatever more you spend, I will repay you when I come back.' 36Which of these three, do you think, proved neighbor to the man who fell among the robbers?" 37He said, "The one who showed mercy on him." And Jesus said to him, "Go and do likewise."

38 Now as they went on their way, he entered a village; and a woman named Martha received him into her house. 39And she had a sister called Mary, who sat at the Lord's feet and listened to his teaching. 40But Martha was distracted with much serving; and she went to him and said, "Lord, do you not care that my sister has left me to serve alone? Tell her then to help me." 41But the Lord answered her, "Martha, Martha, you are anxious and troubled about many things; 42one thing is needful. Mary has chosen the good portion, which shall not be taken away from her."

THE GOSPEL OF JOHN 13

Now before the feast of the Passover, when Jesus knew that his hour had come to depart out of this world to the Father, having loved his own who were in the world, he loved them to the end. ²And during supper, when the devil had already put it into the heart of Judas Iscariot, Simon's son, to betray him, ³Jesus, knowing that the Father had given all things into his hands, and that he had come from God and was going to God, ⁴rose from supper, laid aside his garments, and girded himself with a towel. ⁵Then he poured water into a basin, and began to wash the disciples' feet, and to wipe them with the towel with which he was girded. ⁶He came to Simon Peter; and Peter said to him, "Lord, do you wash my feet?" ⁷Jesus answered him, "What I am doing you do not know now, but afterward you will understand." ⁸Peter said to him, "You shall never wash my feet." Jesus answered him, "If I do not wash you, you have no part in me." ⁹Simon Peter said to him, "Lord, not my feet only but also my hands and my head!" ¹⁰Jesus said to him, "He who has bathed does not need to wash, except for his feet, but he is clean all over; and you are clean, but not all of you." ¹¹For he knew who was to betray him; that was why he said, "You are not all clean."

12 When he had washed their feet, and taken his garments, and resumed his place, he said to them, "Do you know what I have done to you? ¹³You call me Teacher and Lord; and you are right, for so I am. ¹⁴If I then, your Lord and Teacher, have washed your feet, you also ought to wash one another's feet. ¹⁵For I have given you an example, that you also should do as I have done to you. ¹⁶Truly, truly, I say to you, a servant is not greater than his master; nor is he who is sent greater than he who sent him. ¹⁷If you know these things, blessed are you if you do them. ¹⁸I am not speaking of you all; I know whom I have chosen; it is that the scripture may be fulfilled, 'He who ate my bread has lifted his heel against me.' ¹⁹I tell you this now, before it takes place, that when it does take place you may believe that I am he. ²⁰Truly, truly, I say to you, he who receives any one whom I send receives me; and he who receives me receives him who sent me."

21 When Jesus had thus spoken, he was troubled in spirit, and testified, "Truly, truly, I say to you, one of you will betray me." ²²The disciples looked at one another, uncertain of whom he spoke. ²³One of his disciples, whom Jesus loved, was lying close to the breast of Jesus; ²⁴so Simon Peter beckoned to him and said, "Tell us who it is of whom he speaks." ²⁵So lying thus, close to the breast of Jesus, he said to him, "Lord, who is it?" ²⁶Jesus answered, "It is he to whom I shall give this morsel when I have dipped it." So when he had dipped the morsel, he gave it to Judas, the son of Simon Iscariot. ²⁷Then after the morsel, Satan entered into him. Jesus said to him, "What you are going to do, do quickly." ²⁸Now no one at the table knew why he said this to him. ²⁹Some thought that, because Judas had the money box, Jesus was telling him, "Buy what we need for the feast"; or, that he should give something to the poor. ³⁰So, after receiving the morsel, he immediately went out; and it was night.

31 When he had gone out, Jesus said, "Now is the Son of man glorified, and in him God is glorified; ³²if God is glorified in him, God

will also glorify him in himself, and glorify him at once. [33]Little children, yet a little while I am with you. You will seek me; and as I said to the Jews so now I say to you, 'Where I am going you cannot come.' [34]A new commandment I give to you, that you love one another; even as I have loved you, that you also love one another. [35]By this all men will know that you are my disciples, if you have love for one another."

36 Simon Peter said to him, "Lord, where are you going?" Jesus answered, "Where I am going you cannot follow me now; but you shall follow afterward." [37]Peter said to him, "Lord, why cannot I follow you now? I will lay down my life for you." [38]Jesus answered, "Will you lay down your life for me? Truly, truly, I say to you, the cock will not crow, till you have denied me three times.

THE BOOK OF ACTS 2

When the day of Pentecost had come, they were all together in one place. [2]And suddenly a sound came from heaven like the rush of a mighty wind, and it filled all the house where they were sitting. [3]And there appeared to them tongues as of fire, distributed and resting on each one of them. [4]And they were all filled with the Holy Spirit and began to speak in other tongues, as the Spirit gave them utterance.

5 Now there were dwelling in Jerusalem Jews, devout men from every nation under heaven. [6]And at this sound the multitude came together, and they were bewildered, because each one heard them speaking in his own language. [7]And they were amazed and wondered, saying, "Are not all these who are speaking Galileans? [8]And how is it that we hear, each of us in his own native language? [9]Par'thians and Medes and E'lamites and residents of Meso-pota'mia, Judea and Cappado'cia, Pontus and Asia, [10]Phryg'ia and Pamphyl'ia, Egypt and the parts of Libya belonging to Cyre'ne, and visitors from Rome, both Jews and proselytes, [11]Cretans and Arabians, we hear them telling in our own tongues the mighty works of God." [12]And all were amazed and perplexed, saying to one another, "What does this mean?" [13]But others mocking said, "They are filled with new wine."

14 But Peter, standing with the eleven, lifted up his voice and addressed them, "Men of Judea and all who dwell in Jerusalem, let this be known to you, and give ear to my words. [15]For these men are not drunk, as you suppose, since it is only the third hour of the day; [16]but this is what was spoken by the prophet Joel:

[17]'And in the last days it shall be, God declares,
that I will pour out my Spirit upon all flesh,
and your sons and your daughters shall prophesy,
and your young men shall see visions,
and your old men shall dream dreams;

¹⁸yea, and on my menservants and my maidservants in those days
I will pour out my Spirit; and they shall prophesy.
¹⁹And I will show wonders in the heaven above
and signs on the earth beneath,
blood, and fire, and vapor of smoke;
²⁰the sun shall be turned into darkness
and the moon into blood,
before the day of the Lord comes,
the great and manifest day.
²¹And it shall be that whoever calls on the name of the Lord shall be
saved.'

22 "Men of Israel, hear these words: Jesus of Nazareth, a man
attested to you by God with mightly works and wonders and signs which
God did through him in your midst, as you yourselves know—²³this
Jesus delivered up according to the definite plan and foreknowledge of
God, you crucified and killed by the hands of lawless men.²⁴ But God
raised him up, having loosed the pangs of death, because it was not
possible for him to be held by it. ²⁵For David says concerning him,

'I saw the Lord always before me for he is at my right hand that I
may not be shaken;
²⁶therefore my heart was glad, and my tongue rejoiced;
moreover my flesh will dwell in hope.
²⁷For thou wilt not abandon my soul to Hades,
nor let thy Holy One see corruption.
²⁸Thou hast made known to me the ways of life,
thou wilt make me full of gladness with thy presence.'

29 "Brethren, I may say to you confidently of the patriarch David
that he both died and was buried, and his tomb is with us to this day.
³⁰Being therefore a prophet, and knowing that God had sworn with an
oath to him that he would set one of his descendants upon his throne,
³¹he foresaw and spoke of the resurrection of the Christ, that he was not
abandoned to Hades, nor did his flesh see corruption. ³² This Jesus God
raised up, and of that we all are witnesses. ³³Being therefore exalted at
the right hand of God, and having received from the Father the promise
of the Holy Spirit, he has poured out this which you see and hear. ³⁴For
David did not ascend into the heavens; but he himself says,

'The Lord said to my Lord, Sit at my right hand,
³⁵till I make thy enemies a stool for thy feet.'

³⁶Let all the house of Israel therefore know assuredly that God has made
him both Lord and Christ, this Jesus whom you crucified."
37 Now when they heard this they were cut to the heart, and said
to Peter and the rest of the apostles, "Brethren, what shall we do?" ³⁸And
Peter said to them, "Repent, and be baptized every one of you in the

name of Jesus Christ for the forgiveness of your sins; and you shall receive the gift of the Holy Spirit. [39]For the promise is to you and to your children and to all that are far off, every one whom the Lord our God calls to him." [40]And he testified with many other words and exhorted them, saying, "Save yourselves from this crooked generation." [41]So those who received his word were baptized, and there were added that day about three thousand souls. [42]And they devoted themselves to the apostles' teaching and fellowship, to the breaking of bread and the prayers.

43 And fear came upon every soul; and many wonders and signs were done through the apostles. [44]And all who believed were together and had all things in common; [45]and they sold their possessions and goods and distributed them to all, as any had need. [46]And day by day, attending the temple together and breaking bread in their homes, they partook of food with glad and generous hearts, [47]praising God and having favor with all the people. And the Lord added to their number day by day those who were being saved.

From *The Cotton Patch Version of Paul's Epistles*

Clarence Jordan

THE EPISTLE OF THE ROMANS 8

There is, then, no charge outstanding against those who are in (wedlock to) Jesus Christ. For the Spirit's law of new life in Christ Jesus released you from the claims of the law of sin and destruction. For when it became clear that legalism was a failure, due to its weakness in dealing with humanity, God sent his own Son, in an exact replica of a man of sin and for sin, and dealt effectively with human sin. He did this in order that the just aims of the commandments might be realized in us who live not on the level of man but on the level of the Spirit. For they who are man-centered think along human lines, and they who are Spirit-centered think in terms of the Spirit. For man-centered reasoning dead-ends in destruction, but Spirit-centered reasoning leads to life and space. Man-centered reasoning is hostile to God, because it does not subordinate itself to God's plan nor indeed can it do so. People who are man-centered

Clarence Jordan, *The Cotton Patch Version of Paul's Epistles* (New York: Association Press, 1968), pp. 28–30. Reprinted by permission of the publisher.

just can't get along with God. But you all, you are not man-centered but Spirit-centered—provided, of course, that God's Spirit permeates you. If one doesn't have Christ's spirit, he isn't Christ's man. But if Christ *is* in you, the self, because of its sin, is stone dead; but the Spirit, because it is good, is throbbing with life. And if the Spirit of the God who made Jesus to live again permeates you, then this same God will also give life to your hellbent egos by means of his Spirit that permeates you.

It's a fact, then, brothers, that we are under no obligation whatsoever to live a man-centered life. If you do live that way, you're gonna blow yourselves to smithereens. Yet if by the Spirit you utterly smash your selfishness, you will live. For God's sons are they who are led by *God's* Spirit.

Listen, you all didn't get an old master-slave relationship based on fear; instead, you got a father-son relationship in which we are entitled to call God *"Father."* The Spirit himself sings out with our spirit that "WE ARE GOD'S CHILDREN." And if we are his children, we are also his heirs. If, indeed, we are his heirs, then we are Christ's fellow-heirs provided, of course, that we identify with his suffering in order to join in his reward. For I figure that the sufferings we are enduring can't hold a candle to the splendor that's going to become evident in us. In fact, the fondest dream of the universe is to catch a glimpse of real live sons of God. For the universe is in the grip of futility—not voluntarily, but because someone got control of it—and it is hoping against hope that it will be emancipated from the slavery of corruptness into the marvelous freedom of being the *children* of God. For we know that the whole world is agonizing and hurting up to the very present. And not just it, but we ourselves as we anticipate sonship, which means the liberation of our group. In fact, it was our *hope* that got us by. Now hope isn't expecting something you already see, because when one *sees* something, how can he *hope* for it? But if we hope for what we don't see, then it takes patience to wait for it.

Similarly, the spirit also helps us out in our weakness. For example, we don't know beans about praying, but the Spirit himself speaks up for our unexpressed concerns. And he who X-rays our hearts understands the Spirit's approach, since the Spirit represents Christians before God.

We are convinced that God fully cooperates in a good cause with those who love him and who are chosen for his purpose. He has known such people before, and he set them forth, shaping them into the exact image of his Son, who thus became the first boy in a whole line of brothers. It's these whom he set forth that he also invited, and the ones he invited he accepted into fellowship. And it's these whom he accepted into fellowship that he equipped with credentials.

How, then, shall we respond to all this? If God is rootin' for us, who can win over us? If he didn't hold back his own Son, but put him in the game for us all, won't he even more gladly, in addition to his Son, equip us with all we need to win the game?

Who shall reject us when God has elected us? God *accepts* us into fellowship; who banishes us? Does Christ Jesus, the Killed One, or rather, the Risen One, who is God's "right-hand man" and speaks out for us? What shall drive a wedge between us and the love of Christ? Shall trouble or hardship or persecution or drought or poverty or danger or war? It's as the Scripture says:

> For your sake we face death throughout the day;
> We are thought of as slaughterhouse sheep.

And yet—and yet—*we come out on top everytime through him who set his heart on us.* For I am absolutely convinced that neither death nor life, nor angels nor rulers nor the present nor the future nor force nor mountain nor valley nor anything else in the universe shall be able to separate us from the love of God which is in Christ Jesus our Lord.

LIFE IN THE EARLY CHURCH

In slightly fictionalized form, the following passage describes baptism and the Eucharist as they were done in the first and second Christian centuries, when Christians were a minority, sometimes persecuted, within the sprawling Roman Empire. Note the pivotal importance of Easter and the baptism of candidates on Easter eve. Christmas, the other great Christian festival today, was not kept until after this period.

From *Life in the Early Church A.D. 33 to 313*

A.E. Welsford

At last came the day to which Cæcilius had long been looking forward: the Eve of that Easter Day on which he was to be baptized. He had prepared himself, as he had been told to do, by prayer and fasting, and, not only his sponsors, but the whole church had prayed and fasted for his sake and for that of other catechumens. Minucius was one of his sponsors, and Octavius, whose home was in the country, had made

A.E. Welsford, *Life in the Early Church A.D. 33 to 313* (London: National Society and S.P.C.K., 1951), pp. 232–39. (Greenwich, Conn.: The Seabury Press, 1953). Reproduced by permission of S.P.C.K.

a special effort to come up to Rome for Easter, so that he could stand sponsor for him as well. In early times and in the country, baptisms often took place out of doors in shallow streams. Christians preferred to use running water, as being a fitter symbol for the living water of baptism. But in Rome and in other great cities, baptism out of doors was clearly impossible, especially in times of persecution. Often the rain-water tank in the *atrium* of the house where the church was accustomed to meet for prayer must have been used for this purpose; but at least as early as the third century Christians began to build baptisteries—special buildings attached to the house-church where they worshipped. One of the earliest of these baptisteries was in the catacombs, and there the font was a basin hollowed out of the rock, fed with running water from a spring.

In the second century, Easter was celebrated as a great festival of redemption, and in this celebration the baptism of those newly converted had an important place. The whole church, including the catechumens, met on the Saturday night, and kept vigil together until the dawn of Easter morning. Cæcilius and the rest of the competents, who knew that their baptism would take place shortly before dawn, at first found it difficult to fix their attention on the series of readings from the Old Testament, interspersed with chants, with which the intervening time was filled. But, as one passage succeeded another—the Creation, the deliverance of Noah from the Deluge, the sacrifice of Isaac, the safe passage of the children of Israel through the Red Sea, Ezekiel's vision of the dry bones restored to life, Jonah's three days' sojourn in the belly of the whale—Cæcilius became aware that he was watching a great pageant of redemption, scenes from the vast drama of God's dealings with mankind. All these passages were familiar to him now; he had read them for himself; had been instructed in the symbolic meaning of these stories, and had observed them represented with pathetic simplicity upon the grave-stones in the catacombs. He had entered into a great tradition, and was fast making it his own. Much that had at first seemed to him barbarous or childish in this ancient new religion he now saw to be the "foolishness of God", which is wiser than the wisdom of the philosophers.

The reader closed the book of Exodus, from which he had been reading the account of the origin of the Jewish Passover. The last lesson was from the Gospel of St. John, and told of the Crucifixion of our Lord, and then the bishop began his sermon. "Christ our passover is sacrificed for us," he said, quoting from St. Paul, "therefore let us keep the feast." His theme was redemption, and much of what he said was addressed especially to those about to be baptized. When he had finished, the candidates and their sponsors withdrew to the room where the bap-tism was to take place. There the candidates, stripped of their clothes, came forward in turn. In answer to questions from the officiant, Cæcilius affirmed his belief in God, the Father, Son, and Holy Ghost. He then stepped into the shallow basin which served as a font. The officiant poured water over his head three times, saying: "I baptize thee in the Name of the Father, and of the Son, and of the Holy Spirit." After that, his sponsors led him away to clothe him in the white garments which were always worn by neophytes.

In the early Church, it was usual for confirmation to follow immediately after baptism, so Cæcilius and the other neophytes were at once brought before the bishop. The bishop laid his hand on the head of each neophyte, saying: "In the name of the Father, and of the Son, and of the Holy Spirit. Peace be unto thee." Then he anointed him with consecrated oil, called *chrism,* and gave him the kiss of peace. Cæcilius and the others were now full members of the Church and, as such, could join in Christian worship. In a little while they would be making their first communion, for the dawn of Easter morning was approaching. The doors were already shut, and none but the faithful were present, as the bishop summoned the church to prayer. First he guided them in intercession, saying: "Let us pray, my dearly beloved, for the holy Church of God, that our Lord and God would be pleased to keep her in peace, unity, and safety throughout all the world, subjecting unto her principalities and powers, and grant us to live out the days of a peaceful and quiet life in glorifying God the Father Almighty."* Then one of the deacons said: "Let us bow the knee," and all knelt and prayed in silence for a while, until told to rise. Lastly, while all stood, the bishop summed up their prayers in a concluding collect. In a similar way, prayers were offered for the civil government, for the sick, and for the newly baptized. When the prayers were completed, the celebration of the Eucharist began. The bishop greeted the people with "Peace be unto you," and all exchanged the kiss of peace with their immediate neighbours. Then two deacons brought a white linen cloth, and spread it over the stone table at the foot of the dais. While they were doing this, others collected the offerings the laity had brought—little loaves of bread and flasks of wine. Cæcilius had been taught what to expect, yet the warmth and friendliness of the Christian greeting took him by surprise. During the months of his training he had come to love these people, and now he was one of them. It was with thankfulness in his heart that he handed to the deacon the offering of bread and wine which he had brought with him, remembering as he did so to pray that God would accept his life to be henceforth a living sacrifice to him. When the deacons had placed the offerings on the altar, the bishop rose from his throne and, stepping down from the dais, stood on the far side of the altar, facing the people, with his presbyters grouped around him. He added his own gift to the offerings on the altar, and then he, together with his presbyters, silently blessed the oblation.

*Quoted from *The Shape of the Liturgy* by Dom Gregory Dix. This passage is a translation of the old Roman Good Friday intercessions.

"Lift up your hearts", he said to the people.

"We lift them up unto the Lord", the laity replied.

"Let us give thanks unto the Lord", said the bishop.

"It is meet and right", answered the congregation.

The bishop began the prayer of consecration, which was not at this time fixed in a set form, but which always followed traditional lines. He gave thanks to God, through Jesus Christ, for the creation of the world through the Word, for the incarnation of the Word, and for the redemption of the world by the Word. Then he recalled Christ's institution of the Eucharist, saying:

"Who, when he was betrayed to voluntary suffering in order that he might abolish death, and rend the bonds of the devil, and tread down hell, and enlighten the righteous, and establish the ordinance and demonstrate the resurrection, taking bread and making Eucharist to thee, said: Take, eat, this is my Body, which is broken for you. Likewise also the cup, saying: This is my Blood which is shed for you.

"When ye do this, ye do my *anamnesis.*"

He offered the elements in obedience to Christ's command for the *anamnesis*, or recalling of his death and resurrection, and prayed that all who partook might be made one and be fulfilled by the Holy Spirit, and ended with words of praise, saying:

"Through thy Servant Jesus Christ, through whom honour and glory be unto thee with the Holy Spirit in thy holy Church, now and for ever and world without end."

The laity assented with a loud *Amen*, and the communion followed. The bishop broke some of the consecrated bread and made his own communion, and the presbyters and deacons were the next to communicate. The laity came up to the altar in single file and stood, instead of kneeling, as is the modern custom. For Cæcilius and the rest of the neophytes, this was a very special occasion, their first communion, and for them special provision was made. Besides the chalice of consecrated wine and water, there were two other cups, one filled with water and the other with mingled milk and honey. The water symbolized their purification, the milk and honey signified their entry into the "promised land". As the bishop gave a fragment of the consecrated bread to Cæcilius he said: "The Bread of heaven in Christ Jesus", and Cæcilius replied *Amen*. Then he passed on to where deacons were holding the three chalices, and he received from them in turn the water, the milk and honey, and the Eucharistic wine. Each cup was offered to him in the Name of the Father, Son, and Holy Spirit, and from each he sipped three times. Then he returned to his place.

When all had communicated, the deacons received fragments of the consecrated bread to carry to the sick who were unable to come to make their communion. In Rome, where the Christians were too numerous to meet in one place, it was the custom to send fragments of the bread consecrated at the bishop's Eucharist to be placed in the chalice at any other meeting where the Eucharist was being celebrated. Some of the faithful also received portions of the consecrated bread, which they took home and used to make their own communions privately on the days when the Eucharist was not being celebrated. Finally, when the vessels had been cleansed, one of the deacons said: "Go in peace," and the congregation quietly dispersed.

In the weeks and months which followed, Cæcilius took his part regularly in the worship of the Church. From Easter to Pentecost, he and the other neophytes continued to wear their white robes, for this was kept as a season of continuous festival, an anticipation of the joy of heaven. No other special festivals were held, apart from Easter and Pentecost, but Christians met with unfailing regularity on Sunday mornings, even at the risk of their lives. In Asia Minor, the "birthdays" of martyrs were already being kept with special celebrations of the Eucharist, and by the beginning of the third century the custom spread to North Africa and to Rome. The day of a martyr's death was counted as being his birthday in heaven, and was celebrated accordingly as a festival. The Church on earth, conscious of her union with the Church triumphant in heaven, found this a natural and becoming thing to do. Fasting, on the other hand, was left as a matter of private devotion, and the practice of keeping Lent as a penitential season had not yet developed.

Minucius explained to Cæcilius what was the custom of Christians in their private devotions. Those who could do so prayed at the third, sixth, and ninth hours, as well as at dawn and on going to bed. They kept Wednesday and Friday as "station" days—that is, as fasts—and they said grace before and after meals. Obviously many Christians would find it impossible to observe such a rule of life at all strictly—some were slaves, whose time was not their own. These customs had, in fact, been taken over and adapted from Judaism, and were not considered binding by the Church, but they were the expression of an important truth: that religion is concerned with the whole of life. One way in which Christians showed their consciousness of this was by making the sign of the cross, even over the most trivial acts.

> In our coming in and our going out, when we put on our shoes, when we wash, when we eat, when we kindle the lights, when we sleep, when we sit down, whatever business occupies us, we sign our forehead with the sign of the cross.*

Not long after he had been made a full member of the Church, Cæcilius was invited to an Agape of Love Feast. This was held at a private house, but the meal had a religious character, and would not

*Tertullian: *De corona militis.*

have been considered in order unless the bishop or his representative was present. In his unregenerate days he had often taken part in pagan feasts which also had a religious character, but this meal was much more sober, more homely and intimate. It was a custom derived from Judaism, and not from paganism. It was sometimes called "The Lord's Supper" and, like the Eucharist, it had its origin in the last meal which the Lord ate with his disciples. At some time in the first century, probably within the lifetime of the apostles, the rite especially instituted by our Lord, the Eucharist, was separated from the Agape. The behaviour of Gentile converts at Corinth, who called down upon themselves a rebuke from St. Paul for their greed and drunkenness during the Lord's Supper, suggests the reason for this change. In the second and third centuries, an Agape was usually held at the invitation of some wealthy Christian, who wished to make a feast for the whole community, and especially for its poorer members. Cæcilius was particularly struck by the absence of frivolous conversation. The talk was all on religious matters, and consisted for the most part of questions asked by the guests and answered by the bishop. What pleased Cæcilius most was the wording of the blessing which was said over the bread:

> We give thanks unto thee, our Father, for the life and knowledge, which thou didst make known unto us through Jesus thy servant; to thee be the glory for ever. As this broken bread was scattered upon the tops of the mountains and being gathered became one, so gather thy church from the ends of the earth into thy kingdom; for thine is the glory and the power through Jesus Christ for ever.†

This was not the bread of the Eucharist, the Lord's Body, but it was blessed bread of which only the baptized might eat. Cæcilius rejoiced in the sense of fellowship which this common meal gave him, not only with those immediately around him, but also with other Christians all over the world.

THE FATHERS OF THE CHURCH

At the time of its emergence to dominate Europe and the Near East spiritually in the fourth century A.D., the Christian church was also growing in understanding of its faith—often through controversy—even as it grew explosively in numbers. Wise men within the faith sought to define and deepen the articulation of Christian doctrine, and to make it more appealing to people of education by using the language of Greek philos-

†from *The Didache.*

*ophy, even as missionaries found ways to allow it to supersede the reli-
gions of the pagan Greeks, Romans, Celts, and Germanic peoples. One
of the greatest of those early theologians now called the "Church Fathers",
who made the faith of Christ speak the vocabulary of philosophy, was
Athanasius (c. 293–373) of Alexandria. The following passage is on the
reasons for the incarnation, or taking flesh, of the Logos or Word of God
in Jesus Christ. It argues that although mankind, being made in the image
of God; should have been able in theory to know God directly, through
our sinking into wickedness we were not so able, and even the prophets
and the Law were not enough to show us God—since we were attached to
the flesh, we needed to see God in the flesh.*

From *Athanasius: Contra Gentes and De Incarnatione*

Robert W. Thomson

DE INCARNATIONE

12. The grace of being in the image was sufficient for one to know
God the Word and through him the Father.[1] But because God knew the
weakness of men he anticipated their negligence, so that if they failed
to recognize God by themselves, through the works of creation they might
be able to know the Creator. But because the negligence of men sank
gradually to the worse, God again provided for such weakness of theirs
and sent the law and the prophets, who were known to them, so that
if they were reluctant to raise their eyes to heaven and know the Creator,
they would have schooling from those close by. For men can learn more
directly from other men about more advanced things. So they could
lift their eyes to the immensity of heaven, and discerning the harmony
of creation know its ruler, the Word of the Father, who by his providence
in the universe makes the Father known to all men, and for that reason
moves the universe, in order that by him all men should know God. Or
if they were reluctant to do this, they could meet the saints[2] and through
them learn of God the Creator of the universe, the Father of Christ, and
that the worship of idols was godless and full of all impiety. They could
also, by knowing the law, desist from all wickedness and lead lives of

Robert W. Thomson, trans. and ed., *Athanexius: Contra Gentes and De Incarna-
tione* (Oxford: Clarendon Press, 1971), pp. 163–65, 173. Copyright 1971 by Oxford University Press, and reprinted with its permission.

[1]Cf. *c.G.* ch. 2 n. 3.
[2]Ἅγιοι: the prophets of the Old Testament (as opposed to the angels of heaven).

virtue. For the law was not for the Jews only, nor on their account only were the prophets sent—though they were sent to the Jews and persecuted by the Jews—but they provided holy instruction for the whole world about the knowledge of God and the conduct of one's soul. Although, therefore, such was the goodness and mercy of God, nevertheless men, being overcome by their present desires and the illusions and deceits of demons, did not look towards the truth, but sated themselves with many vices and sins, so that they no longer appeared rational beings, but from their behaviour were considered to be irrational. . . .

. . . **16.** For since men's reason had descended to sensible things, the Word submitted to being revealed through a body, in order that he might bring men to himself as a man and turn their senses to himself, and that thenceforth, although they saw him as a man, he might persuade them through the works he did that he was not merely a man but God, and the Word and Wisdom of the true God. This Paul wished to indicate when he said: '*Be firm and grounded in love, that you may be able to understand with all the saints what is the breadth and length and height and depth, and that you may know the love of Christ which transcends knowledge, in order that you may be filled with all the fullness of God.*'[3] For the Word spread himself everywhere, above and below and in the depth and in the breadth: above, in creation; below, in the incarnation; in the depth, in hell; in breadth, in the world.[4] Everything is filled with the knowledge of God.[5] For this reason, not as soon as he came did he complete the sacrifice on behalf of all and deliver his body to death, and resurrecting it make himself thereby invisible. But by means of it he rendered himself visible, remaining in it and completing such works and giving signs as made him known to be no longer a man but God the Word. For in two ways our Saviour had compassion through the incarnation: he both rid us of death and renewed us; and also, although he is invisible and indiscernible, yet by his works he revealed and made himself known to be the Son of God and the Word of the Father, leader and king of the universe.[6]

THE RULE OF SAINT BENEDICT

The importance of monks for the development of Christianity— and civilization—in western Europe can hardly be overemphasized. Monks

[3] Eph. 3: 17–19.
[4] The argument recalls the concept of the cosmic cross. Cf. *Acts of Andrew Laudatio* 46; Irenaeus, *Demonstratio* 34 and *Adv. Haer.* v. 17. 4; also J. Daniélou, *The Theology of Jewish Christianity* (London, Chicago, 1964), pp. 287–8, and H. Rahner, 'The Christian Mystery and the Pagan Mysteries', in *The Mysteries*, ed. J. Campbell (Bollingen Series xxx. 2, N.Y., 1955), p. 374.
[5] Cf. Is. 11:9.
[6] These are the two basic ideas in Athanasius' doctrine of redemption; cf. *c.G.* ch. I n. 3.

preserved and created learning, made wilderness into farmlands, and built monasteries that were refuges in times of chaotic violence. The father of western monasticism was St. Benedict (c. 480–547); his rule and his monastery at Monte Cassino in Italy were models for the monasticism that followed. The passage below gives part of the prologue to his rule for monks, stating the rationale for the monastic life and some sample passages from the rule itself.

From *The Rule of Saint Benedict*
Abbot Justin McCann

Wherefore the Lord also saith in the Gospel: *He that heareth these my words and doth them, shall be likened to a wise man that built his house upon a rock. The floods came and the winds blew, and they beat upon that house, and it fell not, for it was founded upon a rock.*[1] Having given us these instructions, the Lord daily expects us to make our life correspond with his holy admonitions. And the days of our life are lengthened and a respite allowed us for this very reason, that we may amend our evil ways. For the Apostle saith: *Knowest thou not that the patience of God inviteth thee to repentance?*[2] For the merciful Lord saith: *I will not the death of a sinner, but that he should be converted and live.*[3]

So, brethren, we have asked the Lord about the dwellers in his tabernacle and have heard what is the duty of him who would dwell therein; it remains for us to fulfil this duty. Therefore our hearts and bodies must be made ready to fight under the holy obedience of his commands; and let us ask God that he be pleased, where our nature is powerless, to give us the help of his grace. And if we would escape the pains of hell and reach eternal life, then must we—while there is still time, while we are in this body and can fulfil all these things by the light of this life—hasten to do now what may profit us for eternity.

Therefore must we establish a school of the Lord's service; in founding which we hope to ordain nothing that is harsh or burdensome. But if, for good reason, for the amendment of evil habit or the preservation of charity, there be some strictness of discipline, do not be at once dismayed and run away from the way of salvation, of which the entrance must needs be narrow. But, as we progress in our monastic life and in

Abbot Justin McCann, trans. and ed., *The Rule of Saint Benedict* (London: Burns & Oates, 1952), pp. 11–13, 125–33. Reprinted by permission of Sheed and Ward, Ltd.

[1]Mat. vii. 24, 25.   [2]Rom. ii. 4.   [3]Ezech. xxxiii. 11.

faith, our hearts shall be enlarged, and we shall run with unspeakable sweetness of love in the way of God's commandments; so that, never abandoning his rule but persevering in his teaching in the monastery until death, we shall share by patience in the sufferings of Christ, that we may deserve to be partakers also of his kingdom. Amen.

END OF THE PROLOGUE . . .

THE CLOTHES AND SHOES OF THE BRETHREN

Let clothing be given to the brethren according to the nature of the locality in which they dwell and its climate; for in cold districts they will need more clothing, and in warm districts less. It is the abbot's business to take thought for this matter. But we believe that in ordinary places the following dress is sufficient for each monk: a tunic, a cowl (thick and woolly in winter, but thin or worn in summer), a belt for work, and for the feet shoes and stockings. And let not the monks complain of the colour or coarseness of any of these things, but be content with what is to be found in the district where they live and can be purchased cheaply.

Let the abbot see to the size of the garments, that they be not too short for their wearers, but of the proper fit. When the brethren receive new clothes, let them always return the old ones at once, that they may be stored in the clothes-room for the poor. For it is sufficient if a monk have two tunics and two cowls, to allow for a change at night and for the washing of these garments; more than that is superfluity and should be curtailed. And let them return their stockings, and anything else that is old, when they receive new ones. Those who are sent on a journey shall receive drawers from the clothes-room, which they shall wash and restore when they return. And let their cowls and tunics be somewhat better than the ones they wear usually. They shall receive them from the clothes-room when they are starting on their journey and restore them when they return.

For bedding, let this suffice: a mattress, a blanket, a coverlet, and a pillow. The beds should be examined frequently by the abbot, lest any private property be concealed in them. If any brother be found to have anything that he has not received from the abbot, let him undergo the strictest punishment. And in order that this evil of private ownership may be rooted out utterly, let the abbot provide all things that are necessary: that is, cowl, tunic, stockings, shoes, belt, knife, pen, needle, handkerchief, and tablets; so that all pretext of need may be taken away. Yet let the abbot always consider those words of the Acts of the Apostles: *Distribution was made to everyone according as he had need.*[4] So too let

4 Acts iv. 35.

the abbot consider the weaknesses of the needy, and not the ill-will of the jealous. But in all his decisions let him think upon the retribution of God.

OF THE ABBOT'S TABLE

Let the abbot always eat with the guests and pilgrims. But when there are no guests, let him have the power to invite whom he will of the brethren. Yet, for discipline's sake, let one or two seniors always be left with the brethren.

THE CRAFTSMEN OF THE MONASTERY

If there be craftsmen in the monastery, let them practise their crafts with all humility, provided the abbot give permission. But if one of them be puffed up because of his skill in his craft, supposing that he is conferring a benefit on the monastery, let him be removed from his work and not return to it, unless he have humbled himself and the abbot entrust it to him again. If any of the work of the craftsmen is to be sold, let those who have to manage the business take care that they be not guilty of any dishonesty. Let them always remember Ananias and Saphira, and take care lest they, or any others who deal dishonestly with the property of the monastery, should suffer in their souls the death which they endured in their bodies. And, as regards the price, let not the sin of avarice creep in; but let the goods always be sold a little cheaper than they are sold by people of the world, *that in all things God may be glorified.*[5]

THE ORDER FOR THE RECEPTION OF BRETHREN

When anyone newly cometh to be a monk, let him not be granted an easy admittance; but, as the apostle saith: *Test the spirits, to see whether they come from God.*[6] If such a one, therefore, persevere in his knocking, and if it be seen after four or five days that he bears patiently his harsh treatment and the difficulty of admission and persists in his petition, then let admittance be granted to him, and let him stay in the guest-house for a few days. After that let him dwell in the noviciate, where the novices work, eat, and sleep. And let a senior be assigned to

[5] 1 Peter iv. 11.   [6] 1 John iv. 1.

them who is skilled in winning souls, that he may watch over them with the utmost care. Let him examine whether the novice truly seeks God, and whether he is zealous for the Work of God, for obedience, and for humiliations. Let him be told all the hardships and trials through which we travel to God.

If he promise to persevere in his purpose, then at the end of two months let this Rule be read through to him, and let him be addressed thus: "Behold the law under which you wish to serve; if you can observe it, enter; if you cannot, freely depart." If he still abide, then let him be led back into the aforesaid noviciate and again tested in all patience. After the lapse of six months let the Rule be read to him, so that he may know on what he is entering. And, if he still abide, after four months let the Rule be read to him again. And if, upon mature deliberation, he promise to observe all things and to obey all the commands that are given him, then let him be received into the community. But let him understand that according to the law of the Rule he is no longer free to leave the monastery, or to withdraw his neck from under the yoke of the Rule, which it was open to him, during that prolonged delibera-tion, either to refuse or to accept.

Now this shall be the manner of his reception. In the oratory, in the presence of all, he shall promise stability, conversion of his life, and obedience; and this before God and his Saints, so that he may know that should he ever do otherwise he will be condemned by him whom he mocks. He shall embody this promise of his in a petition, drawn up in the names of the Saints whose relics are there and of the abbot who is present. Let him write this document with his own hand; or, if he cannot write, let another do it at his request, and let the novice put his mark to it and place it on the altar with his own hand. When he has placed it there, let the novice himself at once intone this verse: *Suscipe me, Domine, secundum eloquium tuum, et vivam: et ne confundas me ab exspectatione mea.*[7] Let the whole community repeat this after him three times, adding at the end of all the *Gloria Patri.* Then let the novice prostrate himself before the feet of each monk, asking them to pray for him; and from that day let him be counted as one of the com-munity. If he possess any property, let him either give it beforehand to the poor, or make a formal donation bestowing it on the monastery. Let him keep back nothing at all for himself, as knowing that thencefor-ward he will not have the disposition even of his own body. So let him, there and then in the oratory, be stripped of his own clothes which he is wearing and dressed in the clothes of the monastery. But let those clothes, which have been taken off him, be put aside in the clothes-room and kept there. Then, should he ever listen to the persuasions of the devil and decide to leave the monastery (which God forbid), let them take off him the clothes of the monastery and so dismiss him. But his

[7] Ps. cxviii. 116.

petition, which the abbot took from off the altar, shall not be returned to him, but shall be preserved in the monastery.

AUGUSTINE

Probably no writer since New Testament times has influenced the course of western Christianity more than Augustine of Hippo in North Africa; he lived mainly in what is modern Tunisia, 354–430. Not the least interesting aspect of his Christianity is the manner of his coming to it. Although his mother Monica was a Christian, as a brilliant young teacher of rhetoric Augustine kept a mistress and led a sensual life. He had been drawn toward Neoplatonism and Manichaeism, with their view of matter as a lower and ensnaring principle. His conversion was sudden, at least on the surface: he heard a childish voice chanting one evening in a garden, "Take and read, take and read." He took the New Testament and read from Romans 13 " . . . put on the Lord Jesus Christ, and make no provision for the flesh, to gratify its desires." From then on he was Christian.

Augustine's writings as a Christian philosopher, theologian, preacher, and controversialist are voluminous and touch on nearly every area of Christian concern. But two problems were of recurring interest to Augustine: sin versus the grace or divine power by which God draws the fallen individual back to him- or herself, and the relation of Christianity to human society. In the following passage we see him surveying the ideal human state in Eden, then commenting on the fall by which all things human were tainted by lust and violence including sexuality, then presenting the grace by which God will save men and women for his plan nonetheless since his predestined number of saints is unshakeable, and God's power greater than the fall and his love greater than sin, and finally picturing two cities or two societies—that of God and that of human self-love.

From *Saint Augustine: The City of God, Books VIII-XVI*

Gerald G. Walsh and Grace Monahan

Now, the point about Eden was that a man could live there as a a man longs to live, but only so long as he longed to live as God willed

Gerald G. Walsh and Grace Monahan, *Saint Augustine: The City of God, Books VIII–XVI* (Washington, D.C.: Catholic University of America Press, 1952), pp. 405–11. Reprinted by permission of the publisher.

him to live. Man in Eden lived in the enjoyment of God and he was good by a communication of the goodness of God. His life was free from want, and he was free to prolong his life as long as he chose. There were food and drink to keep away hunger and thirst and the tree of life to stave off death from senescence. There was not a sign or a seed of decay in man's body that could be a source of any physical pain. Not a sickness assailed him from within, and he feared no harm from without. His body was perfectly healthy and his soul completely at peace. And as in Eden itself there was never a day too hot or too cold, so in Adam, who lived there, no fear or desire was ever so passionate as to worry his will. Of sorrows there was none at all and of joys none that was vain, although a perpetual joy that was genuine flowed from the presence of God, because God was loved with a 'charity from a pure heart and a good conscience and faith unfeigned.'[1] Family affection was ensured by purity of love; body and mind worked in perfect accord; and there was an effortless observance of the law of God. Finally, neither leisure nor labor had ever to suffer from boredom or sloth.

How in the world, then, can any one believe that, in a life so happy and with men so blessed, parenthood was impossible without the passion of lust? Surely, every members of the body was equally submissive to the mind and, surely, a man and his wife could play their active and passive roles in the drama of conception without the lecherous promptings of lust, with perfect serenity of soul and with no sense of disintegration between body and soul. Merely because we have no present experience to prove it, we have no right to reject the possibility that, at a time when there was no unruly lust to excite the organs of generation and when all that was needed was done by deliberate choice, the seminal flow could have reached the womb with as little rupture of the hymen and by the same vaginal ducts as is at present the case, in reverse, with the menstrual flux. And just as the maturity of the fetus could have brought the child to birth without the moanings of the mother in pain, so could connection and conception have occurred by a mutually deliberate union unhurried by the hunger of lust.

Perhaps these matters are somewhat too delicate for further discussion. It must suffice to have done the best that I could to suggest what was possible in the Garden of Eden, before there was any need for the reins of reticence to bridle a discussion like this. However, as things now are, the demands of delicacy are more imperative than those of discussion. The trouble with the hypothesis of a passionless procreation controlled by will, as I am here suggesting it, is that it has never been verified in experience, not even in the experience of those who could have proved that it was possible. Actually, they sinned too soon and brought on themselves exile from Eden. Hence, today it is practically impossible even to discuss the hypothesis of voluntary control without

[1] 1 Tim. 1.5.

the imagination being filled with the realities of rebellious lust. It is this last fact which explains my reticence; not, certainly, any lack of proof for the conclusion my mind has reached.

What, in any case, is certain is this, that God Almighty the ultimate and supremely good Creator and Ruler of all living creatures, the Giver of grace and glory to all good wills, and the God who abandons bad wills to the doom they deserve, was not without His own definite plan of populating the City of God with that fixed number of saints which His divine wisdom had ordained, even though the City had to be filled with citizens chosen from the ranks of a fallen human race. Of course, once the whole mass of mankind was, at it were, cankered in its roots,[2] there was no question of men meriting a place in His City. They could only be marked out by His grace; and how great that grace was they could see not only in their own deliverance but in the doom meted out to those who were not delivered from damnation. For, no one can help but acknowledge how gratuitous and undeserved is the grace which delivers him when he sees so clearly the contrast between his privileged, personal immunity and the fate of the penalized community whose punishment he was justly condemned to share.

Here we have an answer to the problem why God should have created men whom He foresaw would sin. It was because both in them and by means of them He could reveal how much was deserved by their guilt and condoned by His grace, and, also, because the harmony of the whole of reality which God has created and controls cannot be marred by the perverse discordancy of those who sin.

What I have just said applies to both angelic and human sinners. They can do nothing to interfere with 'the great works of God which are accomplished according to His will.'[3] God who both foresees all things and can do all things, when He distributes to each of His creatures their appropriate endowments, knows how to turn to good account both good and evil. Hence, there was no reason why God should not make a good use even of the bad angel who was so doomed to obduracy, in punishment of the sin that issued from the primal bad will, that a return to good will became for him impossible. This God did by permitting the bad angel to tempt the first man who had been created good, in the sense of having a will that was good by nature.

The point here is that the first man had been so constituted that if, as a good man, he had relied on the help of God, he could have overcome the bad angel, whereas he was bound to be overcome if he proudly relied on his own will in preference to this wisdom of his maker and helper, God; and he was destined to a merited reward if his will remained firm with the help of God, and to an equally deserved doom if his will wavered because of his desertion from God. Notice here that, whereas

2. . . . *universa massa tamquam in vitiata radice damnata.*
3Cf. Ps. 110.2.

the reliance on the help of God was a positive act that was only possible by the help of God, the reliance on his own will was a negative falling away from favors of divine grace, and this was a possibility of his own choice.

There is an analogy to this in living. The act of living in a body is a positive act which is not a matter of choice but is only possible by the help of nourishment; whereas the choice not to live in the body is a negative act which is in our human power, as we see in the case of suicide. Thus, to remain living as one ought to live was not a matter of choice, even in Eden, but depended on the help of God, whereas to live ill, as one ought not to live, was in man's power; therefore, man was justly responsible for the cutting short of his happiness and the incurring of the penalty that followed.

Since, then, God was not without knowledge of man's future fall, He could well allow man to be tempted by the angel who hated and envied man. God was in no uncertainty regarding the defeat which man would suffer; but, what matters more, God foresaw the defeat which the Devil would suffer at the hands of a descendant of Adam, and with the help of divine grace, and that this would be to the greater glory of the saints. Now, all this was so accomplished that nothing in the future escaped the foreknowledge of God, yet nothing in the foreknowledge compelled anyone to sin. God's further purpose was to reveal to all rational creatures, angelic and human, in the light of their own experience, the difference between the fruits of presumption, angelic or human, and the protection of God. For of course, no one would dare to believe or declare that it was beyond God's power to prevent the fall of either angel or man. But, in fact, God preferred not to use His own power, but to leave success or failure to the creature's choice. In this way, God could show both the immense evil that flows from the creature's pride and also the even greater good that comes from His grace.

What we see, then, is that two societies have issued from two kinds of love. Worldly society has flowered from a selfish love which dared to despise even God, whereas the communion of saints is rooted in a love of God that is ready to trample on self. In a word, this latter relies on the Lord, whereas the other boasts that it can get along by itself. The city of man seeks the praise of men, whereas the height of glory for the other is to hear God in the witness of conscience. The one lifts up its head in its own boasting; the other says to God: 'Thou art my glory, thou liftest up my head.'[4]

In the city of the world both the rulers themselves and the people they dominate are dominated by the lust for domination; whereas in the City of God all citizens serve one another in charity, whether they serve by the responsibilities of office or by the duties of obedience. The one city loves its leaders as symbols of its own strength; the other says to its God:

4Ps. 3.4.

'I love thee, O Lord, my strength.'[5] Hence, even the wise men in the city of man live according to man, 'and their only goal has been the goods of their bodies or of the mind or of both; though some of them have reached a knowledge of God, 'they did not glorify him as God or give thanks but became vain in their reasonings, and their senseless minds have been darkened. For while professing to be wise' (that is to say, while glorying in their own wisdom, under the domination of pride), 'they have become fools, and they have changed the glory of the incorruptible God for an image made like to corruptible man and to birds and four-footed beasts and creeping things' (meaning that they either led their people, or imitated them, in adoring idols shaped like these things), 'and they worshipped and served the creature rather than the Creator who is blessed forever.'[6] In the City of God, on the contrary, there is no merely human wisdom, but there is a piety which worships the true God as He should be worshiped and has as its goal that reward of all holiness whether in the society of saints on earth or in that of angels of heaven, which is 'that God may be all in all.'[7]

THOMAS AQUINAS

The major expression of Christian philosophy in the Middle Ages was Scholasticism, and its greatest exponent was Thomas Aquinas (1224–74). His thought synthesized the Greek philosophers Plato and Aristotle with Augustine and other church fathers, and added insights to them out of his own acute intellect. His major work, the Summa Theologica, *manifests a masterful sense of order, system, and logical sequence as it brings together vast areas of Christian thought. Thomas's basic premise is that the realm of nature is knowable to reason and philosophy; and above it is the realm of supernature, including God and those aspects of human experience related to one's ultimate meaning and destiny, knowable instead by faith and revelation. God, however, can be known by reason, although once one recognizes the key fact of God's existence through unaided reason, one should then be driven to seek out God's special and saving revelation. Following are Thomas's famous five arguments for the existence of God. Note the combination of references from Aristotle (the* Metaphysics*), the Bible, and Augustine.*

[5] Ps. 17.2.
[6] Rom. 1.21–25.
[7] 1 Cor. 15.28.

From *Introduction to Saint Thomas Aquinas*

Anton C. Pegis

WHETHER GOD EXISTS?

We proceed thus to the Third Article:—

Objection 1. It seems that God does not exist; because if one of two contraries be infinite, the other would be altogether destroyed. But the name *God* means that He is infinite goodness. If, therefore, God existed, there would be no evil discoverable; but there is evil in the world. Therefore God does not exist.

Obj. 2. Further, it is superfluous to suppose that what can be accounted for by a few principles has been produced by many. But it seems that everything we see in the world can be accounted for by other principles, supposing God did not exist. For all natural things can be reduced to one principle, which is nature; and all voluntary things can be reduced to one principle, which is human reason, or will. Therefore there is no need to suppose God's existence.

On the contrary, It is said in the person of God: *I am Who am* (*Exod.* iii. 14).

I answer that, The existence of God can be proved in five ways.

The first and more manifest way is the argument from motion. It is certain, and evident to our senses, that in the world some things are in motion. Now whatever is moved is moved by another, for nothing can be moved except it is in potentiality to that towards which it is moved; whereas a thing moves inasmuch as it is in act. For motion is nothing else than the reduction of something from potentiality to actuality. But nothing can be reduced from potentiality to actuality, except by something in a state of actuality. Thus that which is actually hot, as fire, makes wood, which is potentially hot, to be actually hot, and thereby moves and changes it. Now it is not possible that the same thing should be at once in actuality and potentiality in the same respect but only in different respects. For what is actually hot cannot simultaneously be potentially hot; but it is simultaneously potentially cold. It is therefore impossible that in the same respect and in the same way a thing should

Anton C. Pegis, ed., *Introduction to Saint Thomas Aquinas* (New York: Random House, 1948), pp. 24–27. Reprinted by permission of the publisher.

be both mover and moved, *i.e.*, that it should move itself. Therefore, whatever is moved must be moved by another. If that by which it is moved be itself moved, then this also must needs be moved by another, and that by another again. But this cannot go on to infinity, because then there would be no first mover, and, consequently, no other mover, seeing that subsequent movers move only inasmuch as they are moved by the first mover; as the staff moves only because it is moved by the hand. Therefore it is necessary to arrive at a first mover, moved by no other; and this everyone understands to be God.

The second way is from the nature of efficient cause. In the world of sensible things we find there is an order of efficient causes. There is no case known (neither is it, indeed, possible) in which a thing is found to be the efficient cause of itself; for so it would be prior to itself, which is impossible. Now in efficient causes it is not possible to go on to infinity, because in all efficient causes following in order, the first is the cause of the intermediate cause, and the intermediate is the cause of the ultimate cause, whether the intermediate cause be several, or one only. Now to take away the cause is to take away the effect. Therefore, if there be no first cause among efficient causes, there will be no ultimate, nor any intermediate, cause. But if in efficient causes it is possible to go on to infinity, there will be no first efficient cause, neither will there be an ultimate effect, nor any intermediate efficient causes; all of which is plainly false. Therefore it is necessary to admit a first efficient cause, to which everyone gives the name of God.

The third way is taken from possibility and necessity, and runs thus. We find in nature things that are possible to be and not to be, since they are found to be generated, and to be corrupted, and consequently it is possible for them to be and not to be. But it is impossible for these always to exist, for that which can not-be at some time is not. Therefore, if everything can not-be, then at one time there was nothing in existence. Now if this were true, even now there would be nothing in existence, because that which does not exist begins to exist only through something already existing. Therefore, if at one time nothing was in existence, it would have been impossible for anything to have begun to exist; and thus even now nothing would be in existence—which is absurd. Therefore, not all beings are merely possible, but there must exist something the existence of which is necessary. But every necessary thing either has its necessity caused by another, or not. Now it is impossible to go on to infinity in necessary things which have their necessity caused by another, as has been already proved in regard to efficient causes. Therefore we cannot but admit the existence of some being having of itself its own necessity, and not receiving it from another, but rather causing in others their necessity. This all men speak of as God.

The fourth way is taken from the gradation to be found in things. Among beings there are some more and some less good, true, noble, and the like. But *more* and *less* are predicted of different things according as they resemble in their different ways something which is the maximum, as a thing is said to be hotter according as it more nearly resembles that which is hottest; so that there is something which is truest, something best, something noblest, and, consequently, something which is most being, for those things that are greatest in truth are greatest in being, as it is written in *Metaph.* ii.[1] Now the maximum in any genus is the cause of all in that genus, as fire, which is the maximum of heat, is the cause of all hot things, as is said in the same book.[2] Therefore there must also be something which is to all beings the cause of their being, goodness, and every other perfection; and this we call God.

The fifth way is taken from the governance of the world. We see that things which lack knowledge, such as natural bodies, act for an end, and this is evident from their acting always, or nearly always, in the same way, so as to obtain the best result. Hence it is plain that they achieve their end, not fortuitously, but designedly. Now whatever lacks knowledge cannot move toward an end, unless it be directed by some being endowed with knowledge and intelligence; as the arrow is directed by the archer. Therefore some intelligent being exists by whom all natural things are directed to their end; and this being we call God.

Reply Obj. 1. As Augustine says: *Since God is the highest good, He would not allow any evil to exist in His works, unless His omnipotence and goodness were such as to bring good even out of evil.*[3] This is part of the infinite goodness of God, that He should allow evil to exist, and out of it produce good.

Reply Obj. 2. Since nature works for a determinate end under the direction of a higher agent, whatever is done by nature must be traced back to God as to its first cause. So likewise whatever is done voluntarily must be traced back to some higher cause other than human reason and will, since these can change and fail; for all things that are changeable and capable of defect must be traced back to an immovable and self-necessary first principle, as has been shown.

FRANCIS OF ASSISI

Another side of medieval Christian life is revealed in the life and legends of St. Francis (1181–1226), the "Little Poor Man" of Assisi in Italy. Francis was neither scholar nor philosopher but the son of a well-to-do cloth merchant who felt called to live a life of Gospel simplicity and love. This he did, not as a grim ascetic but with a spontaneity and

[1]*Metaph.* Ia, i (993b 30).
[2]*Ibid.* (993b 25).
[3]*Enchir.,* XI (PL 40, 236).

poetic grace that made him a knight or troubadour of his Lady Poverty. His Christian piety was warmly devotional; he and the Franciscan move-ment did much to spread such practices as making models of the manger scene at Christmas, venerating the cross on Good Friday, and honoring the presence of Christ in the consecrated bread of the Eucharist with devotions. But the most mysterious episode in Francis's career was the vision he experienced toward its very end, an overpowering vision that left him with the stigmata, or wounds identical to those of Christ, on his own body. Here is an account of this vision from the earliest life of Francis, composed by Thomas of Celano (c. 1200–55) in 1228–29. It is followed by a discussion of the vision by a modern Roman Catholic writer of great distinction.

From *The Lives of S. Francis of Assisi* by *Brother Thomas of Celano*

A.G. Ferrers Howell

While he dwelt in the hermitage which, from the place in which it is situate, is called Alverna, two years before he gave back his soul to Heaven, he saw in a vision of God a man like a seraph having six wings, standing over him with hands outstretched and feet joined to-gether, fixed to a cross. Two wings were raised above his head, two were spread out for flight, and two veiled the whole body. Now, when the blessed servant of the Most High saw this, he was filled with exceeding great wonder, but he could not understand what this vision might mean. Yet he rejoiced greatly and was filled with vehement delight at the be-nign and gracious look wherewith he saw that he was regarded by the seraph, whose beauty far exceeded all estimation; but the crucifixion, and the bitterness of the seraph's suffering smote him altogether with fear. Thus he arose, so to speak, sorrowful and glad; and joy and grief alternated in him. He anxiously pondered what this vision might portend, and his spirit laboured sore to come at the understanding of it. And while he continued without any clear perception of its meaning, and the strangeness of the vision was perplexing his heart, marks of nails began to appear in his hands and feet, such as he had seen a little while before in the Man crucified who had stood over him.

His hands and feet seemed pierced in the midst by nails, the heads of the nails appearing in the inner part of the hands and in the upper

A.G. Ferrers Howell, trans., *The Lives of S. Francis of Assisi by Brother Thomas of Celano* (London: Methuen & Co., 1908), pp. 92–94. Reprinted by permission of the publishers.

part of the feet, and their points over against them. Now those marks were round in the inner side of the hands and elongated on the outer side, and certain small pieces of flesh were seen like the ends of nails bent and driven back, projecting from the rest of the flesh. So also the marks of nails were imprinted in his feet, and raised above the rest of the flesh. Moreover his right side, as it had been pierced by a lance, was overlaid with a scar, and often shed forth blood, so that his tunic and drawers were many times sprinkled with the sacred blood. Alas! how few were found worthy to see the sacred wound in his side while the crucified servant of the crucified Lord was yet alive! But happy was Elias who was found worthy to see it somehow while the Saint was living; and not less happy Rufino who touched it with his own hands. For once, when brother Rufino had put his hand into the most holy man's bosom that he might scratch him, his hand (as it often chances) slipped down to Francis' right side, and he happened to touch that precious scar, at which touch the Saint of God was not a little distressed, and, pushing the hand away, he cried to the Lord that He might forgive him (Rufino). For he concealed the stigmata most diligently from strangers, and from those about him he hid them so carefully that even the brethren at his side and his most devoted followers were for a long time unaware of them. And though the servant and friend of the Most High saw himself adorned with such and so many of these pearls (as with most precious jewels), and distinguished in wondrous fashion beyond the glory and honour of all men, he was not vain in his heart, nor did he seek to gratify [the curiosity] of any concerning this matter from lust of vainglory, but, that man's favour might not rob him of the grace bestowed on him he exerted himself in every way he could to hide it. For his custom was to reveal his chiefest secret to few or none; fearing that if he revealed it to any, these persons treating his confidence as a mark of special affection would disclose it to others (as favourites are wont to do,) and that thereby he would suffer some loss in the grace that had been given him. Accordingly he ever had in his heart and often on his lips that saying of the Prophet, "I have hidden Thy words in my heart that I should not sin against Thee".

From St. Francis of Assisi

G. K. Chesterton

There were some at least who listened to the saint "as if he had been an angel of God"; among them a gentleman named Orlando of

G.K. Chesterton, St. Francis of Assisi (London: Hodder & Stoughton, 1923), pp. 155–57. Reprinted by permission of Miss D.E. Collins.

Chiusi, who had great lands in Tuscany, and who proceeded to do St. Francis a singular and somewhat picturesque act of courtesy. He gave him a mountain; a thing somewhat unique among the gifts of the world. Presumably the Franciscan rule which forbade a man to accept money had made no detailed provision about accepting mountains. Nor indeed did St. Francis accept it save as he accepted everything, as a temporary convenience rather than a personal possession; but he turned it into a sort of refuge for the eremitical rather than the monastic life; he retired there when he wished for a life of prayer and fasting which he did not ask even his closest friends to follow. This was Alverno of the Apennines, and upon its peak there rests for ever a dark cloud that has a rim or halo of glory.

What it was exactly that happened there may never be known. The matter has been, I believe, a subject of dispute among the most devout students of the saintly life as well as between such students and others of the more secular sort. It may be that St. Francis never spoke to a soul on the subject; it would be highly characteristic, and it is certain in any case that he said very little; I think he is only alleged to have spoken of it to one man. Subject however to such truly sacred doubts, I will confess that to me personally this one solitary and indirect report that has come down to us reads very like the report of something real; of some of those things that are more real than what we call daily realities. Even something as it were double and bewildering about the image seems to carry the impression of an experience shaking the senses; as does the passage in Revelations about the supernatural creatures full of eyes. It would seem that St. Francis beheld the heavens above him occupied by a vast winged being like a seraph spread out like a cross. There seems some mystery about whether the winged figure was itself crucified or in the posture of crucifixion, or whether it merely enclosed in its frame of wings some colossal crucifix. But it seems clear that there was some question of the former impression; for St. Bonaventura distinctly says that St. Francis doubted how a seraph could be crucified, since those awful and ancient principalities were without the infirmity of the Passion. St. Bonaventura suggests that the seeming contradiction may have meant that St. Francis was to be crucified as a spirit since he could not be crucified as a man; but whatever the meaning of the vision, the general idea of it is very vivid and overwhelming. St. Francis saw above him, filling the whole heavens, some vast immemorial unthinkable power, ancient like the Ancient of Days, whose calm men had conceived under the forms of winged bulls or monstrous cherubim, and all that winged wonder was in pain like a wounded bird. This seraphic suffering, it is said, pierced his soul with a sword of grief and pity; it may be inferred that some sort of mounting agony accompanied the ecstasy. Finally after some fashion the apocalypse faded from the sky and the agony within subsided; and silence and the natural air filled the morning twilight and settled slowly in the purple chasms and cleft abysses of the Apennines.

The head of the solitary sank, amid all that relaxation and quiet in which time can drift by with the sense of something ended and complete; and as he stared downwards, he saw the marks of nails in his own hands.

JULIAN OF NORWICH

Another style of medieval mysticism is represented by the English-woman Julian of Norwich (c. 1342–1416). Like much of late medieval mysticism, her writing is somewhat influenced by Christian Neoplatonism. It is also influenced by rich personal experience, which occurred as Julian was recovering from serious illness. She spent the latter part of her life as an anchoress—a contemplative dwelling in a cell within a church—but she was scarcely isolated from human life in spirit. In her inimitable writings, profound metaphysical learning and mature faith are expressed in a clear, charming, and deceptively simple style. The first passage below describes all that is made as no larger than a tiny hazelnut beside God; the second culminates in the famous words, "But all shall be well, and all shall be well, and all manner of thing shall be well." The lines from Augustine cited in the modern editorial note at the end are from the same work, the Enchiridion, *to which Thomas Aquinas makes reference in the selection from his works.*

From *Revelations of Divine Love Recorded by Julian Anchoress of Norwich A.D. 1373*

Grace Warrack

"God, of Thy Goodness, give me Thyself;—only in Thee I have all."

In this same time our Lord shewed me a spiritual[1] sight of His homely loving.

I saw that He is to us everything that is good and comfortable for us: He is our clothing that for love wrappeth us, claspeth us, and all

Grace Warrack, ed., *Revelations of Divine Love Recorded by Julian Anchoress of Norwich A.D. 1373* (London: Methuen & Co., Ltd., 1901, 1909), pp. 10–11, 55–57.

[1]MS. "ghostly," and so, generally, throughout the MS.

encloseth[2] us for tender love, that He may never leave us; being to us all-thing that is good, as to mine understanding.

Also in this He shewed me a little thing, the quantity of an hazelnut, in the palm of my hand; and it was as round as a ball. I looked thereupon with eye of my understanding, and thought: *What may this be?* And it was answered generally thus: *It is all that is made.* I marvelled how it might last, for methought it might suddenly have fallen to naught for little[ness]. And I was answered in my understanding: *It lasteth, and ever shall [last] for that God loveth it.* And so All-thing hath the Being by the love of God.

In this Little Thing I saw three properties. The first is that God made it, the second is that God loveth it, the third, that God keepeth it. But what is to me verily the Maker, the Keeper, and the Lover,—I cannot tell; for till I am Substantially oned[3] to Him, I may never have full rest nor very bliss: that is to say, till I be so fastened to Him, that there is right nought that is made betwixt my God and me.

THE FIRST REVELATION

It needeth us to have knowing of the littleness of creatures and to hold as nought[4] all-thing that is made, for to love and have God that is unmade. For this is the cause why we be not all in ease of heart and soul: that we seek here rest in those things that are so little, wherein is no rest, and know not our God that is All-mighty, All-wise, All-good. For He is the Very Rest. God willeth to be known, and it pleaseth Him that we rest in Him; for all that is beneath Him sufficeth not us. And this is the cause why that no soul is rested till it is made nought as to all[5] things that are made. When it is willingly made nought, for love, to have Him that is all, then is it able to receive spiritual rest.

Also our Lord God shewed that it is full great pleasance to Him that a helpless soul come to Him simply and plainly and homely. For this is the natural yearnings of the soul, by the touching of the Holy Ghost (as by the understanding that I have in this Shewing): *God, of Thy Goodness, give me Thyself: for Thou art enough to me, and I may nothing ask that is less that may be full worship to Thee; and if I ask anything that is less, ever me wanteth,—but only in Thee I have all.*

And these words are full lovely to the soul, and full near touch they the will of God and His Goodness. For His Goodness comprehendeth all His creatures and all His blessed works, and overpasseth[6] without end. For He is the endlessness, and He hath made us only to

---

2"Becloseth," and so generally.
3*i.e.* in essence united.
4"to nowtyn."
5"nowtid of." de Cressy: "*naughted* (emptied)."
6surpasseth.

Himself, and restored us by His blessed Passion, and keepeth us in His blessed love; and all this of His Goodness. . . .

. . . "Often I wondered why by the great foreseeing wisdom of God the beginning of sin was not hindered: for then, methought, all should have been well." "Sin is behovable—[playeth a needful part]—; but all shall be well"

After this the Lord brought to my mind the longing that I had to Him afore. And I saw that nothing letted me but sin. And so I looked, generally, upon us all, and methought: *If sin had not been, we should all have been clean and like to our Lord, as He made us.*

And thus, in my folly, afore this time often I wondered why by the great foreseeing wisdom of God the beginning of sin was not letted: for then, methought, all should have been well. This stirring [of mind] was much to be forsaken, but nevertheless mourning and sorrow I made therefor, without reason and discretion.

But Jesus, who in this Vision informed me of all that is needful to me, answered by this word and said: *It behoved that there should be sin;*[7] *but all shall be well, and all shall be well, and all manner of thing shall be well.*

In this naked word *sin*, our Lord brought to my mind, generally, *all that is not good,* and the shameful despite and the utter noughting[8] that He bare for us in this life, and His dying; and all the pains and passions of all His creatures, ghostly and bodily; (for we be all partly noughted, and we shall be noughted following our Master, Jesus, till we be full purged, that is to say, till we be fully noughted of our deadly flesh and of all our inward affections which are not very good;) and the beholding of this, with all pains that ever were or ever shall be,—and with all these I understand the Passion of Christ for most pain, and overpassing. All this was shewed in a touch and quickly passed over into comfort: for our good Lord would not that the soul were affeared of this terrible sight.

But I saw not *sin:* for I believe it hath no manner of substance nor part of being, nor could it be known but by the pain it is cause of.

And thus[9] pain, *it* is something, as to my sight, for a time; for it purgeth, and maketh us to know ourselves and to ask mercy. For the Passion of our Lord is comfort to us against all this, and so is His blessed will. And for the tender love that our good Lord hath to all that shall be saved, He comforteth readily and sweetly, signifying thus: *It is sooth*[10] *that sin is cause of all this pain; but all shall be well, and all shall be well, and all manner [of] thing shall be well.*

These words were said full tenderly, showing no manner of blame

---

[7]"Synne is behovabil, but al shal be wel & al shal be wel & al manner of thyng shal be wele."

[8]Being made as nothing, set at nought.

[9]S. de Cressy has "this" instead of *thus.*

[10]*i.e.* truth, an actual reality.

to me nor to any that shall be saved. Then were it a great unkindness[11] to blame or wonder on God for my sin, since He blameth not me for sin.

And in these words I saw a marvellous high mystery hid in God, which mystery He shall openly make known to us in Heaven: in which knowing we shall verily see the cause why He suffered sin to come. In which sight we shall endlessly joy in our Lord God.[12]

MARTIN LUTHER

The greatest figure of the Protestant Reformation of the early six-teenth century was the German Martin Luther (1483–1546). Many factors lie in the background of the Reformation: tension between northern and southern Europe, tension between the old feudal society and the new merchant class, the disruption and partial discrediting of the old society wrought by the plague and papal schisms, the long-standing trend in Germany especially toward mystical or inward religion. But at the heart of the Reformation as a religious movement lay the spiritual experience of Martin Luther; the Reformation would not have taken the shape it did without his towering personality.

Luther entered a monastery as a young man, but rather than finding peace he was tormented by crushing anxiety as to whether he had or could do enough to satisfy God's demands. That burden was lifted when, in studying the scriptures, he came to the words, "The just man shall live by faith," and these words made him feel, he said, as though he had been born again and the gates of paradise were opened to him. What he

---

[11]As it were, an unreasonable contravention of natural, filial trust.

[12]See also chap. lxi. From the *Enchiridion* of Saint Augustine:—"All things that exist, therefore, seeing that the Creator of them all is supremely good, are themselves good. But because they are not like their Creator, supremely and unchangeably good, their good may be diminished and increased. But for good to be diminished is an evil, although, however much it may be diminished, it is necessary, if the being is to continue, that some good should remain to constitute the being. For however small or of whatever kind the being may be, the good which makes it a being cannot be destroyed without destroying the being itself. . . So long as a being is in process of corruption, there is in it some good of which it is being deprived; and if a part of the being should remain which cannot be corrupted, this will certainly be an incorruptible being, and accordingly the process of corruption will result in the manifestation of this great good. But if it do not cease to be corrupted, neither can it cease to possess good of which corruption may deprive it. But if it should be thoroughly and completely consumed by corruption, there will then be no good left, because there will be no being. Wherefore corruption can consume the good only by consuming the being. Every being, therefore, is a good; a great good, if it cannot be corrupted; a little good, if it can, but in any case, only the foolish or ignorant will deny that it is a good. And if it be wholly consumed by corruption, then the corruption itself must cease to exist, as there is no being left in which it can dwell."

realized is that it is not by what we do—for we could never do enough—that we are made right with God, but by the faith which God himself puts into our hearts, thanks to the saving work of Jesus Christ. This realization was the religious center of Luther's theology and of the Reformation. Luther expounds this theology with customary vigor and clarity in the following passage from his commentary on Galatians; this selection is on the part of Gal. 2:16 that says " . . . a man is not justified [reckoned righteous] by works of the law but through faith in Jesus Christ." Luther alludes here to a favorite theme of his, that the Old Testament Law actually cannot be performed perfectly by human beings as they are, and so serves to show up our incapacity and sin apart from grace and faith. He also attacks medieval doctrines about congruity and condignity, which, as he understood them, suggested that there were prior acts humans could perform to prompt or earn God's grace.

From *Luther's Works, Vol. 26:*
Lectures on Galatians, 1535
Jaroslav Pelikan

Now the true meaning of Christianity is this: that a man first acknowledge, through the Law, that he is a sinner, for whom it is impossible to perform any good work. For the Law says: "You are an evil tree. Therefore everything you think, speak, or do is opposed to God. Hence you cannot deserve grace by your works. But if you try to do so, you make the bad even worse; for since you are an evil tree, you cannot produce anything except evil fruits, that is, sins. 'For whatever does not proceed from faith is sin' (Rom. 14:23)." Trying to merit grace by preceding works, therefore, is trying to placate God with sins, which is nothing but heaping sins upon sins, making fun of God, and provoking His wrath. When a man is taught this way by the Law, he is frightened and humbled. Then he really sees the greatness of his sin and finds in himself not one spark of the love of God; thus he justifies God in His Word and confesses that he deserves death and eternal damnation. Thus the first step in Christianity is the preaching of repentance and the knowledge of oneself.

The second step is this: If you want to be saved, your salvation

Jaroslav Pelikan, ed., *Luther's Works, Vol. 26: Lectures on Galatians, 1535* (Saint Louis: Concordia Publishing House, 1963), pp. 126–27, 133–34. Reprinted by permission of the publisher.

does not come by works; but God has sent His only Son into the world that we might live through Him. He was crucified and died for you and bore your sins in His own body (1 Peter 2:24). Here there is no "congruity" or work performed before grace, but only wrath, sin, terror, and death. Therefore the Law only shows sin, terrifies, and humbles; thus it prepares us for justification and drives us to Christ. For by His Word God has revealed to us that He wants to be a merciful Father to us. Without our merit—since, after all, we cannot merit anything—He wants to give us forgiveness of sins, righteousness, and eternal life for the sake of Christ. For God is He who dispenses His gifts freely to all, and this is the praise of His deity. But He cannot defend this deity of His against the self-righteous people who are unwilling to accept grace and eternal life from Him freely but want to earn it by their own works. They simply want to rob Him of the glory of His deity. In order to retain it, He is compelled to send forth His Law, to terrify and crush those very hard rocks as though it were thunder and lightning.

This, in summary, is our theology about Christian righteousness, in opposition to the abominations and monstrosities of the sophists about "merit of congruity and of condignity" or about works before grace and after grace. Smug people, who have never struggled with any temptations or true terrors of sin and death, were the ones who made up these empty dreams out of their own heads; therefore they do not understand what they are saying or what they are talking about, for they cannot supply any examples of such works done either before grace or after grace. Therefore these are useless fables, with which the papists delude both themselves and others. . . .

. . . But where Christ and faith are not present, here there is no forgiveness of sins or hiding of sins. On the contrary, here there is the sheer imputation and condemnation of sins. Thus God wants to glorify His Son, and He Himself wants to be glorified in us through Him.

When we have taught faith in Christ this way, then we also teach about good works. Because you have taken hold of Christ by faith, through whom you are righteous, you should now go and love God and your neighbor. Call upon God, give thanks to Him, preach Him, praise Him, confess Him. Do good to your neighbor, and serve him; do your duty. These are truly good works, which flow from this faith and joy conceived in the heart because we have the forgiveness of sins freely through Christ.

Then whatever there is of cross or suffering to be borne later on is easily sustained. For the yoke that Christ lays upon us is sweet, and His burden is light (Matt. 11:30). When sin has been forgiven and the conscience has been liberated from the burden and the sting of sin, then a Christian can bear everything easily. Because everything within is sweet and pleasant, he willingly does and suffers everything. But when a man goes along in his own righteousness, then whatever he does and suffers is painful and tedious for him, because he is doing it unwillingly.

Therefore we define a Christian as follows: A Christian is not someone who has no sin or feels no sin; he is someone to whom, because of his faith in Christ, God does not impute his sin. This doctrine brings firm consolation to troubled consciences amid genuine terrors. It is not in vain, therefore, that so often and so diligently we inculcate the doctrine of the forgiveness of sins and of the imputation of righteousness for the sake of Christ, as well as the doctrine that a Christian does not have anything to do with the Law and sin, especially in a time of temptation. For to the extent that he is a Christian, he is above the Law and sin, because in his heart he has Christ, the Lord of the Law, as a ring has a gem. Therefore when the Law accuses and sin troubles, he looks to Christ; and when he has taken hold of Him by faith, he has present with him the Victor over the Law, sin, death, and the devil—the Victor whose rule over all these prevents them from harming him.

JOHN CALVIN

John Calvin (1509–64) was the most important Reformation personality after Luther. He was raised in France, but is most associated with Geneva, where he lived much of his life and which he dominated spiritually and politically. Calvin's theology shaped the Protestant tradition generally called "Reformed." The social consequences of his thought have deeply influenced the cultures of several countries, including Great Britain and the United States. Calvin was more concerned than Luther to reform church government and simplify services, particularly the sacraments. The emphasis on Bible study and self-government in Calvinist churches had a marked impact on the development of modern education and democracy.

The principal emphasis in Calvin's theology is on the absolute sovereignty of God, who saves whom he will by his grace, producing invincible faith in them, a theme from Augustine implicit in Luther's insistence that it is by faith given by God (that is, grace) and not by our own works that we are made right with God. But Calvin and the Calvinist tradition explored this theme more fully and put it in stronger terms, talking of the predestination of some to heaven and some to hell, and of the irresistible grace that made sure the salvation of the elect. At the same time, Calvinism also emphasized the "total depravity" of fallen humankind. It pointed out that apart from God's grace all human works are worth nothing and unable to save anyone. In the following passage from Calvin's major work, we see the spiritual power of this tradition at its brightest, in its emphasis on the omnipotent power of God behind all nature and all human affairs.

From *Calvin: Institutes of the Christian Religion*
John T. McNeill

There is no such thing as fortune or chance.

That this difference may better appear, we must know that God's providence, as it is taught in Scripture, is opposed to fortune and fortuitous happenings.[1] Now it has been commonly accepted in all ages, and almost all mortals hold the same opinion today, that all things come about through chance. What we ought to believe concerning providence is by this depraved opinion most certainly not only beclouded, but almost buried. Suppose a man falls among thieves, or wild beasts; is shipwrecked at sea by a sudden gale; is killed by a falling house or tree. Suppose another man wandering through the desert finds help in his straits; having been tossed by the waves, reaches harbor; miraculously escapes death by a finger's breadth. Carnal reason ascribes all such happenings, whether prosperous or adverse, to fortune. But anyone who has been taught by Christ's lips that all the hairs of his head are numbered [Matt. 10:30] will look farther afield for a cause, and will consider that all events are governed by God's secret plan. And concerning inanimate objects we ought to hold that, although each one has by nature been endowed with its own property, yet it does not exercise its own power except in so far as it is directed by God's ever-present hand. These are, thus, nothing but instruments to which God continually imparts as much effectiveness as he wills, and according to his own purpose bends and turns them to either one action or another.

No creature has a force more wondrous or glorious than that of the sun. For besides lighting the whole earth with its brightness, how great a thing is it that by its heat it nourishes and quickens all living things! That with its rays it breathes fruitfulness into the earth! That it warms the seeds in the bosom of the earth, draws them forth with budding greenness, increases and strengthens them, nourishes them anew, until they rise up into stalks! That it feeds the plant with continual warmth, until it grows into flower, and from flower into fruit! That then, also, with baking heat it brings the fruit to maturity! That in like manner trees

John T. McNeill, ed., *Calvin: Institutes of the Christian Religion*, Volume XX, The Library of Christian Classics, trans., Ford Lewis Battles. (Philadelphia: The Westminster Press, 1960). Used by permission of the publisher. Copyright MCMLX by W.L. Jenkins.

---

[1]*"Fortunae et casibus fortuitis."* Cf. I. v. 11; I. xvi. 8, and accompanying notes.

and vines warmed by the sun first put forth buds and leaves, then put forth a flower, and from the flower produce fruit! Yet the Lord, to claim the whole credit for all these things, willed that, before he created the sun, light should come to be and earth be filled with all manner of herbs and fruits [Gen. 1.3, 11, 14]. Therefore a godly man will not make the sun either the principal or the necessary cause of these things which existed before the creation of the sun, but merely the instrument that God uses because he so wills; for with no more difficulty he might abandon it, and act through himself. Then when we read that at Joshua's prayers the sun stood still in one degree for two days [Josh. 10:13], and that its shadow went back ten degrees for the sake of King Hezekiah [II Kings 20:11 or Isa. 38:8], God has witnessed by those few miracles that the sun does not daily rise and set by a blind instinct of nature but that he himself, to renew our remembrance of his fatherly favor toward us, governs its course. Nothing is more natural than for spring to follow winter; summer, spring; and fall, summer—each in turn. Yet in this series one sees such great and uneven diversity that it readily appears each year, month, and day is governed by a new, a special, providence of God.

God's providence governs all.

And truly God claims, and would have us grant him, omnipotence—not the empty, idle, and almost unconscious sort that the Sophists[2] imagine, but a watchful, effective, active sort, engaged in ceaseless activity. Not, indeed, an omnipotence that is only a general principle of confused motion, as if he were to command a river to flow through its once-appointed channels, but one that is directed toward individual and particular motions. For he is deemed omnipotent, not because he can indeed act, yet sometimes ceases and sits in idleness, or continues by a general impulse that order of nature which he previously appointed; but because, governing heaven and earth by his providence, he so regulates all things that nothing takes place without his deliberation. For when, in The Psalms, it is said that "he does whatever he wills" [Ps. 115:3; cf. Ps. 113 (b): 3, Vg.] a certain and deliberate will is meant. For it would be senseless to interpret the words of the prophet after the manner of the philosophers, that God is the first agent because he is the beginning and cause of all motion;[3] for in times of adversity believers comfort themselves with the solace that they suffer nothing except by God's ordinance and command, for they are under his hand.

But if God's governance is so extended to all his works, it is a childish cavil to enclose it within the stream of nature. Indeed, those as much defraud God of his glory as themselves of a most profitable doctrine who confine God's providence to such narrow limits as though he allowed all things by a free course to be borne along according to a universal law of

---

[2]*"Sophistae."* The word is used by Calvin, in common with the other Reformers and with many Humanists, to designate the Scholastic writers when these are treated adversely.

[3]Cf. I. xiii. 18, note 39, and Aquinas, *Summa Theol.* I. xix. 6: "An effect cannot possibly escape the order of the universal cause."

nature.[4] For nothing would be more miserable than man if he were exposed to every movement of the sky, air, earth, and waters. Besides, in this way God's particular goodness toward each one would be too unworthily reduced. David exclaims that infants still nursing at their mothers' breasts are eloquent enough to celebrate God's glory [Ps. 8:2], for immediately on coming forth from the womb, they find food prepared for them by his heavenly care. Indeed, this is in general true, provided what experience plainly demonstrates does not escape our eyes and senses, that some mothers have full and abundant breasts, but others' are almost dry, as God wills to feed one more liberally, but another more meagerly.

Those who ascribe just praise to God's omnipotence doubly benefit thereby. First, power ample enough to do good there is in him in whose possession are heaven and earth, and to whose beck all creatures are so attentive as to put themselves in obedience to him. Secondly, they may safely rest in the protection of him to whose will are subject all the harmful things which, whatever their source, we may fear; whose authority curbs Satan with all his furies and his whole equipage; and upon whose nod depends whatever opposes our welfare. And we cannot otherwise correct or allay these uncontrolled and superstitious fears, which we repeatedly conceive at the onset of dangers. We are superstitiously timid, I say, if whenever creatures threaten us or forcibly terrorize us we become as fearful as if they had some intrinsic power to harm us, or might wound us inadvertently and accidentally, or there were not enough help in God against their harmful acts.

For example, the prophet forbids God's children "to fear the stars and signs of heaven, as disbelievers commonly do" [Jer. 10:2 p.]. Surely he does not condemn every sort of fear. But when unbelievers transfer the government of the universe from God to the stars, they fancy that their bliss or their misery depends upon the decrees and indications of the stars, not upon God's will; so it comes about that their fear is transferred from him, toward whom alone they ought to direct it, to stars and comets. Let him, therefore, who would beware of this infidelity ever remember that there is no erratic power, or action, or motion in creatures, but that they are governed by God's secret plan in such a way that nothing happens except what is knowingly and willingly decreed by him.

THE RADICAL REFORMATION
AND GEORGE FOX

The Lutheran and Calvinist churches quickly became established and conservative institutions, for the most part state churches. The same

---

[4]Andreas Hyperius discusses this opinion adversely in his posthumously published *Methodus Theologiae* (Basel, 1568), pp. 232 ff., 252. Hyperius (1511–1564) was a Reformed scholar, and professor in Marburg.

can be said of the Church of England, although it retained more ancient and medieval Catholic features than the continental Reformation churches, and, although influenced by both Lutheranism and Calvinism, was not officially aligned with either.

But the yeasty life of Protestantism could not be contained along such staid pathways. Outside and inside the official Protestant churches tumbled a host of other movements—perfectionists, anabaptists, pietists, unitarians. These movements flourished on the continent but perhaps no where more than in the England of the sixteenth through eighteenth centuries. Out of that time and place came several denominations now very widespread—Congregationalists, Baptists, Quakers, Methodists. This "free" wing of the Reformation is diverse, but has certain points in common: emphasis on inwardness, on individual conversion, on felt devotion to Christ, on individual interpretation of scripture, on great freedom in church life and stress on the local congregation as its basic unit, and often belief in the lively possibility of perfection in one's Christian life here and now. Sacraments and other ordinances are often closely tied to felt inwardness; for example, the Baptists felt that baptism should come only after conversion as a sign of it, and the Quakers rejected all "outward" sacraments altogether in favor of inward, spiritual baptism and communion.

No better example of this strand of Protestantism can be found than in the figure of George Fox (1624–91), founder of the Society of Friends (Quakers). His journals provide a vivid picture of his inner life. He rejected "steeple houses," "hireling priests," and "professors" (that is, those who profess Christian life but fall short of perfection in it) for divine grace directly experienced inwardly, and he preached as the Lord gave him utterance, calling for experience rather than creed or doctrine or impressive churches. This passage from an abridged edition of Fox's Journal, describing events in 1647–48, early in his career, gives an example of his way of life and his conversion experiences; one clearly perceives the volcanic inward realities, the impatience with outward "professing" Christianity, the direct dependence on scripture and the inner light, which so deeply compelled Fox.

From *Passages from the Life and Writings of George Fox, Taken from his Journal*

Now after I had received that opening from the Lord, that to be bred at Oxford or Cambridge was not sufficient to fit a man to be a minister of Christ, I regarded the priests less and looked more after the dis-

From *Passages from the Life and Writings of George Fox, Taken from his Journal.* (Philadelphia: Friends' Book-Store, 1881), pp. 18–27.

senting people. And among them I saw there was some tenderness; and many of them came afterwards to be convinced, for they had some openings. But as I had forsaken all the priests, so I left the separate preachers also, and those called the most experienced people; for I saw there was none among them all that could speak to my condition. And when all my hopes in them and in all men was gone, so that I had nothing outwardly to help me, nor could tell what to do, then, O! then I heard a voice which said, There is one, even Christ Jesus, that can speak to thy condition. And when I heard it, my heart did leap for joy. Then the Lord did let me see why there was none upon the earth that could speak to my condition, namely, that I might give Him all the glory. For all are concluded under sin and shut up in unbelief, as I had been, that Jesus Christ might have the pre-eminence, who enlightens and gives grace and faith and power. Thus, when God doth work, who shall let it? And this I knew experimentally. My desires after the Lord grew stronger, and zeal in the pure knowledge of God and of Christ alone, without the help of any man, book, or writing. For though I read the Scriptures that spake of Christ and of God, yet I knew Him not but by revelation, as He who hath the key did open, and as the Father of Life drew me to his Son by his Spirit. And then the Lord did gently lead me along and did let me see his love, which was endless and eternal, and surpasses all the knowledge that men have in the natural state, or can get by history or books. And that love did let me see myself as I was without Him. And I was afraid of all company for I saw them perfectly where they were, through the love of God which let me see myself. And I had not fellowship with any people, priests, nor professors, nor any sort of separated people, but with Christ, who hath the key, and opened the door of light and life unto me. And I was afraid of all carnal talk and talkers; for I could see nothing but corruptions, and the life lay under the burden of corruptions. And when I myself was in the deep, under all shut up, I could not believe that I should ever overcome; my troubles, my sorrows, and my temptations were so great, that I thought many times I should have despaired, I was so tempted. But when Christ opened to me how He was tempted by the same devil, and had overcome him and bruised his head, and that through Him and his power, light, grace, and Spirit I should overcome also, I had confidence in Him. So He it was that opened to me when I was shut up, and had not hope nor faith. Christ it was who had enlightened me, that gave me his light to believe in, and gave me hope, which is himself, revealed himself in me, and gave me his Spirit and gave me his grace, which I found sufficient in the deeps and in weakness. Thus in the deepest miseries and in the greatest sorrows and temptations that many times beset me, the Lord in his mercy did keep me. And I found that there were two thirsts in me—the one after the creatures, to have gotten help and strength there, and the other after the Lord the Creator and his Son Jesus Christ. And I saw all the world could do me no good. If I had had a king's diet, palace, and attendance, all would have been as nothing; for nothing gave me comfort but the Lord by his power. And I saw professors, priests, and people were whole and at ease in that condition, which was my misery;

and they loved that which I would have been rid of. But the Lord did stay my desires upon himself, from whom my help came, and my care wast cast upon Him alone. Therefore all wait patiently upon the Lord whatsoever condition you be in; wait in the grace and truth that comes by Jesus; for if ye so do, there is a promise to you, and the Lord God will fulfil it in you. And blessed are all they indeed that do indeed hunger and thirst after righteousness; they shall be satisfied with it. I have found it so, praised be the Lord, who filleth with it and satisfieth the desires of the hungry soul. O let the house of the spiritual Israel say, His mercy endureth forever! It is the great love of God to make a wilderness of that which is pleasant to the outward eye and fleshly mind, and to make a fruitful field of a barren wilderness; this is the great work of God.

At another time I saw the great love of God, and I was filled with admiration at the infiniteness of it. And then I saw what was cast out from God, and what entered into God's kingdom; and how by Jesus, the opener of the door by his heavenly key, the entrance was given. And I saw death, how it had passed upon all men, and oppressed the seed of God in man and in me; and how I in the seed came forth, and what the promise was to. Yet it was so with me, that there seemed to be two pleadings in me, and questionings arose in my mind about gifts and prophecies; and I was tempted again to despair, as if I had sinned against the Holy Ghost. And I was in great perplexity and trouble for many days, yet I gave up myself to the Lord still. And one day, when I had been walking solitarily abroad and was come home, I was taken up in the love of God, so that I could not but admire the greatness of his love. And while I was in that condition, it was opened unto me by the eternal light and power, and I therein clearly saw, That all was done and to be done in and by Christ; and how He conquers and destroys this tempter, the devil, and all his works, and is atop of him; and that all these troubles were good for me, and temptations for the trial of my faith which Christ had given me. And the Lord opened me, that I saw through all these troubles and temptations. My living faith was raised, that I saw all was done by Christ, the Life, and my belief was in Him. And when at any time my condition was vailed, my secret belief was stayed firm, and hope underneath held me as an anchor in the bottom of the sea, and anchored my immortal soul to its bishop, causing it to swim above the sea, the world, where all the raging waves, foul weather, tempests, and temptations are. But oh, then did I see my troubles, trials, and temptations more than ever I had done. As the Light appeared, all appeared that is out of the Light—darkness, death, temptations, the unrighteous, the ungodly,—all was manifest and seen in the Light. Then after this there did a pure fire appear in me; then I saw how He sate as a refiner's fire and as the fuller's soap. And then the spiritual discerning came into me, by which I did discern my own thoughts, groans, and sighs; and what it was that did vail me, and what it was that did open me. And that which could not abide in the patience nor endure the fire, in the Light I found to be the groans of the flesh, that could not give up to the will of God, which had vailed me. And I discerned the groans of the Spirit, which did open me, and made intercession to God.

In which Spirit is the true waiting upon God for the redemption of the body and of the whole creation. The divine light of Christ manifesteth all things, and the spiritual fire trieth all things and severeth all things. John, who was the greatest prophet that was born of a woman, did bear witness to the Light with which Christ the great heavenly prophet hath enlightened every man that cometh into the world, withal, that they might believe in it and become the children of light, and so have the light of life, and not come into condemnation. For the true belief stands in the Light that condemns all evil and the Devil, who is the prince of darkness, who would draw out of the Light into condemnation. And they that walk in this Light come to the mountain of the house of God, established above all mountains, and to God's teaching, who will teach them his ways. These things were opened to me in the Light.

Ye who know the love of God and the law of his Spirit and the freedom that is in Jesus Christ, stand fast in Him in that divine faith which He is the author of in you; and be not entangled with the yoke of bondage. For the ministry of Christ Jesus and his teaching bringeth into liberty and freedom; but the ministry that is of man and by man and which stands in the will of man, bringeth into bondage and under the shadow of death and darkness. And therefore none can be a minister of Christ Jesus but in the eternal Spirit, which was before the Scriptures were given forth; for if they have not his Spirit, they are none of his. Though they may have his light to condemn them, that hate it, yet they can never bring any into unity and fellowship in the Spirit except they be in it. For the seed of God is a burthensome stone to the selfish, fleshly, earthly will, which reigns in its own knowledge and understanding that must perish, and in its wisdom that is devilish. And the Spirit of God is grieved and vexed and quenched with that which brings into the fleshly bondage; and that which wars against the Spirit of God must be mortified by it; for the flesh lusteth against the Spirit and the Spirit against the flesh, and these are contrary the one to the other. The flesh would have its liberty and the Spirit would have its liberty; but the Spirit is to have its liberty and not the flesh. If therefore ye quench the Spirit and join to the flesh and be servants of it, then ye are judged and tormented by the Spirit; but if ye join the Spirit and serve God in it, ye have liberty, and victory over the flesh and its works. Therefore keep in the daily cross, the power of God, by which ye may witness all that to be crucified which is contrary to the will of God, and which shall not come into his kingdom. These things are here mentioned and opened for information, exhortation, and comfort to others, as the Lord opened them unto me in that day. And in that day I wondered that the children of Israel should murmur for water and victuals; for I could have fasted long without murmuring or minding victuals. But I was judged sometimes that I was not contented to be sometimes without the water and bread of life, that I might learn to know how to want and how to abound.

And I heard of a woman in Lancashire that had fasted two and twenty days; and I travelled to see her, but when I came to her I saw that she was under a temptation. And when I had spoken to her what I had from the Lord, I left her, her father being one high in profession. And passing on, I went among the professors at Duckenfield and Manchester, where I stayed awhile and declared truth among them; and there were some convinced, who received the Lord's teaching, by which they were confirmed and stood in the truth. But the professors were in a rage, all pleading for sin and imperfection; and could not endure to hear talk of perfection and of an holy and sinless life.

About this time there was a great meeting of the Baptists at Broughton in Leicestershire with some that had separated from them; and people of other notions went thither, and I went thither also. Not many of the Baptists came, but abundance of other people were there. And the Lord opened my mouth, and his everlasting truth was declared amongst them; and the power of the Lord was over them all. And I went back into Nottinghamshire, and there the Lord showed me that the natures of those things which were hurtful without, were within, in the hearts and minds of wicked men. The natures of dogs, swine, vipers, of Sodom and Egypt, Pharaoh, Cain, Ishmael, Esau, etc. The natures of these I saw within, though people had been looking without. And I cried to the Lord, saying, Why should I be thus, seeing I was never addicted to commit those evils? And the Lord answered That it was needful I should have a sense of all conditions; how else should I speak to all conditions? And in this I saw the infinite love of God. I saw also that there was an ocean of darkness and death; but an infinite ocean of light and love which flowed over the ocean of darkness. And in that also I saw the infinite love of God; and I had great openings. And as I was walking by the steeple-house side in the town of Mansfield, the Lord said unto me, That which people do trample upon must be thy food. And as the Lord spake, He opened it to me how that people and professors did trample upon the life; even the life of Christ was trampled upon; and they fed upon words and fed one another with words, but trampled upon the life; and trampled under foot the blood of the Son of God, which blood was my life; and they lived in their airy notions, talking of Him. It seemed strange to me at the first, that I should feed on that which the high professors trampled upon; but the Lord opened it clearly to me by his eternal Spirit and power.

Then came people from far and near to see me; and I was fearful of being drawn out by them; yet I was made to speak and open things to them. There was one Brown who had great prophecies and sights upon his death-bed of me. And he spake openly of what I should be made instrumental by the Lord to bring forth. And of others he spake that they should come to nothing, which was fulfilled on some that then were something in show. And when this man was buried, a great work of the Lord fell upon me, to the admiration of many, who thought I had been dead; and many came to see me for about fourteen days' time; for I was very much altered in countenance and person, as if my body had been new moulded or changed. And while I was in that condition I had a sense and discerning given me by the Lord, through which I saw plainly, that when many people talked of God and of Christ, etc., the serpent spake in them; but this was hard to be born. Yet the work of the Lord went on in some, and my sorrows and troubles began to wear off and tears of joy dropped from me, so that I could have wept night and day with tears of joy to the Lord, in humility and brokenness of heart. And I saw into that which was without end and things which cannot be uttered, and of the greatness and infiniteness of the love of God, which cannot be expressed by words. For I had been brought through the very ocean of darkness and death, and through the power and over the power of Satan by the eternal, glorious power of Christ; even through that darkness was I brought which covered over all the world, and which chained down all and shut up all in the death. And the same eternal power of God which brought me through these things, was that which afterwards shook the nations, priests, professors, and people. Then could I say I had been in spiritual Babylon, Sodom, Egypt, and the grave; but by the eternal power of God I was come out of it, and was brought over it and the power of it into the power of Christ. And I saw the harvest white, and the seed of God lying thick in the ground, as ever did wheat that was sown outwardly, and none to gather it; and for this I mourned with tears. And a report went abroad of me that I was a young man that had a discerning spirit; whereupon many came to me from far and near, professors, priests, and people; and the Lord's power brake forth; and I had great openings and prophecies, and spake unto them of the things of God, and they heard with attention and silence, and went away and spread the fame thereof. Then came the tempter and set upon me again, charging me that I had sinned against the Holy Ghost, but I could not tell in what. And then Paul's condition came before me, how, after he had been taken up into the third heavens and seen things not lawful to be uttered, a messenger of Satan was sent to buffet him again. Thus by the power of Christ I got over that temptation also.

In the year 1648, as I was sitting in a friend's house in Nottinghamshire (for by this time the power of God had opened the hearts of some to receive the word of life and reconciliation), I saw there was a great crack to go throughout the earth and a great smoke to go as the crack went, and that after the crack there should be a great shaking; this was the earth in people's hearts which was to be shaken before the seed of God was raised out of the earth. And it was so; for the Lord's power began to shake them, and great meetings we began to have, and a mighty power and work of God there was amongst people, to the astonishment of both people and priests.

EASTERN ORTHODOXY

The predominant form of Christianity in Greece, Cyprus, the Balkans, and Russia is the Eastern Orthodox church. It or related Eastern

*churches, such as the Armenian church and the Coptic churches of Egypt
and Ethiopia, are also strong in various parts of the Near East. Immigra-
tion has brought Eastern Orthodoxy to North America as well.*

*Seeing itself as the oldest Christian tradition, Eastern Orthodoxy
is conservative in doctrine and worship. Its most striking expressions of
Christianity are in its liturgical worship and the mystical piety of its saints
and monks. Eastern Orthodox celebrate the service of bread and wine in
an atmosphere of incense, soaring sacred music, and colorful churches suggesting the glory of heaven; they feel Christian worship should lift one's
senses above, and be a foretaste of, paradise. Orthodox mystics are inwardly caught up in heaven; theirs is the spontaneity and radiance of the
divine. Orthodox worship and spirituality both, in fact, present a remarkable combination of formality and informality. The long and splendid
worship service is stylized, yet during it worshippers pray or move about
with a freedom more suggestive of a home than an institution. The Orthodox saints, especially in old Russia, were independent souls who lived
by the Gospels and direct experience of God, sometimes acted unpredict-
ably, and were venerated by high and low alike.*

*The following passage is about one of the greatest of Russian saints,
Seraphim of Sarov (1759–1833).*

From *A Treasury of Russian Spirituality*

G.P. Fedotov

FRAGMENTS FROM THE LIFE OF SAINT SERAPHIM

Prochor Moshnine was born in Kursk in 1759, into a family of provincial merchants. His family had the piety typical of its class, and early
in childhood Prochor began to read the Bible and other devotional literature. For a time he assisted his brother in business, but the work made no
appeal to him. His was rather a contemplative nature, even as a child he
had had visions of the celestial world. At the age of nineteen he entered
the Sarov monastery as a novice, receiving the name Seraphim in religion;
in due course he was tonsured and received holy orders. It is said that he
had to abandon the celebration of Holy Mass because he lost consciousness of his surroundings during the raptures which were of frequent occurrence to him. In 1794, with the "blessing" of his superior, Seraphim
removed to his "desert," i.e., to the forest which environed the monastery.

G.P. Fedotov, ed., *A Treasury of Russian Spirituality* (London: Sheed & Ward,
1952), pp. 246–49, 251–53. Reprinted by permission of the publisher.

The following excerpts are translated from the materials published by Chichagov.

St. Seraphim's Life as a Hermit (1794–1810)

The cell—called "the desert"—in which Father Seraphim sought salvation was located in a dense pine wood, on the bank of the river Sarovka. It was set on a hill, some five or six versts from the monastery, facing the east, where the winter sun rises. The hermitage consisted of a shack, containing a stove, and a porch, with a small vestibule attached. Around the shack, Father Seraphim had planted a small vegetable garden and put up a fence. At one time he even had a bee-hive which yielded delicious honey. Half way between the desert and the monastery, other hermits lived in isolated huts—the igumen Nazarius, the priest-monk Dorotheus, and the schema-monk Mark. These scattered dwellings were somewhat reminiscent of Mount Athos, which is composed of several hills, with a number of monasteries and separate hermit cells set in dense woods; Father Seraphim therefore called his desert hill Athos; as to the other isolated sites in the woods, he named them, with spiritual significance, after various holy places, such as Nazareth, Jerusalem, Bethlehem, Thabor, the brook Cedron, the river Jordan, and so on.

Throughout his heremitical life, Father Seraphim wore the same poor garments: a loose white linen robe, leather mittens, and rough leather gaiters, rather like stockings, over which he wore sandals of plaited bark; on his head a shabby calotte. On his chest hung a cross—the one with which his mother had blessed him when she let him go away from home—and on his back he bore a sack containing the book of the holy Gospels. The bearing of the cross and the Gospels had, of course, a deep symbolic meaning. During the winter frosts, he would cover his chest with a rag or a stocking. He never bathed. His exterior exercises consisted in prayers, the reading of sacred books, physical labor, the observance of the prayer rule of St. Pachomius, and so on. In cold weather he would start a fire in the stove in his cell and would chop wood for it, but at times he voluntarily suffered the cold. In summer he tended his vegetable beds and fertilized them with moss collected from the swamps. At such times he went without clothing, except for a loin-cloth, and the insects relentlessly stung his flesh, which would grow swollen and blue and encrusted with blood. The staretz underwent these sufferings voluntarily, in the name of God, guided by the examples of the hermits of long ago. In the beds fertilized with moss Father Seraphim planted the seeds of onion and other vegetables, on which he subsisted all through the summer. Physical labor produced a good-humored disposition in him, and he chanted prayers, *troparia*, and canons as he worked.

If Father Seraphim met anyone outside his cell in the Sarov woods, he would usually bow most humbly and go his way, without entering conversation. "No one has ever repented of silence," he afterwards said in his teachings.

A layman once asked him, out of the simplicity of his heart, "Father, have you ever seen evil spirits?" The staretz answered, with a smile, "They are hideous! . . . Just as it is impossible for a sinner to look upon an angel, even so it is an awful thing to look upon the devils, for they are hideous."

In the dense wood half way between the cell and the monastery, there was a very large stone. Calling to mind the lives of the holy stylites, Father Seraphim decided to take this kind of mortification upon himself. To this end, and to fortify his life of prayer, he stood on that stone at night, in order to avoid notice. He would pray, either standing or kneeling, with his arms raised, as St. Pachomius used to do; and he would cry out in a contrite voice: "God, have mercy on me, a sinner!" And to equal by day the mortifications of the night, Father Seraphim kept another stone in his cell; on this stone he prayed from morning until nightfall, leaving it only to recover from exhaustion and to sustain himself with a little food. He engaged in this practice of mortification and prayer for a thousand days and nights.

He was reluctant to advise others to live in the desert. One who lives in the desert, he warned, must be like a man nailed to the cross; and he added that if, in the struggle against the Enemy, monks in a monastery fought as though they contended with doves, the man in the desert had to fight like one contending with lions and tigers.

After the death of the prior Isaias, Father Seraphim did not alter his mode of living, and he remained in the desert. He only undertook an even greater mortification, that of complete silence. . . . No longer did he go out to meet visitors. If he chanced to encounter anyone suddenly in the forest, the staretz would fall on his knees, his head bowed, and would not rise until the passer-by had retired from his sight. In this manner he observed silence for three years, and for some time he gave up his custom of visiting the monastery on Sundays and feast days. One of his novices would come to the desert to bring him food, especially in winter, when Father Seraphim had none of his own vegetables. The food was taken to him once a week, on Sundays. In winter it was difficult for the novice to carry out this mission, for there were no roads to Father Seraphim's desert. The novice would have to struggle through knee-deep snow-drifts and in storms as he carried the weekly supply for the staretz bound to silence. Entering the vestibule, the novice would say a prayer; thereupon the staretz responded, mentally, "Amen," and opened the door of his cell. Folding his hands crosswise on his chest, he would stand by the door, with head bowed and eyes fixed on the ground; he would not bless the brother or even look at him. And the brother, having prayed according to custom, bowing low before the staretz, would put the food on a tray placed on a table in the vestibule. In the same way, Father Seraphim would place on the tray a piece of bread or a little cabbage, and the brother would have to take careful note of this, for it was thus that Father Seraphim silently let his visitor know what he required for the next week—bread or cabbage. And when he had prayed again and bowed low, requesting the hermit's prayers, the novice would return to the monastery, having heard not a single word from Father Seraphim's lips. . . .

. . . Michail Vasilievich and Elena Vasilievna Manturov lived on their old homestead near the village of Nutcha. They were landowners and gentlefolk. Michail Vasilievich had been stricken with such a severe illness that he was forced to leave the State service and settle down on his estate. When the disease from which he suffered reached the stage at which the bones of his feet were splintering, and his condition was critical, he resolved to follow the advice of friends and acquaintances and visit Father Seraphim at Sarov. His serfs carried him painfully into the vestibule of Father Seraphim's enclosed cell. After Manturov had recited the ordinary prayers, the staretz came out of his cell and asked, graciously, "What, you have come to look upon poor Seraphim?"

Manturov fell at Father Seraphim's feet, weeping, and implored the staretz to cure his terrible disease. Then the staretz spoke to him with the most intense sympathy and paternal affection, asking him three times, "Do you believe in God?" And when he had three times received, in answer, Manturov's most sincere, confident, and devout assurance of his absolute faith in God, the great staretz said to him: "My Joy! If you believe so deeply, then believe also that for one who has faith everything is possible from God. Believe, therefore, that you too will be healed by God; as for me, poor Seraphim, I will pray." Then Father Seraphim seated Manturov near the coffin which stood in the vestibule and withdrew into his cell. After some time he returned, carrying the holy oil. He ordered Manturov to undress and uncover his feet. As he prepared himself to rub them with the holy oil, he said: "With the grace given me by God, you are my first patient." Father Seraphim anointed Manturov's feet and drew over them a pair of hemp stockings. Then he brought from his cell a great quantity of bread crusts. He stuffed Manturov's pockets with the crusts and ordered him to go to the monastery guest-house carrying this burden. Manturov set out to obey the Father's command with some apprehension, but soon, convinced of the miracle which had been performed on him, he was filled with unutterable joy and a sort of sacred awe. In his joy he threw himself at Father Seraphim's feet, kissing them and thanking the staretz for his cure. But the great recluse lifted Manturov to his feet and said to him, severely: "Is it Seraphim's task to inflict death or to give life? To send a man down to hell or to raise him out of it? How, now, good Father! This is the work of the One God, who fulfills the wishes of those who fear Him, and who listens to their prayers. May you offer your thanksgiving to God the all-powerful, and to His immaculate Mother."

. . . Some time had passed, and suddenly one day Manturov reminded himself with terror of the sickness he had suffered from, and which he had by now well-nigh forgotten. He resolved to visit the staretz once more and receive his blessing. On his way, Manturov said to himself: "I must indeed thank the Lord, as Father Seraphim told me to." As soon as he arrived at Sarov, and entered Father Seraphim's quarters, the great staretz greeted him, saying: "My Joy! You promised to thank the Lord for giving us back our lives." Surprised by Seraphim's insight, Manturov answered: "I do not know, Father, how, and through what deeds, to thank Him." Then Father Seraphim said, gaily: "Well, my Joy, give away to God all that you possess and take on voluntary poverty." Manturov was filled with confusion. But, guessing his thoughts, the clairvoyant staretz went on: "Give up everything, and do not worry about the things which occupy your thoughts; God will not forsake you, either in this life or in the one to come. You will not be rich, but you will receive your daily bread."

Manturov answered immediately: "I am willing, Father; what is it you want me to do, and to give me your blessing for?" But the great staretz, in his wisdom, wishing to try the impetuous Manturov, replied: "Well, my Joy, let us pray, and I shall tell you to what God has inspired me."

After this they parted. With Father Seraphim's blessing Manturov sold his estate and liberated his serfs. Keeping the money for the time being, he presently invested it in a piece of land near the village of Diveyevo. The plot—fifteen desiatins or more in area—was one which Father Seraphim had pointed out to him, giving him strict orders to keep this land, never to sell it or give it away, and to leave it, on his death, to his [Seraphim's] monastery. It was on this land that Manturov settled with his wife and underwent the trials of poverty. He likewise endured much mockery from friends and acquaintances, and the reproaches of his wife, Anna Michailovna.

ROMAN CATHOLIC THOUGHT

The largest Christian church is the Roman Catholic. Perhaps the basic theme of Roman Catholic Christianity is affirmation that God's grace is experienced not only inwardly but through outward forms as well; through sacraments like baptism and holy communion, through saints infused each in his or her own way with grace, through the visible structure of the church as an organic and hierarchical body headed by the pope as visible vicar of Christ on earth. The following passage is a sensitive and profound explication of this understanding of Christian life in the church by a modern Roman Catholic theologian. Views of the church like those here expressed underlie much of the modern renewal in Roman Catholicism.

From *The Christ of Catholicism*
Aelred Graham

"A man's body is all one, though it has a number of different organs; and all this multitude of organs goes to make up one body; so it is with Christ . . . And you are Christ's body, organs of it depending upon each other."[1] St. Paul's comparison of the mystical Body to a human body should be understood rather as a parable than an allegory. In other words, he is illustrating the likeness between the two on a broad principle of similarity, not entering into the details of the mystical anatomy. We are not meant to ask what the various subordinate organs signify: the ears, the eyes, the feet, the hands and the rest. The essential point is that the diversity of organs in a human body is not only an element of its beauty, it is a condition of its life. This unity in variety does not arise, in the members of the mystical Body, from the fact that they are Christians, since in this respect there is no difference between them; nor is it due to the diversity of natural characteristics, although these, when perfected by grace, can form a contributory factor. Its source lies in those gratuitous gifts which the Holy Spirit grants to the faithful for the common good of the Church: the apostolate, prophecy, discourses marked by wisdom and learning, discernment of spirit, power to heal the sick and to work miracles, aptitude for administration, teaching, helping the poor, consoling the afflicted and performing other works of mercy. Moreover, this diversity is also manifested in the respective functions of the ecclesiastical hierarchy, and in the inequality, which the difference in their cooperation with the various calls of grace produces, among the members of the Church.

What is emphasized here is the supernatural counterpart of the truism that man is by nature a social being. If each of the body's organs could instinctively attract everything to itself, the whole organism would quickly perish. It is the same with the social body; hence nature warns us against selfishness. We learn by experience that no man is sufficient to himself, that each member of society has his own contribution to make, that those who are intrinsically the least honourable are often treated with the greatest honour, that the general health depends upon the proper

[1] 1 Cor. 12:12, 27; cf. Pius XII, pp. 212–13.

working of the whole, and that the welfare of all is bound up with the good condition of each. But we must not stop short at such obvious considerations as these; St Paul furnishes us with the true formula of Christian altruism—all must live and act together *"in Christ."* "Each of us has one body, with many different parts, and not all these parts have the same function; just so we, though many in number, form one body in Christ, and each acts as the counterpart of another."[2] The other members of the Body are not strangers to us; they are part of us; they work for us just as we work for them; we need their help and we owe them ours.

Community of life is thus the nerve and sinews, the very life-blood, of the mystical Body. The individual member does not live by his own life, but by the life of the Body. Hence he must be united, not only to the Head, from whom the living influx flows, but also to the other members, each of whom, in his own sphere, transmits that life to him. Separated from the Head, the member inevitably dies; isolated from the other members, he leads only a precarious and impoverished life. It is from the Head that the whole Body draws its nourishment and, as a compact structure, grows up unto God.[3] In this context we may notice the characteristically Pauline emphasis in the exposition of a truth held in common with St John. We have already remarked on the evident kinship of thought between the mystical Body and the similitude of the Vine and its branches.[4] In both instances the supernatural life is compared to the growth of a living being, a growth deriving from an internal source and wholly dependent upon its union with the centre of life. But in St John the branches draw their sap from the vine-stock to which they are directly joined; while in St. Paul the members, united to the Head by the other members, reciprocally give and receive the flow of life with reference to each other. The first considers primarily the individual life of believers, while St Paul's standpoint is that of the communal life of the Church. But in St John and St Paul alike the agent of the supernatural life is Christ and the Holy Spirit.

The foregoing consideration on the Church as the fulness and complement of Christ, together with their practical bearing upon the co-operation demanded of the members of the mystical Body, are admirably summed up in the words of Pope Pius XII. Not only does Christ fulfil himself through his Vicar on earth, the successor of St Peter, "but also while he himself is invisibly ruling the Church, our Saviour desires to be helped by the members of his mystical Body in furthering the work of the Redemption. This is not on account of any need or insufficiency in him, but rather because he has so ordained it for the greater honour of his spotless Bride. Dying on the Cross, he bestowed upon his Church the boundless treasure of the Redemption without any co-operation on her

[2]Rom. 12:4–5.
[3]Col. 2:19.
[4]John 15:1–11.

part; but in the distribution of that treasure, he not only shares this work of sanctification with his spotless Bride, but wills it to arise in a certain measure out of her labour. This is truly a tremendous mystery, upon which we can never meditate enough: that the salvation of many souls depends upon the prayers and voluntary mortifications offered for that intention by the members of the mystical Body of Jesus Christ, and upon the co-operation which pastors and faithful, and especially fathers and mothers of families, must give to our divine Saviour."[5]

The union of the mystical Body reaches its culminating point in the Eucharist, which is the divinely efficacious symbol of the Church's sacrificial life.[6] We have a cup that we bless; is not this cup we bless a participation in Christ's blood? Is not the bread we break a participation in Christ's body? The one bread makes us one body, though we are many in number; the same bread is shared by all."[7] Here we may note that the Greek word translated by "participation" is κοινωνία, from which we get our "communion." For the Jews, as for the ancient peoples generally, to eat food offered in sacrifice was to share in that sacrifice. The religious banquets held in honour of the heathen gods were a form of ritual worship;[8] this is the context of St Paul's words to the Christians at Corinth, for they were not yet immune from these idolatrous practices. In their case such indulgence amounted to an apostasy from Christ. But St Paul concedes that there is truth in the idea itself—"do not those who eat their sacrifices associate themselves with the altar of sacrifice?"[9] The heathen worship was perverse, not necessarily in itself, but because it was directed to a wrong object, paying tribute to a false god. Yet the underlying principle was applicable to the Christians: to eat food that had been sacrificed to the true God implied a recognition of him and his lordship; it promoted fellowship with him in a common life.

TRADITIONAL
ROMAN CATHOLIC DEVOTION

Another important side of Roman Catholicism is that of private prayer, or devotions other than sacraments. These cover a wide range, but particularly before the changes associated with the Second Vatican Council in the early 1960s, they centered largely on rosary prayers, pil-

[5]P. 213.
[6] 1 Cor. 10:16–17.
[7] 1 Cor. 10:18.
[8]Cf. *ibid.*, pp. 232–33.
[9]Cf. Judges 9:27.

grimages, novenas, and other devotions directed toward the Blessed Virgin Mary, mother of Jesus. Today there are Roman Catholics to whom material like that below would sound somewhat old-fashioned, but it represents a style of Christian piety immensely influential at least from the late middle ages up to the midtwentieth century, and which has a unique beauty and depth. This selection presents the teachings of St. Louis Grignon de Montfort about why true devotion to Mary is the best way to attain union with Christ, and his form of self-dedication to Mary. Louis Grignon de Montfort (1673–1716) was a French priest and founder of charitable works; he was canonized by Pope Pius XII in 1947.

From *To Jesus through Mary: True Devotion to Mary According to Saint Louis Grignon de Montfort*

MARY, OUR CHANNEL OF GRACE

In proof of his assertion that Mary is the means ordained by God through which we receive all good and every grace, St. Louis Grignon reasons as follows:—

First Reason

Mary alone has found grace with God both for herself and for every child of Adam. The angel said to Mary, "Thou hast found grace with God; behold, thou shalt bring forth a Son, and thou shalt call His Name, Jesus."

St. Louis Grignon de Montfort says that *God has chosen Mary for the treasurer,* the administratrix and dispensatrix of all His graces, so that all His graces and all His gifts pass through her hands, and no gift is bestowed on men by heaven except through her virginal hands. Many doctors of the Church hold the same opinion.

Second Reason

Mary has given being and life to the Author of all grace, and on this account she is called the "Mother of grace." In Mary resides the fulness of grace, Jesus Christ, that she may impart grace to the members of Jesus Christ, her true children, as is taught by St. Bernard and St. Jerome.

To Jesus through Mary: True Devotion to Mary According to Saint Louis Grignon de Montfort (Clyde, 1953). Reprinted by permission.

Third Reason

God the Father, from whom every perfect gift and all grace comes, in giving His Son to Mary gave her all His graces. "God has deposited in Mary the fulness of all that is good," says St. Bernard, "so that if we have any hope, any grace, any salvation, we should know that all comes to us by Mary. Take away the sun which illuminates the earth, and what will become of the day? It will vanish with all its brightness, light and blessings. Take away from the vast universe, Mary, the resplendent Star of the Sea, and what will remain but dense darkness, shadows of death and total obscurity of spirit? Let us therefore venerate Mary with a fervent heart, with deepest affection and with all the desire of our soul, for it is the will of Him who willed that we receive all things through Mary. It is His will, I say, but to our advantage."

Fourth Reason

As in the natural order a child has a father and a mother, so, in the order of grace, a true child of the Church must have God for his Father and Mary for his Mother. If anyone glories in having God for his Father without at the same time having a tender, filial love for Mary, he deceives himself and is still far from the way of truth.

Fifth Reason

The Holy Spirit, having espoused Mary, produced in her this masterpiece, Jesus Christ, the Incarnate Word: and as He has never repudiated her, He continues to produce in her and by her, in a real, though mysterious manner, His elect, whose names are written in the book of life.

Sixth Reason

Mary has received from God a special dominion over the children of God. St. Augustine affirms that during their present life all the predestinate are hidden in the womb of the most holy Virgin, in order to be conformed to the image of the Son of God. There they are guarded, nourished, and made to grow by that good Mother until she has brought them forth to glory after death, which the Church calls the *birthday* of the saints. Consequently, as the child draws all its nourishment from its mother, who gives it to the child in proportion to its weakness, so in like manner do the predestined draw all their spiritual nourishment and strength from Mary.

Seventh Reason

On the festivals of the Blessed Virgin, the Church applies to her the words of Holy Scripture contained in chapter twenty-four of the Book of Ecclesiasticus: "Let thy dwelling be in Jacob, and thy inheritance in Israel, and take root in my elect." It is as though the Heavenly Father said to Mary, "My Daughter, let thy dwelling be in Jacob," that is to say, in My elect, typified in Jacob. It is as though God the Son said to her, "My dear Mother, let thine inheritance be in Israel," that is to say, since Israel, the chosen people of the Old Law, typifies the predestined of the kingdom of heaven, "thine inheritance shall be the predestined." Lastly, it is as though the Holy Spirit said to Mary, "Strike thy roots, My faithful Spouse, in My elect." Whosoever, then, is elected and predestined for life eternal, has the holy Virgin dwelling with him, in his soul;* he is her inheritance, her possession, her entire property. He allows her to strike in his soul the roots of her unshaken faith, her profound humility, her all-embracing mortification, her sublime prayer, ardent charity, firm hope, and all her other virtues.

Eighth Reason

In Mary, and in Mary alone, God became man without ceasing to be God. In a similar manner man also can be spiritually remodeled in Mary, and, nowhere as in her, be transformed into God, in as far as human nature is capable, through the grace of Jesus Christ. Mary, together with the Holy Spirit, has produced the most sublime Being which ever was or ever will be—the God-man; and *she will consequently produce the greatest saints toward the end of time,* as the most fervent servants of Mary are destined for the time of greatest tribulation.

FORMULA OF CONSECRATION TO JESUS THROUGH MARY

O Eternal and Incarnate Wisdom! Sweetest and most adorable Jesus! True God and true Man, only Son of the Eternal Father, and of Mary ever Virgin! I adore Thee profoundly in the bosom and splendors of Thy Father during eternity; and I adore Thee also in the virginal bosom of Mary, Thy most worthy Mother, at the time of Thy Incarnation.

"I give Thee thanks for having annihilated Thyself, taking the form of a slave in order to rescue me from the cruel slavery of the devil. I praise and glorify Thee for having been pleased to submit Thyself to Mary, Thy holy Mother, in all things, in order to make me Thy faithful slave through her. But alas! ungrateful and faithless as I have been, I have not kept the promises which I made so solemnly to Thee in my baptism. I have not fulfilled my obligations. I do not deserve to be called Thy child, nor yet Thy slave; and as there is so much in me that merits Thine

---

*St. Louis de Montfort does not here infer that Mary is present in our soul as God is present by sanctifying grace, but *morally* present by her attentiveness to our needs and her co-operation with the Holy Spirit in forming Jesus in our soul.

anger and Thy repulse, I dare not come by myself before Thy most holy and august Majesty.

"It is on this account that I have recourse to the intercession of Thy most holy Mother, whom Thou hast given me for a mediatrix with Thee. It is through her I hope to obtain of Thee contrition, the pardon of my sins, and unfailing wisdom.

"Hail, then, O Immaculate Mary, living tabernacle of the Divinity, where the Eternal Wisdom willed to be hidden and to be adored by angels and men! Hail, Queen of heaven and earth, to whose empire everything is subject under God. Hail, sure refuge of sinners, whose mercy fails no one. Hear my desire to be united with thy Son, the Divine Wisdom. And for that end, receive the vows and offerings which in my lowliness I present to thee.

"I, N., a faithless sinner, renew and ratify today in thy hands the vows of my baptism. I renounce forever Satan, his works and vain displays; and I give myself entirely to Jesus Christ, the Incarnate Wisdom, to carry my cross after Him all the days of my life, and to be more faithful to Him than I have been hitherto.

"In the presence of all the heavenly court I choose thee this day for my Mother and my Mistress. I deliver and consecrate to thee, as thy slave, my body and soul, my goods, both interior and exterior, and the value of all my good actions, past, present, and future. I leave to thee the entire and full right of disposing of me and all that belongs to me, according to thy good pleasure, for the greater glory of God, in time and in eternity.

"Receive, O benignant Virgin, this little offering of my slavery, in honor of, and in union with, that subjection which the Eternal Wisdom deigned to have to thy maternity; in homage of the power which both of you have over this poor sinner; and in thanksgiving for the privileges with which the Holy Trinity has favored thee. I declare that I wish henceforth, as thy true slave, to seek thy honor and to obey thee in all things.

"O admirable Mother, present me to thy dear Son as His eternal slave, so that as He has redeemed me by thee, by thee He may receive me. O Mother of mercy, grant me the grace to obtain the true wisdom of God: and for that purpose receive me among those whom thou dost love, teach, lead, nourish, and protect as thy children and thy slaves.

"O faithful Virgin, make me in all things so perfect a disciple, imitator, and slave of the Incarnate Wisdom, Jesus Christ, thy Son, that I may attain, through thy intercession and example, to the fulness of His manhood on earth, and of His glory in heaven. Amen.

A MODERN MISSIONARY

One of the best known of all Christian missionaries today is Mother Teresa, a Roman Catholic nun world-famous for her work among the desperately poor of Calcutta, India. Born Agnes Gonxha Bejaxhiu of Albanian parents in what is now southern Yugoslavia in 1910, she left for India as a missionary when she was only seventeen. Later she founded the Missionaries of Charity, an order dedicated to comforting, nursing, and above all simply showing Christian love for the poorest of the poor of India's teeming millions. Widely regarded as a living saint by Christians, Hindus, and Muslims alike, Mother Teresa has centered her work on the awareness that what the starving and lonely need most of all is a sign of deep and sacrificial caring for them as individual persons, despite their ugly rags and emaciated bodies.

Christianity has generally been a missionary faith, concerned with a calling to carry the gospel to the ends of the earth. During the nineteenth and twentieth centuries, among both Roman Catholics and Protestants, this has been a movement of immense consequences: not only has it made Christianity at least a minority in virtually every country of Asia, Africa, and the Pacific as well as giving the older Christian countries of Europe and the Americas a world perspective, but through its educational and social work has greatly influenced the modern history of the countries to which missionaries have gone. The following passage about the work of Mother Teresa can represent the work of all missionaries, Roman Catholic, Protestant, and Eastern Orthodox. The emphasis on caring and serving and following in the footsteps of Christ, and also the understandable pride in missionary statistics, on the growth and success of the work, alike reflect the mentality of missionary work in the modern world.

From *Mother Teresa: Her People and Her Work*

Desmond Doig

In the parlour of the Mother House of the Missionaries of Charity hang three boards. On one is displayed the four vows that the Society takes in pursuing 'Jesus's Way of Life'. The vows are poverty, chastity, obedience and charity. Another board, illustrated by photographs, explains what is required of the Congregation as they walk 'In the Footsteps of Christ'. The photographs show the Sisters at work in the slums, in homes for the abandoned and dying destitutes, in schools, among lepers and in mobile dispensaries. Inscribed above and below the photographs are Mother Teresa's own prayers, 'Make us worthy, Lord, to serve our fellow-men through the world who live and die in poverty and hunger. Give them, through our hands, this day their daily bread, and, by our understanding, love, peace and joy.'

Desmond Doig, *Mother Teresa: Her People and Her Work.* (New York and London: Harper & Row, Publishers, 1976), pp. 113–14. Copyright 1976 by Nachiketa Publications. Reprinted by permission of the publishers and of William Collins Sons & Co., Ltd.

'Let each Sister see Jesus Christ in the person of the poor; the more repugnant the work or the person, the greater also must be her faith, love and cheerful devotion in ministering to our Lord in this distressing disguise.'

The third board outlines the structure of the Society, founded in 1950 by Mother Teresa. Its idea is 'To quench the thirst of Jesus Christ on the Cross for love of souls by the Sisters' observance of the four vows of poverty, chastity, obedience and charity'. It attempts to tell at a glance how many Aspirants, Postulants and Professed Sisters there are, and to give in some detail the places in India and abroad where branch Houses of the Missionaries of Charity have been established, together with the dates of their founding. So numerous and urgent are the calls on the Missionaries of Charity, and so fast does the Order expand that this board can never hope to be up-to-date.

When Mother observed us copying down the figures from the board, she warned us that they were not correct, so we asked Sister Agnes if she could help us with the latest statistics. She did, but even as we read them, press reports on the opening of yet another Home for dying destitutes in the once princely city of Hyderabad made the latest list obsolete. The report went on to say that Mother would be visiting the cities of Bombay and Poona before returning to Calcutta via Patna where unprecedented floods had almost submerged the city causing loss of life and untold hardship.

Quoting at random from Sister Agnes's impressive list of statistics, the Missionaries of Charity have sixty-one foundations in India (fifty-one manned by Sisters and ten by Brothers) and twenty-eight abroad. They have eighty-one schools, three hundred and thirty-five mobile dispensaries, twenty-eight family planning centres, sixty-seven leprosy clinics, twenty-eight Homes for abandoned children and thirty-two Homes for dying destitutes. The Order has some nine hundred and thirty-five Sisters and one hundred and eighty-five Brothers. Sister Agnes puts the number of patients treated by the mobile dispensaries at about one million six hundred thousand, and the number of inmates at present in Homes for dying destitutes at two thousand, against which is a note explaining that the number of admissions and deaths have been omitted. Over forty-three thousand lepers are being treated at the leprosy clinics and the Missionaries of Charity are, at this moment, taking care of nearly two thousand abandoned children. Not mentioned are the millions of starving people who have been, and are being, fed by the Missionaries of Charity every day. I doubt that the good Sisters could count the numbers themselves.

Mother Teresa explains that she came to India because it was a mission country, but then happily adds that Indian missionaries are now to be found on all five continents, even in the most affluent countries of the West. 'In England, they suffer from loneliness. They have no need for bread, but they need human love. That is the hungry Christ for us.' She told us of old people dying alone in their often well-to-do homes and their bodies being found days afterwards. 'In the Yemen, the Sisters are called "carriers of God's love." It's wonderful, eh? There is now a church, a tabernacle, in the Yemen after eight hundred years. A person there told me that the presence of the Sisters has breathed a new life into the people.'

EVANGELICAL PROTESTANTISM

The basic religious thrust of Protestantism, that which underlies all that is distinctive about it, is generally said to be belief that one is justified or made right with God by faith. Protestantism asserts that what God looks for, so to speak, is not holy acts or good deeds or even pious feelings—works—but one's inner disposition as far down as one can go toward the source of outward manifestations. What matters is whether this hidden inward source is turned toward or away from God. If it is touched by God's grace and so turned Godward, the person is a person of faith, is accounted righteous, and his or her acts should demonstrate that prior fact.

This central idea undoubtedly does best explain the underlying unity of Protestantism, for it also accounts for its tremendous diversity. Understanding of the nature of such an inward faith and how it should manifest itself obviously can vary immensely. The notion of inward faith still leaves unanswered such questions as: Does true faith appear in commitment to clear laid down doctrine and morals, or in freedom from outward forms in such matters to let faith and grace be their own guides? What kind of worship and church life best comports with it? How does it relate to the authority of the Bible? On issues like these, Protestants have taken nearly every conceivable position.

One side of Protestantism, often called evangelical, emphasizes that Christian faith has to center on Jesus Christ and accept the Bible as normative. It stresses the absolute need for a definite personal commitment to Christ, and the power of Christ to make a new person of those who commit themselves to him. The following passages by the well-known American evangelist Billy Graham clearly state this position.

From *World Aflame*

Billy Graham

Twentieth-century man asks the same question that man has always asked. It is old, but it is ever new. It is just as relevant today as in the past.

Billy Graham, *World Aflame* (New York: Doubleday & Company, 1965), pp. 148–49, 152–53, 158–60. Reprinted by permission of Doubleday & Company, Inc., and of World's Work Ltd. Copyright 1965 by the author.

Just what must one do to be reconciled to God? What does the Bible mean by such words as conversion, repentance, and faith? These are all salvation words, but so little understood.

Jesus made everything so simple and we have made it so complicated. He spoke to the people in short sentences and every-day words, illustrating His messages with never-to-be-forgotten stories. He presented the message of God in such simplicity that many could not understand what He said.

In the book of Acts the Philippian jailer asked the Apostle Paul: "What must I do to be saved?" Paul gave him a very simple answer: "Believe on the Lord Jesus Christ and thou shalt be saved" (Acts 16:30, 31). This is so simple that millions stumble over it. The one and only choice by which you can be converted is your choice to believe on the Lord Jesus as your own personal Lord and Saviour. You don't have to straighten out your life first. You don't have to make things right at home or in your business first. You don't have to try to give up some habit that is keeping you from God. You have tried all that and failed many times. In our crusades when I give the invitation to receive Christ, we sing the hymn entitled "Just As I Am," and you come to Christ just as you are. The blind man came as he was. The leper came as he was. Mary Magdalene with seven devils came as she was. The thief on the cross came as he was. You can come to Christ just as you are. . . .

. . . Faith is described in the Bible as "the substance of things hoped for, the evidence of things not seen" (Heb. 11:1). Faith is not just hanging on. It is laying hold of Christ, for Christ is the object of our faith. It is not simply a subjective feeling, but an objective act.

The two words "belief" and "faith" are translated from the same Greek word in the New Testament, and it is a word that is never used in the New Testament in the plural. Christian faith does not mean believing in a number of things; it means a single, individual disposition of mind and heart toward Jesus Christ.

The most obvious thing about saving *faith is that it believes something*. It does not believe everything or just anything. It is belief in a person, and that person is Christ. Neither is faith antagonistic to reason or knowledge. Faith is not anti-intellectual. It is an act of man that reaches beyond the limits of our five senses. It is the recognition that God is greater than man. It is the recognition that God has provided a way of reconciliation that we could not provide through self-effort.

The psychiatrist tells us that before he can be of any help to his patient, the patient must come to him sincerely, asking for help and yielding to his guidance. The patient cannot be coerced or forced. Spiritually this is just as true with faith. . . .

. . . The question that comes to many minds is this: Just what must I do actually to receive Christ? I wish it were posssible for me to wrap it up in a neat little formula and hand it to you, but that is impossible. As I have already suggested, each person's experience is different from all others. Just as there are no two snowflakes alike, there are no two experiences with Christ exactly the same. However, there are certain guidelines in the Bible that will help to guide you to accept Jesus Christ as your Saviour. Therefore, let me summarize what you must do.

First, you must recognize that God loved you so much that He gave His Son to die on the cross. "For God so loved the world, that he gave his only begotten Son, that whosoever believeth in him should not perish, but have everlasting life" (Jn. 3:16). "The Son of God . . . loved me, and gave himself for me" (Gal. 2:20).

Second, you must repent of your sins. Jesus said: "Except ye repent, ye shall . . . perish" (Lk. 13:3). He said: "Repent . . . and believe" (Mk. 1:15). As John Stott, pastor of All Souls Church in London, wrote: "The faith which receives Christ must be accompanied by the repentance which rejects sin." Repentance does not mean simply that you are to be sorry for the past. To be sorry is not enough; you must repent. This means that you must turn your back on sins.

Third, you must receive Jesus Christ as Saviour and Lord. "But as many as received him, to them gave he power to become the sons of God, even to them that believe on his name" (Jn. 1:12). This means that you accept God's offer of love, mercy, and forgiveness. This means that you accept Jesus Christ as your only Lord and your only Saviour. This means that you cease struggling and trying to save yourself. You trust Him completely, without reservation, as your Lord and Saviour.

Fourth, you must confess Christ publicly. Jesus said: "Whosoever therefore shall confess me before men, him will I confess also before my Father which is in heaven" (Matt. 10:32). This confession carries with it the idea of a life so lived in front of your fellowmen that they will see a difference. It means also that you acknowledge with your mouth the Lord Jesus. "If thou shalt confess with thy mouth the Lord Jesus, and shalt believe in thine heart that God hath raised him from the dead, thou shalt be saved" (Rom. 10:9). It is extremely important that when you receive Christ you tell someone else about it just as soon as possible. This gives you strength and courage to witness.

It is important that you make your decision and your commitment to Christ now. "Now is the accepted time . . . now is the day of salvation" (II Cor. 6:2). If you are willing to repent of your sins and to receive Jesus Christ as your Saviour, you can do it now. At this moment you can either bow your head or get on your knees and say this little prayer that I have used with thousands of persons on every continent:

> O God, I acknowledge that I have sinned against Thee. I am sorry for my sins. I am willing to turn from my sins. I openly receive and acknowledge Jesus Christ as my Saviour. I confess Him as Lord. From this moment on I want to live for Him and serve Him. In Jesus' name, Amen.

If you are willing to make this decision, if you have to the best of your knowledge received Jesus Christ, God's Son, as your own Saviour, then according to the preceding statements of Scripture, you have become a child of God in whom Jesus Christ dwells. Altogether too many people make the mistake of measuring the certainty of their salvation by their feelings. Don't make this serious mistake. Believe God. Take Him at His Word.

LIBERAL PROTESTANTISM

Another side of Protestantism, commonly called liberal, emphasizes that liberating inward faith transcends any set categories, including even any set concept of the nature of Christ or the authority of the Bible. It emphasizes that the outward expression of faith in ideas, doctrines, understanding of the Bible, and deeds can continually change, and should to relate to current social, philosophical, and scientific concepts and to make the essence of Christian faith understandable to contemporaries. Liberal Protestantism generally accepts nonliteral interpretations of the Bible more readily than evangelical. It greatly exalts freedom of thought as an expression of the freedom given by true faith. Liberal Protestants have often been associated with liberal movements in society as well. The following passage from the distinguished theologian Paul Tillich shows how the "Protestant principle" of not absolutizing anything under God releases, in Tillich's view, the true freedom that Christianity brings.

From *The Protestant Era*

Paul Tillich

What makes Protestantism Protestant is the fact that it transcends its own religious and confessional character, that it cannot be identified wholly with any of its particular historical forms. Thus, if there is an incongruity between Protestantism in its present status and the situation of the proletariat, it does not follow that the incongruity belongs in essence to Protestantism. Protestantism has a principle that stands beyond all its realizations. It is the critical and dynamic source of all Protestant realizations, but it is not identical with any of them. It cannot be confined by a definition. It is not exhausted by any historical religion; it is not

Paul Tillich, *The Protestant Era*, abridged edition, trans. James Luther Adams. (Chicago: The University of Chicago Press, 1957), pp. 162–63, 169–70. Copyright 1948 and 1957 by the publisher, and reprinted with its permission.

identical with the structure of the Reformation or of early Christianity or even with a religious form at all. It transcends them as it transcends any cultural form. On the other hand, it can appear in all of them; it is a living, moving, restless power in them; and this is what it is supposed to be in a special way in historical Protestantism. The Protestant principle, in name derived from the protest of the "protestants" against decisions of the Catholic majority, contains the divine and human protest against any absolute claim made for a relative reality, even if this claim is made by a Protestant church. The Protestant principle is the judge of every religious and cultural reality, including the religion and culture which calls itself "Protestant."

The Protestant principle, the source and judge of Protestantism, is not to be confused with the "Absolute" of German idealism or with the "Being" of ancient and recent philosophy. It is not the highest ontological concept derived from an analysis of the whole of being; it is the theological expression of the true relation between the unconditional and the conditioned or, religiously speaking, between God and man. As such, it is concerned with what theology calls "faith," namely, the state of mind in which we are grasped by the power of something unconditional which manifests itself to us as the ground and judge of our existence. The power grasping us in the state of faith is not a being beside others, not even the highest; it is not an object among objects, not even the greatest; but it is a quality of all beings and objects, the quality of pointing beyond themselves and their finite existence to the infinite, inexhaustible, and unapproachable depth of their being and meaning. The Protestant principle is the expression of this relationship. It is the guardian against the attempts of the finite and conditioned to usurp the place of the unconditional in thinking and acting. It is the prophetic judgment against religious pride, ecclesiastical arrogance, and secular self-sufficiency and their destructive consequences. . . .

. . . The Reformation struggled against two ideologies, that is, against two ways of concealing the true human situation, namely, the Catholic and the humanistic ideology. Catholicism claims to offer a secure way of overcoming the separation of man from his divine ground through sacramental graces and ascetic exercises, the efficacy of which is guaranteed by the hierarchy and its sacramental powers. Humanism denies the perverted character of the human situation and tries to achieve essential humanity on the basis of human self-determination. Over against these two ideologies—the religious and the secular—Protestantism must insist upon the unveiled and realistic recognition of the perennial situation of man. Historical Protestantism, however, has not escaped the ideologizing of its own principle. Protestant orthodoxy and Protestant idealism represent the sacramental and the humanistic forms of the old ideologies. In both forms a "man-made God" has been substituted for the true God, a God that is either inclosed in a set of doctrines or is believed to be accessible through morals and education.

In the power of the Protestant principle, Protestantism must fight not only against other ideologies but also against its own. It must reveal the "false consciousness" wherever it hides. It must show how the "man-made God" of Catholicism was in the interest of the feudal order, of which the medieval church was a part; how the ideology of Lutheranism was in the interest of the patriarchal order, with which Lutheran ortho-doxy was associated; how the idealistic religion of humanistic Protestant-ism is in the interest of a victorious *bourgeoisie*. The creation of these ideologies—religiously speaking, idols—representing man's will to power, occurs unconsciously. It is not a conscious falsification or a political lie. If this were the case, ideologies would not be very dangerous. But they are dangerous precisely because they are unconscious and are therefore objects of belief and fanaticism. To reveal these concrete ideologies is one of the most important functions of the Protestant principle, just as it was one of the main points in the attack of the prophets on the religious and social order of their time. Theology, of course, must provide general insight into human nature, into its distorted character and its proneness to create ideologies. But this is not enough. A religious analysis of the concrete situation must unveil concrete ideologies, as Luther and the Reformers did when they unveiled the all-powerful Roman ideology.

PENTECOSTALISM

A form of Christianity that has grown explosively in the twentieth century is Pentecostalism. It started in its modern form in America at the turn of the century. First expressed through several distinctively Pente-costal denominations, around midcentury it took hold in "main line" Protestant denominations and in the Roman Catholic church. Pente-costalism has also spread vigorously overseas, and in many parts of the "Third World" represents the strongest or fastest growing form of Christianity.

Pentecostalism's most distinctive usage is "speaking in tongues"— the practice of using words not those of ordinary language in prayer, praise, and preaching. The "gift of tongues" is said to be bestowed by the Holy Spirit as a sign of full conversion and of the presence of real New Testament Christianity. Where Pentecostalism is found, there is usually also an evangelical emphasis on conversion and commitment to Christ, and an informal and spontaneous atmosphere. Spiritual life may well be centered in small prayer groups rather than in large churches.

The passage below is from a book by the Pentecostal minister David Wilkerson, famous for his work with young people involved in drugs and gangs in New York City. In this passage some of those whose lives were changed by Pentecostal experience are telling a visitor about what happened to them. The boy Roberto had received the baptism of the Spirit that same evening.

From *The Cross and the Switchblade*
David Wilkerson

The first was a twelve-year-old girl named Neda. We had found her on Coney Island, wandering around as if lost. Linda Meisner learned from her that sex and alcohol were the centers of her revolt against her family. "I used to drink a lot," she said now, "and to run around with any boy who looked that way at me. I hated my parents, especially my mother. Linda brought me here to the Center and I sat in the chapel and listened to all the other kids talk about how Jesus helped them when they were tempted. When I had problems, like being with a boy, I used to break up and get disgusted, but these dope addicts had problems, too, worse than mine. 'We still get tempted,' they say, 'but now we always run into the chapel and pray.' When they prayed, they spoke in another language but they looked happy and were sure of themselves. And when they got up from their knees, their temptation was gone.

"So they made me want the same thing. I went into the chapel one day to pray by myself. I started telling God all about my problems and I asked Him to come into my life like he had to those drug addicts. Like a blinding light, Jesus burst into my heart. Something took over my speech. It made me feel like I was sitting down by a river that somehow was flowing through me and bubbled up out of me like a musical language. It was after this that one of the workers showed me in the Book of Acts what it was all about. It was the most wonderful thing that ever happened." . . .

. . . The boy's name was Roberto. Roberto was sixteen years old; he had been on heroin for two years, and on marijuana before that; he had been in jail four times, once for stabbing another gang member in a street fight. The boy had lived, but Roberto was afraid that some day he might kill. Unlike many of the boys who come to the Center, Roberto had parents who stood by him. They tried everywhere to get help, but Roberto's downhill slide only increased its pace.

That afternoon I met Roberto in the chapel. I guessed from the way he was fidgeting and moving around restlessly that he was about to go out for a fix.

David Wilkerson, *The Cross and the Switchblade* (New York: Bernard Geis Associates, 1963), pp. 197–98, 199–202. Reprinted by permission of the publisher.

"I've got problems, Davie," he said, quietly lacing and unlacing his fingers. When an addict says he has problems, he means that he has to make contact and shoot it up—and soon.

So I started talking to Roberto again about the baptism of the Holy Spirit. "Nicky will be preaching about it tonight. Be there, and let the Spirit come upon you."

"I don't know, Davie. I've got to get some fresh air. I'm not feeling so good."

I had to let him go, and frankly I didn't expect to see him again. But that night he was in the chapel when I arrived. I could tell from the way he continued to suffer that he had made it without getting a fix. I sat down beside him, and watched him carefully as several of our ex-gang-members and drug addicts arose and quite simply told of the wondrous things that were happening to them. Nicky preached about the need of every drug addict to have the baptism of the Holy Spirit.

"If you want power in your life . . . if you are on the needle and really want to change, then listen to this. The Holy Spirit is what you need. And when you receive Him, you will also receive ten special gifts which you can depend on. I'm going to tell you about them. If you have a pencil and paper you can copy down the Bible references that show where I got them.

"First of all you will have power. You can read that in Acts 1:8. You shall have power when the Holy Spirit comes upon you.

"Then, you're going to have a Comforter. John 14:26. A Comforter doesn't mean someone who will make you comfortable, it means someone who will stand by you and give you strength.

"Next you will have protection. Read in Acts 16:6 how the Holy Spirit forbids the apostles to take a step which would have been tragic. He will guide you like this, too.

"And here's an important one: you will no longer be hounded by the mind of the flesh, but you will have spiritual values. Read it in Ephesians 2:3–6.

"You will have life. Now you are headed for death, but with the Holy Spirit, it says in Second Corinthians 3:5–6 that you will have new life.

"And you will be living with the Spirit of Truth. The needle holds out a promise to you that is never fulfilled. You don't get release in a drilling session, it just gets worse. John 16:13 tells you that you will have Truth.

"Access to the Father will be yours. Read Ephesians 2:18.

"And the last three: You will have Hope. How many of you have that now? Not many. You will have Hope, says Romans 15:13.

"And the point of all this is found in Second Corinthians 3:17. You, you boys out there now, will have liberty!

"And how does this come about? Through a dramatic, sudden, overpowering experience. Read about it for yourselves in Acts 10:44."

Then Nicky stopped. His voice dropped and he spoke in almost a whisper. "That's what's ahead for you in this new life," he said. "But here tonight I don't think we want to *read* about it. And we don't want to *talk* about it. We want to *do* it!

"If you want this change and power and hope and freedom in your life, get on your feet and come up front. I'm going to lay my hands on your head just like St. Paul did and the same thing is going to happen to you that happened to the new Christians in his time. You're going to receive the Holy Spirit!"

Roberto took one look at me and leaped to his feet; and my heart leaped with him.

"I want everything God has for me," he said. "I want to make it through and never come back."

Roberto fairly ran to the front of the chapel. He grabbed Nicky's hands and put them on his own head. Almost immediately the same thing happened to this boy that had happened to my Grandfather; he began to tremble as if current were flowing through him. He fell to his knees, and the other boys stood around him, praying.

It was like reliving a scene from the Book of Acts. In less than two minutes a new language was flowing from Roberto's lips. It poured out like a spring bubbling up out of dry land.

Of course, everyone was rejoicing. All the other drug addicts came around Nicky and Roberto and began saying, "He's going to make it. He's coming through." Nicky kept saying, "Thank you, Lord. Thank you for helping these boys."

Then others picked it up.

"Thank You, Lord. Thank You for helping these boys."

"Thank You. Thank You. Thank You, Lord."

X

SOLDIERS AND SAINTS OF GOD: THE STRAIGHT PATH OF ISLAM

Islam means submission in Arabic, and it is the faith of those who accept Muhammad as the final prophet of God and who submit their lives to that God. (An adherent of Islam is called a Muslim.) Islam is the predominant religion in northern Africa, western and central Asia, several important nations of south and southeast Asia, and has significant minorities elsewhere. It is a dynamic faith that often inspires intense commitment; it has spread at a remarkable rate at certain times in the past, and today is growing rapidly in Africa.

Islam presents two images to the world. On one hand, it seems like an army of men and women following conscientiously a spiritual regimen of certain fundamentally simple practices. These practices affect all of life and make distinctions between sacred and secular, personal faith and social order, almost meaningless. This image is suggested by the sight of rank on rank of the faithful rising and falling down in prayer in the great mosques of Cairo or Teheran, or uniting in the pilgrimage to Mecca, or struggling to create distinctively Islamic societies where laws and customs derived from the Koran are observed.

But there is another image of Islam too, the image formed by its mystics and saints—the Islam of tombs of holy men, gnomic Sufi sayings, whirling dervishes, or exquisite poetry of divine love. For the mystics and their disciples, outer observances are less important than inner holiness (although the outer are not usually neglected), and for them religion is not only obedience to God but also friendship with him leading to mystic union. The popularity of saints has often provided powerful foci for Islamic loyalty and has been the vehicle for the spread of Islam to many lands. For the saints often have been immensely influential spiritual teachers with something of a divine grace about them. They have led spiritual orders, received pilgrims, and left tombs that have been magnetic centers of devotion after their deaths.

The two sides of Islam have two fundamental features in common. One is absolute monotheism. The Muslim God is called Allah (simply meaning *"The* God"). God for Islam is absolutely supreme, sovereign, and personal, and there is none beside him. To deviate in the slightest from living under this reality is for the Muslim to fall into the greatest and most basic sin, idolatry—the worship or service of something other than the one God. The absolute reality of the one God, beside which all else has only a highly contingent existence, is expressed through the finality of God's will for all of his creation, and in the sheer presence everywhere of his being. The Koran gives rules, therefore, that God wishes humankind to follow to implement his will, and it also reminds us that "Whichever way you turn there is the face of Allah."

The ordinary Muslim expresses the oneness and absoluteness of God by following the commandments, centered on the "Five Pillars of Islam:" the short "creed" that says, "There is no god but God (Allah), and Muhammad is the envoy of God;" prayer five times daily; almsgiving; keeping the fast of Ramadan; and the pilgrimage to Mecca.

The Muslim mystic probably does these, but is even more concerned to know the *being* of God as the absolute presence in and through all things.

Yet the two ways are not inconsistent; they both are responses to absolute monotheism, to experience of the unconditioned *oneness* of God, and each way could be seen as presupposing the possibility of the other.

The second fundamental unifying feature of Islam is its historical experience. Islam is founded on the life and work of Muhammad (570–632), a native of Mecca in Arabia. When he was about forty years of age, Muhammad began to have a strange series of experiences in caves in the mountains where he had gone to meditate. A darkness would come over him, a luminous figure would appear, words would be recited to him. He remembered those words: they became the Koran, the book of God's last and greatest self-revelation to humankind. Its central message is the oneness of God, a message in contrast to the then-prevailing polytheism of Arabia. Muhammad implored his fellow Meccans to accept this message, with little success. But in 622 he went to Medina, and there gathered a following. From then the phenomenal expansion of Islam was underway. Ten years later, at the time of his death, Muhammad and Islam were masters of Arabia; within another century Islamic faith and rule had spread from Spain to India.

Muslims call Muhammad the "seal of the prophets," for he is believed to be the last of a line, the biblical lineage of Abraham, Moses, and Jesus. All prophets were sent to restore the original pure monotheism, religion in its simplest and highest form. In Muhammad and the

Koran, the simplest, and so highest, way to keep the original pure religion of humankind is shown, and so there will need to be no further revelation of it from God until the Day of Judgment.

THE KORAN

This passage from the Holy Koran, which to Muslims is (in the original Arabic) the very words of God and expressive of his personality as well as his message, suggests something of the Koran's tone and content. We here see the vivid and forceful language, and the rapid movement from one theme to another. But we perceive also that the Koran is all centered on one basic revelation: God is absolutely one and absolutely sovereign. Several other motifs basic to Islam appear in this passage: the judgment; the creation of humankind from sperm and clots of blood through the life in the womb; the tortures of the wicked and the paradise of the blessed; the special state of "People of the Book" like Jews, Christians, and Magians (Zoroastrians); the importance of Mecca, with its place of worship established by Abraham, the patriarchal monotheist, at God's command, and its pilgrimage and sacrifice. Finally, we read that the supreme sin is idolatry, and the supreme good is faith in the one God and submission (islam) to him.

From *The Koran Interpreted*

Arthur J. Arberry

THE PILGRIMAGE

In the Name of God, the Merciful, the Compassionate

O men, fear your Lord!
Surely the earthquake of the Hour is a mighty thing;
on the day when you behold it, every suckling woman shall
neglect the child she has suckled, and every pregnant woman
shall deposit her burden, and thou shalt see mankind drunk,
yet they are not drunk, but God's chastisement is terrible.

Arthur J. Arberry, *The Koran Interpreted*, Vol. 2. (London: George Allen & Unwin, 1955), pp. 27–31. Reprinted by permission of the publisher and of Macmillan Publishing Co., Inc.

And among men there is such a one
that disputes concerning God without knowledge
        and follows every rebel Satan,
against whom it is written down that
whosoever takes him for a friend, him he
leads astray, and he guides him to the
        chastisement of the burning.
                        O men,
if you are in doubt as to the Uprising,
        surely We created you of dust
                then of a sperm-drop,
                then of a blood clot,
then of a lump of flesh, formed and unformed
        that We may make clear to you.
        And We establish in the wombs
        what We will, till a stated term,
        then We deliver you as infants,
        then that you may come of age;
                and some of you die,
        and some of you are kept back
unto the vilest state of life, that after
knowing somewhat, they may know nothing.
And thou beholdest the earth blackened,
then, when We send down water upon it,
it quivers, and swells, and puts forth
        herbs of every joyous kind.
That is because God—He is the Truth,
and brings the dead to life, and is powerful
                over everything,
and because the Hour is coming, no doubt of it, and
God shall raise up whosoever is within the tombs.

And among men there is such a one
that disputes concerning God without knowledge
or guidance, or an illuminating Book,
turning his side to lead astray
from God's way; for him is degradation
in this world, and on the Resurrection Day
We shall let him taste the chastisement
        of the burning:
'That is for what thy hands have forwarded
and for that God is never unjust
        unto His servants.'

And among men there is such a one
as serves God upon the very edge—
if good befalls him he is at rest in it,

but if a trial befalls him he turns
completely over; he loses this world
and the world to come; that is indeed
        the manifest loss.
He calls, apart from God, upon that
which hurts him not, and which neither
profits him anything; that is indeed
        the far error.
He calls upon him who is likelier
to hurt him, rather than to profit him—
an evil protector indeed, he,
        an evil friend!

God shall surely admit those who believe
and do righteous deeds into gardens
underneath which rivers flow; surely God does
        that He desires.

Whosoever thinks God will not help him
in the present world and the world to come,
let him stretch up a rope to heaven,
then let him sever it, and behold
whether his guile does away with what
        enrages him.

Even so We have sent it down as signs,
clear signs, and for that God guides
        whom He desires.
Surely they that believe, and those of Jewry,
the Sabaeans, the Christians, the Magians
and the idolaters—God shall distinguish
between them on the Day of Resurrection;
assuredly God is witness
        over everything.
Hast thou not seen how to God bow all who are in the heavens
        and all who are in the earth,
the sun and the moon, the stars and the mountains,
        the trees and the beasts,
and many of mankind? And many merit the chastisement;
        and whom God abases,
there is none to honour him. God does whatsoever He will.

These are two disputants who have disputed
concerning their Lord. As for the unbelievers,
for them garments of fire shall be cut,
and there shall be poured over their heads
        boiling water
whereby whatsoever is in their bellies

and their skins shall be melted; for them await
        hooked iron rods;
as often as they desire in their anguish
to come forth from it, they shall be restored
into it, and: 'Taste the chastisement
        of the burning!'
God shall surely admit those who believe
and do righteous deeds into gardens
underneath which rivers flow; therein
they shall be adorned with bracelets of gold
and with pearls, and their apparel there
        shall be of silk;
and they shall be guided unto goodly speech,
and they shall be guided unto the path
        of the All-laudable.
Those who disbelieve, and bar from God's way
and the Holy Mosque that We have appointed
equal unto men, alike him who cleaves to it
        and the tent-dweller,
and whosoever purposes to violate it
wrongfully, We shall let him taste
        a painful chastisement.

And when We settled for Abraham the place
of the House: 'Thou shall not associate
with Me anything. And do thou purify
My House for those that shall go about it
and those that stand, for those that bow
        and prostrate themselves;
and proclaim among men the Pilgrimage,
and they shall come unto thee on foot
and upon every lean beast, they shall come from
        every deep ravine
that they may witness things profitable to them
and mention God's Name on days well-known
over such beasts of the flocks as He has
provided them: "So eat thereof, and feed
        the wretched poor."
Let them then finish with their self-neglect
and let them fulfil their vows, and go about
        the Ancient House.'
All that; and whosoever venerates
the sacred things of God, it shall be better
for him with his Lord. And permitted
to you are the flocks, except that which is
recited to you. And eschew the abomination

of idols, and eschew the speaking
of falsehood,
being men pure of faith unto God,
not associating with Him anything;
for whosoever associates with God anything,
it is as though he has fallen from heaven
and the birds snatch him away, or the wind
sweeps him headlong into a place
far away.
All that; and whosoever venerates
God's waymarks, that is of the godliness
of the hearts.
There are things therein profitable
to you unto a stated term; thereafter
their lawful place of sacrifice is by
the Ancient House.

We have appointed for every nation
a holy rite, that they may mention
God's Name over such beasts of the flocks
as He has provided them. Your God is One God,
so to Him surrender.

MUHAMMAD

This passage from the work of a distinguished twentieth-century scholar well summarizes a major theme of the religious message of the prophet Muhammad (or Mohammed)—the judgment. The judgment of the last day is the most tremendous expression of the fundamental motif of Islam, God's absolute oneness and sovereignty.

From *Muhammad: The Man and his Faith*

Tor Andrae

MOHAMMED'S RELIGIOUS MESSAGE

The basic conviction of Mohammed's preaching, and the heart of his prophetic message, is the certainty that he alone, in the midst of a

Tor Andrae, *Muhammad: The Man and his Faith* (New York: Charles Scribner's Sons, 1936), pp. 71–76. Reprinted by permission of George Allen & Unwin Ltd.

light-headed and thoughtless generation, sees the fateful event which awaits all of those who are now jesting and laughing so carelessly. The threatening storm-cloud which already darkens the horizon, the disaster which seems so near that he regards himself as the "naked messenger," or the courier who arrives in tattered garments to give warning of the catastrophe which is already about to strike, is the *last day*—the day of judgment and retribution.

For him the Day of Judgment is not an occurrence far off in the hazy uncertain future, belonging to a different sphere from that of mundane events. It is a reality which is threateningly near. He speaks of it in the present tense. He seems to see how the heavens are being folded back above the heads of his careless countrymen, and how the black mountains of lava surrounding the city are collapsing like rubbish-heaps in terror before the advent of the Judge. Of course, Mohammed never stated directly that the judgment would fall upon his own generation, but rather that Allah alone knows when it will fall, and that no one, not even the Prophet, can say whether it is immediately impending. But, on the other hand, he often shows that he regarded it as possible that he himself might yet experience it.

His listeners misunderstood his use of the prophetic present tense. Days, months, and years passed, and the catastrophe did not arrive. They believed his prophecy to be false. "When will the day really arrive which you have proclaimed?" his enemies scornfully inquired. To some extent the Prophet himself was to blame for this misunderstanding. For from the very beginning he spoke, in connection with his prophecy of the judgment, of actual punishments which God had inflicted upon godless cities and nations that refused to believe the warnings of the prophets. Like Christian preachers, Mohammed regarded these earthly punishments as precursors and preliminary steps to the final great judgment. And when he spoke of the flood, of thunderbolts, and of cyclones which came upon the generation of Noah and the generations of other prophets of old, he always concluded with a warning to his own nation: "Thus shall the day of judgment come also upon this generation." It was not until his last days in Mecca that the Prophet, now in utter despair over the unbelief of his countrymen, began definitely to suggest that Allah was preparing a special punishment for the rebellious cities, a punishment which would occur even before the day of judgment.

What the merchants of Mecca could not understand, and what certain learned Orientalists of our own day also find it hard to understand, is that Mohammed had no desire to be an apocalyptic seer, or a clairvoyant who foretells the exact time of the advent of the day of judgment. The present tense which he used expressed the unshakable certainty of his religious faith. The important thing for him is not *when* the day is coming, but the certainty that it *will* come. Man should so live, think, and act as though that day were already visible to the eye, being more certain of its reality than of anything else in this transient world.

In short and breathlessly stormy sentences, often with poetic rhythm

and power, the earliest Suras of the Koran describe the great day of judgment, and the retribution which is sure to follow it. But the Prophet does
not portray the events in a definite sequence as does a theologian who sets
forth a dogmatic creed. He speaks as a messenger whose purpose is to
awaken and to grip his listeners. In these scattered lines we see passing
before us, as in a panorama, the tremendous imaginative religious experience which inspired the heart and conscience of Mohammed and made
him a prophet.

A horrible natural catastrophe to which Mohammed gives various
mysterious names—such as a thunderclap, a cry, a crash—will usher in the
judgment. Either it will come simultaneously with a trumpet-sound which
will call men before the Judge, or the trumpet-sound will produce it. The
earth will be shaken by a terrific earthquake; it will be torn open, and
will reveal what is hidden in its very depths. The mountains will be
moved from their places; they will fuse together as in a mirage, will col-
lapse into dust and ashes. The heavenly vault will totter and break, showing gaping fissures, or will be rolled up like a scroll. The edges of the disc
of the sun will bend together, the moon will split apart and be darkened,
the stars will be extinguished, and will fall in myriads to the ground.
Thus Mohammed believed that the end of the world would be heralded
by a tremendous earthquake. Further, the idea of a world conflagration
is not absent from his thought. The heavens "will give out a palpable
Smoke" (44, 9) and a bright flash of fire, and molten brass will be hurled
down upon men (55, 35).

At the first sound of the trumpet all living men, except a few of the
very elect, will fall stunned to the ground. At the second sound of the
trumpet all will arise, and the dead will emerge from their graves. The
resurrection will occur in the twinkling of an eye. Quickly, "as in a race,"
the dead will leave their graves.

Behind the heavens, which have fallen down or have been rolled
back, the throne of Allah will appear, borne by eight angels. The heavenly hosts will stand ranked in columns, and all men will gather before
the throne. The good will be placed on the right, and the wicked on the
left. Amid oppressive silence the trial will begin, and will be based upon
the notes which are written in the Book of Deeds. Pious men will receive
mild treatment, but sinners will be treated with the strictest justice. Their
dark, dusty, and gloomy faces will speak against them, whereas the faces
of the just will be radiant with joy because they are permitted to meet
their Lord. No man can deny his sins. In addition to the words of the
Book, the bodily members of the sinners, their hands, their feet, and their
tongues, will testify against them. But Allah will watch carefully to see
that no soul receives unjust treatment. The prophets will be called forth,
and they will testify that they proclaimed their messages of warning. Thus
no man will be able to make the excuse that he was not warned. Sinners
will seek in vain to place the blame upon the *jinn*—the devils who are
supposed to have enticed them to idolatry. For the *jinn* will desert their
former disciples, and will assert that these men have worshipped idols

absolutely of their own free will. In their despair the unfortunate will seek help; but all in vain. In the judgment no soul can bear the burden of another; a father will not be able to do anything for his son, nor a brother for his brother. The doctrine of the mediation of the Prophet, according to which he will save each one of his disciples "in whose heart there is only a speck of goodness," is not confirmed by the Koran. There it is often stated that no mediation will be permitted and that none will avail on the day of judgment. There is only one hint that "with Allah's permission" mediation may be possible, and in this case the angels are apparently thought of as the mediators.

ISLAMIC PHILOSOPHY

This passage from the work of al-Ghazali (1058–1111), the greatest of the philosophic theologians of Islam, well expresses the Muslim experience of God's absolute oneness and sovereign power. Because God is absolutely different from anything created, al-Ghazali taught God cannot be known by natural means but only by revelation from himself. The "major" revelation is the scripture, the Koran, and "minor" revelations can be found in the saints of God in all generations. Al-Ghazali started as a young man in skepticism, went through the study of philosophy, and ended with the mystical Islam of the Sufis. He found himself in the end thrown back on divine revelation only. Even the highest revelation, he realized, cannot show us the very being of God, God as he knows himself. For God is unique—absolutely different from anything else—in every respect, and our intellects cannot comprehend such a thing as that, although the mystic saints can come to it in their own way. But revelation can at least show us God's will, the fundamental aspect of God we are capable of knowing.

The passage below is from a short exposition by al-Ghazali of the Muslim "creed"—"There is no god but God, and Muhammad is his envoy."

From *Development of Muslim Theology, Jurisprudence and Constitutional Theory*

Duncan B. MacDonald

We say—and in God is our trust—Praise belongeth unto God, the Beginner, the Bringer back, the Doer of what He willeth, the Lord of the

Duncan B. MacDonald, *Development of Muslim Theology, Jurisprudence and Constitutional Theory* (New York: Charles Scribner's Sons, 1903), pp. 300, 302–03.

Glorious Throne and of Mighty Grasp, the Guider of His chosen creatures to the right path and to the true way, the Granter of benefits to them after the witness to the Unity (*tawhid*) by guarding their articles of belief from obscurities of doubt and opposition, He that bringeth them to follow His Apostle, the Chosen one (*al-Mustafa*), and to imitate the traces of his Companions, the most honored, through His aid and right guidance revealed to them in His essence and His works by His beautiful qualities which none perceives, save he who inclines his ear. He is the witness who maketh known to them that He in His essence is One without any partner (*sharik*). Single without any similar, Eternal without any opposite, Separate without any like. He is One, Prior (*qadim*) with nothing before Him, from eternity (*azali*) without any beginning, abiding in existence with none after Him, to eternity (*abadi*) without any end, subsisting without ending, abiding without termination. He hath not ceased and He will not cease to be described with glorious epithets; finishing and ending, through the cutting off of the ages and the terminating of allotted times, have no rule over Him, but He is the First and Last, the External and the Internal, and He knoweth everything. . . .

. . . We witness that He is a Willer of the things that are, a Director of the things that happen; there does not come about in the world, seen or unseen, little or much, small or great, good or evil, advantage or disadvantage, faith or unbelief, knowledge or ignorance, success or loss, increase or diminution, obedience or rebellion, except by His will. What He wills is, and what He wills not is not. Not a glance of one who looks, or a slip of one who thinks is outside of His will: He is the Creator, the Bringer back, the Doer of that which He wills. There is no opponent of His command and no repeater of His destiny and no refuge for a creature from disobeying Him, except by His help and His mercy, and no strength to a creature to obey Him except by His will. Even though mankind and the Jinn and the Angels and the Shaytans were to unite to remove a single grain in the world or to bring it to rest without His will, they would be too weak for that. His will subsists in His essence as one of His qualities; He hath not ceased to be described through it as a Willer, in His infinity, of the existence of things at their appointed times which He hath decreed. So they come into existence at their appointed times even as He has willed in His infinity without precedence or sequence. They happen according to the agreement of His knowledge and His will, without exchange or change in planning of things, nor with arranging of thoughts or awaiting of time, and therefore one thing does not distract Him from another.

ISLAMIC MYSTICISM

The spirit of the Sufis, as Westerners generally call the Muslim mystics who experience the oneness of God through devotion and ecstasy,

*is best expressed in their poetic writing. Here we see examples from
the work of Jalal al-din Rumi (1207–73), one of the most brilliant of the
writing mystics. Note that he uses highly sensuous imagery, and also
the image of the Ka'ba or place of pilgrimage in Mecca, but transmutes
their meaning to express the spiritual relation of the devotee to God.
Jalal al-din Rumi was born in Balkh, now western Afghanistan, but later
went to Konya in Turkey. He was not only a poet but also a practitioner
of mystical techniques who instituted the whirling dances, which perhaps began the tradition of dancing dervishes or devotees in Islam. He
founded the Sufi order of Maulavis, or "Whirling Dervishes."*

From *Readings from the Mystics of Islam*
Margaret Smith

O hidden One, Who yet dost fill the world from East to West and
art high above the light of the sun and moon. Thou Thyself art a
mystery, yet Thou dost reveal our inmost secrets. Thou dost cause the
rivers to flow forth, by Thy power. O Thou Whose Essence is hidden,
while Thy gifts are manifest, Thou art like the water, while we are
like the mill-stone: Thou art as the wind and we as the dust. The wind
is concealed and the dust it produces is manifest to all. Thou art the
Spring, we are like a garden fresh and fair: the spring is not seen, but
its gifts are evident. Thou art as the spirit, we are as the hand and foot:
the grasping and loosing of the hand are by the will of the spirit. Thou
art like the reason, we like the tongue: the tongue takes its power to
speak from the reason. Thou art as joy and we as laughter, for the result
of joy is our laughter. All our actions are a profession of faith, for they
bear witness to the glory of the Everlasting God.

O heart, why do you lie bound in this transient world? Fly out
from this cramped space, for you are a bird that belongs to the world
of spirits. You are a friend that would always be alone, with the Beloved,
abiding behind the veil of mystery. Why do you stay in this world, which
is passing away? Consider what state you are in, escape from your captivity in this material world and go forth to the grassy lawns of spiritual
reality. You belong to the Divine world, you would be welcome in the
assembly of Love: it would be grievous for you to remain in this abode.
Each morning there comes a voice from heaven calling: "You will find
the road clear for passage, when you make the dust to lie on it." On the

Margaret Smith, *Readings from the Mystics of Islam* (London: Luzac & Company, 1950), pp. 102–03, 104–05, 109. Reprinted by permission of the publisher.

way to the *Ka'ba* of union with Him, you will see at the root of every thorn, thousands who gave up their young lives for the sake of love. Thousands fell wounded on this road and there did not come to them any breath of the fragrance of union, or sign from the abode of the Beloved. . . .

. . . Every form which you see has its original in the Divine world, where is no place. If the form passes away, it is of no consequence, since its original was from eternity. Be not grieved that every form which you see, every mystical saying which you have heard, has passed away, because that is not so. Since the fountain-head is abiding, its channel is always bringing forth water. Since neither ceases, why should you complain? Consider the spirit as a fountain and these creatures as rivers: while the fountain remains, the rivers flow from it. Put regret out of your thoughts and keep on drinking from the rivulet. Do not be afraid that the water will cease to flow: for this water is limitless.

From that time when you came into the world of created beings, a ladder was set before you, so that you might pass out of it. At first you were inanimate, then you became a plant: afterwards you were changed into an animal: why should this be hidden from you? At last you became man, possessed of knowledge, intelligence and faith. See how that body has become perfect, which was at first an atom from the dust-heap. When you have made your journey from man, without question you will become an angel. Then you will have finished with this world and your place will be in the heavens. Be changed also from the station of an angel: pass into that mighty deep: so that the one drop, which is yourself, may become a sea which would hold a hundred seas of 'Umān. Give up this polytheism of yours, say "God is One" with your whole heart and soul. If your body has become old, why grieve when your spirit is young?

By love bitter things are made sweet: copper turns to gold. By love, the sediment becomes clear: by love torment is removed. By love the dead is made to live: by love the sovereign is made a slave. This love also is the fruit of knowledge: when did folly sit on a throne like this?— The faith of love is separated from all religion: for lovers the faith and the religion is God. . O spirit, in striving and seeking, become like running water: O reason, at all times be ready to give up mortality for the sake of immortality. Remember God always, that self may be forgotten, so that your self may be effaced in the One to Whom you pray, without care for who is praying, or the prayer. . . .

. . . O lovers, the time has come to depart from the world: the drum is sounding in the ear of my spirit, calling us to the journey. Behold, the camel-driver has bestirred himself and set his camels in their ranks and desires us to let him start. Why are you still sleeping, O travellers? These sounds which we hear from before and behind betoken travel, for they are the camel-bells. Each moment that passes, a soul is passing out of life and starting for the Divine world. From these gleaming stars and from these blue curtains of the heavens, have come forth a wondrous people, so that marvellous things of mystery may be made known. From these revolving orbs came a heavy sleep to you: beware of this so-transient life, have a care of this heavy sleep. O heart, depart towards the Beloved, O friend, go to your Friend. O watchman, keep awake, for sleep is not becoming to a watchman.

A DERVISH ORDER

Here is a nineteenth-century account of the Maulavi order founded by Jalal al-din Rumi, as it was in Constantinople (Istanbul), Turkey. The takia, *or local lodge of the order, is essentially a closely knit society of laymen gathered around a spiritual master called the shaikh or pir. Some men in the society lived an almost monkish life as close disciples of the master in the lodge. The Qabiri is a comparable order. Orders and spiritual leaders like these have had an immense role in spreading and popularizing Islam. Note the integration of the normal Islamic devotions done by everyone into the more elaborate and ecstatic practice of the order. Note also the reference to God as the Friend both in the poetry of Jalal and the cries of his order.*

From *The Darvishes*
John P. Brown

The *Hazrat-i-Maulavī*, viz. Jalāl-ud-Dīn, stated that he was not of the body which the *'āshiqs* or devout 'lovers' of God beheld; "Perhaps I am that Joy and Delight which the *murīds* experience when they cry out, 'Allāh! Allāh!' therefore seek that delight and taste of that joy; hold to it as to riches, and be thankful that it is me". He once is said to have remarked that a bird which flies upward does not reach the skies, yet it rises far above the roof of the house, and so escapes. So it is with one who becomes a Darvish, and though he does not become a perfect Darvish, still he becomes far superior to common men, and far exalted above ordinary beings. He likewise becomes freed from worldly cares and anxieties, and is exhilarated above all ordinary human sensations.

John P. Brown, *The Darvishes* (London: Frank Cass & Co., Ltd., 1968), pp. 251–53. Originally published 1868. Reprinted with permission of the publisher.

Each *takia* of every Order of Darvishes has a particular day or days in the week for the performance of the religious exercises of the brethren. As there are several *takias* of the same Order in Constantinople, the brethren of one are thus enabled to visit and take part in the ceremonies of the others. The brethren of other Orders frequently join in the services of the *takias* not their own, nothing forbidding it, except, as with the Maulavīs, the want of practice and skill.

A Qādirī who can perform the services of a Maulavī, on entering a *takia* of the latter, goes to the *hujra,* or cell, of one of the brethren, and receives a cap called a *sikka,* or cap made in a 'mould', from which it takes this name. It is made of camel's hair, or otherwise wool; he also receives a *tannūra,* which is a long skirt like that of a lady's dress, without arms, and a *dasta gul* (literally a bouquet of roses), or a jacket with sleeves made of cloth or other material; around his waist is fastened the *alif-lām-and,* or girdle of cloth some four fingers in width, one and a half *archins*[1] in length, edged with a thread (*chārit*[2]), and a piece of the same at its ends serves to tie it round the body; over the shoulders is thrown a *khirqa* or cloak (mantle), with long and large sleeves, and thus equipped he enters into the hall of the *takia,* called *samā'-khāna.*

With regard to their services, it may be said—1. that they all perform the usual *Islām namāz*; 2. that they offer up certain prayers, of the same character; 3. the Shaikh proceeds to his seat, his book lying in the direction of the *qibla* (that of Makka); then standing upright, he raises his hands, and offers a prayer for the *pīr,* asking his intercession with God and the Prophet in behalf of the Order.

4. The Shaikh then leaves his *pōstakī,* or sheepskin seat, and bends his head in humility to the *pīr* towards the side of the *pōstakī,* and then makes one step forward, and turning again towards the same seat on his right foot, bows to the same, as that of the *pīr,* were he in existence. After this he continues round the hall, and the brethren, in turn, do the same, all going round three times. This ceremony is called the *Sultān Walad Daurī,* after the son of *Hazrat-i-Maulānā,* their founder or *pīr.*

5. The Shaikh next takes his position, standing in the *pōstakī,* his hands crossed before him, and one of the brethren in the *mutrib*[3] (upstairs) commences to chant a *na't-i-sharīf,*[4] or holy hymn, in praise of the Prophet. At its termination the little orchestra in the gallery commences

---

[1]Archin, for Turk. *arshūn* or *arshīn,* an ell, about 28 or 29 inches in length.
[2]Chārit, doubtless Turk. sharīt, 'a ribbon or strip'. In Arabic *sharīt* means a rope made of palm bark fibre.
[3]Mutrib = 'minstrel' or 'singer', or who or what causes to 'dance and skip'. On p. 257 *infra mutrīb* is translated 'place of excitement', but the dictionaries give no noun of place from *tariba,* 'was excited' (cf. Johnson, p. 1202). The word should apparently be *mutrib-khāna,* 'musicians' room' (Evliya, i. p. 181).
[4]Na't, lit. 'laud' : *na't* = 'encomium'.

performing on the flutes (called *nāis*), the *kamāns*[5] and *qudūrs*[6] (the latter small drums).

6. One of the brethren, called the *samā'-zan*, goes to the Shaikh, who has proceeded to the edge of his seat, and bows to him, his right foot passing over the other—kisses the hand of the Shaikh, recedes backwards from him, and standing in the middle of the hall, acts as a director of the ceremonies about to commence.

7. The other Darvishes now take off their *khirqas*,—let fall their *tannūrīs*,—go in single file to the Shaikh, kiss his hand, make an obeisance to the *pōstakī*, and commence turning round on the left foot, pushing themselves round with the right. If they happen to approach too near each other, the *samā'-zan* stamps his foot on the floor as a signal. Gradually the arms of the performers are raised upward, and then extended outward, the left hand turned to the floor, and the right open, upward to heaven; the head inclined over the right shoulder, and the eyes apparently closed. The Shaikh, in the meantime, stands still on his *pōstakī*. The brethren, whilst turning round, continually mutter the inaudible *zikr*, saying *Allāh! Allāh!* and the musicians play for some twenty minutes or half an hour, chanting a hymn called the *'ain-i-sharīf*. Often they perform only some ten minutes, when having reached a certain part of the chant, in which are the words *Hai Yār!* (O Friend!), they cry it out loudly, and suddenly cease. The Darvishes below at the same time stop in their course, so that the *tannūra* wraps around their legs, so as to quite conceal their feet, and all inclining lowly, perform obeisance again to the Shaikh. The *samā'-zan* taking the lead, they all march slowly round the hall, bowing low to the Shaikh, turning completely round as they pass him. If any fall, overcome by the performance, this repose affords them an opportunity to withdraw, which some few do; soon after this the music recommences, and the same performance is renewed until arrested as before. This is done three times, after which they all sit down, and the *samā'-zan* covers them with their mantles.

ISLAMIC LAW

Islam, submission to God, is guided for the faithful Muslim by an extensive legal tradition which shows how this submission is to be made in all areas of life; acceptance of the authoritative guidance of the law is inseparable from being a Muslim and a part of the Islamic community. The law was built up gradually over the years through the work of codi-

---

[5]Kamān, in Turk. 'a violin'.
[6]Qudūr, pl. of *qidr*, lit. 'a pot or kettle'.

fying lawyers. It was based on four sources: the Koran *itself;* traditions *about the practice and sayings of the prophet to illuminate matters not clear or not mentioned in the Koran; the* consensus *of the whole Muslim community, which was held to be correct when truly unanimous, and, when consensus cannot be obtained, the agreement of the preponderance of reputable authorities; and finally* analogy—*determining the law for a new situation by finding the closest parallel to it in the precedents.*

The following passage is from a handbook of Islamic law compiled by a Russian nobleman of the last century who governed for the czar a province by the Caspian Sea containing many Muslims. It shows something of the tone of Islamic law, and deals with salat, *or the prayer done five times daily, which is one of the Five Pillars of Islam. This prayer-practice begins with purifying oneself with water, or sand if none is available, and is done in a prescribed manner, with several deep bows or prostrations, facing in the direction of Mecca. It centers verbally on the opening lines of the Koran, a short ascription of praise to God and petition that he may "guide us in the straight path." It is an act of formal* islam *or submission, in essence, rather than a prayer for particular benefits; it follows definite form and faces Mecca because it is a rite of membership in the community of Islam and a formal expression of one's own submission. It should be remembered that Islam also teaches that one should pray inwardly freely wherever he is and whatever he is doing, and that God is really everywhere, not just in Mecca.*

From *Le Droit Musulman*

Nicolas de Tornauw

Prayer is the most important of all the practices of the Muslim religion; it is only by prayer that the soil is purified and approaches near the throne of God.

Rules concerning the manner of the formal prayer are distinguished according to whether they deal with what is done before or during the prayer. In jurisprudence they are called respectively *tos we mek* and *ken ters,* words which do not mean anything in themselves, but are composed of the first letters or syllables of the most important and imperative of the precepts about prayer. . . .

Before formal prayer, one must:

    I. Purify oneself.

    II. Remove himself from all impure things.

From Nicolas de Tornauw, *Le Droit Musulman.* Translated from Russian into French by M. Eschbach. (Paris: Cotillon, 1860). Translated from French by R.S.E. Some Arabic and Persian terminology omitted.

Observation of these two points is absolutely prescribed; failure in the same renders the prayer useless, or contrary to the law. . . **III.** Be covered during prayer with proper clothing. For men, it suffices that during prayer they cover the sexual parts. But women must be completely dressed, even to not allowing the face, the hands, or the feet up to the ankles to be visible,

The clothing ought to have these qualities:

1. Be the legitimate property of the one praying;
2. Be free of all impurity;
3. Not made of the skin or hair or an animal reputed impure. [e.g. the pig, which Muslims are not to eat];
4. Not made of pure silk; and finally
5. Without any special ornamentation.

It is not permitted to wear ornaments made of gold, silver, or precious stones during prayer.

IV. Prayers are ordinarily made daily; there may also be special prayers.

The times daily for prayer are five in number. But a qualification can be made regarding these times. The recitation of the formal prayers at the prescribed times is considered the exact following of the written rules, and is spoken of as the "preference" or the "sublimity." But if against his will the believer is hindered by his occupation or physical impediment from praying at the prescribed times, the recitation of the prayers at other times is just as meritorious.

The five daily prayers are:

1. The prayer at noon.
2. The prayer at the setting of the sun, before it has completely disappeared.
3. The prayer after the setting of the sun, from dusk to dark.
4. The prayer before midnight.
5. The prayer before sunrise.

Besides these prayers there are:

1. The Friday Prayers.

These prayers are recited at noon on Fridays, amid the gathering of many believers in the principal mosque of each town by the clergyman called the imām. His function is to begin the prayers of the faithful gathered in the mosque, who then continue on their own.

The local imam is chosen by the highest spiritual authority, a superior imām who holds temporal and spiritual power, or if there is none the sovereign of the country, or someone delegated by him. According to the book *Kadi Chan*, the sovereign ought to be a Muslim of good morals; according to other authors, the nomination of the local imām always pertains to the sovereign, unless he is not a Muslim. If it is impossible to obtain the nomination of an imam by the sovereign, the people name him according to their own inclination, and the Friday prayers will still be legal, but such an election of an imām should subsequently be ratified by the sovereign.

The local imām should be of age, possessed of all his intellectual faculties, of free birth, male, and capable of reciting the prescribed prayers precisely and distinctly. Opinion is divided on the point of whether he must be of good morals; the best opinion prefers that the local imām be of conspicuous piety and irreproachable conduct. Among the Shiites, this condition is rigorously required. However, the nomination by the sovereign of an unworthy subject to this function, who is nonetheless able to recite the Friday prayers, imposes on all Muslims the obligation to recognize him as the local imām, and to admit the perfect legality of these prayers and recitations. . . .

> 2. The prayers on the two feast days, that which falls on the tenth day of the month of pilgrimage to Mecca, and the day immediately after the fast of Ramadan.
> 3. Prayers in time of catastrophe, for example, in time of earthquakes, hurricanes, avalanches, tempests, etc.
> 4. Prayers recited over the dead, at the place of burial before the body is interred.
> 5. Prayers during the pilgrimage.
> 6. Prayers in fulfillment of vows, for aid and assistance, etc.

V. The place of formal prayer ought to be in its nature pure and authorized by the law. Preferred above all other places is one specially set aside for prayer, as the mosque, or places that are not private property such as a desert or an uncultivated field. It is not permitted to pray on private property without the consent of the owner.

The place of prayer ought to be pure, above all the place where the forehead touches in prostration. It is best for the forehead to touch the ground or objects especially consecrated. [This explains the special prayer mats or rugs commonly used by Muslims.]

Men and women may pray together; nonetheless the women ought to be separated from the men, and to take places behind the latter. It is forbidden for a man to look at a woman during prayer; this dissipates his thoughts, disturbs his recollection, and renders the prayer ineffective.

These are the restrictions to be observed regarding the choice of a place intended for prayer:

> 1. It is forbidden to prayer where the dead are interred, and at the least the place where the forehead touches the ground must be no less than ten paces from a tomb. But among the Shiites, it is permitted to pray at the tombs of imams, although one must take care to have the tomb at one's back.

2. If one must pray on a public road one should place something in front of him to keep the traffic passing by from disturbing his prayers.

3. It is forbidden to pray in a stable or a place intended as a shelter for animals, or

4. In a place where people gather to eat or drink, or to enjoy wine; or in a place where wine is kept; or in general in any place where forbidden things occur.

5. Finally, prayer is not permitted while moving on horseback, or operating a ship, etc.

Also one ought not to have near him any illuminated lamp or fire when he prays. These should be at some distance or placed behind him. One is counseled to recite his prayers at different places in the house or mosque, for then at the Last Judgment these different places will testify that these prayers have been recited.

Concerning the direction during prayer, *kebleh*, the Muslim ought to have his face turned toward the *kaaba*, that is, toward the temple of Mecca. This direction is fixed for each different place by the calculations of the clergy and the astronomers.

RAMADAN

One of the five pillars of Islam obligatory on all Muslims is keeping of fast of Ramadan, when no food or drink is taken during the day. At night meals are eaten, and the pious try to rest during the day and spend the night in eating, religious study, and prayer, often in small groups. The end of Ramadan is marked by a great festival. Here is an account of the practice.

From *Muslim Institutions*

Maurice Gaudefoy-Demombynes

Pre-Islamic Arabia had no religion sufficiently organised to provide for any sort of ritual fasting. It knew only those abstentions from food

Maurice Gaudefoy-Demombynes, *Muslim Institutions* (New York: Barnes and Noble, 1950), pp. 102–04. Reprinted by permission of Barnes and Noble, Inc., and of George Allen & Unwin Ltd.

or wine that were imposed by religious tabus, or adopted in consequence of individual vows. Muhammad, at the beginning of his residence in Medina, that is to say, at the time when he counted on the conversion of the Jews, prescribed the fast of '*Ashūrā*', which copied the Jewish fast of *tishri*. When Muhammad had broken with the Medina Jews, the Muslim fast, under the influence of the Christian Quadragesima, was turned into an abstinence of one lunar month's duration, that of *ramadān*, which, in the old Arab calendar with its solar corrections, fell in Summer, but which, by the time the fast came to be properly organised, had slowly moved back towards Winter. Muhammad did not foresee that the Muslim calendar would continue to move ramadān through the whole course of the year, nor that the severe obligation of a complete daily fast (*saum*) would coincide, by thirty year cycles, with the longest days of the year.

From sunrise till sunset, more precisely, taking as the limit the instant in which it is possible to distinguish a white thread from a black one, or, according to one interpretation, a line of light on the horizon against the darkness of the sky as a whole, the believer is required to abstain entirely from food, drink, tobacco, perfumes, etc., as well as from sexual relations. But, during the night, all prohibitions are removed, and the faithful, wearied by long abstinence, make the best possible use of their recovered liberty. Needless to insist on the depressing consequences of such a régime, especially when enforced on men who work during the day. All Europeans who have maintained regular relations with the Muslim world are aware of the physical and mental effects of the fast of Ramadān.

The opening of the month of Ramadān is fixed, as in the case of all other months, by the appearance of the new moon. The beginning of the fast, and also its end, are, therefore, dependent on an astronomical observation that no previous forecast can replace. The state of the atmosphere, not to speak of an astronomic delay that could be foreseen, sometimes makes impossible or difficult the direct observation of the event. It is permissible to accept the affirmation of two trustworthy witnesses. But, in the towns, it is the religious authority, usually the qādī, who gives a definite decision. Local circumstances can give rise to disputes on this point between personages of equal authority. The fast can thus last for twenty-eight, twenty-nine, or, at most, thirty days.

In the towns the exact instants of the beginning and end of the fast are announced each morning and evening by the appearance of a green flag on the tops of the minarets of the mosques, and by a cannon shot. After the evening signal, it is customary to break the fast by a light meal called *fatūr*, and to end the night with a last collation, the "dawn meal" (*ṣaḥūr*). A special crier, called *muwaqqit* or *musaḥḥir*, announces, in the towns, the last hour at which this repast may be taken.

The fast is obligatory only on adults in full possession of their physical and mental faculties, *'āqil, bāligh*. Are exempt, therefore, the sick, feeble old men, pregnant or nursing women. For other reasons a dispensation is given to travellers. But such dispensations are not irrevocable and, as soon as material conditions permit, the believer must accomplish his fast throughout any other month, or give expiatory alms (*fidya*). The voluntary violation of the sexual tabu is paid for by the freeing of a slave, or by a fast of two months, or by feeding sixty poor persons.

In the accomplishment of the fast, as in every other duty of Islam, it is the intention (*nīya*) of the faster that counts. The mosques are specially well attended during the month of Ramadān. In the evening, after the Prayer of the *'ishā'*, the faithful gather in groups and, led by an imām, say a Prayer of at least twenty *raka'āt*, of which each group of four is separated by a pause. Hence its name, *salāt al-tarāwīh*. It is accompanied by recitations from the Qur'ān and pious conversation, which may last until dawn. Some writers, Ibn Jubayr for example, have described these ceremonies interspersed with meals, which the faithful return home to eat, or have brought to them in the mosques.

Tradition asserts that the fast was instituted in Ramadān because it is during this month that the Revelation (*tanzīl*, Q. 2.181) "came down" to the earth, more exactly in the night of fate, *laylat al-qadr* (Q. 97, 1–3), in which, in popular belief, human destiny is determined for the whole year. The date of the night of fate is not precisely indicated. Consequently, the nights of the days of odd numbers, from the 21st to the 27th of Ramadān and especially this last day, are honoured by invocations and Qur'ānic recitations.

The "breaking" of the fast, which occurs on the first of the month of *Shawwāl*, is the occasion of a feast, *'īd al-fitr,* called in the Maghrib the Little Feast, *al 'īd al-saghīr*. Like the Great Feast of the tenth of *dhu l-hijja*, the feast of the breaking of the fast involving a solemn Prayer, called *salāt al-'īd*, consisting of two *raka'āt* with numerous *takbīr* and two *khutba*.

It is on that day that the statutory alms that mark the breaking of the fast must be given (*zakāt al-fitr*), which must not be confounded with the *zakāl* properly so called, of which we shall speak in the next chapter. Each head of a family must, in respect of each individual for whom he is responsible, give to the poor a *sā'a* of four *mudd* of the customary food of the country.

The feast is the occasion of domestic rejoicings that continue for three days. New clothes are worn. People congratulate and embrace each other.

The feast of Ramadān is one of the most living institutions of Islam. Muslim towns observe it strictly, and public opinion judges severely any individuals who seek secretly to avoid it.

THE HAJJ

Perhaps the pillar of Islam best known to non-Muslims is the Hajj, the obligation of all Muslims who are able to make a pilgrimage once in a lifetime to Mecca. Islamic tradition makes Mecca, in Saudi Arabia, the place where the creation of the world began, where Abraham, the paradigm of true primal monotheism, built his shrine, and where the prophet received the Koranic revelation renewing and confirming that ancient faith. The importance of Mecca and the Hajj in unifying Islam can hardly be overestimated. As hundreds of thousands of pilgrims stand together on the slopes of Mt. Arafat, where Muhammad preached on his last visit to the holy city, Islam is truly visible as a vast army drawn out of many peoples but united in obedience to God.

From *The Hajj: An Appreciation*

Ismail Ibrahim Nawwab

In response to God's injunction to mankind prescribing the Pilgrimage to Mecca (the Koran, Sura III, verse 97), countless followers of Islam, rising yearly from the global ocean of humanity, have sallied forth to make the Hajj for almost 14 centuries. Considering the uniqueness of this phenomenon, with its rich kaleidoscope of symbol and significance, appearance and reality, past and present, and the innate, almost universal barrier to empathy in religious matters, few non-Muslims can be expected to have any inkling of what the Pilgrimage really means to the believer.

What *does* the Hajj mean? Is it a sterile ritual? A formality, perhaps? Or, as one of the five pillars of Islam—that is, one of the requirements imposed on Muslims—is it merely an obligation to be discharged as quickly and perfunctorily as possible?

Nothing could be further from the truth. Indeed, it is no exaggeration to say that the Hajj, to the average Muslim, is the emotive goal and the climactic experience of his temporal existence. It is a form of spiritual

Ismail Ibrahim Nawwab, "The Hajj: An Appreciation," *Aramco World Magazine*, 25, No. 6 (Nov.–Dec. 1974), 12–13. Reprinted by permission of Arabian American Oil Company.

fulfillment which he shares and simultaneously celebrates with the entire world of Islam. But to explain why—and to attain some understanding of the symbolism and function of the Hajj—one must go back to the historical and sociological highlights of the Islamic traditions in which its origins are embedded.

It all begins with Abraham.

In Islam, Abraham—the same Old Testament Abraham familiar to Judaism and Christianity—plays an important role. He is regarded as a prophet and venerated as a zealous advocate of monotheism, as a relentless foe of idolatry and as builder of the Ka'bah, "the House of God," focal point for Muslim worship of the One God. With respect to the Hajj specifically, Abraham, his son Ishmael and his wife Hagar are central to some of its holiest rites.

But the Hajj only *begins* with Abraham; it is affirmed by Muhammad, the Prophet of Islam, who, in making the Pilgrimage begun by Abraham, found that it had degenerated into a soulless idolatrous ritual and purged it. To Muslims this continuous monotheistic strand holding together the time of Abraham and the era of Muhammad is a symbol of the unity of God which permeates Muslim religious thought. Thus the yearning to behold, at least once in their lifetime, the pivotal Ka'bah, the center of the cosmos and *Qiblah* or focus of all prayer, symbolizes to a Muslim humanity's movement toward unity in the quest for God.

The rites of the Hajj—which are precisely those followed or approved by Muhammad during his Pilgrimage—are few in number, simple in execution, but rich in meaning. The major ones are: Donning the *Ihram*, "the Circling" of the Ka'bah, "the Running" at al-Mas'a and "the Standing" at 'Arafat. Other essential rites include Throwing the Pebbles and the Sacrifice. Since the Prophet of Islam did allow his disciples some flexibility in ritual sequence during the Pilgrimage, the order and even the manner in which these rites are performed can vary. The believer is thus free to follow the sequence most convenient to him as long as he is guided by the practice of the Prophet and his Companions.

The first rite of the Hajj is Donning the *Ihram*, a physical manifestation of the pilgrim's entering into a state of consecration. This act is accompanied by the uttering of the *Talbiyah*. This phrase, "Doubly at Thy service, O God," is a Declaration of Pilgrimage and is frequently repeated during the Hajj.

"The Circling" (*Tawaf*) of the Ka'bah in the vast courtyard of the Sacred Mosque in Mecca signifies that the Muslim's life must focus on unity—the unity of God and mankind. Neither the Ka'bah nor the Black Stone it contains are objects of worship. Although Muslims do kiss the Black Stone, this is done only to cherish the memory of the Prophet, who planted his kiss on it.

The ceremonial procession, or "the Running," between the hillocks of al-Safa and al-Marwa in Mecca is a reenactment of Hagar's frantic search for water for her infant Ishmael when they were lost in the desert;

it commemorates the anguished love of motherhood and the decisive role of womankind in history.

The hours passed at 'Arafat on the ninth day of *Dhu al-Hijjah*, the month of the Pilgrimage, are precious. They are devoted to profound self-examination of the ends and means of a Muslim's earthly existence, to sincere application, to genuine repentance for one's sins, and to moving prayers for the dead and the living. At no other place and on no other occasion in his lifetime does the believer feel so intensely and confidently that he is approaching a merciful, responsive and loving God. It is well-nigh impossible to convey the vividness of the experience and the sense of elation of the pilgrim during this essentially *personal* apprehension of Divine presence and grace. At 'Arafat, a Muslim's devotional life reaches its culmination. It is the feeling of many that this is the closest man can come to an encounter with God on earth. Besides, it was on this day that the Prophet delivered the Farewell Sermon by the rocks of the Mount of Mercy to the multitudes who witnessed the first, and last, Pilgrimage made by Muhammad. Often compared with the Sermon on the Mount, the Prophet's address gives glimpses of the religious, moral and legal amalgam so characteristic of Islam.

> O People, listen to and understand my words for I do not know whether I shall ever meet you in this place after this occasion . . .
>
> Your life and property are sacrosanct and inviolable until you stand before your Lord on the Day of Judgment, as this day, this month and this place are sacred . . .
>
> All usury is hereby abolished . . .
>
> Satan has despaired of ever being worshipped in this your land, although if he is obeyed in other matters, he will be pleased even with the inconsequential lapses on your part . . .
>
> You have your rights over your wives and they have rights over you . . .
>
> Know that every Muslim is every other Muslim's brother. Nothing belonging to his brother is lawful to a man, unless it be given freely and with good grace.
>
> So wrong not yourselves . . .
>
> I have delivered God's message to you and have left with you a clear command: the Book of God and the Practice of His Prophet. If you hold fast to this you will never go astray . . .

The lapidation ceremony—throwing pebbles at three stone pillars in Mina—is another commemoration of Abraham's practices. Some associate it with Satan's efforts to dissuade Abraham from sacrificing his son as commanded by God. By stoning the spots where Satan appeared to the Patriarch, the pilgrim symbolically rejects evil and disobedience to God.

The sacrifice of animals, also at Mina, is in recollection of Abraham's willingness to sacrifice even his beloved son to fulfill God's command. It also symbolizes the Muslim's preparedness to part with what is dearest to him in order to attain God's pleasure. The act of sacrifice is an encapsulation of the spirit of Islam: *submission* to the will of God—which is the literal meaning of the word Islam.

But quite apart from the historical and symbolic significance of the Hajj, the institution of the Pilgrimage serves two main functions for the Muslim, both as an individual and as a member of society.

The unassuming *Ihram* worn by the pilgrim serves a social purpose as well. For at least once in the believer's lifetime, the idea of equality among Muslims becomes a visible fact. Philosopher and fool, patrician and plebeian, millionaire and beggar alike wear this unsewn garment— and become indistinguishable. The social status or privileged rank of the believer are of no consequence in the sight of God. During the Pilgrim- age, as a result of this simple sartorial device, neither are they of conse- quence in the sight of man.

Also on the social plane, the major, unparalleled contribution of Islam is in the area of racial harmony and the brotherhood of the faith- ful. The Hajj is Islam's key instrument for creating and strengthening fraternal ties among millions of its followers. Pilgrims representing every conceivable color, country and tongue yearly converge upon Mecca. Here, they share common objectives and beliefs, and perform the same devo- tions. They also get acquainted with one another, and learn of, and grow to care for, the conditions of their brethren in other countries. The Hajj inspires in the believer an unrivalled sense of solidarity, a feeling of iden- tification in a world of alienation. The believer feels himself a part of the whole system of the cosmos. Whether in Mina or Michigan, 'Arafat or Zululand, no man, no woman and no nation is an island. In this re- union, convened annually by God from the time of Abraham, ties of brotherhood and love are forged among people representing the nations of the earth.

SHIAH ISLAM

Shiah (Shi'a) is the form of Islam predominant in Iran and southern Iraq, and is represented by minorities elsewhere. It differs from Sunna, the other main tradition, in a belief that the leadership of Islam should be held by a hereditary line of Imams descended from the prophet; the last visible Imam is said by the majority of Shiites to have been the twelfth, who went into hiding but who will return to establish righteous- ness in the world. The rightful place of the Imams was usurped, Shiites say, by the caliphs; for the Shiah Muslim, the world is a dark place where evil has temporarily triumphed. Never was this clearer than at the emo- tional heart of Shiah, the battle of Karbala (680 A.D.), when the third Imam, the princely Husain, was killed by the wicked forces of the caliph.

This event, celebrated at the turning of the year, has overtones of being a cosmic drama between good and evil and the salvation-giving sacrifice of a young and innocent hero. Here is an account of the celebration of the death of Husain in Muharram, the first month of the Muslim calendar, in modern Shiah.

From *Muhammadan Festivals*

G.E. von Grunebaum

It would be incorrect to say that Husain stands in the center of Shî'a dogma, but it is unquestionably true that contemplation of his personality and fate is the emotional mainspring of the believers' religious experience. The principal and most characteristic festival of the Shî'a is built around his death, which has made him, in the phrase of an early mourner, "the bond of reconciliation with God on the Day of Judgment."

Toward the end of the Muslim year, black tents are pitched in the streets. These tents are adorned with draperies, arms and candelabra. Here and there wooden pulpits are erected. On the first of Muharram, when the festival proper begins, mourning clothes are donned; people refrain from shaving and bathing, and a simple diet is adopted. From the pulpit the beginning of Husain's story is narrated with as much detail and elaboration of episodes as possible. The listeners are deeply affected. Their cries of "O, Husain, O, Husain!" are accompanied by groans and tears. This kind of recitation continues throughout the day, the mullahs taking turns on the several pulpits. At one time the notables of a quarter would fit out a tent and pay a mullah to recite in it, while the listeners were served food and drink. During the first nine days of Muharram groups of men, with their half-naked bodies dyed black or red, tour the streets. They pull out their hair, inflict sword wounds upon themselves or drag chains behind them, or perform wild dances. Not infrequently fights with Sunnites or other adversaries will develop, resulting in casualties and even deaths.

The celebration culminates on the Tenth of Muharram in a big procession originally designed as a funerary parade to reenact the burial of Husain. The center of this procession is formed by the coffin of Husain,

G.E. von Grunebaum, *Muhammadan Festivals* (New York: Henry Schuman, 1951), pp. 87–90. Copyright 1951 by Henry Schuman. Reprinted with permission of Abelard-Schuman, publisher.

carried by eight men and accompanied on each side by a banner-bearer. Four horses and some sixty blood-smeared men march behind the coffin and sing a martial tune. They are followed by a horse, representing Dul-dul, the war-horse of Husain. In the rear there is usually a group of per-haps fifty men rhythmically beating two wooden staves, one against the other.

The poet Qâ'ânî (d. 1853) has given dramatic expression to the thoughts and feelings of the Shî'ites in his catechism-like elegy on the death of Husain. The poem begins:

> *What rains down? Blood! Who? The Eye! How? Day and*
> *   Night! Why?*
> *From grief! What grief? The grief of the Monarch of Kerbela!*
> *What was his name? Husain! Of whose race? 'Ali's!*
> *Who was his mother? Fâtima! Who was his grandsire?*
> *   Mustafâ [Muhammad]!*
> *How was it with him? He fell a martyr! Where? In the plain*
> *   of Mâriya!*
> *When? On the tenth of Muharram! Secretly? No, in public!*
> *Was he slain by night? No, by day! At what time? At noon-*
> *   tide!*
> *Was his head severed from the throat? No, from the nape of*
> *   the neck!*
> *Was he slain unthirsting? No! Did none give him to drink?*
> *   They did!*
> *Who? Shimr! From what source? From the source of death!*

It has been pointed out that this ritual, which is without parallel in Islam where a saint is never commemorated by a re-enactment of his funeral, incorporates rites of an earlier cult. A number of details regard-ing the arrangement and the symbolism of the procession corroborate the general parallelism of the ceremony with the festival of Adonis-Tammuz. The violent death of that god on the approach of summer, symbolizing the decline of nature's productive force under the searing rays of a merci-less sun, was followed by a mourning of seven days after which the body was washed, anointed and shrouded to be carried abroad in a procession and finally interred. The fact that the Husain festival did not originate in Persia, but in Mesopotamia where as far as we know the first Tenth of Muharram procession with "solemn wailings and lamentations" was held in 962, localizes it in the region where in various disguises the Adonis tradition was to show some sporadic vitality more than two centuries later. The historian Ibn al-Athîr (d. 1234) records that in 1064 A.D. "a mysteri-ous threat was circulated from Armenia to Khuzistan, that every town which did not lament the dead King of the Jinn should utterly perish."

In 1204, the same writer tells us, an epidemic ravaged Mosul and Iraq, "and it was divulged that a woman of the Jinn, called Umm 'Unqûd [Mother of the Grape-Cluster] had lost her son, and that every one who would not make lamentation for him would fall a victim to the epidemic."

While the Tenth of Muharram procession remained confined to the Shî'ite world, the veneration of Husain has spread into Sunnism. The Fâtimids (969–1171) had Husain's head transferred to Cairo and the Mosque of the Hasanain (literally: of the two Hasan—that is, Hasan and his brother Husain) was erected over the relic and still preserves a reputation of especial sanctity. While the mourners in the Shî'a procession are all men, the crowd that assembles in the Hasanain Mosque on the occasion of 'Ashûrâ is composed almost exclusively of women who gather apparently in order to witness a *dhikr* meeting.

At a comparatively recent date—it was first witnessed by a European in 1811—the *ta'ziya*, or Passion play, the only drama to be developed in either Persian or Arabic literature, became the real climax of the Shî'ite Tenth of Muharram celebrations. The stage requires few properties besides a large *tâbût* (coffin), "receptacles in front to hold lights," and Husain's arms and banner. The poet speaks the introduction and, supported by a choir of boys, chants a *khutba*-like lamentation. Another male choir, dressed as mourning women, utters the wailing of the women and mothers. The spectators are given cakes of earth from Kerbela, steeped in musk, "on which they press their foreheads in abject grief." To defray the expense for a *ta'ziya* is a meritorious work, with which the donor "builds himself the palace in Paradise."

The play consists of a loose sequence of some forty to fifty scenes. Dramatic suspense would be absent even if the events were not known to the audience, for they are foretold by Gabriel to the prophets, foreseen in dreams, and frequently narrated at length before being acted on the stage. The performance is highly realistic, especially in the portrayal of Husain's sufferings from thirst and in the battle and death episodes. Old Testament figures are introduced to typify the events of Husain's Passion. National animosity against the Arabs expresses itself on occasion, but the true villains are Caliph Yazîd, who gives the order to kill Husain, and Shammar, or Shimr, who is believed to have struck the fatal blow.

The excitement of the audience reaches such a pitch that the spectators not infrequently try to lynch the actors representing the murderers of Husain. Anti-Sunnite feeling is said to be such that no Sunnî would be knowingly tolerated among the spectators. The final scenes usually depict the progress of the martyr's severed head to the Court of the Caliph. On the way, the cortège halts at a Christian monastery whose abbot, upon the sight of the head, swears off his faith and professes Islam. The sight of the head produces the same effect on some Christian ambassadors who happen to be at the Court of Yazîd when it arrives. Not only Christians, but Jews and pagans are affected in the same way; even a lion is seen to bow low before Husain's head.

ISLAMIC SAINTS

One of the most important aspects of popular Islam is the venera-
tion of wali, *or saints. The saints have a special role in the divine admin-*
istration of the world. Their presences while living, and their tombs after
death, are radiant with a holy power that draws the faithful from near
and far. The following passage, based on a study of Islam in the Sudan,
well summarizes belief and practice about saints in Islam.

From *Islam in the Sudan*
J. Spencer Trimingham

Ho, verily upon the friends (*awliyā'*) of Allah there is
no fear neither do they grieve. (Qur'ān, x. 63.)

Every Muslim believes that beside the visible order of believers there
exists an invisible order of saints who, under the direction of Allāh, manage the affairs of the world for Him. So bound up are the saints with the
religious life of Islam in the Sudan that to think of Allāh without His
intermediaries is impossible.

Men of piety attracted attention through their alleged powers from
the beginning of Islam, but no regular theory about them nor special cult
developed until the rise of the dervish orders in the twelfth century A.D.
All authority then came to be invested in the shaikh of the order who
claimed to have powers of intercession with God and to perform miracles.
Naturally when dead his followers continued to venerate him still as a
'friend' of God and their protector.

The word *wali* in its religious sense may have to be translated as
'saint,' but we must avoid reading our own conceptions into the word.
The idea of 'nearness' (to God)[1] which lies behind it needs to be brought
out because it is essential in the development of the Muslim theory of

J. Spencer Trimingham, *Islam in the Sudan* (Oxford: Oxford University Press, 1949), pp. 125–28, 141–45. Reprinted by permission of the publisher.

[1] *Walī*, plur. *awliyā'*, is derived from *walā*, to be near.

saintship. In the Qur'ān *walī* does not have a strict meaning,[2] but in the course of time it came to be applied to those who were felt to have a personal relationship with God. The word then lays stress not on saintliness but on personal relationship with God. The *awliyā'* are those who live in the presence of God.

As a result of the development of this usage of the term *walī*, the theory developed that God has granted to some of them special powers which even make the subsistence and governance of the world depend upon them.

'Alī al-Hujwīrī states that God has chosen the saints to manifest His actions:

> God, then, has caused the prophetic evidence (*burhān-i-nabawī*) to remain down to the present day, and has made the Saints the means whereby it is manifested, in order that the signs of the Truth and the proof of Muhammad's veracity may continue to be clearly seen. *He has made the Saints the governors of the universe*; they have become entirely devoted to His business, and have ceased to follow their sensual affections. Through the blessing of their advent the rain falls from heaven, and through the purity of their lives the plants spring up from the earth, and through their spiritual influence the Muslims gain victories over the unbelievers.[3]

This government of the world has a mighty meeting of the saints, both dead and living, as its directive organization. Their head is the *Qutb* (Axis) who is a saint living on earth in different incarnations. He is God's official administrator in the world and constitutes the most vital link in the chain of union between the Creator (*al-Ḥaqq*) and the creatures (*al-khalq*).

Many of the Sūfīs have asserted heretically that by virtue of having attained unity with God the saints are higher than the prophets in rank. In actual fact to the masses they are. A prophet is certainly of less value to the community than a saint, for in the saint is embodied that longing for salvation which is inherent in all men. He is regarded as an embodiment of saving power quite apart from his personal piety or impiety. This is because the Muslim idea of a holy man has nothing to do with his personal merit, or attainment of holiness through pain and suffering, prayer and meditation; it is rather a mechanical conception and does not involve the personal will. The saints are people 'honoured' by God with His special favour, and the way in which this honour is manifested is through their possession of *baraka*, whereby miracles (*karāmāt*) are performed on

---

[2] *Walī* in the Qur'ān is applied to God as 'Patron' or 'Guardian' (ii. 258, iii, 61, xlv. 18, &c.); it is used for 'guardian' in a general sense (ii. 282); and as 'Friend' or 'Ally' of God (x. 63). The popular sense of the word became common during the ninth century A.D.
[3] *Kashf al-Mahjūb*, trans. R. A. Nicholson, p. 213.

their behalf. A miracle (*karāma*) is an honour.[4] The purity of a saint's life or doctrine is of secondary importance; if he can work miracles, that is enough, he is a saint and therefore one to be feared and one whose protection is to be sought.[5] A saint without miracles is no saint at all; but when it is remembered that converting a sinner, clairvoyance, telepathy, and *firāsa* (the art of divination from the physiognomy or actions of a person) are *karamāt*, and that these are the commonest of phenomena among ecstatics, it will be seen that it is not difficult to attain to *walī*-ship. It is absurd to look for ethical signs of saintship, for if the holy one's consciousness is absorbed into God, his body can hardly be held account-able for its actions. This does not mean that the ascetic virtues are not admired, but that they have nothing to do with the holiness.

Baraka, literally 'benediction', means holiness in the Muslim sense of something given by God. The whole conception has its roots in pre-Islamic beliefs in a wonder-working force, re-set in a new form in Islam, and therefore with new tendencies, through it being regarded as a '*bless-ing*' from God. *Baraka* is possessed in its highest degree by the saints and is bestowed arbitrarily by God regardless of merit; although the concep-tion is not absent that exceptional piety and asceticism, can, as it were, force God's hand and make Him bestow it. It is universally believed in the Sudan that the *baraka* of a saint can also be transmitted to his pos-terity. This accounts for the fact that men whose conduct is so vile as to offer the worst possible example to others, are yet venerated because they are regarded as having inherited this supernatural power from a *walī* ancestor. Thus we get in the Sudan whole feki villages which live to a large extent on the credulity of the masses. *Baraka* can also be claimed by certain acts such as the recitation of the *Fātiha*, which is caught by the symbolic act of raising the hands during the recitation and then trans-ferred by drawing the palms down over the face. . . .

. . . The people may not always be sure of the efficacy of the *baraka* of living fekis, but they have a blind faith in that of their dead saint, normally spoken of as 'our shaikh' and always as though he were living. He is in fact supposed to be slumbering and manifests himself to people in dreams or trances. His powers to bless or blight cover almost every category of human need.[6] His power is testified by the miracles performed

[4]D. B. Macdonald has pointed out that the *karāmāt* (thaumaturgic gifts) of the saints are closely akin to the χαρίσματα of I Cor. xii. 9, worked by divine grace. *Mu'jizāt* has become synonymous with *āya* (sign), i.e. miracles in the conventional sense, which are recognized by orthodox Islam only in the prophets and are Acts of God performed through a prophet to prove his mission (*da'wa*).

[5]The same attitude is adopted to the tombs of Christian saints in Muslim countries, many of whom, of course, are in the Muslim calendar. In the Sudan, which does not have indigenous Christian saints, the only example is that of the festival of Mār Jirjis (the Prophet al-Khidr of popular Islam) at the church dedicated to him in Halfāya.

[6]In view of this universal veneration for the saints it is surprising to discover this proverb 'I supposed the *qubba* held a saint' (*ana qāyil fi'l qubba shaikh*) as the equiv-alent of 'all that glitters is not gold'.

on behalf not only of one's dead ancestors, but also of one's living family. It is impossible to manage one's affairs properly without his help, whether it is the curing of a sick child, the winning of a wife, or the blessing of children.

The tombs of these holy men are to be found chiefly along the Main Nile north of Khartoum and the Blue Nile from Khartoum to Sennār, they are less frequent on the White Nile and there are others scattered in most settled districts. In Kordofān the various local fekis are buried under a tree with only a couple of stones and a few fluttering flags to mark the site.

There are various kinds of shrines, for any place that is in some way connected with a saint may partake to some degree of his *baraka*.

1. There is the *qubba*, the domed tomb of a noted saint. It may be a square *jālūs* building with an egg-shaped dome,[7] or a high *tukl* of the same conical shape. This is erected over his grave which is often the place where he died. His *baraka* must naturally be strongest at the place where he lived and died and still spends a great deal of his time. Not every *qubba*, however, marks the burial place. Sometimes it may be no more than a memorial shrine, or it may be the place where the placenta of the saint was buried.[8] There is one such at Jadīd where Bakrī wad Idrīs was born, others are that of Bakrī b. 'Abd Allāh b. Hasōba at Sōba Bakrī who is buried at Umm Laban on the White Nile; also at Bāra that of Al-Hasan, son of the founder of the Mirghaniyya, who is buried at Kasala. *Qubbas* are usually in charge of a feki who is a descendant of the dead saint sometimes the khalīfa appoints the guardian. He is maintained by the community and the gifts of pilgrims.

2. Secondly, there are simpler mud buildings with a flat roof or a *tukl* in the form of an ordinary *quṭṭiyya* (often called *ḍarīḥ*); others with no roof at all, just a plain *turba* marked at head and foot and with four mud walls around it. Especially numerous are shrines called *bayān* (manifestation) which mark the places where a saint has been seen in a dream. Omdurman, not having many saints' tombs, is full of them. There is one outside my house and I have been told that some devotee dreamt that he met a *walī* called Shaikh Mas'ūd at that spot. The *walī* told him that his *baraka* would adhere there to help people and to receive honour. The man then built a mud wall and women visit it and leave their *karāma* in the form of small coins, coffee, &c., which are then taken by the poor or children. At Wad Medanī there is an unusual *bayān* to Hasan the son of Muhammad 'Uthmān al-Mirghanī which is built of brick with a roof of reeds. Inside is a

---

[7]This type of Sudanese *qubba* also appears among the nomads of the High Algerian Plateau and 'follows the local style of building in clay of the nomad country with the egg-shaped dome and the usual tapering lower structures' (*Enc. Is.*, Suppl. vol., 128). Burckhardt (*Nubia*, 274) gives a sketch of a cone-shaped tomb and remarks that he only saw two such during his journeys. The *qubba* of Shaikh Idrīs al-Majdhūb at Kuēka is of the stepped *mastaba* form almost as old in Egypt as the First Dynasty.

[8]Seligman believed that in ancient Egypt the placenta was regarded as the double, physical and spiritual, of the infant it had nourished (*Hamitic Problem*, p. 658). Among sections of the conglomerate of Omdurman a similar belief prevails.

turba, though there is no body there, covered with a purple pall, at one end of which is a hole containing earth to be taken to the sick to bestow his *baraka*. *Bayāns* to Sīdī Hasan, as he is known, are very numerous: I have seen three at least in in Omdurman. Some *banayāt* are visited for special services. There is one in Khartoum of Shaikh Maḥmūd Abū Shaiba, who is buried at Nōfalāb, which is visited by bridegrooms on their wedding night, as also are the tombs of Khōjalī and Ḥamad at Ḥalfāya.

3. There are shrines marked by neither building nor *turba*, except perhaps a ring of stones or a cairn sometimes with a stick and a flag. Such enclosures are often *bayānāt*, or they may mark the spot where a saint went into retreat or performed a miracle.

4. There are further various holy places and objects which are associated with saints and partake of his *baraka*; or, in districts till recently pagan, they may be objects, such as trees, springs, wells, rocks, once associated with pagan worship, now personified or identified with saints.

The *qubba* is always a sanctuary (*ḥaram*), and sometimes the fenced area around it. It therefore acts as an asylum for people fleeing from vengeance or justice. There is a general feeling too that wild animals should not be killed near a tomb; for it is possible that such an animal may have some connexion with the saint, many of whom granted their protection to certain animals. Among the Bishārīn and 'Abābda is the curious belief that animals sacrificed at a tomb turn into gazelles or ibex which enjoy the protection of the *walī*, who punishes any attempt to shoot them.[9]

The saint, too, protects objects deposited at his tomb for safe-keeping. Ploughs will be left by cultivators whose *dura*-patches are scattered over a wide area. MacMichael mentions having seen such articles as a hair-tent, bowls, grindstones, left by Arabs at the tomb of Ḥasan wad Ḥasūna until their return at the end of the season.[10] Merchants going to Egypt still leave surplus goods at the grave of Abū Ḥamad as when Caillaud passed in 1821. Hair, nail clippings, and teeth are often left to prevent others getting them for purposes of witchcraft. Dust or stones taken from their graves also protect. They are usually attached to the crossbeam of an unused *sāqiya* (water-wheel) to prevent its being stolen. The most solemn oath that can be taken for most people is that at their saint's tomb, whereas they do not mind swearing falsely on the Qur'ān.

The manner of worship at tombs is very simple in character. It is quite free, with no fixed forms of devotion, though since most are connected with a *ṭarīqa*, there are set methods of saying the Fātiha, special Qur'ānic passages and *murāqabāt* (meditations). Visiting a tomb is called a *ziyāra*. If regular visits are not paid to them the saints tend to appear in dreams to complain and utter threats. The visitor at his first sight of the shrine 'draws' the blessing of the saint by first saying the Fātiha hold-

9G. W. Murray, *Sons of Ishmael*, p. 154.
10*Hist.* ii. 287.

ing out and looking at the palms of his hands, then raises his hands and draws them down his face (*at-tabarruk*).

Two types of visits are paid to the tomb: one for the benefit of the saint and the other for the worshipper. The first is the paying of honour to the saint merely by the visit and the repetition of the Fātiha, but usually offerings (*zuwāra*) are brought—food, candles, incense, &c. Gifts are usually made at the various stages of life, such as the shaving of a child's head, circumcision, marriage, to secure their protection. Failure to do so might cause harm to fall on the child. The people firmly believe that the saint enjoys the immaterial 'substance' of the food, &c., offered him. Orthodoxy says that, since the distribution of food is a pious work, the 'merit' of this, which normally would be received by the alms-giver, is transferred to the saint. The materials must be consumed, either burnt in his honour (candles, oil, incense) or eaten by a living person, preferably the feki in charge, the poor, or children. The important thing is the *intention* to transfer the 'substance' or the 'merit' to the saint.

For the second, the worshipper sits or stands facing the shrine and tells the saint of his desires or troubles and, in order to move his compassion more effectively, makes a conditional vow (*nadhr*) that if the saint is gracious, he will return and hold a Qur'ān-reading, or make a sacrifice (*dhabīḥa*), or whitewash his tomb, or give money to the poor. The night of 27th Ramadān (*Lailat al-Qadr*) is believed to be especially propitious for making requests. When a vow is made, sometimes they go alone, sometimes with a few friends, or, if it is a very special desire, in procession. Failure to carry out the vow after the granting of the request would be visited with the direst of consequences, such as the illness or death of a son who has been granted. Stories of such catastrophes are common. Amongst most groups visits are paid to the shaikh's tomb during marriages, circumcisions, and other festivals. Sick animals are also taken to a tomb and driven around it seven times.

Contact with a shrine is believed to be beneficial, therefore in order to keep the saint in mind of the request something which has been in contact with the person is usually left. Normally this is a piece of rag attached to the door or to sticks planted in the walls for that purpose.

A saint is believed to retain his living characteristics after death. Therefore if he was noted for a particular miracle during his life he continues to exercise that power. Sometimes a particular cure becomes his speciality only after his death. Thus the *qubba* of Al-Khōjalī at Halfāya is good for children cutting teeth, that of 'Abd al-Ma'rūf at Berber for evidence; most people will be very chary of swearing falsely at his tomb. Mud from the tomb of Ahmad wad at-Taraifī near Wad Medani is good for curing dog bites, hence the saint is called Ahmad Dābī as-Sa'ar (the viper, i.e. enemy, of rabies). If you have been robbed, a nail driven into the ground before the *bayān* of Shaikh Zinzīr in Khartoum will result in the Shaikh visiting you during sleep and showing you or telling of the thief.

SAYINGS OF SAINTS AND SUFIS

The citations below are sayings or stories attributed to the saints and mystics of Islam. They express something of that which is universal in the Sufi way.

From *The Way of the Sufi*
Idries Shah

A MEETING WITH KHIDR

Khidr is the 'unseen guide' of the Sufis, and it is he who is believed to be the anonymous Guide to Moses in the Koran. This 'Green One' is often referred to as 'the Jew' and he has been equated in legend with such figures as St George and Elijah. This tale—or report—is characteristic of the supernormal functions attributed to Khidr, both in folklore and among the dervish teachers.

Once, while standing on the banks of the Oxus river, I saw a man fall in. Another man, in the clothes of a dervish, came running to help him, only to be dragged into the water himself. Suddenly I saw a third man, dressed in a robe of shimmering, luminous green, hurl himself into the river. But as he struck the surface, his form seemed to change; he was no longer a man, but a log. The other two men managed to cling to this, and together they worked it towards the bank.

Hardly able to believe what I was seeing, I followed at a distance, using the bushes that grew there as cover. The men drew themselves panting on the bank; the log floated away. I watched it until, out of sight of the others, it drifted to the side, and the green-robed man, soaked and sodden, dragged himself ashore. The water began to stream from him; before I reached him he was almost dry.

I threw myself on the ground in front of him, crying: 'You must

Idries Shah, *The Way of the Sufi* (New York: E.P. Dutton & Co., 1970), pp, 161–62, 219–22, 227. Copyright 1968 by the author. Reprinted by permission of the publisher and of Collins-Knowlton-Wing, Inc.

be the Presence Khidr, the Green One, Master of the Saints. Bless me, for I would attain.' I was afraid to touch his robe, because it seemed to be of green fire.

He said: 'You have seen too much. Understand that I come from another world and am, without their knowing it, protecting those who have service to perform. You may have been a disciple of Sayed Imdadullah, but you are not mature enough to know what we are doing for the sake of God.'

When I looked up, he was gone, and all I could hear was a rushing sound in the air.

After coming back from Khotan, I saw the same man. He was lying on a straw mattress in a rest-house near Peshawar. I said to myself: 'If I was too raw the last time, this time I'll be mature.'

I took hold of his robe, which was a very common one—though under it I thought I saw something glow green.

'You may be Khidr,' I said to him, 'but I have to know how an apparently ordinary man like you performs these wonders . . . and why. Explain your craft to me, so that I can practise it too.'

He laughed. 'You're impetuous, my friend! The last time you were too headstrong—and now you're still too headstrong. Go on, tell everyone you meet that you've seen Khidr Elias; they'll put you in the madhouse, and the more you protest you're right the more heavily they'll chain you.'

Then he took out a small stone. I stared at it—and found myself paralysed, turned to stone, until he had picked up his saddle-bags and walked away.

When I tell this story, people either laugh or, thinking me a story-teller, give me presents. . . .

To Be a Sufi

Being a Sufi is to put away what is in your head—imagined truth, preconceptions, conditioning—and to face what may happen to you.

Abu Said

What Must Come

To those who seek truth in conventionalized religion:

Until college and minaret have crumbled
This holy work of ours will not be done.
Until faith becomes rejection
And rejection becomes belief
There will be no true believer.

Abu Said

Worship

O Lord!
If I worship you from fear of hell, cast me into hell.
If I worship you from desire for paradise, deny me paradise.

Rabia

The Door

Salih of Qazwin taught his disciples:
'Whoever knocks at the door continually, it will be opened to him.'
Rabia, hearing him one day, said:
'How long will you say: "It will be opened"? The door has never
  been shut.'

Like Calls to Like

Hasan of Basra went to see Rabia. She was sitting in the midst of a
  number of animals.
As soon as Hasan approached, they ran away.
Hasan said:
'Why did they do that?'
Rabia answered:
'You have been eating meat. All I had to eat was dry bread.'

Fruit and Thistles

To an ass, a thistle is a delicious fruit.
The ass eats the thistle. It remains an ass.

Habib el-Ajami

When Avicenna Met Abu Said

When the philosopher and the Sufi met, Avicenna said:
'What I know, he sees.'
Abu Said remarked:
'What I see, he knows.'

The Sufi Call

Answer the Sufi Call, as best you are able, in this world, with a
  loving heart and honestly. Then you are truly safe in this world
  and in all the other worlds.

Salik Hamzavi

Bread

If you are entertaining a dervish, remember that dry bread is
  enough for him.

Harith Muhasibi

Benefit

Most of humanity do not know what it is in their interests to know.
They dislike what would eventually benefit them.

Al-Nasafi

Point of View

To the sinful and vicious I am evil;
Bu to the good—beneficent am I.

Mirza Khan, Ansari

Teachers, Teachings, Taught

Teachers talk about teachings.
Real teachers study their pupils as well.
Most of all, teachers should be studied.

Musa Kazim

Service and Mastership

He who does not know about service knows even less about Mas-
tership.

Tirmizi

Perception and Explanation

For him who has perception, a mere sign is enough.
For him who does not really heed, a thousand explanations are not
enough.

Haji Bektash

To a Would-be Dervish

My heart has become confused from the world and what is in it.
Within my heart there is nothing but the Friend.
If perfume from the rose-garden of Unity comes to me
My heart, like a rosebud, will burst its outer skin.
Speak to the recluse in his solitude and say:
Because the very edge of our prayer-niche is as the curve of the
    Eyebrow
There is no real difference between the Kaaba and the idol-house
—Wherever you may look, there equally is HE.
The being of a dervish is not in what his beard and head are like:
The Path of the dervish is in qualitative exactitude.
A dervish may easily shave his head without regrets
But he is a dervish who, like Hafiz, gives up his head.

Khwaja Hafiz of Shiraz

Sufism

Sufism is truth without form.

Ibn el-Jalali

Where it Went

I saw a child carrying a light.
I asked him where he had brought it from.
He put it out, and said:
'Now you tell me where it is gone.'

Hasan of Basra